Advance Praise

"It is such a pleasure to see two erudite thinkers opening their minds to the other's perspectives and to watch them learn from one another even as they are teaching their students. This book is a rare and shining example of religious tolerance, theological inquiry and spiritual education—such an important offering in these times of religious and secular polarization. What a breath of fresh air!"

—Isa Gucciardi, Ph.D., Founding Director of the Foundation of the Sacred Stream, author of *Coming to Peace*

"Anyone drawn to both Tibetan Buddhism and Christian spirituality owes themselves some serious time with *The Lotus and the Rose*...a series of engaging conversations between two close friends who dive into the spiritual depths of their respective traditions and find all sorts of resonance and connection in what they've discovered....Their talk ranges from banter to philosophic discursus, [and] is full of engaging stories and often awash in laughter. Rather than being otherworldly and cut off from daily life, these two spiritual explorers are socially conscious and fully engaged....It covers a bookshelf of issues and history and spiritual exploration, like an extraordinary class that opens a host of doors to a subject you hadn't realized was so important to you."

—Paul Chaffee, Editor of *The Interfaith Observer*

"There are many paths that lead to the same destination. *The Lotus & The Rose* is an exciting new chapter in the intentional practice of finding understanding, beauty, and value across cultural and religious divides that once seemed unbridgeable. The wisdom gleaned from the conversations between Buddhist Lama Tsomo and mystical Christian Matthew Fox gives hope to our shared values of compassion, respect, and friendship."

—Robert Funk, Student

"As humanity evolves toward a spiritual understanding grounded in the truth of inter-being, theological divisions begin to melt and the common heart emerges. The danger in this inter-spiritual movement is that we risk losing the treasures that lie at the core of all the world's great religions. Blessedly, beings like Matthew Fox & Lama Tsomo serve as 'Keepers of the Jewels' so that what is most relevant and life-giving in each faith is preserved and shared. To listen in on the conversation between these two wise friends is to bear witness to sacred inquiry and living love. Through their willingness to inquire deeply into their own traditions, we reap the best of them both, opening a portal to the quintessence of all wisdom ways."

—**Mirabai Starr was an adjunct professor of Philosophy and World Religions at the University of New Mexico-Taos for 20 years, and is a critically acclaimed speaker, writer, and teacher.**

"Lama Sangak Yeshe Tsomo and Radical Reverend Matthew Fox are tireless spiritual dialoguers. They are committed re-enchanters of the Mystical and the Sacred at a time in the world when most people have an elementary school view of religion and see 'spirituality' as a contagious disease. In this secular age—intensely self-interested and determined to disconnect from the old hat 'sacred' and any form of organized religion—'Lotus and Rose' lively interfaith exchanges and dovetails are essential, especially for young people of conscience with their lives ahead of them."

— **Charley Linden Thorp has researched and taught in Europe and Asia. Author of five books, she says she longs to return in her writing and research to the Golden Era of Hindu Philosophy "when sacred was the norm and secular plurality had not even been dreamt of."**

THE
LOTUS
& THE
ROSE

A Conversation Between
Tibetan Buddhism
& Mystical Christianity

Reverend Matthew Fox
Lama Tsomo

Namchak

PUBLISHING

The Namchak Foundation supports the study and practice of
the Namchak Lineage of Tibetan Buddhism.
Namchak.org.

Library of Congress Control Number: 2018947950

Book design and typography by Mary Ann Casler
Editorial by Michael Frisbie
Cover art: Chantall/Shutterstock.com

Cataloging-in-Publication Data
is available from the Library of Congress

First printing, September 2018
ISBN: 978-0999577004
Printed in Canada on recycled paper

10 9 8 7 6 5 4 3 2 1

CONTENTS

Why "the lotus and the rose"

LAMA TSOMO • THE LOTUS: The lotus has great symbolism in Buddhism. For one thing, it has its roots in the muck of a swamp or pond, yet its flower is pristine—unsullied by the muck—and faces the sky. This represents us as human beings, being able to span such vast levels of consciousness, of being. Interesting fact: scientists have imitated the unique structure of the lotus flower cells to create paints that resist dirt far better than others.

In Tibetan Buddhism the lotus has particular significance since Padmasambhava (literally meaning "lotus-born") was the master of transformation, who transformed Tibet into a Buddhist country. The Tibetans of the Nyingma tradition consider him the reincarnation of the Buddha Shakyamuni. His name refers to his having appeared as an eight-year-old child, sitting on a lotus.

MATTHEW FOX • THE ROSE: To me the rose has several meanings within my tradition. I have learned that the rose is an archetype that stands for the mystic Center, the heart, the garden of Eros, the paradise of Dante, the emblem of Venus and the Beloved. It also stands for blood such as that which Jesus shed while teaching compassion to an Empire that did not want to hear about it.

In the Litany to Mary (which by the way finds a beautiful parallel in the twenty-one practices and names of the Green Tara in Tibetan Buddhism), she is referred to as the "Mystical Rose" and I recall vividly how this image captured me when I was a teenager. Thus the rose becomes a door to invite the Divine Feminine in. The rose is also a mandala and is thus a centering device reminding us that all work is meant to operate from the inside out—it honors inner work while recognizing diverse outer manifestations of our inner lives.

In addition, Meister Eckhart says we should all "live like the rose which lives without a why." A rose exists…to be rose…and that seems not only sufficient but wonderful and special. Roses do not last long but they do display their beauty of color and smell and geometry with abandon— generously we might say. And so we too are invited to live without a why, live in order to live and love in order to love and work in order to work.

Foreword

One lustrously snowy winter afternoon a few years back, Lama Tsomo and Matthew Fox were asked to describe their connection, their mutual regard. Here's a bit of what they had to say about each other.

I first met Matthew Fox through his book, *Original Blessing*. I was struck both by his brilliance and by the truth of what he was saying in the book. When our mutual friend said he could make an introduction, I was excited and I thought, "My gosh—I can actually meet this person and talk to them." By that time I had obviously steeped myself in the Tibetan Buddhist tradition. But when we were actually in dialogue, I was once again struck by his brilliance, his sense of humor, his mind that flashes all over the place. But there's also a depth of knowledge of the things he's talking about. Then I got to appreciate him on another level as a personal friend more and more as we kept talking. It's just that joy of conversation and interaction and the adventure of inquiry that both of us are so passionate about.

I'm struck that he actually lives a lot of what he believes in. He's a truly compassionate, good-hearted, good-spirited person. I think anyone who's seen him speak is aware of his quick wit and sense of humor. They may not know about his generosity of heart.

Lama Tsomo

I appreciate working with Lama Tsomo for a lot of reasons. One is that she's down to earth, she's a mother, she's taken some big leaps—courageous leaps—in terms of leaving her own culture to learn a very different language and culture and to immerse herself deeply into the practice and philosophy of Buddhism. And I think she's come back with a fine capacity for articulating to Westerners what the wisdom of this profound tradition is all about.

I also find her open to listening to the traditions of the West and the mystical tradition of Christianity, which is what draws me. I just find her fun to be with and challenging and not superficial. She enjoys good food and laughter and the gifts of nature in its many manifestations. And of course her stories about her own teachers and spiritual companions are captivating. She's a good friend!

Reverend Matthew Fox

Acknowledgments

From Lama Tsomo

First I want to thank Matthew Fox for conceiving of the idea to do this dialog and for inviting me to do it with him. When he asked, I didn't feel nearly as qualified as others to represent the Buddhist side. So I tried to talk him out of it—but clearly did not succeed. One of the many blessings of having joined with Matthew in these dialogs is that we have become friends since that early invitation. Matthew is a fine poster child for the lineage he represents. As for my lineage, I thank Tulku Sangak Rinpoche for bringing it to me in the first place, and continuing to share so much of it with me, so generously, for decades. His brother, Namchak Khen Rinpoche, has done the same as well, also tirelessly, for many years. And there's still so much I want to learn! Long before I encountered Tibetan Buddhism I was Jewish, and our Rabbi, Herman Schaalman, was also a family friend. His wisdom and personal example laid a strong foundation for my future spiritual endeavors. I've been very lucky.

Many thanks to the many people who passionately worked to help Matt and me to manifest this dialog in the form you now have in your hands. Our editor, Michael Frisbie, has brought his prodigious intelligence, skill, and dedication to this project, doing far more than editing. We couldn't have done it without him! I so appreciated Karen Everett's enthusiasm as she filmed the first three locations of the dialog, since I was new to such a project. Thanks to Katy Garton and her team at Sprout

Films, for her superb job of filming, and the deep caring brought to the countless hours of editing that rendered the beautiful videos distilled from the many hours of filming. Thanks also to Linda Devendorf for proofreading, and being a pleasure to work with. Mary Ann Casler brought her skill, her constant goodwill, and a passion for the project to her fine design and layout work.

On our Namchak team, I want to thank Kelly Hughes for wrangling all of us—yes, I live in Montana, where we wrangle!—to pull our many threads together in time to finally publish this sprawling work of many places over many years. Thanks to Janna Glasser, our legal counsel and perennial enthusiastic supporter, for keeping us from any legal missteps. Jessica Larson, our Director of Education and Outreach, continues to help us to bring this work to the world, as will Anne Tillery of Pyramid Communications, who so generously brings her array of skills to many of our efforts at Namchak.

Thanks too, to the various entities who hosted the installments of our dialog: The Academy for the Love of Learning; the Upaya Zen Center for allowing us to film that portion there; the Jung Center of Houston, which hosted us thanks to the efforts of Jo Sandlin and Jim Hollis; and Stanford University.

And finally I want to express great appreciation to my dear friend Aaron Stern, founder of the Academy for the Love of Learning, for being my co-conspirator in life in general and countless things in particular. They say that we all need a witness to our lives. I certainly do. And I couldn't ask for a better one than Aaron.

From Matthew Fox

I want to thank Michael Frisbie, Kelly Hughes, Jessica Larson and all the people working with Namchak Publishers for their steadfastness, imagination and perseverance in seeing this long process to a happy ending. And I wish to thank the many Buddhist teachers in my life, both formal and informal.

Thanks also to the following: Surely to the Dali Lama, in whose presence I have sat more than once, and Thich Naht Hanh, who graced our University of Creation Spirituality by his presence and teaching and stories, and who also shared his walking meditation sessions in Oakland's Lake Merritt Park. To Joanna Macy for her wonderful teachings and the several occasions we co-taught both in the US and in Germany. To Robert Thurman for his writings and our delightful dialog at Spring Center in Berkeley, and to Isa Gucciardi, founder of Spring Center, who sponsored our event. To Father Bede Griffiths for his pioneering work in Deep Ecumenism and to Aaron Stern, co-founder of the Academy for the Love of Learning, whom Lama Tsomo introduced me to—and to David Korten, who introduced me to Lama Tsomo.

To Dom Aelred Graham whose book *Zen Catholicism* was my introduction to Buddhism in the early 1960's, and to Thomas Merton for his fruitful efforts to bring Buddhism and Christianity together, including his *Zen and the Birds of Appetite*, which features our common friend Meister Eckhart. And of course a special shout out to Meister Eckhart (and Thomas Aquinas too, on whose shoulders he stands) whose frequent Buddhist-like teachings awakened Merton and make this marriage of East and West so real. Also to Dr. Suzuki, Merton's mentor in introducing Eckhart to him and who recognized the deep connection between Eckhart's wisdom and that of the East. To friends Kyle and Max for incarnating the beauty of Buddhist values in their daily lives, and to Matthieu Ricard, whose book on *Happiness* Tsomo and I studied together in one of our shared sessions recorded in this book.

And finally to Lama Tsomo for her good and earnest company and her enthusiastic embrace and understanding of the Tibetan Buddhist lineage that speaks so deeply to so many in our time.

To all, a Big Thank You!

Introduction

Whenever they get together, Lama Tsomo and the Reverend Dr. Matthew Fox bring to the conversation their lively passion for their individual spiritual traditions, and a shared personal history as colleagues and long-time friends.

The Lotus & The Rose presents these traditions, these individuals, this friendship in a unique set of conversations that spans a decade and a range of venues and audiences. This volume includes full transcripts of presentations to audiences at Stanford University, The Jung Center in Houston, and the Upaya Zen Center in Santa Fe. Also included is a private, more casual conversation between just Tsomo and Matthew, as well as two new individual interviews.

Lama Tsomo and Matthew Fox have both taken less-traveled spiritual paths, giving them each an unusual combination of expertise in their traditions along with a fresh perspective informed by their own routes and the nature and challenges of today's world.

Lama Tsomo was born into an American Jewish household, retaining those roots as her spiritual search eventually led to her immersion in Tibetan Buddhism, culminating in her 2005 ordination as a Tibetan Buddhist lama, one of the few Americans so recognized. She has taught hundreds of students in the West and in Asia, and is the author of the award-winning book *Why Is The Dalai Lama Always Smiling? A Westerner's Introduction and Guide to Tibetan Buddhist Practice.*

Matthew Fox was a member of the Dominican Order for 34 years and continues as an internationally recognized voice and catalyst for Mystical Christianity. He is a scholar, a reinventor of worship, an activist, the author of more than 35 books, and the force behind the *Fox Institute of Spirituality* and *The Order of the Sacred Earth*. The late historian and theologian Thomas Berry wrote that "Matthew Fox might well be the most creative, the most comprehensive, surely the most challenging religious-spiritual teacher in America."

The Lotus & The Rose isn't static words on a page, a text carefully crafted by two writers. It is a true record of real conversations in real time. It is about images in your mind's eye, movement imagined, voices—Tsomo's, Matthew's, their audiences'—alive with enthusiasm and curiosity and interplay. So in creating this transcript, we've been faithful to the rhythms and expression of these voices, letting you hear in your mind's ear what was said just as it was spoken, with all the colloquial eloquence and interaction and digressions and discovery.

And, of course, the best way of all to get a sense of these conversations and presentations is to enjoy the hours of video available, offering extensive excerpts from each of these sections. While this book is a great opportunity to read and ponder *everything* that was said in these conversations, the video selections let you appreciate the full dynamic of the ideas and personalities.

www.namchakpublishing.com/lotusrose/videos
PASSWORD: LotusRoseLive

You don't need to read *The Lotus & The Rose* straight through. Each section gives you an overview of the topics covered, so you can use those as a guide, but also feel free to wander: skim, flip, return, dog-ear as you wish. And most important: enjoy!

For more information, or to share your ideas and questions, you can check out **www.namchak.org**

UPAYA ZEN CENTER
SANTA FE, NEW MEXICO

In November of 2006, the Academy for the Love of Learning invited Lama Tsomo and Matthew Fox to give a presentation in Santa Fe, New Mexico. Because the Academy had not yet completed construction on its own facility, Matthew, Tsomo, and their audience met in the home of Joan Halifax, founder of the Upaya Zen Center, a setting that lent a particular warmth to the gathering.

The gathering was welcomed by Aaron Stern, the founder of the Academy for the Love of Learning. He is a musician, teacher, and consultant on learning. Aaron shared a brief introduction of his friends, Tsomo and Matt, for the audience.

CHAPTER INDEX

Introduction

AARON STERN: Let's start with Tsomo, who's a student of Gochen Tulku Rinpoche. Some of you know him as Tulku Sang-ngag Rinpoche. He says that she is his foremost American student. And Tsomo recently had her "lama-nation," we called it, when she became a lama in Montana. She's certainly a very dear friend of mine, and what most touches me about her work is that she brings a kind of "kitchen table" wisdom. She's the mother of three and the grandmother of one, and spent a lot of her life mothering, building houses with her own hands, farming with her own hands, going to school and becoming a psychologist in the Jungian tradition, did her master's, wrote a really wonderful book on interpretations of fairy tales from the feminine, not feminist, perspective. It's just a wonderful book.

She went on after many, many years of meditation and practice and found her way into the Vajrayana tradition, found herself a great teacher and really went deeply into it, and now is a lama. So it's one of those great American stories: a Jewish lama.

And Matt, what do we say about Matt? Let's see. He's a troublemaker, a wisdom teacher, formerly a Dominican priest silenced by the Vatican, and renewer of Creation Spirituality. We know he had the audacity to speak of the feminine or elevate the feminine to its proper place, and went on to write, I don't know, 30 books, maybe, the most recent on education. My image of him is this man who walks around with his briefcase, going from speech to speech to speech, telling this story and waking people up. So it's a great honor to introduce both of these two extraordinary human beings.

MATT: Well, thank you, Aaron, and it's good to be here with you at this wonderful Academy for the Love of Learning—with the best name of any school in the world and good people to measure up to it. The theme of our dialogue today is "The Lotus and the Rose." There's a story behind this title, which we've had to struggle with a bit because the first proposal was that it be called "The Lotus and the Cross," and I feel that the cross has received far too much attention already, so I vetoed that. Tsomo and I were talking, and I talked about how one of the archetypes, one of the names of Mary, the goddess in Christianity, is "Mystical Rose." And she latched onto that because part of what we are talking about is bringing the feminine and the masculine into a healthier balance. Meister Eckhart says, "All the names we give to God come from the understanding of ourselves." So if we just run around with male versions of the Godhead in our heads, then something's amiss in our own souls.

I realized, walking into this space here, we've got Our Lady of Guadalupe. Not only is she surrounded by roses, but part of the story is that she unveiled a mantle full of roses when she encountered this young indigenous man who told us the story. I think "*The Lotus & the Rose*" carries a lot of beauty with it and meaning from both West and East. And I'm sure Tsomo could talk eloquently about the lotus part.

I'm supposed to begin by saying what our outline is, and a few opening remarks, and then Tsomo will lead us in a chant. Then I'll ask a question or two of the group to find out who's here, and then each of us will take 15 minutes to talk about our autobiography—where we come from in terms of our own mystical experience, what brings us to this table, together. Following that, we'll each take about 12 minutes apiece to discuss our lineages: where we come from in terms of our ancestral, spiritual trees. Then Tsomo will lead us in an experiential meditation for about 15 minutes, and we'll have a break. We'll regroup and we'll dialogue around a few topics, including what is the goal, what are the methods, of each of our traditions, and the role of silence, and maybe something about God-talk. Then we'll have an open discussion with yourselves. Then we'll close with my leading of a meditation that we believe John the Baptist taught Jesus and Jesus taught his disciples, but no Christians have heard of it in 1,900 years—that's the sad part of it. You people will participate in that, and it's quite an act of meditation. It's not a particularly quiet meditation; it's Jewish after all. It's from Ezekiel. That's kind of our map so you know where we're going.

So, just a few words of opening. I've been struck for years by that statement by the late historian Arnold Toynbee, who said shortly before he died that "the greatest event of the twentieth century will be the coming together of Buddhism and Christianity." Of course he died before the end of the twentieth century, and now we're into the twenty-first, but I think the fruits of that prophetic statement still need to be harvested, that Buddhism and Christianity, and more broadly East and West, with their wisdom traditions, have to go deeper and also connect more profoundly. That's what I'm hoping our dialogue will contribute to here. So, with that, then, I think we can move into an opening chant.

Tsomo: I'm going to suggest that we do something very simple: We're going to say one syllable again and again. This syllable is from Sanskrit, which was never actually just a commonly spoken language. The mantras that the Tibetans chant are generally Sanskrit because they're sound formulas. This syllable is the heart syllable "HUNG." I'm pronouncing it in the Tibetan style, "HUNG," so it's like "H-U-N-G." And if you notice— just try saying it once—where it vibrates in you.

[*"HUNG"* . . .]
You feel it literally vibrates in the heart area. And in contrast, "OM." If you try that, see where it vibrates.

[*"OM"* . . .]
That's associated with the chakra in the pineal gland area. So this is a dialogue that's based on our experience, and, after all, in Tibetan Buddhist understanding, the seat of the mind, the mind that goes between lifetimes, is in the heart. This is what we're going to really bring forth at this time with the seed syllable. So please join me.

[*"HUNG"* . . .]
Powerful syllable!

Matt: Why don't you say a few words about the lotus part of our theme here, "*The Lotus & the Rose*"? What's so special about the lotus?

Tsomo: Well, there are a couple of things about it. One thing that has always struck me about it is that the lotus is a wonderful metaphor for the human being. It has its roots, its feet, down in the muck. It lives in ponds, and so it's down in the gushy muck, right? It's got this stem, and then of course the leaves and the flower are up on top of the water facing the sun and the sky. The human being has an amazing capacity to span so many levels of

awareness. And this is something that has always struck me about the lotus. In the Vajrayana tradition particularly, Guru Rinpoche, who brought
Buddhism to Tibet, was not born in the normal way. He appeared
on a lotus as an 8-year-old boy on a milk lake, so he is known as the
"Lotus-born." PEMA JUNG NAY is another name for him, and it
means "Lotus-born." The lotus also represents transformation because
Guru Rinpoche brought Buddhism to Tibet. Tibet had had its own indigenous religion that was quite profound in itself, but Guru Rinpoche
transformed that country into a Buddhist country. He also transformed
dust into gold and his own body into light. So the lotus, to me, also signi-
fies transformation.

MATT: We want to begin by asking what traditions are represented in this
room. Perhaps both your birth tradition and where you're from now, or
how would you identify yourself now in terms of tradition? So, for example,
how many come out of a Jewish tradition? And how many come out of a
Christian tradition? And what other traditions do people come from besides
those two? Any other tradition represented in terms of birth? Agnostic?
Okay, and how would you identify yourselves today "Multi"—how many
would use that term, that they're multi? And other traditions to be named?
How many would call themselves "practicing Christians" today, if you want
to put it that way? Uh huh. Don't be so shy. And practicing Buddhists, how
many people call themselves "practicing Buddhists"? How many call themselves "practicing Jews" or "Jewish Buddhists"?

STUDENT: *You know, as a Jew, you never actually stop practicing.*

MATT: There you go. I think it's true for Catholics, too. You never quite
get over it.

STUDENT: *No, you never do. A recovering Jew.*

MATT: Okay, well, I'm glad we have diversity in the room. I am reminded
of a contemporary sociologist who writes about these post-modern times.
Walter Truett Anderson is his name, and he says, "Today we all belong
to so many communities at once. We should all write "e-t-c period" after
our names." That's another way of talking about what you were talking
about. The pluralism and the coming together of these traditions is, I
think, what's going on, and I think it's important to acknowledge that.

So our first topic is to go into our own experiences, and I was chosen

CHAPTER 1

Personal History

to go first with a flip of the coin or something, and I lost.

MATT: I was raised in a large Catholic family of seven children. I was in the middle, the neurotic middle, three brothers and three sisters, and I grew up in Madison, Wisconsin. I know that just being on the land there was very important to my own spiritual experiences as a child. I had a lot of Native American dreams, for example, and the Native American spirituality has always been profound for me and important in my own growth and survival even over the years. Years ago, I had a wonderful experience with an elder here in Santa Fe, in his *kiva*, talking about how hard it is to find good rattlesnakes to pray with these days in Santa Fe, because with all the building going on, the snakes are disappearing. It was a marvelous conversation.

When I look back at my own life, things really blew open for me spiritually as a teenager. I remember when I was a ninth-grader, a freshman, walking in my living room and someone was playing Beethoven's 7th, and all I wanted to do was dance. My whole soul just wanted to dance. It was a mystical moment. I've remembered it ever since. I remember reading Tolstoy's *War and Peace* between my junior and senior high school in summertime. And I told a friend that blew my soul wide open and I wanted to explore what happened to me. And of course, it was a mystical experience, and I didn't have words for it then, but that really had a lot to do with my going into the Dominican Order a few years after high school because I wanted to explore the spiritual experience. Shakespeare also had that effect on me in high school.

Another important element in my own growing up was having polio when I was 12 years old. I lost my legs, and the doctors couldn't tell me if I'd ever walk again. My father was a football coach in Madison, Wisconsin, for many years and my older brothers were all state football players, and I thought that's what I was going to be, too, and all of a sudden I couldn't walk. So my whole life shifted, and while I was in the hospital for many, many months as I was, this fellow would come to visit me who was a Dominican brother and very contemplative. He was from New Orleans and spoke with this Southern accent I had never heard in my life in Madison, Wisconsin. But he was very contemplative. He ended up being a Trappist monk for many years. Then he left and got married and has five kids, but that's another story. But the point is, he brought this other version of masculinity into my life just by his joy. He was a very joyful person, but also had his contemplative side. My father was not contemplative. He was much more something else—choleric, I guess. So all that kind of added up. Now, my legs came back to me after about a year, and I remember, when they came back, being overwhelmed with a sense of gratitude to the universe for having legs that worked. I remember saying to myself two things. One, "I'm never taking my legs for granted again," and number two, "I don't want to take my life for granted," because a friend of mine had died of polio the year before, and I thought it was a good deal to get life back and my legs back.

I think that had a lot to do with my mystical development of my own vocation because one way I define the mystic is: "The mystic is one who doesn't take for granted." I think that's why there's such an emphasis on meditating with breath in many traditions: because we tend to take breath for granted, but it's a little bit primal to take for granted for too long. So I think those were all formative developments in my own mystical journey, and I went into the Dominicans, as I say, to explore the mystical side of things. And while they had a lot of spiritual practices, including vegetarianism and a lot of meditation, a lot of chanting, sleep deprivation, celibacy, all that, they had it in their agenda, but they didn't talk about it. It was just kind of there. And after several years, I went to my superiors and I said, "Hey, you know, my generation is not going to be interested in religion. We're going to be interested in spirituality." This was the mid-1960s, and I said, "We're not getting any in the classes. We're not talking about these things, so why don't you send someone on to study it, and I'm glad to go." A few years later, they came to me and said, "Okay, you can go to Europe and study spirituality." So I was fortunate to do that. And from Thomas Merton, the Catholic monk, I got the advice to go to Paris, and they didn't want to send me to Paris. They said, "We never sent anyone to France that came back again." Then when I did come back and started teaching, they wished I hadn't come back again. So it goes to show you can never please all the people all the time.

But it was in Paris that I met my mentor, Père Chenu, a wonderful old French Dominican. I had him his last year that he was teaching. He was 75. He is a grandfather of liberation theology. He also named the Creation spiritual tradition for me, which made all the difference because I did come of age in the 1960s with the Civil Rights Movement and the Anti-War Movement and all of that. And my big question was, "How do I connect mysticism with social action and justice issues, and can you connect them?" He really helped me answering my question by naming this tradition. Really, all my work since has been exploring the Creation spiritual tradition and finding these amazing figures in the West, such as Meister Eckhart, and Hildegard of Bingen, and Thomas Aquinas, and the historical Jesus, and the Cosmic Christ, Nicholas of Cusa, and others who are really living out an authentic mystical practice that was also engaged in its struggle for justice. So that's been a great joy for me. When I returned, of course, the Women's Movement was very strong, and I taught for four years in a women's college, at Barat College in Lake Forest, Illinois. That really made me a feminist, just learning the stories of women and what they had been through in terms of their own development and needs. And of course, the Ecological Movement, the Gay and Lesbian Movement, all of this was going on in the 1970s. So to integrate that with the mystical was very important for me, and, really, all of my writings have been in some way, I think, an effort to articulate the relationship of spiritual practice to the work of justice and healing.

I also found early that you can't teach spirituality in a European model of education. It's all head. It leaves the heart out and the lower chakras. So immediately I designed a program after four years in this (undergraduate) women's college. I was invited to join the masters at Mundelein College in

Chicago, and I said, "Well, you have to take me and my program." So I designed this program, and the first one I hired for it was a dancer who led us in circle dancing. Far more important to me than biblical scholars are dancers because I learned early that if you don't bring the body in, it's not real. And this is precisely what European education forbids us to do. So from the start, our program—that was about 29 years ago we started that—it had great energy because we were bringing left and right hemisphere of the brain together, the body and the mind, and the heart, and social justice, and mystical practice. A lot of scientists came on board, and others. A lot of artists came on board. I remember one artist telling me, "You know," he said, "I've taught for 25 years, and this is the first time I've felt that I was teaching my whole soul in class, that I was allowed to," because we taught art as meditation, so you could bring all that into the classes and spiritual practice.

After seven years in Chicago, at Mundelein, we moved to California because that's where the science and mystical dialogue was going on in America, and also because we had outgrown our place in Chicago. We went to Holy Names College and had a wonderful 10 years there. The president was a great, strong, big Scotswoman, Celtic nun, president of the college, and she supported us. The Vatican was trying to shut us down for 10 years, and she stood by us and we survived it. Then she retired—she was a sociologist—and they had a new president. Within two years we were gone. And also I was expelled from the Dominicans and so forth. Then we moved after 12 years at Holy Names College, we moved to downtown Oakland, starting the University of Creation Spirituality. We were there for nine years.

Again, all of that was part of my spiritual practice because I learned to integrate my work and my spirituality. And seeing students come alive was—well, what can I say—as much enlightenment as I needed at that time in my life, to see students come alive and go on their journeys and to carry these practices into their work worlds. I remember lecturing in Australia toward the end of our tenure at Holy Names, and a young man stood up and asked, "Does Creation Spirituality have a strategy for social transformation?" For me that was a marvelous question. It got me to articulate. I was writing my book on the Reinvention of Work, and I concluded if we can reinvent work and reinvent education and reinvent forms of worship, we could have ourselves an awakening as a species and as a culture. So that, in a nutshell, is some of my personal journey, and to have encountered Tsomo this last year of my life.

Tsomo: Well, I first encountered your work when I read about original blessing, and I thought what a wonderful concept that is. At the time, I was mothering and homesteading in the country just west of Madison, Wisconsin.

Matt: Wow, good things happen in Wisconsin.

Tsomo: Yes, people don't understand. Anyway, they just laugh at the accent.

So, just going a little bit back to my Jewish roots and my education in that, I was so fortunate when I was a tiny little girl. We were living in a small town in Ohio, and there were only five Jewish families, and there weren't enough people to have a temple. So every Sunday everybody would trade off, going round-robin around these five different houses, and parents would trade off sitting with the kids and telling Bible stories and talking about the meaning of them. And I loved it. I just soaked it up. Then we moved to Chicago, where then, of course, there were bona fide temples. So my brother and I were sent to temple, and we used to hide to try to not be seen by the carpools, so we wouldn't have to go because the meaning, the spirituality was missing. We were being taught the Hebrew alphabet, we were being taught history but in a very dull, dry, lifeless way, and it was completely meaning-free. The 15 minutes of recess, I would dash down to the library and check out books for kids on Bible stories and things like that and go home and spend the week reading them. I finally got out of going to temple altogether.

Fortunately our family was friends with the rabbi, and my dad, who was a confirmed agnostic, would have these amazing debates, really debate discussions, with the rabbi. I grew up in a typical Jewish household, and debate was very much a part of learning. I would watch this debate go on, trying to get to the bottom of, well, what is the nature of God that he might or might not believe in. And the description that the rabbi gave was not the God that I normally was hearing about. It wasn't the guy with the white beard and the puppet strings. It was much more profound than that. This rabbi had studied the Kabbalah and had come from Germany, escaping Hitler, and was quite an amazing rabbi who was in a leadership position among American rabbis, really internationally. I was lucky that this was happening in the kitchen when I was growing up.

As far as restoring the feminine in my own life, I didn't really identify myself as a feminist. When they were burning bras, I was grateful to have one. And I was nursing. But I was homesteading; I was living in the country and living from the land. I went to "the Mother" in the sense of the Earth. For the little bit that I did in planting seeds and getting the weeds out of the way, I received so much. And it was much more than that. It was a natural place. It wasn't very easy to farm there because it was very hilly in that part of Wisconsin, so there were lots of forests and lots of fields. I was able to just restore for myself, as a modern person, my connection with "the Mother."

I'm going to doubleback. In high school, I was lucky enough to run into the work of Carl Jung. And so I studied Jung as a high-schooler and was fascinated with how the mind worked. And people would tend to come to me with their problems, and I'd listen. I was always fascinated, first of all, with what were their true motivations and so on, but I also was moved by what I was hearing, and if there was any way that I could help them just by even listening in a certain way, I found that just made my day. So I decided to become a psychotherapist, and I found that the work of Jung was the only work that I found that incorporated the soul in psychology, which after all is named after the soul, the *psyche*.

So I did study that and got my master's degree and then the equivalent of a second master's degree in body-centered psychotherapy, because I noticed that just talk therapy alone didn't quite do it. It does need to include the body. And I was searching for spirituality that would incorporate both masculine and feminine. I actually put out prayers every day for my teacher; that was part of my meditation practice. And when I first met my teacher it was actually in Santa Fe. I had already discovered Vajrayana Buddhism by then. I'd done some Hinayana and then Mahayana Zen, and then was trying on Vajrayana for size and working with an American lama, and I met Gochen Tulku Rinpoche. He was actually teaching and giving an empowerment for the next practice that I was going to be doing in this series of practices—and I didn't get that this was the answer to my prayers.

The next time I met him he was on my doorstep—then I got it. And

I was struck by the fact that he incorporated debate in the learning process. It was a very alive process. There was sound, color, archetype, all of these things that I felt were so important to me. And the central figures in the set of practices, the preliminary practices in his tradition, were the primordial Buddha in masculine and feminine form in union. Kind of the Tibetan yin and yang, you might say. I felt that I had found something that goes beyond psychology and what it could do. Psychology, I found, is very important for those of us who are tripping over our mental furniture in the dark. It gives us one of those little headlamps and helps us to sort of move that chair so we're not stubbing our toe every time we go over there. But after we've rearranged the furniture a certain number of times, Buddhism, I found, could show me the door out. And it gave me a much larger context. It also gave me, in Vajrayana particularly, a wealth of methods and practices to work with all kinds of neurotic emotions.

CHAPTER 2

Wave Metaphor

TSOMO: I'm going to mention a little bit about this context because I think it's important to talk about today. I'm going to use a metaphor because it's probably the best way to convey the most: A picture is worth a thousand words.

If we imagine true reality to be an ocean of awareness, just this one huge phenomenon, this ocean of awareness that is constantly creating waves, then we could say the deeper part of the ocean might be like what's known as the *Dharmakaya*, or truth body. It's pure awareness. It's emptiness, but it's not a vacant void; it's this aware emptiness. And since there's no sense of separation, then there's ultimate compassion—that's a quality that completely pervades this ocean of awareness. This emptiness also is constantly making waves. That's the nature of the ocean, to make waves. The emptiness constantly flashes forth luminosity, manifestation, and it does it through a stage we might call the *template* level of reality, or the *archetypal* level. It differentiates more and gets more complex until it reaches more of a manifested level, and that's called the *emanation body*, or *Nirmanakaya*. What I'm calling the archetypal level is the *Sambhogakaya*. So you've got the Dharmakaya, that emptiness, and then in the luminosity department you've got Sambhogakaya and Nirmanakaya. This is really like two sides of one coin. You can't really separate them. You've got the ocean and the waves, but how could you ever take the waves apart from the ocean? It's the nature of the ocean to make waves, and the waves are not separate from the ocean.

But if we imagine one of these waves, just one little wave, getting a little confused and saying, "Okay, I'm me, and then there are all the other waves and the rest of the ocean," and identifying just as me, myself, this wave, then there's a separation that happens. The "I" and "other" come into play. And this then leads to sort of a domino effect. If I'm just this one splinter of reality, and there are all these other waves and the rest of the ocean, all of a sudden I have a lot of need. Because when I was the whole ocean, there's no such thing as need. What could I need? But if I'm just this one little piece of reality, then all of a sudden I have all kinds of needs. I have to take care of this, that, and the other, and I'm rushing to get this and that. We eat and then we get hungry again, so we have to provide more food for ourselves, and then there's shelter and clothing and Maslow's hierarchy of needs that go on and on, and we never seem to quite collect all of them. There's this huge, deep longing that we all have to go home to the whole ocean, and yet we'll do anything to preserve our separateness. It's a very strange phenomenon about us sentient beings.

So the first of the three categories of neurotic emotions that the Buddha talked about—he talked about 84,000 of them, but they are often grouped into three categories—the first one is *marigpa*, the term in Tibetan meaning "lack of awareness," sometimes called ignorance. Anything having to do with lack of awareness, narrow-mindedness, sleepy torpor, laziness, this kind of thing, that's all in that category. That was the first one because we had a lack of awareness concerning who we were and how reality really was.

The first one led to the second one I mentioned, which was neediness, clinging, desire, any of those, and I think addiction falls into that one. That's the second category.

And then that one quite naturally leads into the third category. There are things we're grasping after, and then there are the things we don't want. We're constantly reaching for happiness and wanting to push away suffering. This is something that the Buddha observed all beings are constantly trying to do. Even if you stop and really observe your thoughts, the train of thought that you're having generally is pursuing happiness or trying to find a way to push suffering away. So the third category has to do with pushing suffering away. It also has to do with aggression. I discovered this in what I thought was my perfect child, when she first began playing with other children. When you get two children and one block, desire can lead to aggression. And she pulled the other kid's hair. I was so embarrassed. So there it is, the third one. One domino just sort of leads to the other.

Buddha Nature

TSOMO: Hearing neurotic emotions spoken of in a much larger context like this and then trying out these skillful means, of which there are so many in Vajrayana, and finding them to succeed was just a huge opening up for me. Remembering back to "original blessing," "original purity" is the term that they use in Tibetan Buddhism quite often, *kadak*, and if we understand that all of reality is Buddha Nature, what would be outside of that? So then we too are actually, in our true selves, Buddha Nature, but these neurotic emotions are like clouds covering the sun. Even though it's not our true nature, there it is. And one of these leads to the other, and then that leads to action. *Karma* means "action" in Sanskrit, and these are actions of body, speech, and mind. They all count. Intention definitely counts. So when we then take action, coming from these neurotic emotions and these misperceptions of reality, that then plants seeds that will come back in a reaction, you could say. This is another level of physics that the physicists haven't figured out yet, but in the universe there is the law of karma. And the way it tends to follow you, I thought was really interesting. I asked Rinpoche, "When we die and we go back into the ocean of awareness, this Dharmakaya, why is it that our habits of mind and our past actions follow us?" First of all, I want to say that our perception of reality is kind of like splatterings on the windshield. We get more and more obscured, and we can't see reality as it truly is. So, you know, I think this is a solid table. I see water: It's something to drink. But a fish, which has different karma, is looking through a different windshield, and they see water as home and something to breathe. And the beings in the god realms see water as *amrita*, wisdom nectar. And so it goes.

Well, getting back to what happens when we die, I'm going to use a piece of paper as Rinpoche did for illustrative purposes. I said, "How is it that this follows us?" And he said, "If you take a piece of paper and roll it up and it gets in that habit, and imagine that it happens for a long time, then it's not quite so flat. It's now got this shape. And I can do this for a moment, but it comes back up. A karmic action might be like a crease in the paper. And now, even if I do this, the crease is still there. So this is why we call it *cyclic existence.*" *Korwa* is the name for it in Tibetan. We keep going around and around in korwa because we keep reaching for happiness and trying to push away suffering, but we're ignorant of how to do this properly. So we then take actions that cause us more suffering and keep happiness further away. Ultimate happiness would be going back home to the whole ocean, which is not to ignore the existence of the waves at all; it's the whole thing. So if we come back to that, that's ultimate happiness. We just keep finding ourselves going around and around and never getting to that. We just keep dreaming this dream, whether we're waking or sleeping, that we call *Samsara.*

When I heard things like this, they struck me as true. I thought, "Okay, I found my teacher, I found a path that makes sense to me, I get to debate. I'm quite comfortable with that, being Jewish." And so off I went. And I've done lots and lots of retreat, generally three months of retreat a year, for many years. And I just felt as though I was standing under a waterfall with my mouth open, trying to catch as much as would come, because Rinpoche could just give me all kinds of amazing, profound teachings. Then I would go and practice, put these things actually into practice, spending long times in silence and prayer and doing specific practices that included body, speech, mind, all of the senses, directing them toward improving my state of mind. I found that they worked, so then I wanted to do more. Then he'd give me more, and so then I'd do more. One thing led to another, and the next thing I knew I was "lama-nated."

Lineage

TSOMO: For our next section, we're going to be talking about lineage. Especially because we're in America—how can I say this?—people don't usually go so deeply into one particular lineage. I myself have been in the sweat lodge many times. I live on an Indian reservation, and I'm very fortunate to know a medicine person, so I'm able to do that. And I actually tasted quite a bit of the spiritual smorgasbord for years before I settled on Vajrayana. But this reminds me a little bit of a gathering of mystics that happened a number of years ago. They came from different traditions, different lineages, but they were all deeply rooted in their own. They were debating back and forth about their different lineages and how truth is, and theological discussions were rampant. But when they talked about their transcendent experiences, they were all saying the same thing. It's as though many paths lead up the mountain from many different angles, so the terrain looks different on the way up, but the peak experience, you could say, is one point.

So here we are today, coming from our different lineages. As we do this, just think for yourselves, notice if any of your own peak experiences come into your mind at all. And also, just listen for possibly the fruits of following a particular lineage for a good long ways up the mountain.

We decided that I would go first for this part, so I'm still talking. So I explained, basically, the answer to the question that you may not have known you had, which was "What is Samsara, and how do we get here, anyway?" Now I'm going to talk a little bit about the Buddha's methods for how to get out because that's the lineage that I practice. I feel myself to be tribally Jewish and culturally Jewish, but the methods that I use are Buddhist, Vajrayana in particular.

The Buddha himself was moved by the suffering that he was seeing around him of everyone wanting happiness. All beings, not even just human beings, but everybody wanting happiness, nobody wanting to suffer, and yet, the harder they tried and the more they pursued that, the more happiness seemed to be beyond their grasp except in very temporary ways. And there was a lot of suffering involved. I mean, if you identify as the wave, what happens when other waves crash into you and mess you all up? If you identify as the wave, what happens when you go up on the shore and that's the end of that wave? Death is a terrifying thing. Sickness is a terrifying, miserable experience.

So he went on a journey. And finally, after studying many techniques, he was able to see himself, reality as it really was, and he had to take away all of the clouds that were blocking his own Buddha Nature. He had to eliminate all identification with his ego until he was to the point where all that was left was identifying with the whole ocean. Then he saw reality as it really was. The group of students that had gathered around him when he emerged from the last meditation under the *bodhi* tree said, "Can you tell us what is reality like? We want to be enlightened, too." And he said, "Words carry concepts, and what I've experienced is far beyond concept. So I can't tell it to you and have you understand and then become enlightened." And they said, "You can't just leave us here. You have to give us something." So he began teaching, and he set forth 84,000 *sutras* and thousands and thousands of *tantras*. He set forth three main branches of Buddhism, which are paths to enlightenment, ways that we can step-by-step reach that goal.

The first of those was what's known as the lesser vehicle, Hinayana, and that has a particular way of handling things. It mostly avoids the poisonous emotions—they're called the "three poisons," these three categories of neurotic emotion—and tries to avoid creating more karma and to reach enlightenment for one's self.

But in the greater vehicle, Mahayana, there are two purposes: enlightenment for self and others. So there's much more of the element of compassion in that, of course, thinking, "I can't just have enlightenment for myself and leave everybody else behind to suffer." The methods for working with the poisonous emotions are also different. There are antidotes applied. So for example, if you're feeling jealous, meditate on and practice sympathetic joy—sort of turning that around. For anger, there's forbearance, and so on and so forth. There are the applications of antidotes, which transform the emotion.

In Vajrayana, which is a subcategory of Mahayana, you actually take that emotion itself onto the path. You hold that emotion and then just very skillfully peel away the layers of the onion, the drama around the emotion, and get to the pure quality of it. What you come to are the five aspects—because there are also five categories, you can subcategorize anger into two more—you come into the five facets of primordial wisdom, which is a quality that pervades the Dharmakaya, the emptiness level of reality. You actually then use that emotion toward enlightenment in a very powerful, efficient way. So for example, with anger, yeah, there's the drama around it and the feeling self-righteous and the stories and the talking and the mind, but if we get past all that and we look to the true essence of it, it simply has this very crisp, sharp quality to it. And so it is what's known as—well, *yeshe* is the word for primordial wisdom. You could say its mirror-like yeshe, or mirror-like wisdom. And there are the other wisdoms. This is also true for when we feel desire or clinging. We can actually see to the essence of it, through all of these, which I won't go into now.

So these are some of the things that we work with in the path that I've been on, the Vajrayana path. Another aspect is the use of the lama. Because when you're doing this particular kind of practice, where you're carrying these neurotic emotions onto the path and actually using them themselves as the basis for enlightenment, it's very easy to fool yourself. So it's very important to have a highly trained, highly realized lama who is working closely with you. They'll often prescribe practices for this or that particular student because they see the inclinations of that mind and where someone might be fooling themselves and might need work. They'll apply particular archetypal deities to meditate on. And these meditations include visualization and sound, and they can include prostrations and working with a *mala*, so that all of our senses are brought onto the path.

The lama also provides another very important function, and I discovered this when I was meditating early on in my experience with Gochen Tulku Rinpoche. I was doing guru yoga and then going into a meditation space, and I found, as I was meditating, that it wasn't just my usual mind and my usual awareness. It was far greater and clearer than that, and a far higher level of realization than I normally was at. And I could tell it wasn't just me. So the next time I had a chance to get to a translator, because at that time I didn't know Tibetan, I asked him, "What was going on here in this meditation?" He said, "You were doing guru yoga, right?" "Yeah." "Well, you joined your mind in loving connection with the lama's mind. So, in a sense, you were piggybacking on his level of awareness." Again, a very efficient path up the mountain—you might say, a gondola. So I feel that lineage bushwhacks the path up the mountain, and some of these methods feel like a gondola taking you much further up the path than you could under your own steam.

CHAPTER 3

Christian Mystics

MATT: Your journey's obviously so rich. And you're part of a tradition that's so profound and rich—I mean, 84,000 sutras, that's enough to kind of . . .

TSOMO: Not to mention the tantras.

MATT: Yes, exactly. It's enough to kind of, you know, make you pause. Now we know why reincarnation is so important in your tradition—you can only take 20,000 each time, and that's if you're smart. There are two of your images that I'd like to pick up on. One is, of course, the ocean, us all being part of the ocean. And the other is about the Buddha Nature, all of us carrying the Buddha Nature.

Because, for me, coming out of the Christian mystical tradition, I've been pleased to see what's happening lately with the latest scholarship on the historical Jesus. Of course that quest has been going on for, like, 200 or 300 years, and they're finally to a point where they think they know who the historical Jesus was, and which words he really said, and which ones he didn't say. And, in fact, it's only 15 percent of the words ascribed to Jesus in the Gospels that we can really say with certainty were his words. The other 85 percent came from the community. But that's stunning in itself, I think, because that shows, hey, these people were turned on, and they didn't mind putting words in Jesus's mouth, which is really amazing. The chutzpah of that, you know? So it didn't matter to them whether they said it or Jesus said it, they were turned on. And that's important information.

Most recently, these very scholars who've been in the books for centuries, really—because it's been a lineage, it's been a process—are now turning to Paul. One of them, John Dominic Crossan, in his recent scholarship on Paul, [paraphrasing], says, "For Paul, you cannot be a Christian without being a mystic, and not just any kind of mystic, but a cosmic mystic, the Cosmic Christ." And one scholar, equally valid, Bruce Chilton, says, for Paul, his Christ is "metacosmic," which I think is great. I don't know what it means, but it's bigger than cosmic—that's really big. Metacosmic, well, that's the Buddha Nature, you see. And the way I see it, like you talked about the lotus in the water, I see it in terms of light, the metaphor. We always talk in metaphors when we talk about something important. As I tell my students, nothing important should be taken literally, whether it's spirit, or life, or death, or love, or sex. What's important is this metaphor, and this is the real stumbling block in fundamentalism, that they're trying to tie metaphors down to something literal. And that kills. Paul said that: He says, "The letter kills, the spirit gives life."

But the awareness that first of all you can't be a Christian without being a mystic—and, well, Paul is not Jesus by any stretch of the imagination. He is the first writer in the Christian Bible. He is the first one to write, and his favorite name for the Christ is Sophia, Lady Wisdom, which is shocking. It was shocking in the first century to the empire and to the Jewish establishment, if you will, and is shocking still today, that the Christ is Lady Wisdom. Again, it taps into the whole tradition of the goddess, and the Guadalupe, and the Black Madonna, and so much else.

So I feel, frankly, at this time in history, very touched and grateful that I've lived long enough to see these scholars begin to talk about serious things like mysticism. Because to say you can't be a Christian without being a mystic—just one implication of that is that every seminary in the world should shut down now overnight because there's not one that's teaching mysticism that I know of in a healthy way. The implications of that are just huge—they have to kind of regroup. I would like to see the seminaries shut down for six months and then take every faculty member, staff, and student and train them in spiritual practice, then put them back in, and we would have a real rejuvenation of lineage.

When I did my master's studies in theology, I chose to work on Jesus and prayer in a biblical context. And what I learned from that was how

Jewish Jesus was in his prayer, but also how, when you're dealing with the subject of prayer, you're really dealing with the essence of what we call *spirituality*. And so in my first book, *On Becoming a Musical Mystical Bear*, from a dream I got while writing it, and now called *Prayer: A Radical Response to Life*, I'm trying to deal with prayer and its essence, get down to what it really is. And ultimately I say it is our *yes* to life, which is our mysticism. And it is our *no*, and that is our prophetic side, our standing up to injustice and the forces of life that interfere with life, such as necrophilia and all of its manifestations, including, of course, many of the things you're talking about in terms of addiction and self-pity and ignorance and so forth. I see that struggle for falling in love with life as our *yes*. And it is a struggle because history is not as kind as we would like, often, and life itself is a struggle. It contains suffering for all beings, obviously. It's roses with thorns, not just the wonderful smells of roses. And roses themselves, are as you know, well, impermanent.

In my own discovery, Meister Eckhart has played a huge role. And even though Eckhart was a Dominican, I never heard about him in my 11 years of training as a Dominican, and that's because he was condemned by the pope a week after he died. I heard about him a bit in my studies in Paris, but very little. I really discovered him after my return, and it happened in two ways. I was reading a book by Kumar Swami, a Hindu, on arts and spirituality, and there was a chapter in there on Eckhart, and there were quotes from Eckhart that I had published in a book I had written the year before, and this freaked me out. I didn't finish Kumar Swami's book. I was so freaked out, I put it back on the shelf. I thought, this is scary. A few months later I went back and I picked it up and I finished the essay on Eckhart, and there were more quotes that I had published that year in an article I did on sacred space and sacred time. I looked over my shoulder, you know, for these ghosts in the room, which turned out to be angels.

Well, then I had kind of a shift, and I said, "You know, this isn't something to be scared about. I have a brother here," because I had already published several books and there was a bit of flurry out there—and now here's a brother. So I started to look more deeply into Eckhart. And then I was in a serious car accident. To make a long story short, I had an operation, and Eckhart came to me during the operation, and we went walking together on the beach. Nothing said, complete silence. It was the most transcendent dream of my life, and he really entered my world in a fuller way there. Then I really went after him, after his works, Latin and German, and I found there, as I say, a real brother. He talks about the ocean simile time and time again when he's talking about compassion, and he says compassion is an ocean and that we're born in compassion. He says "the first outburst of everything God does is compassion." He has a beautiful sermon, which I call "God Compassion as an Ocean," our origin and it is our destiny. There, too, I think the metaphor that you and your tradition comes up with very much plays with this language from Eckhart, and experientially so.

Now, in terms of method, it wasn't just Eckhart. Eckhart led me to Hildegard. And Hildegard, in many ways, had been silenced for about 700 years. A few authors who wrote about her said she was crazy because she invented her own language and all this, but I found in Hildegard a real, dynamic Renaissance woman who was scientist and healer and mystic and painter, and a great musician, and a prophet. She was writing letters to the popes, telling them they were surrounded by evil and to get off their papal throne, and she was writing letters to abbots and archbishops, saying they were drying up. And that's the only sin anyway, is drying up, she said, so better do something. She was amazing. So I got into her and kind of helped bring her forward, and then a lot of others got on board, of course. Hildegard is really present in our consciousness today.

Then I went back to Aquinas, whom I'd had years of study with as a Dominican because he was a Dominican, but they had never introduced us to the mystical side of Aquinas. And of course I learned why when I got into Aquinas. They had never even bothered to translate his most mystical works. His first work, *Commentary on Denis the Areopagite*—was never translated into German or French or English. And many of the biblical works, never translated—his commentary on Isaiah, for example. Brilliant work. So I translated these and did a work on Aquinas's mysticism. *Sheer Joy: Conversations with Thomas Aquinas on Creation Spirituality* So here were three heavyweights, Aquinas, Hildegard, and Eckhart, who are all in a lineage. Aquinas quotes Hildegard, and Eckhart was very much a student of Aquinas because he came into the Dominicans right after Aquinas died.

These people were drawing on this Cosmic Christ tradition, the tradition of the Buddha Nature in all of us. The Cosmic Christ tradition, here's how I see it in terms of light. Jesus as an individual, like the historical Buddha, was a light, a particle. We now know that light is both particle and wave, and the scientists fought about that, I think, for a 100 years. Is it particle, or is it wave? It's both. So that's how I see the Buddha and I also see Jesus and the Christ. That as an individual, Jesus is a particle of light, but as Christ, the risen Christ if you will, or the spirit of Christ, like the Buddha Nature, it is a wave. And so I, too, as an individual, I am a particle, but as part of the whole, your metaphor of the ocean—the Christ wave breathes through me as the Buddha Nature breathes through other beings. And the fact that science now is telling us that photons and light waves are in every atom in the universe, for me, affirms the mystical intuition of John: 1 that says Christ is the light in all being. So for me the name "the Christ" or "the Buddha Nature" hardly matters because they're both inadequate, but they both carry weight. They both carry historical substance because both of these beings lived, struggled, and taught, and because others have followed their teachings. So it does carry that kind of weight, but we should never get bogged down with concepts or with names. They're all inadequate.

Aquinas says the most important thing we know about God is that we do not know God. It's that sense of humility that I think is so lacking in so many crusades, inquisitions, and religious dogma.

CHAPTER 4

Cosmic Christ Lineage

MATT: The Cosmic Christ tradition didn't begin with Jesus. It comes from the Wisdom tradition of Israel. And, again, the latest scholarship on Jesus is that as an historical student, he comes from the Wisdom lineage of Israel. And of course, Wisdom in Israel is feminine, it's nature based, and it's cosmological, and it's very mystical.

When I was a child, especially a teenager in the Catholic Church, we were a practicing Catholic family, and I derived a lot from Catholicism. That's why I went into the Dominicans. I was in a public high school. My best friends were Jewish, agnostic, or Protestant, and we had all these debates about philosophy and God. I would go to my parish priest, who was Dominican, and he would have me reading Aquinas and Chesterton and some intelligent Catholic writers. And that had a lot to do with my interest in the Dominicans because they had this intellectual side to the lineage, and that was very important to me. And Madison was of course a university town, so there was this kind of heat around the intellectual discussion that I appreciated. Not unlike, I think, Tsomo your experience with the rabbi who was knowledgeable and debating with your father.

So, again, for me the lineage has grown from being just Jesus. I remember concluding my master's thesis on Jesus's prayer by saying there's no way to renew Christianity without becoming more Jewish. And in many ways, I would say all my work has been about bringing Christianity back to its Jewish roots, and now we're discovering Jesus himself comes out of Wisdom's editon of Grace. It's the Wisdom liturgy that was on Saturday morning in the Catholic Church in the 1950s. When I was a teenager, Saturday's Mass was always dedicated to Mary, and what they used for the readings were these beautiful passages from Wisdom literature like Proverbs or Sirach. "I was by God's side, a master crafts person, playing with God day after day, delighting to be with the sons and daughters of the human race." That's Proverbs. Or Sirach, saying, "Before the hills were formed, I was there. Before the oceans were there, I was there. I walked the vaults of the sky and I walked on the sands of the ocean." This sense of cosmology, that's Wisdom. It totally turned me on. I preferred Saturday Mass to Sunday Mass because of that. And I didn't know why at the time. I couldn't say, "This is mysticism, this is the feminist tradition, we're not getting anyplace in our culture." No, I couldn't say that. All I knew was, I was turned on, and it was the goddess that was turning me on in the Catholic Church. And to Catholicism's credit, you see, it is pre-modern, so it kept alive this pre-modern awareness of the goddess and of the feminine and of mysticism. Because Protestantism came along at the time of the modern era, and it cut off the goddess explicitly. Luther turned the tap off on Mary, and Calvin was even worse. So Protestants suffer from that lack of the feminine and the mystical and the ocean: *la mère*, the mother, the ocean, La Mer.

As a Catholic, I did not suffer in the 1950s from that lack. In fact, I was drinking it in, and that's part of the lineage. And for me, the effect of the aesthetic in Catholicism was primal. When I was thinking about becoming a Dominican, and a senior in high school, I went on a retreat in the Dominican House of Studies in Dubuque, Iowa. And what I appreciated was three things. One was a sense of community. Another was the seriousness of the scholarship and the study. But above all, it was hearing the monks chant, and it was in Latin, and chanting the Psalms, which is Wisdom literature. It was the aesthetic of that that totally moved me and drew me in and kept me in. Again, a lot of that has been lost when they put the liturgy into the vernacular, and you realized how prosaic a lot of what's being sung is about. You see, when it was in a foreign tongue, it's much more mystical because you're not stuck on the meaning of the words. You're feeling the sounds at other levels of your chakras.

So for me there's been an explosion of my lineage to realize how Jewish it is, how profoundly mystical it is. It was a Hindu, Kumar Swami, who got me into Eckhart, but it was a Buddhist, Suzuki, who got Thomas Merton into Eckhart. In 1958, when Suzuki and Merton had their dialogue on Buddhism and Christianity, at the end, Suzuki threw up his hands and said, "I can't help you, Tom. You're a typical Western dualist. The only outside chance you have of getting Buddhism is to read that one Zen thinker of the West, Meister Eckhart." And Merton said, "But he's been condemned by the Church." Suzuki said, "Well, I can't help that, can I?" Merton thought it over, and to read Zen poetry and Eckhart. And he totally shifted. The Merton of the 1950s was a very dualistic, guilt-ridden, Augustinian monk. The Merton of the 1960s is confident, he's Buddhist, and he's prophetic. And in his journal that he wrote on his last trip to Asia—his only trip to Asia, but his last trip in this lifetime because he died there—he was writing in his journal [paraphrasing], "Eckhart is my lifeboat. Eckhart is my lifeboat." So Eckhart was profound; he brought on the shift in Merton's whole consciousness.

For me, then, this lineage of Eckhart goes right though Karl Marx. Marxim's scholar, Ernst Bloch, in his last book, says that Eckhart was a big influence on Marx. This lineage of the Creation mystical tradition is older than Jesus. It's Jesus. It's Paul when he is recognized at his best. Paul had his bad moments; he is culturally determined like a lot of us. But, at his best, Paul is talking about how in Christ—and you can translate it "in the Buddha"—there is no distinction between male and female, Jew and Gentile, slave and free, and so forth: this recognition of the ocean part, not the individual piece.

One thing that I want to make explicit because so many Westerners are unaware of is how, for me—this is an affirmation of the universality of Buddha's teaching—how they are dealing at the level of archetype and even deeper level of being. Both Eckhart and Aquinas have in their writings pure Zen, or pure Buddhist, teachings, and their methodology is a very simplified form of letting go of all thoughts and letting go of all images.

And so in this one passage, Eckhart says, "How should you love God? Love God mindlessly, without a mind. Love God as God as a 'not God,' a 'not person,' a 'not thing.' Separate yourself from all twoness and sink into the unity with God."

That's just one passage from Eckhart. But it's not only Eckhart, even Aquinas talks about letting go of the "discursive mind" and about sinking into wisdom, playing with wisdom. He says that's what contemplation is: playing with wisdom. He says you do this by letting go of all images of God and of all images at all, quieting the mind and playing with the heart. I actually have some of these passages here. I think I'll take a couple of minutes to share a brief sentence or two so you get this, because this is the lineage but it's not out there. Christians, even Dominicans, students, Thomists, are not in touch with this lineage. That's the problem. The Dalai Lama says, "The number one obstacle to interfaith is a bad relationship with your own faith tradition." And if today's scholars in Christianity are saying, "Hey, you can't be a Christian without being a mystic," well, where are the mystics? We should look and see what our lineage teaches us about the methodology, how to get into this practice that takes us beyond compulsions.

So Aquinas says, "God exceeds all speech. God is ineffable. Nobody can sufficiently sound God's praises. We know God through ignorance, and we get into this ignorance. It happens when our mind, receding from all other things, lets itself go, lets even itself go, and becomes united to the super-resplendent rays of the deity. Thus, in as far as it knows, God exists not only beyond all the things that are within it, but even beyond it and beyond all the things that can be comprehended by it. Knowing God in this way in such a state of knowledge, one is illuminated by the very profundity of divine wisdom, which we cannot examine thoroughly. The depth of God is called 'hidden' and 'unknown essence' of God."

And then here's his teaching on meditation: "The first requirement then for the contemplation of wisdom is that we should take complete possession of our own minds before anything else does, so we can fill the whole house with the contemplation of wisdom. It's necessary to be fully present there, concentrating in such a way that our aim is not diverted to other matters. And then you enter the house, and in that house you find rest, and in that house you play."

He says that "There are two kinds of distractions in the soul caused by the variety found in external things. The first, we leave behind external things in order to enter into the soul itself, but the second distraction that has to be removed is the one caused by discursive reasoning. So we have to abandon discursive reasoning, fix the soul's gaze on the contemplation of one unified truth. And then after these two steps, a third act of oneness occurs, and that is knowing that being still we see that I am God," quoting the Psalms.

The West Catches Up

MATT: So what I'm saying is there are practices in Christianity that to me are pure Buddhism, but what this proves to me is that the Buddha found universal truths. Eckhart and Aquinas also found them without going East because they didn't have that opportunity. They found it in their own meditation practice. So you have an Eastern discovery and a Western discovery coming together here. And for me this is stunning because we are now talking about human nature. We're not talking about Buddhism or Christianity or Judaism. We're talking about what it is to be human, and what it is to safeguard what is most valuable in the human heart, and what it takes. It does take practice. It does take effort. And it does take teachers.

The West has a lot of catch-up to do. This is why a lot of serious Westerners have gone East, including Tsomo. But I think this catch-up is doable for two reasons. One is, we're in such a crisis as a species that there's nothing like necessity to get human beings off their duffs and working. But, secondly, is that we have access to Eastern teachings and to indigenous teachings, and to Western teachings that we've never had access to before. The Creation spiritual tradition has been condemned, it's been underground, it's been a minority opinion in Western theology for centuries—many, many centuries.

But that's what a paradigm shift means, as Thomas Kuhn says. What used to be on the edge moves to center stage. Now wisdom is moving to center stage. Part of it is the Women's Movement and feminist theologians who are bringing it forward, and part of it is our desperation, part of it is cosmology, and part of it is a yearning that you spoke of: the yearning for mysticism and for the return to unity and the ocean. So we have a lot going for us to move into our healthy human-hood again.

But in terms of lineage, I'm emphasizing lineage here, let me share with you this one passage from Eckhart, and this is just one of his passages on meditation, if you will. I gave my own paraphrase, but here are his exact words. "How then should one love God? You should love God mindlessly, that is so that your soul is without mind and free from all mental activities. For as long as your soul is operating like your mind, so long does it have images and representations. But as long as it has images, it has intermediaries. And as long as it has intermediaries, it has neither oneness nor simplicity. Therefore, your soul should be bare of all mind, it should stay there without mind. For if you love God as He is God, or mind, or person, or picture, all that must be dropped. How then should you love God? Love God as God is: a 'not God,' a 'not mind,' a 'not person,' a 'not image.' Even more as God is a pure, clear, one, separate from all twoness, and we should sink eternally from something to nothing into this one. May God help us to do this." So that's the ocean. And notice, he's sinking. That's ocean-talk. We are sinking into this oneness.

So I think that you were going to lead us into an experience to get us into the sinking, maybe.

Tsomo: Exactly. We have methods. And some of the methods involve insight forms of meditation coming at it, others are just calming the thoughts enough that we come to it, and others through giving rise to *bodhicitta*, which means "the heart mind of awakening."

A: PRACTICE—*Dying Meditation*

Tsomo: I was thinking to do a bodhicitta one where we could feel how we're not separate through the exercise of compassion. But somehow, as you were talking, I thought, maybe I'll pick another one where we can just experience it in more of an insight way. We can feel the connection coming at it from so many different ways. But I thought this would be a good one probably for all of us who come from agnostic traditions or sort of polyphonic traditions, and different traditions that we all come from. In order to peel away the layers of this onion and get to our very true essential nature, there are some simple imagery things that we can do.

When I first was working with my lama on calm-abiding meditation and insight meditation, I would say, "What do you suggest I do when my mind wanders? You know, it happens from time to time." And he said, "You can go at it from two different ways. You can stop and look directly at the thought and see what is it, really. What is its true essential nature? Or you can turn the lens inward and look at the thinker and do the same thing with the thinker." So I invite us to do that second one today.

The way I did it, and I found it really helpful, was to actually rehearse dying, the dying process, because in that process a lot of the layers of the onion are going to be peeled away, and a lot of the things we identify as "me" get peeled away.

If you can, just sit with your backs straight but relaxed. I prefer, in this case, to close my eyes, although most of the meditations are with open eyes. So either way is fine.

But just imagine, now, that it's time for you to leave this life. What does that mean? What falls away? Well, the body of course falls away. So let's really feel that happening as much as we can. Now we feel with that body falling away, we also lose many of the things that we learned in this life: the piano lessons, the books that we read, foreign languages that we learned. English falls away. Many of our neuroses that we've dealt with all this life fall away, the experiences that caused them. The people we attach these experiences to fall away. Our personality falls away. We leave behind our name, being American or whatever country we're from. And yet, what is there? Perhaps we could call it "my awareness." But where is the "my?" Just "awareness." So resting in just awareness for a moment. If you haven't opened your eyes yet, slowly open them, keeping that "just awareness" in your awareness, and also allowing manifested reality to coexist in your awareness: the ocean and the waves simultaneously, indistinguishably present. This kind of emptiness I call the pregnant emptiness, and it is full of compassion. We can feel some qualities of this emptiness. And so as we emerge from this contemplation, please remember, if you can, some of those qualities in your encounter with your true self.

CHAPTER 5

Compassion and Generosity

MATT: So, in terms of some dialogue, Tsomo, the other day, proposed we talk a little bit about goals. When I look at goals, in terms of my lineage, two words rise to the surface: one is *compassion*, and one is *generosity*.

For me, compassion very much comes out of mysticism because it comes out of our awareness—the term we ended with—awareness of interdependence. Once we recognize how truly interdependent we are, compassion just happens. It flows. It's absolutely natural. Eckhart put it this way: "What happens to another, whether it be a joy or a sorrow, happens to me." That's compassion. It is our common joy and our common sorrow. And it's also an effort to relieve the sorrow to the extent we can, to relieve suffering to the extent that we can, the work of relieving ignorance or relieving physical pain through healing and medicine and so forth. That, of course, is the Jewish tradition, from Isaiah, of what we call the works of mercy.

And after all, Jesus said in his Sermon on the Mount, as translated in Luke's Gospel, as remembered by the Luke tradition, "Be compassionate as your creator in heaven is compassionate." Now that's calling us to our divinity because in the Jewish tradition, God is the compassionate one. So for Jesus to say, "Hey, we've got this in us," is an amazing challenge. It's a challenge that, 2,000 years after his teaching has only sporadically been fulfilled, but it has been fulfilled in some honorable beings that we all recognize and praise, talking about Martin Luther King, Jr., or his influence from Gandhi, or the other people we call saints and heroes—Dorothy Day—people who carry the work of compassion into the world.

So I think there's a wonderful coming together, then, of what the East would call "non-action and action," and what the West, I think, would call "being in action." Meister Eckhart says, "We should worry less about what we do and more about who we are, because if our being is just, we will be just. If our being is joyful, we will be joyful." This reintegration of being and action and doing, if you will, is part of the accomplishment of a mystical lineage and of our own practice.

Also in the West, Eckhart is very Jewish when he says, "Compassion means justice." Compassion is not just about feeling for people, it is about creating structures that allow people to emerge, allow their deeper self, this ocean with all of us, to emerge, to allow the Buddha Nature to emerge, to allow the Cosmic Christ, the Christ Nature in all of us to rise to the surface. And for that, obviously, we need justice. We need fairness. An unjust relationship does not hold. Eckhart put it this way: "There is no love between a master and a slave. For love, there has to be equality." He said, "Your life has to be about either living equality or making equality happen." With that, compassion flows, the joy flows, the empathy flows, and the work to relieve the suffering flows.

For me, *generosity* has become a very important word lately. It's an amazing word in English when you look it up etymologically. I end my book called *Sins of the Spirit, Blessings of the Flesh*, with an essay on *generosity*, the word. It's amazing. From this word we get *genesis, generativity*—it's from the Greek word. Generosity includes creativity; you can't be generous without being creative. Indeed, creativity is a giving away of our gifts. It's like the Native American give-away. That's generosity. But it's more than that. Also in the word is the word *genus*—and *lineage* and *kin*-ship, from which we got the word *kind*. *Kindness* is related to the word *kin*, and *kin* is related to the word for genus and kind, what we come from. Our species is a kind. Our families are a kind and kinship. Kindness is related to the word *kin*. So all of this is also from our talk about the mammal brain, about our capacity for compassion, for kinship.

So when I explore this word *generosity*, it just gets me very excited because it has to do with cosmology, our genesis, where we come from, our beginnings as well as our creativity. And again, we have to go beyond the lineages that are human—even beyond the thing called Buddhist lineage, beyond the thing called Christian or Jewish lineage, to all the other beings that have brought us here. And now we can name them. You know, the galaxies and the supernovas and the fireball and the atoms. This is our lineage. Think about their generosity. If you ever come up short looking at human generosity, think about this: The sun—the entire earth system runs on one billionth of the energy that the sun gives out every day. That's pretty darn generous. There's at least one generous being there, and it's the sun, folks.

And we have to realize how generous the other beings are—plants that we eat, food that we eat, the fish or the animals, if you eat fish and animals. There is this generosity going on, and the whole point is that we continue the cycle and not interfere with it by stopping it with our stomachs and our greed and our needs, you see, that we are called upon to be generous also. It is a cycle. But, again, it's easier to understand. It's not just a commandment for the two-legged ones: Be generous. No. The commandment is how we ended the last meditation. Be aware. Be aware of how much generosity is going on, on the part of all beings on a daily basis. And this has been going on forever.

And there's one word that I kind of want to resurrect. I think it's been badly beaten up and abused in the modern era, and that is the word *sacrifice*. I think that when there is slave-master relationships of any kind, the word *sacrifice* gets abused: You are sacrificing for someone else. But the real word *sacrifice* means "to make holy." And you do make holy by being generous, by giving away, by not just seeking your own perfect serenity or security, which of course in our civilization is such an issue. So *sacrifice*, I think, is a word worth redeeming. It is about making holy by deeds that come from our being.

When I read Buddhist literature, it's interesting how smoothly generosity and compassion glide together in the writings. And I think that's as it should be, because when you come to, down to this bottom question, "Who are human beings?" I think all the great teachers, the Buddhas, and the Lao Tzus, and the Isaiahs, and the Jesuses, and the Dorothy Days and all have been trying to remind us that we are generous in our roots. The ocean is a very generous source from which we come, and we are capable of compassion. And I think that as a species we need to continually not just be reminded of this, but be led to this. Part of the struggle we're up against today is that the forces that dominate our awareness—like the media for example, and the powers behind them—their bottom line is anything but generosity and compassion. The world in which we find ourselves, the human-made world, is not conducive to bringing the best out of us. It's conducive to the reptilian brain, not to the mammal brain.

Part of our awareness is to cushion ourselves, buffer ourselves from this energy of greed, which is the opposite of compassion and generosity, and fear, which is the opposite of sharing. Fear, literally, makes us go like this; it tightens us up. In fact, Aquinas says, "Fear is such a powerful emotion for human beings that when fear takes over the soul, all compassion goes out the door." So fear and compassion are incompatible. The compulsion for security or the preaching of fear is the killing of compassion.

The implications of putting these issues forward, compassion and generosity, are huge for our own souls, our own hearts, but our own culture, too. This is going to be a clash, and yet I think that this is what the next level of evolution of our species is all about. Either we learn what our teachers, East and West, have been telling us—that we're compassionate beings and we're generous beings—either we learn this and practice it, or we're probably finished as an experiment on this planet.

TSOMO: So, on that cheerful note . . .

MATT: Well, it was cheerful right up to the end.

TSOMO: I'm going to maybe bring it back to something a little more upbeat, positive.

CHAPTER 6

Enlightenment as Goal

TSOMO: In looking at goals, I was thinking, well, that's a pretty easy one for me, coming from the Buddhist tradition. The goal is enlightenment. But then, of course, we have to define enlightenment—and I began to, earlier on in this dialogue today. We are, in our true selves, this ocean of awareness that constantly makes beautiful patterns of waves all over the place, and whatever we define as ugly is actually having to do more with the splattered bugs in our own windshield, karmic bugs on our windshield, and the twists in the windshield and the colorations. Because reality, as it actually is on its own terms, is more beautiful than we can probably even very well imagine, whether we're talking the Dharmakaya, Sambhogakaya, and Nirmanakaya. The whole ocean and its waves is actually that. And we are simply this piece of reality that is also Buddha Nature, just like everything else, because what isn't? And it's only our own delusion and the neurotic emotions that come from that that we need to clear away. Again, it's like the clouds finally being cleared away from the sun. And then, of course, there's the sun, and that's what we really are: Buddha Nature.

So the methods that the Buddha set out went into all these different iterations and different countries, and the lineages then were passed down mouth-to-ear, mind-to-mind, from one master to another, all the way down to present day, including my teacher, who is a lineage holder. For example, he in a former incarnation was one of the nine close, close students of Guru Rinpoche, who brought Buddhism to Tibet. When he was a young child, he remembered that and other lives. Then he trained his mind so the potential was really brought forth. You talked quite a bit about bringing those Buddha qualities forth through the methods of prayer that you mentioned earlier and silence and so on.

And there were methods that were also handed down. And in Vajrayana, in particular, Guru Rinpoche did quite an amazing thing. He hid what's known as *treasures*, and he hid them in rocks, at the bottoms of lakes, in the air, all over the place. He then wrote, in scriptures, predictions for who would discover these, what names they would be known by, where they would be discovered, and roughly when. They have been discovered all along since he hid them in the 800s CE, right up until present times. The treasure that was revealed for the particular lineage that I'm working with, Gochen Tulku Rinpoche, was hidden at the bottom of a lake. There are amazing, phantasmagorical stories about this treasure revealer, as he was called, who went to the bottom of the lake and retrieved the treasure, and there was *Dakini* writing in the air, and he was saying, "Somebody get a pen, quick." "Oh, we forgot the pen and the paper." So he's dictating as he's reading it from the sky in front of him, and then it's disappearing as they get it. That happened quite a bit actually in the moment of revealing the treasures.

There is usually one who named the treasure revealer who went before, much like John the Baptist with Jesus, interestingly enough. Each of these treasures was a cycle of teachings of a graduated path from starting with where you're at, which is not able to just drop the mind like that, and all the complicated thoughts, and be able to just be in that ocean. If we could do that, oh, wouldn't it be easy? But these teachings meet us where we're at—beings that are stuck on this channel of reality without the channel changer, taking sight, sound, busyness of mind, all of those things, and the neurotic emotions, too, and bringing them onto the path in a very potent set of practices. This is what these *terma* cycles do, these treasure cycles.

I've been studying these paths one at a time, starting with just calm-abiding meditation, being able to rest one's mind on one thing for a while—just pursuing that. Not necessarily achieving it for 20 minutes straight. Then the insight meditation, which you got a glimpse of in the way we worked with that rehearsing of our dying.

There's another meditation that expands our capacity for compassion, which was a Buddha quality. Of course the practices get more and more potent as you go along, and your mind gets more distilled; then you can handle the more potent medicine, until they get quite intense and we're working with archetypal deities. So we're beginning to work with Sambhogakaya, the archetypal realm, and working with pure vision instead of the obscured one, and doing this enough that we get used to it. The word for meditation in Tibetan, by the way, is *gom*, which means "getting used to." We just need to spend a lot of time doing that because we're stuck in this relative truth level of reality and have trouble seeing the ultimate truth level of reality. And those two truths, again, are like two sides of one coin. We can't ignore the waves of the ocean any more than we can ignore the rest of it.

So we keep working with these different aspects and working with the "clearing away the clouds" part, and the "bringing forth the sun" part. The word in Tibetan for "Buddha" is *sangye*, which means "clearing away and maturing." So you have those two processes right there. With compassion meditation, the people who were just taught one as they walked into the lab were then doing, I think it was 30-second breaks and then 90-second meditations. And their gamma waves were measurably increased. You've heard about alpha and beta, theta, and delta waves in the brain, but they also measure gamma waves. They're high-frequency waves that the brain puts out, but usually not so much. And with the long-time meditators, they put out levels of gamma waves that had never ever been recorded before. No one had ever had anything approaching these levels—not only when they were meditating, which was when they were really off the charts, but they were still off the charts in between sessions. And the brain was giving out more coordinated readings between the left and right hemispheres, and between the lobes of the brain, and so on. Talk about taming the lizard.

All these were measured repeatedly, and the way one scientist put it was, "Just as weightlifting and aerobics can sculpt the body, these meditative practices can sculpt the brain." And they had actually measured that. And a lot of those experiments happened in Madison, Wisconsin. Back to the scene of the crime.

In the "proof of the pudding" department, also, people who have practiced these Vajrayana practices have been known to transform their physical bodies into light and leave behind nothing but hair, nails, and the clothes that they were wearing—there's just this heap left on the ground. And that's happened not in long-ago times only, but also even in more recent times. And Rinpoche himself knew somebody who had attained this level, actually, a couple of people.

There was a woman in Lhasa who he met; she was a student of Dudjom Rinpoche's. He went and visited Lhasa even though he had left Tibet some years before that, but he came back and he was doing *korwa*, or circumambulation around the *Jokhang*. Lots of them meet there—that's also a way to run into people. So he said, "Well, how are you doing?" because he knew her from before and she was just this housewife. She said, "I'm doing well, and my practices, I think, are going pretty well, but I just don't know if I'm going to make it to rainbow body before I die." And he's thinking, "Well, she has a pretty high opinion of herself." He then heard that she, not too long after that, passed away, and her body—they didn't move the body—it kept getting smaller and smaller and smaller.

There are different ways of attaining rainbow body. Sometimes it's in an instant; you turn around and there's just hair and nails. But other times, it's more like this. And so her body was getting smaller and smaller, and people were visiting the apartment in throngs. This was a tiny little apartment in Lhasa, and the Chinese did not know what to do with this. But, anyway, her body did continue to get smaller and smaller, and this was somebody Rinpoche knew personally.

There have been other examples as well. There was a woman who was just a housewife and a yak herder. And she was milking the female version of a yak (because a yak is just a male; it's like saying milking a bull). Her daughter was on another lineup, and she was on this lineup, wearing a triangular rain hat—I guess it must have been raining. The daughter thought, "Gee, she is taking an awful long time. I've finished already. What's going on?" The hat is down there under the yaks. Finally, she went over to check and there was just the clothing, the hair, and the nails.

Yeah. There are many stories like this. And my lama's lama, Dilgo Khyentse Rinpoche, when he passed away, they found relics in his bones. He was quite an amazing master.

These things really do work, and I think it would be just wonderful for these exchanges to continue and for us to explore, well, what happens with Christian meditators? I've heard of one woman who was considered quite saintly in Europe, I think it was in Germany, who no longer needed to eat. She just lived on light. So these things are possible for anybody anywhere in the world.

MATT: Well, there are many stories like that in the Christian hagiography, and there's some contemporary ones. I've certainly met people, for example, who have visitations from angels and things like that. But I don't know—I think there's a danger, especially given the way the media triggers our minds these days, with titillation. I think there's a certain danger that extraordinary phenomena becomes some kind of goal instead of compassion. I think, you know, with compassion as the goal, then you can tolerate extraordinary phenomena.

Many of the saints, it bothered them that they bilocated or that they levitated. Teresa of Avila talked about this. She said this isn't important. So I think we can kind of miss the forest for the trees.

TSOMO: Yeah. And the Buddhist masters say the same thing. It's a distraction. That's not the point.

MATT: Also in the West, in the Christian tradition, sometimes odd political movements are built up on these things. For example, Padre Pio, who apparently had this stigmata, or even some of the Fatima appearances, Mary and so forth. These became rallying cries for fascist movements. So, especially in the West, things got a little scary. This is why, again, I think you have to stick to a middle path of justice and compassion, and let the extraordinary phenomena happen as it happens. But what I like most about the stories you told was how we can actually affect the curvature of the brain, if you will, the shape. Because when you talk that way and with the help of science, you kind of help us make this a little bit objective for us. This is a gift in our time that we didn't have before. I get excited about the potential for our schools for raising children and for our species.

Again, as I have said before, if we can teach meditation, if we can retain some control over our consciousness that these ancient peoples and traditions offer us and had and still have, as you say, there lies a lot of hope for our species. And from that point of view, we want to think about democratizing, so to speak, or making more available. Again, I think it's one of the phenomena of our times, and I don't get it, I don't see it talked about that much. One of the great gifts of our times is that the monks are leaving the monastery to boil down and simplify the practices so that a lot of ordinary people can—it's interesting, the examples you gave, those two women, ordinary housewives and so forth—that ordinary people can live their lives with grace and balance.

So there's the fact that Thich Nhat Hanh and the Dalai Lama are making themselves available and training people, but also the late Father Bede Griffiths, who was an authentic Christian monk and mystic for sure. I remember he said to me shortly before he died, "The future of monasticism is with lay people." I think that's very important. The way I picture it is with the end of the Piscean Age, and the Piscean Age was about dualisms: two fish swimming in opposite directions. So we had this big thing about monk distinct from layperson, or ordained distinct from unordained, and male distinct from female. And I think at this time in the Age of Aquarius, it's about the waters. It's about that ocean. It's about all of us tapping into that ocean, because if we don't, we're not going to make it.

That's the exciting news, what you're talking about, that these methodologies, these practices can actually be scientifically verified as well as in terms of story. And, therefore, we ought to be able to make them available even in a culture that makes a big deal about separation of church and state, but is thoroughly interested in what science approves of. So I think that making this headway in terms of the kind of experiments you're talking about, about experimenting with the minds of meditators, has tremendous potential. Both, you may say, politically as well as practically, because it is a political question. How do you get meditation, in its various forms, into education and into government? Instead of having, for example, a chaplain in the House of Representatives, who stands up and says some pious prayer to God knows who, what God in the sky they are praying to, to stand up in the House of Representatives and have them do a meditation that gets everyone there into gamma state and then start passing laws. Now that's interesting. isn't it?

Tsomo: Absolutely.

Matt: That's, I think, within the realm of political imagination.

Tsomo: And imagine if they had to do daily meditation, every time they convened—spend the first half-hour doing that.

MATT: Right. Instead of these prayer breakfasts, have a meditation breakfast. So you see, it's kind of like they've got a forum, but it's perverse right now. But if you could bring something in there with good scientific substance behind it, that's what will rattle the cage in this culture.

TSOMO: That was the genius of the Dalai Lama: He called for this mind-and-life gathering of scientists. He for many years had wanted to see science and Buddhism come together in some of these creative ways. And he also invited Western philosophers and psychologists. So that way, in speaking in the terms of modern times, most people in these days are devout believers in science, that's what they can buy—that's what they'll have faith in.

MATT: And right. And that moves us.

TSOMO: Yeah.

B: PRACTICE—*Chariot Meditation*

MATT: I think our time is running out on us here. Five minutes left. Okay. Maybe we should have discussion.

TSOMO: What about the Jesus chant?

MATT: We'll have to let the Jesus chant go. We've got . . .

TSOMO: But I wanted to hear it, oh no.

MATT: No time for Jesus chant.

STUDENT: *How long?*

MATT: I think it would take seven to 10 minutes. You'd rather do that than ask questions?

STUDENT: *Well, in light of everything . . .*

TSOMO: My vote would be yes.

STUDENT: *My vote would be yes, too.*

MATT: Well, I'll take a shot at it then. Okay, this is from Ezekiel: chapter one. When the Jewish people were in exile, Ezekiel had this vision, and it was a vision of the Ark on wheels. It was a portable temple, if you will, a portable Ark. And the tradition is that this particular meditation makes prophets of people. So it's a very strong meditation, and you shouldn't do it without, you know, some safety precautions. And what we're being told is that this is what John the Baptist taught his disciples, and of course,

John the Baptist ended his life as many prophets do, by being beheaded. And Jesus was one of these disciples, of course. He went to study with John the Baptist as a young man, and probably was with him about five years before John got killed.

The story is that Jesus taught this to his disciples. Here's how the longer phrase goes. "When the living creatures moved, the wheels beside them moved. When the living creatures rose from the ground, the wheels also rose. Wherever the spirit would go, they would go. The wheels would rise along with them because the spirit of the living creatures was in the wheels. When the creatures moved, they also moved. When the creatures stood still, they also stood still. When the creatures rose from the ground, the wheels rose along with them because the spirit of the living creatures was in the wheels." And it goes on like this. So it's a matter of getting into a rhythm and a beat with the chanting of these words. So you go beyond the meaning of the word, really. You get into the beat, into the mantra.

So let's try this out then. [*Matt leads the group in singing the following.*]

The wheels beside them moved . . .
[*Note: Each line is echoed several times by all.*]

MATT: So you echo me. Use your hands, too—so you're moving the wheels.

Okay, now then I'll go like this to stop, and then I'll go to another and then you'll echo me back. Okay?
When the living creatures rose . . .
Wherever the spirit would go . . .
They would go . . .
Then there came a voice from above . . .
High above on the throne . . .
Was a figure like that of a man . . .
He looked like glowing metal . . .
It was full of fire . . .
A brilliant light surrounded him . . .
Like the appearance of a rainbow . . .
Radiance surrounded him . . .
This was the appearance of the likeness of the glory of the Lord . . .
Of the glory of the Lord . . .
[*Note: Echoes fade out, then silence for a few moments.*]

This language about glory, *doxa*, and radiance is the language of the Cosmic Christ, or of the Shekinah, of the Divine Feminine. In our midst, of wisdom, incarnate in our midst.

That was an abbreviated version. If you do it in a large group and you have two choirs going, so one has half of the phrase, and the other the other, and you echo it and everything, it's amazing what happens. I did this the first time at Vancouver School of Theology with a group of, about 300 mostly Protestant ministers. It was at the end of a session, and the next day we met again, and I asked how did it go. Something like 80 percent didn't sleep all night. And I realized, wow, even Protestants can have a mystical experience with scripture if you get your eyes out of the damn text and chant it. Get it into your bodies. It was an amazing break-through. I was stunned—that if you take the Bible and don't read it and look for meaning, but chant it, you're in another space. And no one's told Protestants that for 500 years because we've been living in the modern era, and the modern era means you get the text right instead of the con-text. Sound is about context. The potential of the things like this, putting these scriptures to chants and all that, is huge.

AARON: So with this final message to the Protestants, we close this morning and thank you so much for being here, both of you, and we look forward to your next dialogue, and thank everybody here for . . .

MATT: Thank you, everybody here, for participating.

TSOMO: And thank you for inviting us, and thank you all for holding the quality of space in the way that you did so that in this crucible this could happen.

MATT: Indeed.

AARON: So shall we . . . ?

TSOMO: Might as well bring Zen into it.

STANFORD UNIVERSITY, CALIFORNIA

In 2007, Matthew Fox was teaching a course on Creation Spirituality at Stanford University, a site ideal for the joint weekend workshop offered by Matthew and Lama Tsomo that June. The event engaged participants' minds, bodies, spirits, and voices.

CHAPTER INDEX

Introduction

Day 1

MATT: We thought we'd get started with brief introductions from yourselves, and then Tsomo and I will do a little telling of our stories, the lineages that we represent. That would be about 15 to 20 minutes each, and there will be some practices as we go along, too, from both traditions. In fact, I think we were going to begin with a practice before we go into the naming, or the identifying, or not. Maybe we should do the identifying first.

TSOMO: I like the idea of just opening with—you were going to maybe do a chant.

MATT: Okay. And you were going to speak to the subject of chants.

TSOMO: So Matthew is going to introduce a Christian chant from his tradition, and I just wanted to say a little something about sacred sound as it's used by the Tibetans—and they use it a lot.

The Tibetans, rather than ignoring the senses and ignoring many of the things that we have about us that many people think are sort of antithetical to spirit, they actually bring them onto the path. So they bring sight, sound, smell, the movement of the body, all of these, onto the path. And they do it by bringing them into an archetypal level. They use archetypal sound—and I should explain a little bit what archetype is. As it was defined by Jung, archetypes are, you might say, templates, pure qualities of reality. And archetypal images, then, are things like the Virgin Mary; perhaps that image can evoke the Great Mother. Kuan Yin in China— that image evokes Great Mother. That Great Mother archetype we can then access through sight or through sound. And the Tibetans, when they use mantra, they use Sanskrit actually, not Tibetan, quite often. And this Sanskrit was never a spoken language. It is sound formulas that invoke these archetypes. So I'll just leave it at that and let you begin with yours.

MATT: Okay. When I look at sound and the spiritual practices, it strikes me as very interesting that so many traditions around the world have us chant or, if you will, have us speak the sound "aah" when they're talking about divine figures. So *Adonai*, *Yahweh* in Israel, of course, *Allah*, and *Buddha*, *Krishna*, and with Jesus, *Abba*. The historical Jesus, his favorite name for God, for the Divine, was *Abba*, which means literally "parent" or "papa," really. It's an intimate term of parent or parentage. Eckhart talks about the intimate fatherly heart, and I think that's precisely kind of a naming of the Abba language in the historical Jesus.

A: PRACTICE—*Aah Chant*

MATT: So I thought we might begin then with the "aah" sound. Again, remembering, as Tsomo just said, this is archetypal, and again I think it's striking that this sound is so prevalent in all the world's spiritual traditions.

TSOMO: To that end I just have to add that, in Sanskrit, "aah" is the basic sound. It's understood whenever there is a consonant that it is followed by "aah," and "aah" is just the constant that runs through it. It's the ground out of which everything comes.

MATT: Perfect. So why don't we begin that way, then, with our feet on the floor and back straight to let as much wind to come as possible. Let's just start with the tone "aah," and you can take any tone you want. Just bring the breath up and don't hold back. Don't be shy. Don't be self-conscious, As Eckhart says, "Mysticism is unself-consciousness." He says that getting back to the child state of just making sounds that don't mean anything puts the left brain asleep, gives it a break, you know. After we do this for a bit, then I'll give a signal to move from "aah" to "Abba." Then we're also in the morphic resonance in the charged memory of the historical Jesus because this was his favorite name for God. Okay, ready, then? And you might want to shut your eyes for this just so that you can be with the breath. And, of course, remember *breath* and *spirit* are the same words, not only in Hebrew and in Greek and in the biblical languages of the West, but in African languages, too, and,

I presume, Eastern. Tsomo can tell us that. But breath and spirit are the same words, and wind and air. So, again, when we're taking breath we're taking in the air of the universe as a cosmic act.

[*To arriving group members*] Come on in, folks. Welcome. There are two seats in the front row up here that you're welcome to take. Tsomo has a somewhat gentle, profound but gentle speech, so it's good not to be too far back because the microphone is not working in this room.

TSOMO: Also, when I'm taking you through meditative exercises I'd rather not shout.

MATT: I've never heard her shout in her life. She's not a shouter.

TSOMO: I have three kids, so I can do it.

MATT: You were a shouter at one time. You haven't been a Buddhist all your life.

Okay, we're beginning with a sound together here, the sound being "aah," which is a very universal sound for the divine name. And then we're going to go into the term *Abba*, which was the historical Jesus's favorite name for God, and it means the intimate of "father." Ready, then. Again, eyes shut just so that we're not distracted, and we get on the wave of this breath that is the also spirit and is also cosmic gift of air. Ready?

[*Group chants "Aah."*]

MATT: Keep the sound coming. And now "Abba."

[*Group chants "Abba." Then silence for a few moments.*]

MATT: Then we bow gently in reverence to the sound, the source, and the spirit we brought in to be among us. Thank you.

TSOMO: In the Tibetan tradition, we have bookends to all spiritual endeavors, whether it's a practice session, or a dialogue such as this, or a classroom situation. We want to make sure that we're coming from the best intention, so we normally give rise to *bodhicitta*. And of course, you've all studied your glossary of terms, so you know exactly what I mean when I say *bodhicitta*. But just in case, I thought I'd add a little. *Bodhicitta* literally means "the heart-mind of awakening," so it's the part of us that can feel that we're actually not separate. This illusion of separation, then, is bridged, and we feel how we're connected with all beings—it's often expressed as compassion combined with method, skillful means, and incisive wisdom. This combination, then—if we remember the literal definition, "heart-mind of awakening"—all of these words begin to give us the feeling of bodhicitta. So I ask you to please have that intention, that in a sense, for the sake of all sentient beings, you're sitting here on the front lines exploring spirituality in this way. So we begin with that intention. And then we're going to end this session by dedicating whatever merit we manage to gain from this effort to the eventual enlightenment of all beings.

MATT: Now Tsomo, I think you were going to lead off with your story now and some of the teaching that accompanies it. Is that right?

TSOMO: Yeah, we thought we should share a little bit about our backgrounds, too. And as you listen to us, I was listening to all of you, and there's the question of lineage, the question of the methods that really help us on our spiritual paths. I hear all of you holding these things, and everyone holding the stories that we come with. So as you listen to us, each of us is very strongly rooted in a particular lineage, although we also have inquiring minds and have sort of explored the whole smorgasbord. And for Americans in particular, I think, getting a chance to hear from people who are so strongly rooted in a particular lineage and tradition, you get a chance that's unusual to see what the benefits of that might be, because America does the smorgasbord really well, but as far as going deeply into a particular tradition, that doesn't happen so often. One *geshe* who was advising an American on spiritual pursuits put it really well when he said, "You know, you can dig a hole anywhere and get to water, but if you keep digging shallow holes here and there and start this one and then stop, and start that one and then stop, you never get to water." But what I'm sensing in the aspirations of everybody sitting here is that everybody wants to finally get to water. There was a gathering of mystics from various traditions, each of whom was very deeply rooted in their own tradition. When they talked about their religions, there were all sorts of debates going on and a lot of confusion and irritation and things like that. But when they simply talked about their mystical experiences, their transcendent moments, they all sounded the same. That's sort of like— now I can pick another metaphor and talk about a mountain. Once you get to the top, it's the same point, but the paths leading up can be many and varied, and they look very different on the way up.

I was born in a Jewish family, and I still consider myself tribally Jewish. That's how I put it. So there's no lapsing from that. I've got genetics in my tribe with me. But I did reach a moment as I pursued Tibetan Buddhism more and more deeply when I realized I knew more Tibetan words than Hebrew, and I had a moment of Jewish guilt. I had to stop in my meditation session and say, "Can I go forward? Wait a second." I really had to just sit with myself about that. I finally was able to sort it out by saying, "Well, I am always—my identity is still—a Jewish American, yet these methods were helping me pursue my spiritual life and feel as though I was really making progress." And not just my spiritual life; I was developing more mastery over myself, my emotions, the way I see the world and myself, so that I had more mastery of everyday life as well. So I wasn't going to give that up, and I didn't have to. Luckily, my lama presented it in such a way that he said, "Really, I'm not presenting you with a religion so much as a set of practices, and a graduated spiritual path that can eventually lead you to enlightenment." We know this for a fact because it's proven to be the case. People have done this with these tools.

So, just going back a little bit to my Jewish roots. I remember my family was friends with the rabbi of one local temple, and I didn't realize that apparently he was quite something on a national level. I just remember as a little kid looking way up at my dad and the rabbi talking in the kitchen, nibbling after dinner, about the existence of God. My dad labeled himself agnostic, but he was a practicing atheist, and sort of a reluctant atheist in another way, because I think he wanted the rabbi to convince him that there was a God. So there would be these intense debates in the kitchen, which of course is a very Jewish thing, and it's not fighting. I learned later when I grew up and hung around with other people that they thought I was fighting with them. I thought we were having a great rousing debate. Anyway, here was this debate going on in the kitchen. And the way this rabbi described God was actually then very similar to what I discovered, some of the concepts of the great emptiness out of which all being comes. I was hearing some of that in the kitchen discussions between the rabbi and my father. So it wasn't this fellow with a beard and puppet strings that I was hearing about. It was something much more refined and profound and believable to me. So by the time I had been through the spiritual smorgasbord for many, many years and finally met this lama, who I am still studying under, Gochen Tulku Rinpoche, when he began talking about the *Dharmakaya*, emptiness bringing forth luminosity, there was a little bit of recognition from those kitchen discussions. Also, the fact that he taught through sometimes question-answer, sometimes debate, he expected lots of questions from me, I felt very comfortable with that, growing up in a Jewish household.

Just to give you a little bit of an idea of *Vajrayana* and where it is on the map—I think I should mention that because that's my lineage that I'm here representing. I did Zen for a few years and even a retreat. I did *Theravadan*—so some people have talked about *Vipassana*; that comes from that tradition. It was after I had done those that I came upon Vajrayana Buddhism and especially settled on studying with this lama. The Buddha set out three basic paths, but there were lots of sublineages within those. He felt that he needed to expound 84,000 *sutras*, for example, and then all the *tantras* because everybody is very different. Our minds are very different. We have different habits that we carry with us into this life, we have different karma, different proclivities, so he really wanted to allow for that in the paths that he set out. In Theravada, which I think you got in your glossary of Buddhist terms, as we look at the neurotic emotions and the confused way in which we perceive reality in ourselves, the way that path handles it—I could use a metaphor of poison. You can either avoid the poison altogether and walk around it, keep a big distance from it, or you can pacify it—that's still part of that whole Theravadan tradition. But in *Mahayana*, of which Zen is part, you can transform the poison through antidote, applying an antidote to the poison. So for example, for anger you could apply patience, or forbearance. It's *zöpa* in Tibetan. In Vajrayana, they handle the poison yet differently. Rather than simply antidoting it or avoiding it—what my teacher taught me was to take, for example, anger and actually just hold it lightly and begin peeling away the layers of the onion. You peel away the neurosis, the righteous, dramatic feelings and thoughts, and all of those kinds of things, and get to the pure quality of it. And there's a certain sharpness about anger, just a pure clarity and sharpness about it.

When you peel away any of these neurotic emotions, you actually get to one of the aspects of primordial wisdom. In the case of anger, the Tibetans say that you come down to its true essence, which is mirror-like wisdom, mirror-like primordial wisdom. They categorize these emotions into three basic groups, which I'll talk about later, and sometimes one of them gets two more subcategories. I won't go into all of that, but just to say that Vajrayana handles these poisonous emotions with which we poison ourselves and then commit karmic acts. *Karma* means "action," as you all know from your glossary of terms.

I fought against my training to become a lama the whole way, actually; I really just wanted to learn these techniques. And the more I learned them and applied them, the more excited I got. I have a master's degree in counseling psychology, so I've really always been fascinated not only with spirituality, but the mind and what can transform the mind, what can heal the mind. And these tools were so astonishingly effective. And because of my Jungian background, I could appreciate the highly skilled use of archetype for many of them, so I just wanted to do more and more, honestly, for my own benefit and anybody else I could help, because I enjoy the process of teaching, too.

Fairly early on, Gochen Tulku Rinpoche said, "I want to give you the lama title, and then you can continue teaching." And I said, "Oh, I don't need the title. I'm just interested in these methods." And I did more and more retreat, usually three months a year of strict, classic Tibetan Buddhist retreat. After many years of that, then he finally conferred the title on to me. So I've really studied a lot of these methods, and that's a lot of what I teach, although I have to give the context for it. We're going to be in a very interesting dance here, trying to bring you both the concepts and the experiences of each of our respective lineages today and tomorrow.

MATT: Yeah. Let me say, you know, Tsomo is very humble, but I was at her ceremony when she was made a lama this past summer, a year ago up in Montana. It was very special, and it's very rare that a Jewish North American woman is made a lama in the Tibetan tradition. And she's mastered the language as well over the years, as she says, "better than her Hebrew." She's also a mother of three and a grandmother, just to fill it all out here. I really admire her perseverance and her passion and her profound grounding in this tradition. I like the way she began, about going deeply into our water holes instead of just staying at the surface and never getting to the water. And that conjures up for me a great line from my mentor, Meister Eckhart, who says, "God is a great underground river that no one can dam up and no one can stop." In my book I did a few years ago on the spiritual traditions of the world, I call it *One River, Many Wells*, because my image is that there are many wells into that underground river. There is a Buddhist well, and many Buddhist wells for that matter, or at least Buddhist wells with tributaries. And there's a Sufi well, there's a Christian well, there's a Jewish well, there is a goddess well, there are indigenous wells, and today I think even science, as it turns more toward wisdom and less from just knowledge, is also a well.

Of course, as several people have mentioned, your artistic experiences of music, singing, and other forms of art are also wells. But the point is to go deeply down a well. And I think, sadly, an awful lot of human history has been going to war over the wells. And to me, what was really sad about that is it shows how superficial we are. We're up at the surface saying, "My God's better than your God," or "My God can beat up your Goddess," or whatever it is we're shouting at the top of our voices, and forgetting that we've all got a journey to make, and we've got to go down to the well to that underground river. And once you get there, it is common drinking, as you said. When people from different traditions get together and share their mystical experience, you are talking universal language, if you will, archetypal language, and we're drinking from one source. Because as Aquinas says, "God is the source without a source." And he/she can go by different names. You don't have to call it *God* by any means.

A bit about my own story and what goes behind it. I was raised in a Roman Catholic home in Madison, Wisconsin. Seven children in 10 years is what my parents did—very Catholic thing to do in the 1930s and 1940s. I went to public high school. I was very blown away as a teenager by mystical experiences I had reading Shakespeare, listening to Beethoven, and above all reading Tolstoy's *War and Peace* my junior year in high school in the summer. I told a friend it blew my soul wide open, reading that book. I didn't know what had happened to me. Now I would say, "It's a mystical experience." But I wanted to explore what happened to me. I was at least that self-conscious. What was that that hit me through Tolstoy? So it was on that basis—and also debates I had with my good Jewish and Protestant friends about philosophy of God and theology. And I'd go into my parish priest, who was a Dominican, and he had me reading G. K. Chesterton and Thomas Aquinas, and I realized, "Oh, there's an intellectual tradition here—good." I was drawn by that and by the aesthetic experience of our music and so forth. And I was drawn to the Dominicans because they seem to have such a tradition. So I attended a retreat my senior year of high school in Dominican studies in Dubuque, Iowa. Then they were still chanting, in Latin, the Psalms of David. And I found that aesthetically mind blowing; the Gregorian chant, and the community living, and the intellectual dimension, those three things really. "Hey, these guys got what it takes." So I thought I'd give it a try, which I did then after a couple years of college.

Also, I had an experience when I was 12 when I had polio and I lost my legs, and [the doctors] couldn't tell me if I would walk again. My legs did come back in about a year, or year and a half, and I remember saying to the universe that I wasn't going to take my legs for granted ever again. A friend of mine had died of polio the year before I had it. It was a good experience of facing death and also just facing letting go of a lot, not having legs. So one way I define mysticism today is "not taking for granted." Like even what we did already this morning, a breath is about not taking our breath for granted. Every breath is a gift. None of us made it up, and none of us made the lungs, designed the lungs, that would get the breath just right, or the flowers that fine-tuned the oxygen hundreds of million years ago on this planet so it would be just right for beings like us. So a breath itself is such a miracle. Life is. Everywhere we turn there's a miracle. Legs are miracles. And sometimes the only way you would know it is when you don't have them. So for me, that 12-year-old experience of facing death and polio and all this was also pivotal, in retrospect. I wasn't conscious of what was going on. In fact, I was flattered by the attention I got, finally, in our family of seven kids. My family had to come and visit me outside the hospital window because it was contagious. They weren't allowed in. But they had never come and visited me for anything else in 12 years of living at home. I was stuck in the middle of the family. You're the most neurotic and the most forgotten.

I had a lot of mystical experiences in Wisconsin growing up with nature and, and the Native American tradition. And I had a lot of experiences in my training as a Dominican. We did a lot of chanting, a lot of meditation, a lot of mantras—we called it the Rosary, but they were mantras—and the study. I love to study. And that's very Jewish: the idea that study is itself a prayer, using the brains that God gave you, focus, bring your heart to it. We're told it's just as prayerful as chanting, study is. And having grown up in a university town, I always had that prejudice anyway that God gave us minds, and it's a good thing to use them.

But in my training as a Dominican, there was something amiss because we weren't studying spirituality as such. We were acting out vegetarianism, fasting a lot, celibacy, chanting, all these things were going on, but no one was talking about why we did it or what happens when things happen to you. I was having these experiences and priests could not tell me. I remember one of them said, "You're going to have to find this stuff on your own. There's no priest in this whole community who knows what you're talking about." So I said, "Well, then, send someone to study spirituality." I remember saying, "My generation is not going to be interested in religion. We're going to be interested in spiritual experience." We didn't study the mystics at all in 12 years of training as a Dominican. I never heard Meister Eckhart's name used once, and he was the greatest mystic of the West, in terms of articulating the experience.

To make a long story short, they sent me to Paris, with Thomas Merton's advice, and it was there when I met my mentor, Père Chenu, a wonderful French Dominican, the father of liberation theology, who was silenced by the pope for 12 years in the 1950s, forbidden to write because he was with the Worker-Priest Movement and working with Marxists after the Second World War in France. But the Second Vatican Council brought him back into good graces, if you will, and John XXIII opened the doors. And that's when I came of age. In fact, my first vows were to Pope John XXIII. He was my pope. And so the 1960s were very wonderful, and I was there in Paris from 1967 to 1970, getting my doctorate in spirituality. It was Merton who told me to go study there, and I'm grateful to him for that.

What I want to say about my lineage is, first of all, there is Christian but for me that means Jewish. When I did my master's thesis in my theology training in Dubuque, Iowa, before I went to Paris, I did it on the Prayer of Jesus in the New Testament, because I wanted to reground my experience and that of Christian spirituality in the Scriptures. And it was there that I began to really feel the Jewishness of Jesus and how so many centuries of Christian theology had, in so many ways, cut itself off from the Jewishness of Jesus. A lot of my entire work since has been to try to bring back the Jewish spirituality that really fed Jesus.

CHAPTER 1

Defining Mysticism

MATT: We're living in an amazing time because the scholarship on the historical Jesus has really come around. So people like Marcus Borg or John Dominic Crossan or Bruce Chilton, great scholars today with the Jesus story, they all agreed that Jesus comes from the wisdom tradition of Israel. And the wisdom tradition is the feminist, the cosmological, and the nature mysticism of Israel. It is the Creation spiritual tradition of Israel. This is why I was so turned on, visiting the Dominicans, chanting the wisdom literature that is Psalms, when I was a teenager. The Psalms are so creation centered. They bring in the sky, and they bring in the Earth, and they bring in the feminine. And they bring in eros, therefore. In fact, the Book of Wisdom says, "This is wisdom: to love life." That's the "yes" to life that I think we yearn for as a civilization.

Of course, the whole relationship of social justice and spirituality was absolutely the question for me because I came of age in the 1960s. So the Civil Rights Movement and the Anti-War Movement. And that's when I was in Paris, and the students brought down the government—and de Gaulle—on the streets when I was there. And I was in a certain way part of that. So my question was, "How do you relate social justice and mysticism, or do you, can we?" And really all of my writing has been about that question.

When I did return, I taught four years at a women's college at Barat College in Lake Forest, Illinois, hearing women's stories. Now, my family was different because I had a very strong mother and a strong father, but my father learned feminism early. He did. Before she died, my sister reminded me of a story I hadn't remembered—I have three sisters and three brothers—how when we were teenagers, my dad put us around the table and said, "I don't make enough money to send you all to college. I make enough to send the girls to college. You boys have to go out and find scholarships because it's easier for boys to get scholarships." So my father was pretty well educated by my mother, you see. I had forgotten that story, but it's true. So I had the Dominicans pay for my education, I had another brother who went to West Point and had the Army pay for his, and another brother who had Princeton pay for his. So we got the message. And then the Ecological Movement in the 1970s, and the Gay and Lesbian Movement. Integrating all this with spirituality has been my passion and has gotten me into a little bit of trouble along the way, too.

But what I want to stress is that—and it's been brought up in many of you who came out of Presbyterianism, Catholicism, and so forth—that all of us have been shortchanged when it comes to knowing that there is a powerful Christian mystical tradition, beginning with Jesus himself. Jesus was a nature mystic. In fact, I'll use a word that's been badly abused, because I'll use it to wake you up, he was pagan in that respect. *Paganus* is just a Latin word for a country person. Jesus was a peasant. He was from Galilee, the Wisconsin of Israel, right? The green part of Israel. And the scholarship today is saying, look, he was considered illegitimate in his village, he wasn't allowed in the synagogue on the Sabbath, so he did what you did: While the others were in the synagogue, he went out to nature to pray. That's what he had to do. This is why he was steeped in nature, wisdom nature, mysticism. You see it in all of his parables, all of his stories. He was not with his eyes in the book. His was not a book-oriented religion. Wisdom theology in Israel is—first of all, it's ecumenical from the get-go. It's ecumenical. Wisdom is not restricted to the Jewish people. Nature is not restricted to Jewish people; it's cosmological and it's Earth based. So that's the first point in terms of this lineage, that Jesus was a creation mystic and, of course, his mentor, John the Baptist. That's a very interesting issue we don't have time to go into now, but we will go into it probably later.

The second story today, coming out of the latest scholarship, is this guy Paul. Paul was a very well-schooled, well-educated—unlike Jesus, speaking Greek, writing Greek—Jew who was very zealous. At first he was attacking this Jewish sect, and it was a Jewish sect, calling themselves Christians. Then he had this amazing mystical experience that literally changed history. You can say whatever you want to say about it psychologically, sociologically, or theologically, but Paul being struck on the road to Damascus changed history. As Otto Rank said, Jesus was the introvert and Paul was the extrovert in the origins of Christianity. Paul took the movement into Gentile country, into Rome, and into the educated classes through his Greek experiences. He was an amazing figure. The latest scholarship on Paul is stunning, John Dominic Crossan and his book on Paul that came out last year. Now, Crossan is a Biblical scholar, whose emphasis is on justice and liberation theology. Crossan comes from the Catholic tradition of liberation theology. It's stunning to find in his book this statement that [paraphrasing] "for Paul, you cannot be a Christian without being a mystic." Now that's stunning. Let me say it again. "For Paul, you cannot be a Christian without being a mystic." Paul is the first writer of Christianity. The first guy in the Christian Bible, in terms of date, is Paul. And he's the first Christian theologian and unlike any other theologian, since his stuff is in the Bible. But he's saying, "You can't be a Christian without being a mystic." Well, that's stunning because 99 percent of Christians don't know anything about mysticism. We have these churches, we have these seminaries, we have all these edifices, and, believe me, they're not teaching mysticism. So, whoa, there's some cacophony, and so no wonder so many Christians have had to go East or someplace to find their mysticism. Not only is Paul insisting all Christians have to be mystics, but for Paul, Christ is a cosmic mystic. One scholar today says, "Paul's Christ is metacosmic." I didn't even know what that means, but it's a big, big cosmic. So the Cosmic Christ is the earliest mysticism in the Christian tradition, and it's the cosmic wisdom tradition.

STUDENT: *Would you mind defining mysticism?*

MATT: Well, no one will ever define *mysticism* properly, because mysticism is a right-brain experience and the left brain is what does our defining for us. But I'd be glad to offer a few shots at it. My book, *The Coming of the Cosmic Christ*, Chapter 2, has what I call "21 running definitions" for *mysticism*. So that's the point. You'll never get one that works, but a few. It is our unitive experiences—the experiences you have of unity of all things,

or of you and God, or of you and being. And it can happen on so many occasions. It can happen *through* meditation, for sure, and *in* meditation. It can
happen on a mountaintop. It can happen in nature. It can happen in child-
birth. It can happen in lovemaking. It can happen with music, with art, with
study. As Eckhart says, "For a person who is awake, breakthrough"—that's
one of his words, which is *satori* in the East—"breakthrough does not happen once a year, once a month, once a week or once a day, but many times
every day." So it is about being awake and ready. But *mysticism* etymologically, *mysteuein* in Greek, means two things: "to enter the mysteries," and "to
be cut off from your senses." That doesn't mean to beat up on your senses,
but it means to give them a break and go into a place of deep silence, even
from your senses—instead of taking in, to be with. Again, in our culture
we're so busy-busy, and then we pipe in musak, just in case you're not 100
percent busy-busy, to take over your mind. This is why meditation practices
of so many kinds are so valuable to get back to being. So another definition
of *mysticism* that I would throw around would be "being with being," returning to the level of being. For some people that can happen just by walking
meditation, as some prefer to, or getting into nature, or turning off the TV.
And death is another experience, and being with those who die, and the
union that happens there is part of it, too. But essentially, I see mysticism as
the unitive experience.

Now, to fast-forward from Jesus and Paul to the Rhineland mystics.
Just the last day or two, I read a phrase, I don't remember where, saying
that the Rhine was the Ganges of the West. It was just a wonderful phrase.
Oh, it was in a book by Gaston Bachelard that I was reading recently.
Yeah. I love that [paraphrasing]—the Rhine is the Ganges of the West—
because it's true. The Rhineland mystics, Hildegard of Bingen—Bingen
is right on the Rhine; Nicholas of Cusa—Cues is right on the Rhine; and
Eckhart, who worked on the Rhine, both in Cologne, he studied in Cologne in the north, and in Strasbourg in the south. The Rhineman mystic,
and, of course, the Celts settled on the Rhine. All this, what I would call
the healthy Cosmic Christ mysticism of the West, is thanks to the Celts,
most of it. They settled on the Rhine and in northern Italy. This gave us
Saint Francis, your redhead Italians. That's the Celtic influence. Dominic,
the founder of the Dominican Order, of which I and Eckhart and Aquinas were members, was a redhead, a redheaded Spaniard. So the Celts

settled in northern Spain, too. And that gave Dominic an intellectual twist to him, a quest about the mind and not just the heart, bringing them together. That was his goal, and that's where Eckhart shines so powerfully, too, and Aquinas.

So these Rhineland mystics in the Middle Ages gave birth to what I would call a rather authentic Christianity. And then the Quakers—some of you mentioned your Quaker connections. The first time I ever lectured on Eckhart was in a Quaker House in Chicago. And when I finished, the big lady who ran the place shouted from the back, "My God," she said, "it sounds just like George Fox!" And of course it's true. Eckhart was condemned the week after he died, and his marrying of the contemplative and the active, the justice and the mysticism, had to go underground in the church because of that condemnation. He was working in the real political movements of his day, which was the women's movement, the Beguine Movement, which was condemned by the pope 17 times. One Pope John XXII, the same guy who condemned Eckhart, condemned the Beguines, the women. They kept growing every time he condemned them, you see.

George Fox represents very much this same tradition of contemplative, active, justice mysticism that was Jesus, that was Paul, and that certainly was Aquinas, and Eckhart, and Francis, and Hildegard, Nicolas of Cusa, Julian of Norwich, the fifteenth-century mystic from England, and some others. This tradition is also not anti-intellectual. It's very pro-scientific because science tells us what's in nature. Aquinas said, "A mistake about nature resulting a mistake about God." Well, for me, that is the most noble thing he could say about the scientist vocation. To put it in a positive way, then, that means what we discover about nature is a discovery about God. Einstein knew that, and he knew it from his Jewish tradition that you can trust the mind to find the universe's secrets and therefore God's secrets. Buddhism is deliciously rich in honoring and using the mind to explore what really counts. This anti-intellectual, anti-mystical, "We're saved, you aren't," "God is a punitive father" and all—that is a dominant version of Christianity, both in the Vatican, sad to say, and in Protestant fundamentalism at this time in history. Although, of course, it has echoes in Islamic fundamentalism, Jewish fundamentalism, Hindu fundamentalism, even Buddhist fundamentalism, and Native American fundamentalisms that are also alive and well at this time in history.

The oldest writer in the Hebrew Bible, the ninth century BC, the J source in the Bible, was creation centered. The wisdom tradition that came later, after the prophets, the prophetic tradition, is also deeply creation centered, and Jesus comes from that as well as the wisdom tradition. And then what Jesus brought together in his practice and his preaching, and then what Paul brought in, and certainly what this medieval mystic, Rhineland mystic movement did. So that's some of my lineage. And as I say, it is ecumenical. Wisdom traditions always have been ecumenical. The Queen of Sheba is praised in the Hebrew Bible, and she was not a Jew by any stretch of the imagination, but she was a wisdom source, and because this acknowledged that wisdom was playing with God before the creation of the world. Well, no matter what your science says, "before the creation of the world" means "before the creation of religions," right? Ergo, wisdom is present in all religions and before them.

Far from being heretical, this tradition, I would propose, is the tradition of Jesus himself. The whole idea of original sin, for example, is not Jewish. Therefore, Jesus never heard of it, no Jew has ever heard of it. It's fourth century AD, Saint Augustine, and it was a detour, a complete detour for the Western Church. And the reason it has hung on so long is that it has served political interests, because it's in that very century that the Church took over the Roman Empire. Not by choice; it was the only one left standing. And you have to give us some credit for holding the monastic tradition, especially holding together some semblance of the inheritance of music, and math, and learning, and everything else, from the fourth century to the twelfth century, when things exploded in new ways. And the sixteenth century, which gave us the printing press and the Reformation and all those things, much of it positive, not all of it, that launched the modern era in a theological sense. I think we're due for a real Reformation, a real Renaissance, today, as a species, not just in terms of our particular denominations. Therefore, I think this mixing that Tsomo and I are doing, that she's already done in her life with her Judaism and her Buddhism, and that we're doing, choosing to kind of focus on Meister Echkart as a spokes-person of the Western tradition, I think it's very needed and very wise.

Just a real quick story and then I'll shut up. Thomas Merton, the great Catholic monk, was very Augustinian and dualistic in his writings of the

1958 and guilt-ridden. But in 1959 he had a correspondence with Dr. Suzuki, the Japanese Buddhist scholar, and at the end, Suzuki threw up his hands and said, "Tom, you are a typical Western dualist. I can't help you. Your one outside chance is to read the one Zen thinker of the West, Meister Eckhart." Merton, in his candor, said, "But Eckhart's been condemned by the Church." And Suzuki said, "Well, I can't help that, can I?" And that was the end of that conversation. Merton learned something. He spent 1960 doing nothing but reading Eckhart and Zen poetry, and writing it. And you look at his writing in the 1960s, and he's completely shifted—his book on the conjectures of a guilty bystander, for example. His books on Eastern mysticism, and the Zen masters, and then his final book done on his travels in Asia, where he met so many Rinpoches, and so he had amazing mystical experiences in Buddhist temples. He kept writing in his journal, which we have [paraphrasing], "Eckhart is my lifeboat. Eckhart is my lifeboat." I believe he actually was assassinated. I think he died a martyr for the Peace Movement. He was the first American religious figure to come out against the Vietnam War. He came out before King did, against the Vietnam War. I believe he was killed by the CIA, and I have a certain amount of proof for that.

His last talk to us before he died was on Karl Marx and monasticism. So he was doing what Eckhart was doing, what I'm trying to do, and this tradition was trying to do—bring together the deep mysticism with the deep compassion that also means justice and healing and taking a stand. It was Merton who sent me to Paris, but this story is a good one because his relationship with Eckhart was very special. Eckhart brought him into the political arena. It brought him out of his Augustinian guilt about being a human, and it brought him into the East. And I think, in a way, we're all, at some point, at that juxtapose of the Buddha's wisdom and the Christ wisdom. And I think we need both. The Buddha lived a full life, died at 84, saw it all. I'm sure he had a midlife crisis, all of it. He was a father, a husband, and all of that. Jesus got himself killed at 30, a rebel, Jewish, outrageous prophet. We need both: the holy patience and the serenity and the wisdom of the Buddha; and we need the holy impatience of the Jewish prophets, such as Jesus. We have to learn how to marry these two, and I think it's a sad thing for our species that we split the two. And we're living in a time when we can marry them, beginning with our own souls and our own practice, and then with our institutions in the way we see the world. Okay, that's my lineage.

Tsomo: Earlier you were talking a lot about the people of your lineage, and I sort of wonder if—would people be interested in just hearing a little bit about—for example, the Buddha and how Buddhism came to Tibet and that sort of thing, because I didn't really go into that. So I'll just quickly do a little catch-up on that.

CHAPTER 2

The Buddha's Journey

TSOMO: There are a lot of stories about the Buddha, so I'm going to make this very brief. He was born a prince in India, and he went on this journey, definitely against his father's wishes. When he was born, there were all kinds of amazing signs, and the royal couple was told that he would either be a great king who was ruler of all the known world, or he would be the creator of a new religion. His father wanted him to go into the family business, so he did everything in his power to try and keep the young prince Siddhartha interested in everyday life and the momentary pleasures of life. He also tried to keep all suffering from the view of this young prince. As the young prince got older, he began to want to go outside of the palace, like any young person wanting to explore beyond the boundaries set by their parents. He finally did go out on several occasions, and on each occasion he saw human suffering. He saw somebody very old and bent down with age and in pain, and was shocked by it, truly struck by it because he had been spared it. Actually, he was more shocked by it than if he had grown up with it all along. So somebody should have advised the king a little differently.

He came back and was deep in contemplation in his room. How could he stop this suffering? Because everyone gets old—either that, or they die young, but those are the two options. Everyone gets sick—and he went out and came upon a sick person. So he realized after a couple of these forays that everyone who is born gets sick, gets old, dies, and there's lots of suffering along the way. Because this was such a shock to him, having already almost grown up before really discovering this, he took it all the more to heart. And because he was such an amazing being, he decided to leave the palace behind. He also came upon, in one of his forays, a mendicant, somebody who was traveling, begging, who was a pursuer of the mystical and the spiritual, and he realized, "This is the only way. I must find out how reality really works. What is the truth?" Because he just knew that if he found out how reality really was, what the truth really was, and the nature of our own minds, that he would eventually come upon the secret to true lasting happiness. So he did leave behind a wife and a newborn child, and pursued this path, and studied under one master after another, always coming closer and closer to the truth, but there was still a bit of a veil.

It was finally when he sat under the *bodhi* tree that he was able to, in a sense, not only clear away his own obscured view and sort of clean his own windshield, but really take away the windshield altogether, and he was experiencing truth absolutely directly. In that moment of awakening—and *Buddha* means "awakened one"—he realized the mistake that we all tend to make. We originally were part of this great ocean of reality—I call it a *pregnant emptiness*—out of which all of what we call *manifested reality* comes, and it's all a very pure process: the flashing forth of appearances out of emptiness. There's no separation of any of it, but at some point, you could say, one wave on the ocean gets a little confused and thinks, "Oh, I'm this wave, and then there are those other waves, and there's the ocean that's apart from me." This is where the confusion begins, and it leads to—well, the Buddha laid forth 84,000 different neurotic emotions.

He categorized them mostly into three categories, one being ignorance, narrow-mindedness, laziness—all of those were in that general category. Another one would be grasping; I think addiction goes into that category, desire, clinging. That would be the second category. The third one would be anger, aggression, aversion. As soon as we mistakenly think we're separate, then we need all kinds of things, and we need to push away all kinds of other things.

So we've got the delusion, that's the first one, the ignorance one; non-awareness is another way it's termed. That naturally leads to the grasping, clinging, desire. And then the pushing away, the aversion. These then swirl around and begin to affect our behavior. You look at a little child who wants this block that happens to be in the hand of another child, right? So you get the delusion of separateness, then you get the desire and clinging, and then you get the aggression—pulling the hair of the other kid to get the block.

Karma, as I mentioned before, means "action," and karma sticks to our souls in a particular way. I asked my teacher about this, and he explained it very articulately by rolling up a piece of paper, which I'm going to do for you now. The habits of mind that carry forth from one lifetime to another, and the karmic traces on our souls, you wonder how they pop up when we melt into the ocean of oneness at the end of life. How do they then pop up again in the next life? This was what I put to Rinpoche when I asked him. So he rolled up a piece of paper, and when he let go, of course, it still had a certain bend to it. And even if I press down on it, it pops up again, yeah? And the karmic traces are sort of like a crease that you would have in the paper, which you can't all see, but you can imagine. Even if I go like this, there's still a crease in the paper. There's the planting of the karmic seed, but until we've lived out the fruits of that seed, exhausted the fruits of that seed, we haven't finished with the story. So it doesn't matter whether we die and are born into another life and maybe go five lifetimes down the road. Finally, that karmic seed, that trace, is going to bubble up to the surface, and we're going to find ourselves living out the fruits of that particular karmic seed.

The Buddha realized all of this, and saw it very clearly, as he sat under the bodhi tree. He realized that once we completely cleared away all of the karmic traces that are on our windshield—and habits of mind color it and shape it and bend reality into whatever it is that we see—once we can clear all of that away, and directly perceive reality with no delusion and none of these emotions coloring our perception, then we'll be returned once again to this great ocean of awareness. And not just seeing, but feeling through the heart that we are not separate from all of these other beings. This is the way that we can come home once again. And we're really on just a very, very long journey home. So he dedicated the rest of his life then to doing his best to explain, really, what is ineffable and inexplicable and beyond words, but he also laid out many, many methods and a graduated path toward enlightenment, and as I said before, in different styles for different people, so that even though he couldn't directly explain to us this reality that's beyond words, he preferred to give us a path by which we could eventually experience this reality for ourselves.

Now, we can have the breakthroughs, the satori moments that you mentioned, but really what the Buddha focused more on was a graduated path by which we can slowly but surely clear away these confused perceptions, and the karma that we've built up, and our neurotic emotions that we carry with us, our habits of mind, clear those *obscurations*, as he often calls it, away, and meanwhile bring forth our innate Buddha Mind, our Buddha Nature. Because what else are we made of? We are a wave on this ocean, an appearance coming out of emptiness. The emptiness suffuses us as it suffuses everything. This ceaseless compassion that is a quality of this ocean of oneness also suffuses everything. It suffuses us, too. And this is our true nature. It's the true nature of everything, so, of course, also us.

MATT: Can I speak to this a little? What you're saying?

TSOMO: Yeah.

MATT: There are two things I want to respond to in terms of the Western tradition. First is the universality of suffering that is so primal in the Buddhist experience in teaching. You notice how that corrects—notice how I'm saying this—it corrects the distortion, or the preoccupation, with the cross in the Western tradition, because the cross theology is presented as saying, "We are the causes of suffering," you see? And what the Buddha is reminding us of is, "No, every being suffers." So there's not a cause and effect. You know, the preoccupation with the cross in Christianity—I don't know if I like saying it, but I say this because it has to be said. Jesus had one really bad day, and they built a religion on it. You know, get over it. Jesus was teaching for years before they hung him on the cross, and they hung him on the cross because he was teaching something powerful like being compassionate, which is good Buddhist teaching, too. But the point is that in many schools of the West, the whole cross thing has been completely distorted, and Buddhism really helps to clean this up, because suffering is part of not just the human experience, it's part of the historical experience of every being that passes through. So that's one very important link, I think, that the cross theology has been distorted. I mean, after all, there was Easter, too, and there was a lot before the cross.

But the second thing you've just said is so important about the original purity, the Buddha Mind, and being part of this origin. That is exactly what I mean by Original blessing. And that, too, has been completely distorted and covered up by original sin ideology in the West, which as I put it earlier, comes from Augustine, not from Jesus, and certainly not from Judaism. Eckhart has the most beautiful sermon that I call "Mysticism as an Ocean," where he talks about, really, being in the fetal waters of union and communion and compassion. It's pure Buddhism, but he gets it from his own tradition. The mystical journey here, too, is about reentering just what you were talking about, that primal ocean. So, here again, we're at the level of universal archetypes. Suffering is an archetype. It's not all cause and effect. We're not responsible for all the suffering in the world. We are responsible for some, and that's where the practices of overcoming what you called the neuroses—and the 84,000 of them, wow, I could swear I only had 83,000. It's a shocker. But the work we have to do on ourselves is precisely, as you said, to lessen the suffering. But I just want to bring in this, to make this dialogical now, this level of teaching.

Tsomo: Well, when you say there isn't cause and effect, Buddhism does teach that there is cause and effect.

Matt: Well, I'm saying that there's not complete cause and effect. There is some. That's why I say we have to do the work to lessen the suffering, on ourselves and then on culture. When Christianity says that we nailed Jesus to the cross, that's a very big burden to put on kids, for example, or anyone else. And it's not exactly historically defensible either, that we're killing the Christ all over again. I would say, for example, that the killing of the rain forest or the whales or the polar bears that's going on today is the Crucifixion of the Christ all over again, but it's not the Crucifixion of Jesus.

Tsomo: Okay. And what I would say is that karma is unerring, because those marks on your soul from the acts that you've committed at some point, 500 lifetimes ago, or five minutes ago, there it is. The traces are there. So if it's historically inaccurate, that's one thing, but cause and effect is 100 percent. Now, there are methods to work with those seeds that have been planted before the causes fully ripen, because otherwise we just turn around and around in Samsara forever.

MATT: And you're going to lead us in such a practice soon.

TSOMO: Actually, we're going to do that a bit later. But what I wanted to get to now—first of all, I was talking about lineage, and if I could just get back to that for a second, because it's a long fast-forward from 2,500 years ago when the Buddha lived to even the 800s CE, when Buddhism came to Tibet and was really established there. There was an attempt earlier. Guru Rinpoche was invited to Tibet. Padmasambhava is another name for him, but the Tibetans tend to call him Guru Rinpoche. He was invited to Tibet by the king, whose name was Trisong Detsen. You don't need to know these names. There's not going to be a test. Guru Rinpoche was quite a powerful master, and I kind of think of him, in archetypal terms, as the master of transformation, because he transformed the gold dust that they brought to him into regular old dust. They were all horrified, especially since that was their meal ticket to get back to Tibet—they were supposed to have some of that gold dust. Several people came to request his presence for the king. Here was this pile of gold dust now, as dust, and he said, "Don't worry about it. I can turn it back again." Then he turned it back again. He did a lot of transforming like that. There were also demons tearing down the temple that the king was trying to build. Every day they would build it. Every night the land spirits, really, which were still against this new religion, were tearing it down, and this went on and on until the king called for Guru Rinpoche. When Guru Rinpoche came, he then had a little session with these land spirits, and then they were continuing the building at night instead of tearing it down. And during the day the regular old Tibetan workers were still building the temple. That's another example of transformation. The final one was the fact that he transformed his body into light, and there were lots of witnesses, literally writing it down as it was happening. He was giving final words of advice and then off he went, with his body fully transformed and still visible.

If you were to look at the myriad practices of Tibetan Buddhism and just break it down to two simple methods, you could say that they are doing two basic things. They are either clearing away the obscurations, or they're helping us to mature and bring forth our Buddha Nature. So I was just going to introduce, then, a practice called *tonglen*, which means "sending and receiving." And this helps us to bring forth our Buddha Nature.

I've talked enough about obscurations; let's go for bringing forth Buddha Nature. And, of course, a very popular Buddha quality is compassion. This is a compassion practice. And you were just talking about compassion. It's just a great basic one, and something that I still do a lot myself.

Buddhahood is not the same thing as these breakthroughs and satori experiences that we've been talking about. Buddhahood is crossing a point of no return where you've finally cleansed away all of these various impurities, and fully brought forth and matured your Buddha Nature. This needs to be done, according to Buddhism, through a long process. We've been knocking around Samsara for however many eons, however many countless lifetimes, and we've got some pretty ingrained habits. We've built up a pretty big karmic debit side of the ledger. So it's going to take some doing to change the habits of mind and change all of this to where we cross that point of no return.

B: PRACTICE—*Tonglen Meditation*

TSOMO: Please get in a reasonably comfortable position with your back reasonably straight. First, let me just give you an overview of this very simple practice. You're going to do two things: With the in-breath, you're going to do one thing; with the out-breath, you're going to do another. If you imagine somebody, and we'll start with somebody you already naturally feel sympathetic to—if you imagine them in front of you, and you imagine them suffering, what do you naturally want to do? You want to take that suffering away from them, and you want to replace it with joy and happiness—preferably not just even temporary joy and happiness, but permanent. Let's say you imagine somebody who is hungry. It may not even be a physical hunger. It may be loneliness, a hunger for companionship. Maybe you can just feel that somebody is very lonely and sad. So if you imagine that person in front of you, and you can see that they're lonely and sad and abandoned, then you want to take that away from them. You're going to breathe that suffering into your heart. It's a very courageous thing to do. *Courage*, coming from the word *heart*, it means the same. You're going to breathe that suffering into your heart, and you're going to use the power of visualization, which brings in then all of your neurological systems and even your muscular systems. They've even proved this in laboratories: Doing these kinds of exercises brings your whole body, all the different parts of your brain, into play.

So you breathe in a dark cloud of suffering. You see this dark cloud of suffering as you breathe it into you. And you want them to be happy, so you breathe out this sparkling, shiny, bright cloud of your wishes for them. You see that cloud then enveloping that person. And now they're relieved of their loneliness, or their hunger, or maybe it's somebody who is physically sick and in terrible pain. So we imagine now their faces lifting because the pain has been lifted away. Now they're feeling well and healthy. Whatever the suffering is, then, you imagine now they're relieved of it and feeling the opposite. But beyond that, as you keep breathing, you don't want them to be happy just for the moment, you want them to be happy permanently. So you imagine this permanent happiness that the Buddha had discovered, that they come home once again to the ocean of oneness and complete enlightenment.

We're going to begin with somebody we really automatically feel sympathy for, and feel it strongly. I had one lady who couldn't feel it for anybody she knew, and I said—I don't know why I had this inspiration—I said, "Do you have a cat?" And she said, "Yes." "Imagine your cat." So, whoever it is—I have a couple of dogs I love a lot—imagine them, imagine their suffering. You naturally want to take it away, and you naturally want to breathe out this joy and all of the good wishes for them. And then we're going to step it out. We're going to begin to imagine more and more people like that, but maybe people we don't know so well. Maybe it's somebody we don't know at all. If we're thinking about somebody who is lonely, we can imagine an orphan on the streets in Bombay, or anywhere. We can really step this out. So we're going to expand our capacity for compassion.

Let's start now.

Who is your first person you're going to start with? What is it that they're feeling? And begin to breathe in that suffering, allowing it into your heart, taking it away from them and into yourself through the breath. Because of your compassion, you can quite easily wish happiness for them, the relief of that suffering and permanent happiness for them. And so the bright, sparkly cloud naturally rides on your breath toward that person, surrounding them, and transforming them as their face lifts into a smile.

And now expand the circle just a little bit. If you've been focusing on yourself, you might be ready now to focus on someone else who you really have sympathy for, and begin sending and receiving with them. Or, if you've already been working on someone else, find yet another.

As you allow yourself to feel the pain and suffering of that person, allow the tears if they come, and the smiles when they come.

Continue expanding this circle out, and think of more people or beings who experience a similar suffering, even if you don't know their names but you still want to take away that suffering, and you still want to give them complete happiness.

We want big, deep breaths. Long breaths in, and long breaths out. And try to keep it even, not just taking in the suffering for a long, big, deep breath, but also just as strongly breathing out your wishes for happiness and seeing the face lit up and transformed.

To expand it even further, we just imagine all beings who at any time have felt a similar suffering. And since time is an illusion, it could be now, anytime previously, or anytime in the future. We just expand the circle all the way out, then, to all sentient beings and continue the breathing.

So now we'll leave this practice. Please finish. And opening your eyes…

What we wanted to do next, so that you could have a chance to digest the experience a little bit, was first open this up for questions. I imagine there might be one or two questions. And then we'll break down into smaller groups, so you all have more of a chance to talk with each other a bit about this. So, are there any questions?

STUDENT: *Why is it necessary to take the suffering into ourselves? Why do we have to take in other people's, others' suffering, rather than just imagine? We all have our own, so we can imagine and empathize.*

TSOMO: Speaking not so much as the engineer of this practice, but more as a practitioner with a lot of years of experience, I think the directness of it in that setup is very powerful and effective. It's also a little scary. And that's part of the purpose of it, to challenge ourselves a little bit and expand our capacity for compassion to the point where we're willing to suffer a bit ourselves in order to relieve the suffering of somebody else.

STUDENT: *I was just wondering if the suffering of another actually isn't our suffering.*

TSOMO: Yeah. I think on an ultimate level it is. There are two forms of compassion actually—or bodhicitta—that are talked about. There's ultimate bodhicitta, which is coming from the place of the whole ocean of oneness, so then, of course, someone else suffering over here is the same as if it were this wave or that wave. So there's that level. And there's also the relative level at which you've still got this other person suffering over here and me over here. I think part of the intent of the exercise is to bridge that gap, that sense of "I-other." Of course, we're always trying to do that one way or another in Buddhism.

MATT: Meister Eckhart[1] says, "What happens to another, whether it be a joy or a sorrow, happens to me." I see this exercise as acknowledging that and taking it in deeper because otherwise, we're spectators. And that's something, but as she says, it's growing your own heart to challenge it or to bring in the darkness of the suffering of others.

TSOMO: In a very real and felt way. Actually, this maturing and growing our Buddha Nature is kind of like pushing the envelope as much as possible, and we're very much doing that in this exercise.

There was a king long ago who was working with a very high Buddhist master. The master was trying to work with him on generosity, and the king said, "But I have absolutely no generosity. I'm not generous. I hate giving." So that's where they had to start. And the master said, "Well, you see that piece of fruit there?" "Yeah." "Okay, well, take that piece of fruit. Okay. You've got the piece of fruit. Now, give it from your left hand to your right hand." He said, "I can do that." So he gave it from the left hand to the right hand. "Great. Just keep doing that for a while." So he just kind of went back and forth, and pretty soon he was able to step it out just a little bit, and a bit more and more. And you notice, we even did that in this practice: stepping out the feelings. Once we had them going really strongly, the compassion then was able to step out to people we had never met before. [*to another questioner*] Yeah.

STUDENT: *I like the phrase, it's interesting that "it's growing your heart," and I understand that as a discipline for one's own practice. But what I'm wondering is that at certain levels can it be, is it understood to be an actual, kind of a healing practice? In other words,*

---

1. Matthew Fox, *Meditations with Meister Eckhart* (Santa Fe, NM: Bear & Co., 1983)

not just an exercise for growing one's own heart, but creating the actual effect of healing on someone else. I am just wondering if, as a practice, does this reach that level?

TSOMO: Um hum, um hum. Well, they have done studies on thousands of people, I think more than one study, on prayer and the effect of prayer in people in ICU and with heart surgery and things like that. And when people, even not necessarily sitting right there, were praying for that person employed that, it didn't matter what religion it was, but the effect still seemed to make itself felt. That they had fewer days in ICU, less depression—which often happens with heart surgery—better rate of recovery, sooner recovery, all of those things, as opposed to the control group. So that would indicate there is some effect. [*To student*] Yeah.

STUDENT: *This is really big. I'm used to this practice as a compassion practice and real positive. How much time do you think should we really, should we spend on a compassion practice as opposed to something else?*

TSOMO: Well, Pema Chödrön talks about this. And again, this is a question of capacity, but certainly, early on, five minutes is plenty. This is a very powerful practice. I can be, you know, both smiling and in tears in no time, and to hold that for longer than we can really hold it, we're gonna just end up in distraction, or in kind of a funny mental place. And it might be good to then move over into Vipassana or *Shamatha*, and then come back to it and do another five minutes. So you can do kind of a round-robin, and that's something that I would recommend, especially in the beginning. These are more questions about the practice? [*to student*] Yeah.

STUDENT: *Yeah, one of my meditation teachers talked about extinguishing the black smoke that you're breathing in, the sufferings of others. When it comes down to the heart, trying to just, letting it extinguish there. So getting back to the question of taking on suffering of other beings, maybe you sort of experience it, you feel compassion, but then you let go of that so that you're not weighed down by that, the suffering of others. Do you know what I'm talking about?*

TSOMO: That's interesting. I haven't heard it put that way. The way I experience it is that there is a natural transformation, an alchemy, that happens. And you can say that the catalyst is the compassion, because if we want the happiness for the other person, then when we breathe in that dark smoke, the next thing we naturally want to do is breathe out happiness for them. And so that's the catalyst. The compassion is the catalyst that turns that energy into this lovely, positive, joyful thing by our very desire for them. So that's how I experience it. But that's a beautiful way it was put. I haven't heard that before. Yeah, Phillip.

STUDENT: *For my experience just now, what I'm getting from this, is that it's a test. The heart chakra, if not the strongest, is one of the strongest chakras, and the archenemy of the heart chakra is fear. So as soon as you imagine taking in somebody's pain, it's a test of your courage. Do you really want to help this person? You're almost taking a split-second sacrifice by allowing their pain to enter your heart. So if you're not willing to do that, then you really don't want to heal them. You really don't. It's not really there. You know what I'm saying? Why would you bring it in? Because you have the power to heal it. You'll see, at that moment, do you really want to heal that person? Are you willing to sacrifice yourself for that person? This is a Buddhist practice, but it also, to me, seems like a "Jesus died for us on the cross" kind of thing. You're taking in the pain to heal everyone else.*

TSOMO: Um hum, uh hum, uh hum. Well, really, I like what you're saying about love and fear being sort of at opposite ends, and one precludes the other. If you're bursting with love, you're not feeling fear in that moment. If you're feeling fear, it's hard to have the love come forth. So this is a great exercise in that and, also, a method for working on that. Also, since identification with ego, in other words, identification as this one separate wave on the ocean, if that's the problem, this certainly is an elegant solution if it's applied again, and again, and again, because we sure applied the problem and the ego way of thinking again, and again, and again. I want to be careful with my words here because I don't think the ego in itself is evil or bad. I think identifying with it is the problem. [*To student*] Yeah.

STUDENT: *Yes. It's related to Ramsey's question with regards to taking on the suffering of another. In my perception, it assumes that they can't deal with their suffering themselves.*

TSOMO: How so?

STUDENT: *Well, if I take it away, I'm the taker as opposed to them healing their own suffering, knowing that their suffering is either an illusion or that they can heal their own suffering. Is there a corollary practice of just knowing their wholeness as opposed to taking this thing away from them?*

ANOTHER STUDENT: *I'm a pediatric nurse, and I would have to say that the children can't necessarily identify and cope with their own suffering, so of course someone else has to take it. This was my issue from the very beginning, even with the book, and dealing with suffering and how to cope with it. What about the children and the babies? So to hear someone say, well, they have to cope with it themselves, or if I take it away then they're not going to develop, that's very hard for me because I deal with babies' and children's suffering all the time. Maybe I don't have the capacity to cope.*

STUDENT: *Actually, I appreciate what you're saying, but I think there's two things that are getting collapsed. Is there a notion in a practice of whole?*

TSOMO: Of seeing people as whole? Yes.

STUDENT: *Yes, that's, I guess, where I was going with it.*

TSOMO: Yeah. And there are various beings that we can feel this compassion for. I still think that there's a very big place for tonglen, for all beings who are suffering. And if they want to work on themselves, they can still do that.

So maybe now would be a good time for us to get into the groups of four, and I'd like you to pick three other people who you don't know, you've never met before.

First of all, sharing what happened in your experience with the tonglen. Was it easy or hard? Happy? Sad? Maybe it was both. I think for me, it's both, actually. Beginning of the exercise, how was that as opposed to the end of it when you did it? Try and take some notes so we can maybe share it with the big group.

And really share your feelings with each other. This is a time when you get a chance to have a taste of *Sangha*. That's the third of the three jewels, which support us in our spiritual journey. The three jewels are the Buddha, who is an enlightened one, he actually reached enlightenment; the Dharma, the map that he put out and gave to us; and the Sangha, our spiritual, fellow journeyers. So allow this to be your little Sangha for the next couple of days, and really share your feelings. This is a feeling exercise that I gave you. See if you can be a little courageous and talk with them about it. After all, you never have to see them again.

TSOMO: [*After the groups have met*] An important distinction that I would like to make—I haven't had a lot of time to really teach this practice to you—is that you don't think of taking on the story around the suffering, it is the actual suffering itself that you're taking in. [*To student*] Yeah.

STUDENT: *It was interesting. We all have different perspectives. It was easy to visualize suffering and to bring that in. For certain people and situations, it's very difficult to visualize them being relieved of the suffering. That was an exercise.*

TSOMO: People usually have more trouble with one or the other. Anyone in this group want to speak?

STUDENT: *Well, we noticed our attention wandered a lot during tonglen, and then I was talking about Shamatha practice and redeveloping sustained attention. It's really a preliminary practice and helps me with all the other meditative practices. Then we got into the question about giving ultimate happiness and the difficulty of kind of being able to visualize that.*

TSOMO: Um hum, um hum. I think that may be why using a white cloud, sparkly cloud, is helpful because it's such a huge, ineffable thing to try and visualize. So you use something that sort of represents that. And, hopefully, the feeling comes with it. [*To student*] Yeah.

STUDENT: *It was interesting, I think for each of us, the practice of the taking-in, and the earlier conversation that we had in the room about the fear of being overwhelmed by it, and feeling helpless to do anything about it, which goes back to what Karen was talking about, trying to do something about it as opposed to just taking.*

TSOMO: Well, and again, if you're not taking in the whole story, just the suffering itself, there's less of that temptation to solve it, because it's not about solving it. And I feel empowered that I am doing something when I breathe out, so that's an added help for me when I do it.

Another benefit I found is, when I am suffering, myself, my lens gets very small, and I'm just seeing my little suffering here. This practice expands, opens my lens to such an extent that by the end, really, my suffering hasn't changed any in size, but the whole view has, so now it's a very different experience. So, you guys back there?

STUDENT: *There was a little bit of struggle with it in the beginning, of taking in the pain, or finding that person. Just taking in the pain, I was describing it as, like a gatekeeper, at the beginning of your practice, trying to stop you from getting extra deep. And I made a note for me of all the people that I thought I could feel suffering for—that was the* *hardest. So it's easier to just, to go to someone else that I can sympathize with. I think it was easier for people to pick people that they know rather than the big scope of everybody.*

TSOMO: Um hum. Well, I don't have the quote exactly right but, "Love thy neighbor as thyself." I think is the quote.

MATT: Eckhart puts it this way. He says, "Compassion begins at home with your own body and your own soul." So it's hard to begin at home. You know, it's almost easier to go out.

TSOMO: But skipping that step, though, truncates our capacity for true, deep compassion. So I would recommend us starting with yourself and then stepping it out from there, because you might find you can afford to feel more compassion then for others. Actually, I get a lot more empathy for others once I've allowed that for myself. So it's a much more juicy practice that way, and the practice then is more successful.

STUDENT: *One person in our group commented that when it got to the point of taking in the suffering of all sentient beings, that that was overwhelming and they didn't do it. I think many of us have some resistance, and it's a radical practice. It's amazing how Pema has presented this—it's not closed-door at all. It's in her books, it's on her tapes. I think we talked about the idea that one of the ways of dealing with that fear of taking on all of that suffering is to first dissolve one's self. And there may even be a way that she presents it, a step where somehow you just see yourself as a filament between heaven and Earth. So, am I taking it into Steve? Well, yes, but not really, because Steve isn't here. So, if we dissolve our sense of self, our sense of ego first, then it's not quite as terrifying. I don't know. Can you unpack that idea a little more?*

TSOMO: Well, I would say it two different ways. Maybe "expanding ego" would be a way to say it, and also I feel myself to be more like a conduit. So I've expanded my lens, and this one here, this wave in the ocean, is like a conduit through which the suffering and the joy is passing. I don't have to be the source of the joy. I don't see myself as the source of the joy. It's passing through me, and the suffering is passing through, and the picture is much bigger. So that's my experience of it.

MATT: I'd like to add something here, too, and this is just one exercise, but it seems to be a parallel one that maybe we're presuming in doing this: to take in the beauty of the world, and the grace of the world, and the joy of the world, because this prepares you. This makes you strong to be able to take in the suffering of the world. Like I say, you don't go into a mine without a lantern. So dare we go into the real hot spots of suffering without the protection of grace, joy, and beauty? Because, like Rabbi Zalman Schacter-Shalomi says, [paraphrasing], "There's more good than evil in the world, but not by much." So that means you do have to meditate on the goodness of the world. And Eckhart says, "Whenever you talk about God, the Creator, you're talking about goodness." You see, blessing, original blessing, or original purity, is about the intrinsic goodness of being. And we can't presume we're there, especially in our culture. I'm given a lot of what I call toxic religious messages. So in my practice, I think I would precede something—and, of course, we don't have time in this brief time together to do all these things—but I think that it may be very worthwhile to precede this practice with taking in the beauty, the grace, and the joy of all beings to sustain you, to get truthful about the suffering of all of it. That's why in the structure of the four paths of Creation Spirituality, the *via positiva*—the goodness, the blessing—precedes the *via negativa*, because it makes you strong. And it is all about strength. And it's just what your group said, they couldn't deal with this. Everybody is suffering, you know, please. So how do we strengthen the heart? I would put that out there, too.

Tsomo: Well, and Pema Chödrön says, as I think somebody over here said, the practice of Vipassana, where you're really resting in the ocean of being, gives you that basis and that joy, and you're experiencing the original purity. Then from that, doing the five minutes of tonglen, and then back into this, that rhythm also helps with the practice. That's in context then. We did this a little out of context.

Student: *I like the way she put it. She said it's like sending a card to somebody. You're just sending good wishes, you're holding them close, and you're sending positive affection to another person. And Trudy has used it a lot with a death of her friend. It has been able to strengthen her through relationships, to help them through their time of suffering. For Garrett and I, it was a new experience for us to, at some point in our practice of tonglen, to discover that not only is all the world us, but that we are also part of all beings—so, learning to be included. In all cases, even if we don't understand all the levels that are going on, the practice itself does feel good. I got to the point where I started* *practicing tonglen on the buses when I was riding on the bus. Anybody who stepped in didn't have to know what was going on for them. I just imagined taking them on. And I found that for me, it was a kind of a trick. Tonglen practice is a trick, because it's like an antidote. The more you relieve the suffering of other people's, the more it's being held within you. And the more you generate compassion for others, the more you learn to generate compassion for yourself. And so it's kind of like taking a little bit of poison and discovering that you are well after all.*

MATT: Building your immune system.

STUDENT: *Yeah, exactly. Tonglen practice, I think, is one of my all-time favorites, and it's the easiest to learn, and it teaches so much.*

CHAPTER 3

Mysticism and Science
RICARD AND ECKHART

MATT: Our idea was to deal the first half of this afternoon with the *Happiness* book by Matthieu Ricard[2]. For me this was a very interesting book, at times more than others. I did feel that it was a bit lengthy at times. But I've studied with the French. I did my doctorate in France, and one of the things I liked about this was he was taking on the French intellectuals with vengeance, Buddhist vengeance, a very gentle vengeance. I like the way he talks about Sartre you know, he's so depressed, and his "being and nothingness," and all this stuff. And, of course, I read a lot of Sartre when I was a young guy.

TSOMO: Did we want to begin this session with giving rise to bodhicitta? That was one thing we were going to open with, just quickly.

MATT: Oh, I'm sorry. I thought you weren't going to do that. Go ahead.

TSOMO: Yeah. With each of the sessions, just to remind everybody of that intention, that the bodhicitta, the heart-mind of awakening, this combination of wisdom and compassion that is bodhicitta, we want to bring that forward so that we can take full advantage of this moment. Not only for ourselves, but for the sake of all beings. Sorry, go on.

MATT: Thank you. And I like that because it puts learning in the context of the heart, and that's the way to wisdom. Too much learning in the

2. From *Happiness: A Guide to Developing Life's Most Important Skill* by Matthieu Ricard © 2006. Reprinted by permission of Little, Brown and Company, an imprint of Hachette Book Group, Inc.

West has fallen into just a context of knowledge, and that's just a weapon. Knowledge by itself is a weapon, but knowledge that serves the heart, that's wisdom, and that's how we have to shift as a species today, for sure. And that's what does it, in this awareness.

So, I did get a kick out of his taking some potshots at people like Sartre and so forth. And just the title *Happiness* is not a favorite French phrase among the French intellectual class, whatsoever. So I found this was kind of behind the scenes in a lot of his writing here, and I did take delight at that.

But specifically what I want to do in the time I have, and then to open it up to discussion, your own and Tsomo's, too, as we go along, is to point out some of the really significant connections that I see between Ricard's writing and Eckhart's, his writing out of his Buddhist experience. First of all, that [Ricard] comes out of science is very important. I alluded to that briefly this morning about how the tradition that Eckhart comes from, the Dominican tradition, Aquinas, and so forth, is very pro-science. Hildegard, too. Hildegard, who was twelfth century—she preceded Aquinas or Eckhart—she says, "All science comes from God." So this is not fundamentalism, you know. Because clearly fundamentalism everywhere, whether it's today's Vatican, or the Jerry Falwell kind, or the Taliban kind, or any other kind, it is always making bogeymen out of science. The fear of knowledge, the fear of science is so prevalent in fundamentalism, but there's not a taint of that in this tradition. In fact, Aquinas was so controversial in his time, because he was bringing in the best scientists of his day, thirteenth century. Who was what? Aristotle. He came from Baghdad, in fact. That's where they were translating Aristotle into Latin. And then they sent it up into Spain. And that's where Dominic, who was very pro-intellect, caught on to the idea of, "Hey, you can be a Christian and bring these exciting new ideas into the universities," which had just been born at that time. And Aristotle had three strikes against him. First, he came from Islam. Another strike against Aristotle was that he was a pagan. Ah, ah, eeeek! Pagan. He wasn't Jewish, and he wasn't Christian. And the third was that he was a scientist. Who needs science? The fundamentalists in the thirteenth century are just like the ones today. Who needs science? Augustine told us everything we had to know. It's all about sin and redemption, sin and redemption. Nothing about creation, nothing about the grace of creation.

So Aquinas took on this history of opposition to science, and he paid tremendously for it. So much so that there were times when the king of France had to get the army out to surround his convent, because Christian priests were whipping up the populace against Aquinas, because he was bringing a pagan scientist baptized by the Muslims, for God's sake, into Christianity in the thirteenth century. Aquinas had real courage, and he did not back down. And his best friend did back down, Bonaventure, who was a Franciscan and Aquinas's contemporary at the University of Paris. He backed down because it was getting so hot, because some Aristotelians were atheist. Siger of Brabant was an atheist. Aquinas was a Christian man and Aristotelian. Hanging out with atheist Aristotelians was like hanging out with Marxists in our time, and you got tainted for it. Aquinas did not back down; Bonaventure did. He gave up on Aristotle. He went back to Plato, and they made him a cardinal. Aquinas was really alone then, and he actually had a nervous breakdown at the end of his life. And the end of his life, his last year of his life, he couldn't talk. It's an amazing story.

But I just bring it out to you because we're going through this again: science versus faith, or versus religion. God of one is God of the other. The God of your right brain, your mystical brain, is a God of your left brain. Duh. So, let's get them both operating. That's what I'm talking about here. So I respect very much that Ricard comes out of his own scientific background, and then he does all this powerful work in Buddhism and mind training, and now he's in a place to be dialoguing with serious scientists. And he's at the forefront, really, of these experiments going on, may I say, in my hometown, University of Wisconsin, in Madison, where they are really testing these meditators to see what, in scientific language, we can describe as going on. And Tsomo knows a lot about that, too. But that's part of who this guy is, and it's great.

TSOMO: I just have to say here that Davidson, for example, is part of the Mind and Life Institute. This was a gathering of scientists, philosophers, and psychologists who were brought together by the Dalai Lama. And together, for the last couple of decades, they've been pursuing truth, comparing notes on truth, you might say. And from this, many books have been spawned, and many studies, including the ones at University of

Wisconsin, Madison, with Davidson. I believe here at Stanford, too.

MATT: In our day it's so important to bring science and spirituality to-gether because, truthfully, many of us don't believe anything unless it has a science "good health seal of approval" on it. I'm doing a conference this summer with 300 or 400 scientists. They call themselves "ISEEM." I don't know if you've heard of them, International Society of Energy and Energetic Medicine. It's a weird title. But there's some very exciting scientists, and they're interested in spirituality, and I'm in a workshop and a keynote there in Boulder in a month or so. I'm looking forward to it a lot. And their theme for this conference—they have one every year—is "Miracles."

One of the points I want to make—I'll be quoting Eckhart, among others—Eckhart says, "Isness is God," you know. And Einstein says, "There are two ways to look at life. Either nothing is a miracle. Or every-thing is a miracle." And I think the modern age, when we shut the cosmos down and called it a machine, then what religion did was define miracle as an intervention in the machine, an intervention of natural laws. And that's the way we think, "Oh, a miracle is 'zap,' you're saved, or 'zap,' you're healed." But surely that's weird. Once the cosmos opens up for what it really is, then you realize that every breath is a miracle. The fact that this Earth happened, that the moon is just the right distance from the Earth for tides to rise and therefore for life to happen, all these facts of science, then, to me, become daily fodder for miracles. And we're not here just asking to be zapped and freed. Life itself has its own wonder about it.

TSOMO: Well, even the things that are considered outright miracles, peo-ple flying through the air and that kind of thing, if you look at it from another point of view, that this is a dream during waking hours, just as we have dreams at night when we're sleeping, there really isn't that much difference after all. Has anybody here experienced realizing they were dreaming during the dream? Okay. And in that moment, then, weren't you able to do anything you wanted? Fly through the air, pass through walls, all these. You can transform anything into anything. You can just play. And the universe is the play of God, and it's known in Buddhism as the play of the Dharmakaya, the ground of all. So we get to play once we realize how it really works. So everything is a miracle and nothing is a miracle, just as you're saying.

MATT: That word *play* is so important to Eckhart and Aquinas, too. Aquinas says, "The nearest word to *contemplation* is *play*." That's the synonym for *contemplation*—that you're playing with wisdom, you're playing with God. And Eckhart says, "When you learn to live without a why, and to love without a why, and to work without a why, what is that? That's play." Play has no why. It has no purpose beyond itself, and that's why recovering play is such a profound and mature spiritual trip, as you're saying. Or another way to put it is don't take anything seriously, especially not your death.

STUDENT: *Interesting you said that word—death—because the thing that I found in the reading mentioned the food chain, and up to the point where food arrives in a can. I find that it's a difficult place for me to consider miraculous, and don't know that people do, or death as being part of the miraculous. Yet, when you're saying that it's all the miraculous, we have to include those things that we wouldn't necessarily find joyous events, or, you know, the process of food processing in this country. But from what you're saying, we have to live with that and entertain that as being part of the miracle of our lives. Or not.*

MATT: Yeah. Well, I think what humans contribute is not always miraculous. It's sometimes demonic, if you will, sometimes very negative. So this is where ethics and morality comes in—what do we do with our play, which is creativity? And Jung says, [paraphrasing], "No creativity without play and fantasy." That's the *via creativa* in the Creation spiritual tradition and the four paths. But we can play destruction, or we can play at beauty, grace, compassion. What do we do with our compassion? What do we do with our capacities of imagination and creativity? So that's where the ethical question comes in. And that's why it's so important, it seems to me, to purify our intentions at play and at creativity, because we are very powerful beings, what we can do for good or bad, destruction or creativity.

Okay, so just getting in with you a little bit about these connections between Ricard, working out of his experience, and Eckhart. A couple of years ago I visited Eckhart's monastery, in what used to be Eastern Germany, and it's almost miraculous that the place stands to this day, because it's certain the Eastern Communist Germans were not busy repairing old religious sites. What's so curious is the old monastery he was in was not destroyed in the Second World War at all, but they added a new church in, I think, the seventeenth century. It was bombed. But his place wasn't. So I actually sat in his stall. We know where he sat, because he was prior in this church, and the prior always sat in this once place. So I sat, and I thought it would be a very peaceful experience, and it was just the opposite. I felt like Fearless Fosdick. I felt all these arrows were going through me and it was just like being on an electric chair or something. But I realized he was in that seat for four years meditating. A part of the Dominican practice is to meditate daily and also to chant daily. And he was there. I had the sense that this is where he learned his Buddhism, right in that seat. It was really moving to me. Because in his "Via Negativa" he's talking pure Buddhist talk, and he didn't get it from going East. There's no evidence that there are texts on the Rhine at that time from the East. He got it from going into his tradition and his own psyche. That to me is part of the wonder and the beauty of Buddhism, that it's more than just Buddhist. I think what's really been found there is universal truths about the human capacity, our human minds and hearts.

Notice on page 24[3], at the bottom, Ricard, speaking from the Buddhist tradition says, "Phenomena exist in an essentially interdependent mode and have no autonomous and enduring existence. Everything is relation. Nothing exists in and of itself immune to the forces of cause and effect." Well, Eckhart says exactly the same thing. Eckhart says that behind everything is relation. He says, "The essence of everything is relation." That quote is not in your little book, but it's in the big book I have on his work. It's an amazing statement for a Westerner to make in the fourteenth century, because in Western philosophy they were looking for the *Ding an sich*, the thing inside the thing, from the fifth century BC up through the twentieth century. And Eckhart says exactly what Ricard says. This is his exact quote, "Essence is a relation of everything that exists."

Note this is also very feminist thinking in terms of relationship—how deep is relationship inside of things? Is relationship just, you know, you and me, we meet, we know each other's names, fine, we go our way? Or is calling on relation really more important than calling on the thing itself? And I'm sure Tsomo will be getting into this, the issue of the transparency

3. From *Happiness: A Guide to Developing Life's Most Important Skill* by Matthieu Ricard © 2006. Reprinted by permission of Little, Brown and Company, an imprint of Hachette Book Group, Inc.

of what she would call the ego of our selfhood, that what really is there is relation. This is what Eckhart is saying in the fourteenth century. It's what Ricard says right here. It's also, I think, what today's physics is saying, that they're finding that you don't just have things inside things inside the microcosmic world. You have relationships, but also in the macrocosmic world. And it is all about interdependence, as Ricard says.

So again, this is a profound side from Buddhism, but it's found in our Western tradition as well. It is interesting to me, in this whole book, he never once mentions Eckhart. So clearly he has never been exposed to some of his Western mystical teachers, which is typical—99 percent of us have not been. We've had to go very out of our way, and if you have been, you often get kicked out of the church for doing it. That's the scandal. And it's like Theodore Roszak says, "During the Enlightenment, the modern era, mysticism was held up for ridicule as the worse offense against science and reason."

So if we're going to get our degrees and get serious, and get grown up, you've got to hide in the closet if you're a mystic. And even on this campus, I know a very renowned professor, a scientist, he runs a program of multi-millions of dollars every year, and he doesn't tell anyone here that in fact he has this profound spiritual experience of sweat lodges. He has a sweat lodge in his backyard. He has sweat lodges with his wife and others on a regular basis. He has a mystical life, but he has to pretend he doesn't, because he is a scientist, he's for serious, he's at Stanford. Well, if they only knew.

Another passage that stands out for me is the bottom of page 52[4], where Ricard's talking about "the denial of the possibility of happiness." Now notice, this is the French intellectual life, but it's also the basic cynicism that courses through Western culture. It's not all a French problem. "The denial of the possibility of happiness seems to have been influenced by the concept of the world as mankind and mankind as being fundamentally evil." Now this is Augustinian and it's Lutheran, Calvin. "This belief stems largely from the notion of original sin." It permeates our culture. That's what he's saying, and I couldn't agree more. I think it's the basis

---

4. From *Happiness: A Guide to Developing Life's Most Important Skill* by Matthieu Ricard © 2006. Reprinted by permission of Little, Brown and Company, an imprint of Hachette Book Group, Inc.

of consumer capitalism. Because what you're being told in this barrage of advertising messages is that you don't have what it takes, you've got to buy salvation outside yourself, you've got to get your prettier teeth, or your more perfect refrigerator, or something that's going to make you right. That's original sin ideology.

So if you move to 205[5], you have him saying in the top paragraph, "Certainly the concept of original sin, which is peculiar to Christian civilization, and its accompanying sense of guilt, are steeped in this thinking of the selfish gene. It has in fact had a considerable influence on Western intellectual thought." Et cetera. Absolutely. But what is the antidote, then, to this pessimism and to this original sin ideology that takes over the Western soul? Both its secular and its religious soul—it does both. And the antidote is the original purity teaching of Buddhism that we can get to. This is not just about "it's out there someplace." Here are some paths there, or in my language, *original blessing*.

Tsomo: Now when you say "paths there," you mean coming back home to it, in a sense.

Matt: Yeah. There are ways to reconnect to your original purity, or to your original blessing. And Eckhart has tremendous teachings on this. He talks about returning to meditation, returning to your "unborn self," where he says you are totally free and where you become the maker of who you are. And he goes on and on in these amazing passages about our unborn self. And what he's saying, then, is that before we entered this world, we were in this state of original purity and original blessing, and you can get back there anytime you want through practices. And also just general awareness, that evil does not have the last word, and that the beauty of creation, the grace of creation, the grace of your creation, is deeper than any brokenness or any damage. And if you've dealt with people who have been very broken, just think, for example, of people going to AA, so alcoholics who have bottomed out, and how many of them have reported back afterwards that this was their first experience of grace, or transcendence, or spirit, or God. It came after they had surrendered and

---

5. From *Happiness: A Guide to Developing Life's Most Important Skill* by Matthieu Ricard © 2006. Reprinted by permission of Little, Brown and Company, an imprint of Hachette Book Group, Inc.

yielded to the bottoming-out. So they had to go through horrible things before they recovered a sense of their own beauty and their own grace.

Obviously it is very important to the Vatican, too, because it was my book *Original Blessing* that especially set them off. But what I'm saying is that I think this ideology of original sin, which Ricard picks up on several times in this book, is pivotal. It's almost like either you accept that ideology, that we're born evil, or you don't, or we're born beautiful and we're capable of evil. And, of course, society is capable of dumping its evil on us. Now I like the language of Otto Rank, who is not Christian but Jewish, when he talks about the "original wound". I think it's much more accurate than original sin, and he defines the original wound that we're all born with, as leaving our mother's womb, that we were content in the womb. There was wholeness and happiness there. But in leaving through the birth canal, and then the suffering that goes on from the moment you take your first breath, we come in the world with a wound, and the wound is having left the womb. So he thinks all of our struggles in life are pushing, re-pushing that button of the original wound of separation. So whether it's death, whether it's divorce, whether it's disease, whatever tends to force itself upon us in negative ways, this is really a replaying of that original wound of separation from the mother.

His solution—these are his words—is that, and Rank was Freud's youngest and most brilliant disciple—his solution is *unio mystica*. That's his language: the mystical union. He says that every mystical union is a healing of that original wound. It is a return, therefore, to the original place of bliss and grace, blessing and purity. And he says [paraphrasing], "Especially in our lives we experience *unio mystica* in acts of love and acts of art." Love and art are the basic paths in which we begin to heal that wound.

CHAPTER 4

The Four Paths of Creation Spirituality

MATT: Now, on 134[6] of Ricard—and again, I'm skipping around; there's a lot here, as you know, and I'm just hitting some parts—in the middle of the page he's quoting some psychologist, and he's talking about this movement of positive psychology. "And a few notable exceptions, and my wish to develop a positive psychology, no aphorism made, invested in cultivating positive attributes of mind from individuals not suffering from mental disorders." I really like that. We don't have a psychology for healthy people. We only have a psychology for sick people. And Buddhism does have that. Buddhism is telling you what your powers are. For me, this is what the four paths of Creation Spirituality do for us, too, especially the *via creativa*. And I wanted to show that there's a formula here. How do we come to creativity? The *via positiva*, which is our experiences of the beauty, and the grace, and the goodness of creation, of life—it's our experiences of awe and wonder. Plus the *via negativa*. The *via negativa* is sometimes about silence, and emptying, and nothingness, which can be a very cool thing, by the way. Nothingness is by no means always a downer. It's a wonderful thing sometimes to be alone. Have you noticed? But the *via negativa* also can be about suffering. It also is about suffering and how we deal. But together they yield creativity. There's a formula here for creativity. That it is the falling in love with life, and it is the awe of life, and it is the

---

6. From *Happiness: A Guide to Developing Life's Most Important Skill* by Matthieu Ricard © 2006. Reprinted by permission of Little, Brown and Company, an imprint of Hachette Book Group, Inc.

letting go of input, therefore entering in the silence of solitude, or also suffering, which is another form of letting go. So both meditation and suffering together, they make you a rich person with something to give back. That's what creativity is, something to give back.

What he's calling the *positive psychology*, it seems to me, would be both this experience of awe and wonder, and falling in love. And not seeing falling in love as just an anthropocentric thing, but falling in love with being, with life, with trees, with animals, with poems, with music, et cetera, as well as with an individual. The *via creativa* has a special relationship with the *via positiva* because in your creativity you're putting more beauty in the universe. You're bringing more awe and wonder into the universe. You're bringing more opportunities for joy into the universe. So I see what he's calling for here, what he calls a positive psychology, which is not to be confused with positivistic or tiptoeing through the roses as if there is no pain and suffering. I see this as very much honored in the four paths of Eckhart and Creation Spirituality, because both of these are saying something about our empowerment, your power to give birth. And how important is that? Eckhart says, "What does God do all day long? God lies on a maternity bed giving birth." So Eckhart's definition of—first of all, it's very maternal, very feminine—but it is also, it's giving us permission. Oh, that's why we're here: to give birth continuously.

Now, the *via transformativa* is so important, too, because this is about compassion and justice. What is it we're giving birth to? And that's what I said earlier. The *creativa* by itself—I mean, you know, inventing gas ovens was a creative act in the 1940s. So you need the *via transformativa* to critique and steer the creativity. Creativity in itself is power, but it can be demonic as well as divine. What way to go with it matters. This is why so many teachers from all the world traditions are holding compassion—the test of compassion and justice—up to us to help us steer creativity and to test it. We have to test our creativity. Above all, you can't turn it over to others. Of course, this happens a lot with our tax dollars, for example. So this too is all about empowerment. Again, I'm just pointing out the parallels between Ricard's teaching here, about the call, because the call, and I couldn't agree more, that psychology has to grow up. I think many psychologists today are being called to be spiritual directors. More than

"What's your problem," it's "What's your divine potential that isn't coming forward that we can help to develop more fully?" That, I think, is the question, and I think that he brings it out here, and I think the four paths help him in a way.

One thing that I like about Tibetan Buddhism is that it's, obviously, not at all iconoclastic or Puritan. Some forms of Buddhism are much less colorful. I love the colors, the sounds, the smells, the vibrancy, the creativity, the rituals. Again, coming from a Roman Catholic tradition, just the smells of beeswax that you used to get, or the feeling you would get from Gregorian chant and all that—it fed the senses. And this was one of the first things you spoke about this morning.

Tsomo: Um hum. Well, when I was in Tibet, the butter lamps were slightly old yak butter, so it was a little different. The incense was better.

Matt: I remember being with Aboriginals in Australia, and they're telling me, "We spend a long time preparing for our rituals. And it's making clothes." And I said, "What's that about?" "Oh," they said, "we have to be as beautiful in our bodies as the snakes are in theirs, and as the birds are in theirs." This is the obligation, you see, to imitate the beauty of the world, and gather as human beings to be as beautiful as these other beings. The whole role of beauty is so palpable in the Tibetan tradition, but it is in, I would say, the best of Christianity, too, or it should be. Okay, so how are we doing time-wise? I've got to stop? Okay.

Tsomo: Just want you to be sure and be able to sort of tie the ribbon.

Matt: I understand. Just one more point. Tie the ribbon. Okay. Let me see, one point: 184[7]. This is a good ending to sort of talk about at the very top end of the paragraph. "If we come to grips with the internal processes that govern them, we may be able to teach people how to take pleasure and live it." Now that's a quote, he's quoting Ruut Veenhoven. How to take pleasure in living. When you have these four paths, the way I picture them is a spiral, an open-ended spiral. Path one, two, three, and then four, but it's open-ended, and then it starts up again. You go from the

---

7. From *Happiness: A Guide to Developing Life's Most Important Skill* by Matthieu Ricard © 2006. Reprinted by permission of Little, Brown and Company, an imprint of Hachette Book Group, Inc.

via transformativa back to the *via positiva*, because what is justice, except an effort to bring more to the table to celebrate life? And this is what the prophets of Israel promised, that the people would gather at the mountains, rich and poor, and the rivers would flow with justice, and everyone would be fed and nourished. The idea, then, that this is not an end in itself, these four paths, it just, it expands—it expands back, then, to the *via positiva*. And I think that's parallel to what he's quoting there, that the empowerment and the—what he calls the pleasure of life, that I call the act of savoring, which is the *via positiva*, and that's a spiritual act to learn to savor. In our culture we're so busy grabbing that we don't realize what a spiritual act it is to enjoy, to savor the graces of life. And it takes a discipline to do that.

I remember years ago I was teaching in Chicago, and one of the young people in the class—I was talking about the *via positiva* and savoring—he went down to the bus station in Chicago and ordered a bowl of popcorn. And he took three hours to eat the bowl. He would pick up one kernel and meditate on it, and then put it on his tongue and turned it over very, very slowly. He savored. He was learning to savor a bowl of popcorn. And during the process he said about fifteen different people—you know, the bus station in Chicago, especially back then, was not the most savory place in the world—they all came up to him and they said, "Where did you learn to eat like that? Where did you learn to enjoy yourself so much?" And he was able to say, "From Meister Eckhart"—that we are here to savor. That's what I hear him saying on page 184 in his book. We're here to savor the beauties of life, and to work that others can do so also. So those are a few connections between Eckhart and Ricard. So, do you want to jump in here, or…?

Tsomo: I thought I'd take us through just a very quick exercise that I did a lot of when I was studying the Vipassana. I'm going to ask everyone to, once again, be courageous—I keep doing that with these exercises—and rehearse the process of dying. And not with lots of "Ow, it hurts here," and all that kind of thing, but actually to try and get past this identification with being "me" in this life now. Again, it's sort of letting go of our tight, tight grip of identification with ego—"I am this person, this wave on the ocean"—which was, if you take the original meaning of *sin*, it literally, the translation that I've heard, is "missing the mark." In Tibetan it's *marigpa*, this moment that we made a mistake when we were one wave in the ocean and thought, "I'm just this wave," rather than we're actually the whole ocean and there's this wave. Dying, then, doesn't become the personal loss when you're the whole ocean, when the wave goes back down, goes up, and down. It's not the big drama that we normally see it to be when we're identified just with this one little wave.

So the purpose of it is to bring insight. Before, we were bringing forth compassion, this Buddha quality of compassion, and now to balance it, let's bring forth a little bit of insight. So let's sit down. And again, have the back straight. There are energy channels, and the mind rides on those energies. So when the back is straight, the channels are straight. When the channels are straight, then the winds can go straight. When the winds are moving in a straight way, then the mind can be straight. So this can up our chances of a good experience. I'm going to just talk you through it, step-by-step. We're going to peel away the layers of the onion that we're all calling *me*. And that's what happens in the dying process. We lose one thing after another. So to help our imaginations, we can close our eyes. It's not necessary.

Imagine now that you're letting go of this life. An obvious thing is that you're going to let go of this body. So with that go the capacities of this body: these hands that hold things and do things, these legs that walk and jump and dance. We're letting go of these particular hands and legs. We're letting go of this life, so we're letting go of all of the parts of the story that shaped the particular personality of this life that we're calling *me*. There go the piano lessons, and algebra, and foreign languages. As a matter of fact, we let go of our own language. We even let go of our name. Really feel the letting go of all of these things, one after another. And we begin to ask, "What remains? Who is this one I've been calling *me*? What is it?" And when we let go of this life, and even our name, perhaps we come down to "my awareness." You might try that on for size: "my awareness." "But what is this 'my' of the awareness?" Perhaps it's just awareness. And in this moment, I ask you to experience this awareness without the boundary of a "me." Boundless awareness. Bring yourselves back now to this localized time and place. Hopefully, this little taste reminds you of other tastes you've had in your own meditative experiences: moments of breakthrough, or satori, and moments in nature, maybe, when those limits we put on ourselves are loosened a little bit.

MATT: Can I ask you a question?

TSOMO: Um hum.

MATT: Eckhart asks that same question, "What remains? What lasts?" and his answer—and he says this more than once, so it's on his mind a lot—his answer is, "What is inborn within me remains." Now, would you say that is very much like awareness? Do you think awareness is something that is inborn within us?

TSOMO: Absolutely. In Tibetan Buddhism the term *sentient beings* means that the being in there experiencing things is being aware of the experiences it's having. So, yeah, I think there's definitely a counterpart. I mean, who is experiencing the suffering? So there's some kind of awareness that is experiencing that.

STUDENT: *Not a self, but awareness.*

TSOMO: Yeah. It's the way I would put it, and then we'd construct a self around it.

MATT: And Eckhart gets that from the passage in John's gospel, where the Christ is saying, "You will bear fruit, fruit that remains." And Eckhart keeps coming back to that. Well, what remains, what fruit remains? That seems to be a very Buddhist question, too, now.

TSOMO: The Buddha talked a lot about the impermanence of things. Anything that is a composite is eventually going to come apart. Well, that would cover a lot of things. What's left? What isn't a composite of things? And what's left is the Dharmakaya, which I assume you all remember from the glossary of Buddhist terms. The Dharmakaya is that pregnant emptiness out of which everything comes, and it never was something put together, and there are no pieces and parts to come together. So how can it fall apart?

MATT: And that is that which is inborn within me.

TSOMO: Yeah, because the quality of this emptiness—there are several qualities of it, and one of them is awareness: knowing. Another quality of it is unimpeded compassion because if there's no sense of separateness, then the feeling of suffering or any sort of experience is felt throughout the whole. So it's ultimate compassion.

MATT: And it seems to me it's creativity. It's a birthing energy.

TSOMO: Constant.

MATT: And I think that's what Eckhart's zeroing in on, too.

TSOMO: I might as well get right into my responses to Eckhart. On page 5 in the Introduction, he's talking, I mean you are talking, the author is talking about *via positiva, negativa, creativa,* and *transformativa.* When I think of *via positiva* and *negativa* in this union that you speak of, I think of, well, a couple of different things. There is sort of like the Tibetan equivalent of yin-yang, for those of you who've studied any Taoism. Everything positive and everything negative, so the same terms. It's personified archetypally in Tibetan Buddhism as the primordial Buddha. And it's in masculine and feminine form: Kuntuzangpo and Kuntuzangmo. So Kuntuzangpo is all positive, masculine. Kuntuzangmo is all positive, feminine. They look like human beings in union. And it's beautiful because he's dark blue, as though he's just emerging out of space, out of emptiness, but actually the one representing the emptiness out of which all being comes is Kuntuzangmo, the all-positive feminine. So this is the union right there of the positive and negative, *positiva* and *negativa,* emptiness and what's called *luminosity.* And this luminosity is this flashing forth of form into being. On this level, it's absolutely pure. There's no confusion, no spattered windshield, and all the other things I was talking about. We're talking just on a very pure level.

I'm going to move now into *creativa,* because as you begin form, then it goes through some steps in the process. So the first step to form, from the emptiness, is the archetypal level, as I call it. And now I'm getting into the three *Kayas* for those of you who were paying attention to your glossary of Buddhist terms. So the Dharmakaya is that emptiness level. Then we come to the template level, or archetypal level, where it's still very pure, and primordial wisdom, which is again a quality of the ground of all, a quality of this emptiness, this primordial wisdom, or *yeshe,* then divides into five facets. So there are different, five different qualities of primordial wisdom.

STUDENT: *A quick question. You said not* via positiva *and* via negativa, *but the Buddhist term for the same thing?*

TSOMO: Kuntuzangpo. Do you want me to write that down? Kuntuzangpo: *Kuntu* means "all"; *zangpo* means "positive" in the masculine.

STUDENT: *You said the male was a dark blue; what was the feminine?*

TSOMO: She's often depicted as white, interestingly enough, even though she's really the emptiness and he's the luminosity. [*Tsomo writes on chalkboard.*] So Kun-tu-zang-po and Kun-tu-zang-mo are in union. This emptiness corresponds with the Dharmakaya. *Dharmakaya* means "truth body," Kaya being "body," and we're speaking of, you could say, the Buddha body or enlightened body of truth. And that's really on the ultimate level.

So I'm just trying to associate those. Then getting into luminosity. [*Tsomo writes on chalkboard.*] Now into form. We have actually two Buddha bodies. The first one we come to is *Sambhogakaya*, which is that archetypal level, the template level, starting with the five wisdoms, the five Buddha families. These are five qualities of primordial wisdom. So now we've differentiated that much, and then we're going to continue to differentiate into lots and lots of complexity until we have the *Nirmanakaya*, which means "emanation body." But right now, I'm speaking on a pure level. On the realized level, it looks quite different from the level that we're all perceiving right now, because we're fixated on the human realm level. We've got all kinds of karma involved. We've got all kinds of neurotic emotions and habits of the mind involved. So what we're seeing right now is very different from what an enlightened being would be seeing if they tuned into this classroom right here. And whereas we're stuck and we can't find the channel changer, they, a fully realized Buddha, have the channel changer and can tune into various levels of reality at will. Great masters have been known to do that, really. And it's written how the Buddha was able to go from one realm to another with freedom, because he had woken up from the dream. When people asked him after his enlightenment, "Who are you? Who are you?" he said, "I'm awake. What I am is awake." And hence the name *Buddha*, "awakened one."

So in looking at these, *via positiva* and *negativa*, it naturally came to *creativa*, so then I thought of the three Kayas. When I looked at *via transformativa*, speaking of justice and how does that fit in with these great, ultimate ideas that we've been talking about, there are really two truths spoken of in Buddhism. There's absolute truth, which is the truth body that is referred to here in Dharmakaya, and there's just one absolute truth. When you get down to the absolute essence of any appearance—and we're all appearances, right?—in the way that I'm speaking of, we're the waves on the ocean, that if we get down to what's underlying all of that, even Western science has come to see that it's actually emptiness, but it's this emptiness that has this endless power to produce all manner of emanations, or appearance, or luminosity, these terms that I'm trying to use. Once we get into the differentiated level, and particularly when we get into the warped version, sentient beings who have gone a little off the mark, when we get into that level, then we speak of the relative truth. So there's absolute truth and then there's relative truth. The truth relative to human beings would have it that water is something we drink, for example. But for even a fish, relative to them, water is something quite different. It's their home where they live; they breathe it. In the winter, they're fine staying in the water. We would die in a few minutes.

Now, in the hell realms, according to Tibetan Buddhism, there are 18 of them: We just don't have one, we have 18. That's okay. We have lots of purelands, too. Anyway, water can be various things, but in the hot hell realms, water would be like molten lava, all sorts of flames coming off of it, and horribly hot. But in a good realm, it would be wisdom nectar flowing along. There are all kinds of unseen channels, you could say, getting back to the channel changer, and other beings are stuck on these other levels, and they're seeing water very differently. So that's relative truth, relative to your point of view. On this differentiated level, then, there is injustice, there is suffering, there are all kinds of stories going on, endless numbers of stories going on, and the Buddha encouraged us to hold tightly to both truths. If we let go of one of them, it's at our peril.

I do know of some practitioners who only gave allegiance to ultimate truth and said, "Well, it's all illusion anyway, so I can get away with whatever I want to." And they did terrible things. I know one of them now who was a very accomplished practitioner. He's possibly not going to live much longer, and all of these acts that he had done for so long thinking, "Oh, it's illusion. It doesn't matter." Now they are coming back to him. And of course, karma plays into this. On the level of relative truth, karma exists. When you do an action, there is a consequence of that action. We can't ignore that fact. At the same time, if we only think in terms of relative truth and ignore ultimate truth, we're also at our peril. We cut off our true route and the chance to find our way home. So we need both truths, and the fact that they're depicted in union, in Tibetan Buddhism, is, I just think, a wonderful use of archetype. And it's used a lot. This is something we meditate on a lot and really take into ourselves.

I want to just tell you a story that happened a very, very long time ago, many, many *kalpas* ago, many eons ago. There were two students, and they came before a teacher, and they were studying and studying, and they learned about ultimate truth. One of them, who was a prince by the way, had this mistaken understanding and thought, "On the level of ultimate truth, all of this is illusion. I can do whatever I want." So he went about doing horrible things, really horrible things: coercing people, killing people, doing anything he wanted. And he was in a position of power to do a lot of terrible things. He was then reborn as a very powerful demon. He went on through many, many lifetimes. He was reborn in a hell realm, but then got more and more power. And this power of creativity without the morality was the story he was living out on fantastic archetypal levels. He ended up filling the hell realms with all kinds of beings, because of his powerfully negative acts. Finally, these great *bodhisattvas*, these very highly realized beings, who were also full of bodhicitta, compassion, and wisdom, got together and said, "We've got to do something about this." So through compassion, the motivation of compassion, along with skillful means and the power that they had, they were able to actually help him to have an experience so that he realized his mistake and was horribly remorseful. And still having the power that he had, but now understanding the need to take into account relative truth and the need for justice and compassion, he then devoted himself, for the rest of eternity, to benefiting beings, and is still a powerful protector in the pantheon of the *Dharma* today.

The other fellow—remember there were two students who studied with this master—the other fellow argued with that first fellow, and they had quite a hot debate. That second fellow took the way of the bodhisattva, and never forgot to hold to both truths, and he then became Vajrasattva, who perhaps some of you know, who have studied Tibetan Buddhism. He is a very important, one of the great bodhisattvas, who has refused to go completely back into the ocean of oneness and melt into that, into complete Buddhahood. He's just this far from it, because he keeps just enough personal intent to serve as a way for us to be able to clear karma for ourselves. Because that's half the story of enlightenment:

clearing the karma away, as well as bringing forth the Buddha qualities. So I wanted to tell that story as an illustration so you could see something about the two truths and how they interplay.

When I was speaking of primordial wisdom, sometimes that term is translated as "timeless awareness." So this ocean is constantly making waves, and the waves are never the same twice. Any nanosecond, they're not the same as they were the nanosecond before. And the waves are going up and down, and up and down. The Buddhists say that manifested reality is like the frames of a movie. There's a flashing forth of that one picture, and then darkness, then flashing forth, and then darkness every nanosecond many, many times. So that we, just as we do with the frames of a movie, we put together a continuum that is not actually the way it is. There is actually this moment of complete darkness, emptiness in between every moment of the flashing forth, all the time, ongoing, right now. Because of that, we're, in a very real sense, dying and being born every nanosecond several times. So there's a chance for enlightenment—to not be confused about the luminosity shining forth from the emptiness, not identifying with a particular pinprick of it. Every moment we have that chance. It's only our habits of mind and our karma, pulling us in a particular way of seeing things, that is stopping us from an enlightened way of seeing.

One quote that I enjoyed from the Eckhart—and now I think you'll begin to understand a little bit of why I enjoyed it so much—"When we say, 'God is eternal,' we mean God is eternally young. God is ever green, ever verdant, ever flowering. Every action of God is new, for he makes all things new. God is the newest thing there is, the youngest thing there is. God is the beginning, and if we are united to him we become new again."

Now, there's another passage here that then takes a bigger arc. "When I dwelt in the ground, in the bottom, in the stream, and in the source of the Godhead, no one asked me where I was going or what I was doing. Back in the womb from which I came I had no God and merely was myself." The next page, I think, speaks of the journey. "And when I returned to God and to the core, the soil, the ground, the stream, and the source of the Godhead, no one asked me where I'm coming from or where I've been. No one misses me in the place where God ceases to become."

This place is sometimes referred to as Yum Chenmo, the Great Mother, Prajnaparamita. This is the, how would you say, the "wisdom gone beyond."

She's also referred to as the "Mother of all the Buddhas," and she's personi-fied as a female goddess. In the Garden of a Thousand Buddhas that my lama is building in Montana, the Buddhas are all about this high, and there's this huge 27-foot-high Yum Chenmo statue that's in the center. So even though there really isn't a form to this on the archetypal level, we can create form. So this is hopefully to invoke that home, which we all started from. We're now on a very, very long journey, around and about, until we come home again. And that coming home again is what we call full Buddhahood. So that's some of the relationship between emptiness and luminosity. And I think I've already talked a lot about the *via negativa*, so responding to more of Eckhart on this, I don't know if that's necessary.

STUDENT: *My question is, in Tibetan Buddhism, awakened ones, are they able to pass through—because you're saying they can go through, they can change the channel and go through different dimensions. In other branches of Buddhism, they describe the nine levels of existence. Like there's the animalistic level of existence as a human being, and then you go up and up until you get to enlightenment. Do you understand where I'm going?*

TSOMO: I think I get the trend, yeah.

STUDENT: *Okay. Now, my question is, are you speaking of life levels or are you speaking of, like, fourth, fifth, sixth, seventh dimension when you go from different levels, you know, change the clicker? Like I'm saying, an enlightened being may be able to go to somebody that's just existing on the third dimension that we are in here now. They can go to somebody that is in an animalistic realm and dwell and chill, and then go to somebody who is in an enlightened realm and all in between. And they can do that where other people can't. It's almost like we have an energetic bubble where we can't pass into these other life levels. So, I'm asking, in the Tibetan, are we going into a mysticism of, "Zoop, I'm not here anymore. You don't see me. I'm in the fourth dimension now, but I'm still watching you"?*

TSOMO: They don't use the term *dimension*. They speak of the six realms. These are realms of being, such as the animal realm, or the human realm, or the god realm, or there's a realm called the hungry ghost realm, which covers actually a lot of different experiences, and then the different hell realms that I was talking about. There's also something called the jealous god realm. Those are the six realms that are referred to in my tradition.

STUDENT: *Are you in your body, or do you go into soul realm?*

Tsomo: A Buddha or a bodhisattva of a very high level can manifest as a fish to help benefit fish. Or not, or just peek in, or tune in, in a sense. Their choice. They have complete choice, because they no longer are stuck in one corner. They're no longer a slave to their desire, anger, karma, ignorance, and all the rest of it. They're free, because they're awake.

Student: *And you can reach that enlightenment within your lifetime?*

Tsomo: Yes. In Vajrayana Buddhism it can be done in one lifetime. And that's been proven in the sense...

Matt: Get moving.

Tsomo: Oh yeah, you'll have to get busy if you have a few eons like the rest of us stuffed in the backpack.

Student: *I've been thinking about this all morning since we introduced ourselves. If this is tomorrow's curriculum, or if it's too personal or something, just say so, but as a Jewish Buddhist, if I may put those two terms together, are you theistic, or are you non-theistic, or are you both, or neither, or something else? And as a follow-up question for Matthew Fox, is mystical Christianity theistic or non-theistic? Because this is for me, a pithy question in reconciling whether one can be a Christian and a Buddhist at the same time, because they seem to be at odds, but on some level I don't think they're necessarily at odds.*

Tsomo: Um hum. Well, you know, a couple things that I could say to that. One is the saying, "There's no such thing as an atheist in a foxhole." When we're in extremes, or even when we're not, we want to be able to pray to somebody. And there is somebody to pray to in Tibetan Buddhism, but that's not the same thing as this ultimate truth that we're speaking of. So there are enlightened beings, and I would say generally they're on the archetypal level, so there are different qualities of beings. You might pray to Guru Rinpoche, the master of transformation, for example, for this or that. And then there's Green Tara, who is the Tibetan version of the Great Mother. Or you might pray to Vajrasattva because you feel terribly guilty about something and now you don't want to just sit there with creeping guilt. You want to do something about it and work with Vajrasattva. There are actually powerful Vajrasattva practices which we're hoping to get around to, the whole process of working with mistaken action, and how do we work with that. We don't want to just sit with creeping guilt or the results of that without having some skillful means. These are various beings to pray to, and yet there is another level of reality where everything comes together in this very root, basic essence. And there is nothing in all of the manifested world that doesn't have that same essence. So you might say it's like the tips of an iceberg, and the iceberg is below the surface. We can't really perceive it so clearly, but that's what the meditation and the various skillful means can hopefully bring us to. So I guess I would sort to have to say both/and, and that they're not mutually exclusive in my mind. I can pray to these various beings and yet they don't, in any way, preclude the existence of the Dharmakaya, its ultimate truth level.

CHAPTER 5

Spiritual Practices

STUDENT: *So if you went to the hospital and they asked you to check your religion, you personally could freely check Jewish and Buddhist, both boxes, or maybe more, or would it not even be a question worth debating, perhaps. I don't know.*

TSOMO: I'm going to go ahead and put it in my terms, because I'm terrible at multiple-choice questions. I always did terribly on those tests. I would say that I am tribally Jewish, and my methods, my path, is Buddhist. They're Buddhist methods, the methods of the Buddha. And fortunately, my teacher presented it that way to me so that I didn't feel as though I had to drop my Jewishness in order to study these methods. He said, "I'm teaching you a set of methods that you can pursue if they work for you." So it was very much in freedom that I was able to step into all this.

MATT: I liked your question a lot, because I think it is very important, especially for Westerners, to get over some of our straitjackets around God talk. And, frankly, no one does this better than Eckhart. He says, "I pray to God to rid me of God." That's a good line. It's a good line. To be rid of the all-male God, if that's your going image, or the all-white God, or the "God with the long white beard" God, or the avenging, punitive father God who runs the spiritual life of everyone from George Bush to Cardinal Ratzinger. And, again, we can thank Buddhism for this because I do think that Buddhism helps by going beyond theism, beyond God talk.

Remember that atheism is a rejection of theism. *A* means "no" in Greek. But panentheism is what mysticism is about. And panentheism,

133

someone here earlier this morning said that she was a pantheist, but it may well be that you are a pan-en-theist. There's a difference. The difference is between being burned at the stake and not being burned at the stake, so you might want to catch this. *Pantheism* says everything is God—two Greek words; "All is God." *Panentheism* says, "Everything is in God, and God is in everything." It is the ocean in the wave, and the wave in the ocean. Or, if you will, the water in the fish, and the fish in the water. I think all mysticism is panentheistic. It is a step away from theism, and I think that's very important. And it's one reason why there's always a tension between religious bureaucrats, if you want to put it that way, and mystics. Because, yes, we're humans, we do need buildings. We do need a few rules to agree on and all that bureaucratic stuff, but in no way is that religion. It's sociological structures. And this is why today we feel this huge tension between spirituality and religion, because religion has become almost empty, or often empty. A lot of form with a lot of money and a lot of stuff, and almost empty, while spirituality is about the riches of what you're calling the *essence* and tuning into the essence of things.

Now, another language path on this that Eckhart has is between God and Godhead. And this, again, is very Buddhist. Eckhart knew two languages: Latin and German. In both of them, *God* is masculine: *Deus* in Latin, *Gott* in German. *Godhead*, in both, is feminine: *Deitas* in Latin, and *Gottheit* in German. So there you have an interesting play of what you were talking about: the dialectic God and Godhead, masculine and feminine. But he says there's this huge difference. In *Passion for Creation*, this big book on Eckhart's sermons, I remind readers that Eckhart says that "God acts." So God is that side of divinity that acts in creation and in history and in redemption. God has got a history, if you will, but the Godhead does not act. The Godhead is about being. It's about mystery. So you have the dialectical history and mystery, history/mystery. And the problem in Western religion is that we've been talking only about God. God acts, God redeems, all this. And where is the Godhead, the God of mystery, the God of silence, the God of being? The image I had of Godhead is the great, big, cosmic mama in whose lap the universe sits, that the universe is God, the Godhead's womb.

So the Godhead is about being and mystery, and God is about history. And we have to get the balance back. The West is totally out of balance in that regard. Then there's also these amazing passages in the

"*Via Negativa*" of Eckhart about this is the ocean, that is so mysterious and deep and it has no name. "God's darkness is a super-essential darkness, a mystery behind mystery. A mystery within mystery that no light has ever penetrated." I don't know a Western thinker that has gone so deeply into the unnameability of the Godhead. This is so Buddhist, and it's so important for Westerners to get it, and it's a surprise to know that you can get it from your own home tradition. You don't have to learn Tibetan to get it, but I praise those who have.

TSOMO: Well actually, in Sanskrit, one of the classic things that is recited is, "*Gate gate paragate parasamgate bodhi soha*." And that chant was exactly what I thought of when I read page 41 because it's saying, "Beyond, beyond, meta-beyond, beyond the meta-beyond, awakeness, so be it," might be a loose translation.

MATT: So 45, just real practical stuff. "How should we love God? I will tell you. Love God as God is. This means love God as God is a not-God, a not-mind, a not-person, a not-image. More than this, love God as God is a pure, clear one who is separate from all twoness. One should love God mindlessly. By this I mean your soul ought to be without mind or mental activities or images or representations. Bare your soul of all mind and stay there without mind." It's pure Buddhism, and it's from a Christian preacher who got condemned a week after he died. That's just proof of pudding. And then, "I advise you to let your own 'being you' sink into and flow away into God's 'being God." Then your 'you" and God's, 'his,' will become some completely one 'my' that you will eternally know with him his changeless existence and his nameless nothingness."

So there is an answer. That's Christian mysticism, folks. Unfortunately, 99.9 percent of people who call themselves Christians, including most current popes, don't have a clue. They don't have a clue.

STUDENT: *I have a question. You say we can find the same mystical philosophy in Eckhart that we do in Buddhism.*

MATT: Not identical, not identical. But the big things.

STUDENT: *A resonance, then.*

MATT: A resonance, absolutely.

STUDENT: *But do we find the same degree of methodologies, of techniques, of exercises to awaken to the unborn state? I don't find it, and I think it's something that's profoundly missing in the Christian mystical traditions, a panoply of practices, a path to take that's really well delineated.*

MATT: Well, I agree. No, I don't totally agree. I agree to an extent. I agree that Buddhism and its many forms—and Buddhism comes, as you've said, in many traditions and lineages—has many, many wonderful practices. But believe me, there are many in Christianity, too, that people don't have a clue about—for example, chanting. One thing I've been developing lately is taking some of the words—well, I actually did this with 300 ministers a year ago at Vancouver School of Theology. I had them chanting some words from the Bible instead of reading them, thinking about them, putting them into chant. And the next day they came back and said half of them didn't sleep all night. They were so charged up by putting these phrases into chant that they had just been reading. So the point is that, in the old days in monastic traditions, in monastic orders, and certainly in Eckhart's time, they were chanting these phrases, and in the chanting something much more cellular and physical happens. So the point is that I think it's mostly from the Enlightenment, from the modern era, when we reduced religion to what's in a book, that we lost the reality. In the Middle Ages, a lot of people were illiterate, but they were able to chant phrases and turn them into spiritual devices, into mantras actually. And, like I say, the Rosary itself, which came from Islam, and is a mantra device of repetition and, therefore, beat and rhythm that goes over and over and puts you into an altered state.

TSOMO: And they got it the Middle East from India, which is where the Tibetans got it. That's where Buddhism came from, was India.

MATT: Ah ha! Well, I guess it all came from India. When I talk to Indians, that's what I'm told—mother India, mother India. What I'm saying is there are a lot more practices than we have today. They've been lost, or at least temporarily suspended. And I think a lot of it, frankly, has been our excessive left brain quest of the last 300 years, and the right brain has kind of atrophied. But it's amazing how fast it comes back. When you can take a couple hundred ministers and get them to stay up all night, because they've just had the first chanting experience of their life. I remember laughing when I heard these stories the next day and them saying, "Oh, Christians can meditate, too." It's a pitiful state that a lot of Christianity is at, where it does not have its practices anymore. But I find that bringing it back, even like this Aramaic prayer of the "Our Father," getting people to dance this, and to chant the very words that Jesus chanted, it really works. It gets people into altered states. So, what I'm saying is, there's a very open field here in which Westerners should be working. And it's not just Christians, you know, as Jews rediscover the Kabbalah, for example, and deal with that at the level of practice, not just what's being said in a book. You're also getting some profound results.

But again, though, I couldn't agree more that Buddhism is much more, what should I say, much more in touch with their practices, at least many of them are. I've actually been told that Buddhism is more alive in North America than it is in Japan today, for example. But they've lost less. I think they've lost less than we have in the West. But again, I'm amazed at how rapidly we can bring it back. It's like it's in our morphic resonance, it's in our cells, and it can be brought back, but it takes some effort and intention. You have to know what you're doing. If you have a ridiculous theology—that religion is about sin and redemption—that's not going to bring anything powerful back. That's the same old bad news. You need the four paths. You need this ancient tradition of wisdom, the wisdom tradition of Israel and the Cosmic Christ tradition.

TSOMO: I think somebody has a question.

MATT: Yeah.

STUDENT: *Yes. I want to ask, that's good because that's right about this. I never was a Catholic, but I thought that was fundamental belief, this belief of salvation, that you are a worm and you need God to, to take care of you, and to save you. You said something this morning about it. Was it in the fifth century that this became part of the...*

MATT: Fourth century.

STUDENT: *Fourth. Excuse me. What happened before? I mean that's of the Jews already with the Adam and Eve and the serpent. And aren't we making short shrift of that idea?*

MATT: No, you see, the Jews have the story about the fall, but they don't have the story about original sin. It was Augustine, the fourth century, that connected the fall to original sin. And that just isn't Jewish. So it's not accurate, because that story comes from Judaism, not from Augustine. The fall is a reminder that humans make mistakes, and that, in fact, we fall to learn. You know, to learn to walk you fall, you skin your knee. That's what it's about. And we make choices that—well, you could use the word *karma*—that have consequences. It's archetypal again. There are many interpretations of the Genesis story, but the idea that it's original sin is a distorted interpretation. It just is.

STUDENT: *What's the difference between original sin and the fall?*

MATT: Original sin says that you're born with a...

STUDENT: *Tragic flaw.*

MATT: ...with a tragic flaw, or that you're born as a worm and not as an immaculate image of God, as a blessing and a powerful image of the divine. And curiously, you see, again, Augustine was a Western theologian. Eastern Christianity isn't invested in original sin, yet they still have baptism. Islam has Genesis, the Old Testament. They don't believe in original sin. So it's strange.

TSOMO: I don't know if I should maybe also speak to this question of methods that you had asked earlier about, the methods of the Tibetan Buddhist path—and this is Vajrayana that I'm speaking of. I listed the *Yanas* quickly. Do people want to know a little bit more about the graduated path of that? Can I have a raise of hands? So we don't have a whole lot of time. Okay. How to say it in 25 words or less? It is a graduated path. There we go. Okay, that's under 25 words. Getting back to the fact that we're trying to clear away the obscurations and to bring forth our true Buddha Nature, those are the two main things that we keep trying to do, but we do develop—how can I say?—more and more potent forms of medicine, if you will, to apply to that as we go along. So we can begin with things like tonglen, which bring forth the Buddha quality of compassion, expand that capacity. And there're other practices on that level that bring forth other Buddha qualities. At the same time that we're doing that, we're developing our ability to settle our mind on one thing and have it stay there. Because until we can quiet the waters of the mind enough, we aren't going to be able to slow down the frames of the movie enough to understand what the mind is doing. We're trying to investigate the mind by using the mind as a tool, so we'd better refine the tool or we're not going to get very far.

Now, this group of scientists, who are working with the Dalai Lama, finally, finally, after a certain number of years, they were willing to try refining this tool, the mind, in order to investigate the mind directly within their own experience. But they admitted that they couldn't do it just right out of the gate, so they began actually doing retreat for some of these sessions when they got together. What they were mainly doing in those retreats was *Shamatha* practice—just slowing the thoughts, the rushing of thoughts, slowing that down, slowing down that timeless moment between the thoughts so that they could begin to understand the movie they were playing. Samsara is like a movie. It's just we're stuck. We don't know we're in the theater. We don't have the channel changer. We are completely at the mercy of this movie, and who's the producer of this movie? Our own mind. There are many words for *mind* in Tibetan and Sanskrit. So the mind that I'm talking about is not the same mind as the one great mind, or enlightened intent as it's sometimes translated, when they're referring to the presence of this huge mind that occupies the Dharmakaya. There are different terms for all of this.

I sort of reached a graduation point in my learning of Tibetan language, when I had been in a strict three-month *dzogchen* retreat, doing very particular practices that sort of took me by the nape of the neck and brought me to these timeless states. And afterward, after experiencing ultimate truth and being able to sit in that a bit, I was trying to carry that into my meal breaks and slowly prepare dinner while hanging onto, you know, seeing the emptiness right under the appearances and seeing that all together like two sides of one coin. Then at the end of retreat, my lama came and he was going to do the rituals that open up the boundaries of retreat. And I had to discuss this with him in Tibetan, first of all, because he doesn't speak English, so it would only be practical. But the other reason was that English doesn't have the differentiated terms that I needed to describe my experiences and to ask him questions about "Now, how do I bring this forward into daily life?"

The aim of Tibetan Buddhism is to hold onto both truths, to have them both really clearly in hand, and it's only then that you can live life with mastery and be able to move through life in a way that doesn't create terrible karmic effects for yourself or another, and you can hold to ultimate truth at the same time. And I could see that he actually, to an astonishing extent, is able to hold those both at the same time while he's on the phone, while he's editing ancient scriptures that have been recovered from Tibet, and so on and so forth. He's really able to hold those both at once.

So now I've given you a hint as to some of the beginning practices. Then after this wide open sort of just holding the spaciousness and slowing down the thoughts, then there is the more incisive one, this question of, "Really, who is the thinker?" which we did just a little taste of today. Also we can do that with the thoughts as they arise, because they're going to come up. It's the nature of the mind to generate thoughts, and that's fine. It's a question of "Do we chase after the thoughts? Do we have to? Maybe we don't. Maybe we can just sit there and let the thought come and go." But if a thought should come and we find ourselves chasing after it, then to penetrate and, with the same kind of focus, say, "What is that thought? What is the true nature of that thought?" And, of course, it's the same thing. Its essence is ultimate truth, Dharmakaya, emptiness. So we just keep using either way to get our way home again: looking at the thinker, looking at the thought. These are all very, very foundational practices.

Then above that, we find more skillful and intensive practices once we've kind of distilled ourselves with these foundational ones, where we can—how can I say?—cleanse the karmic spatters on the windshield very effectively and bring forth the Buddha qualities more effectively. Then we begin working with the channels and the winds directly, where the karmic patterns create knots in the channels. We begin to have the winds flow clearly then, as we do these practices very specifically aimed at that, and can succeed in actually doing that. Then finally we come to dzogchen, or "great perfection." "Great completion" is another translation of *dzogchen*. And those practices bring us to the final place where we can truly have mastery of both of these two truths.

MATT: I'd like to throw in an idea, almost like a question, maybe we could carry overnight or something, too. But speaking from my tradition, what you're calling the absolute truth or the ocean, I see a metaphor for divinity. When I wrote *One River, Many Wells*, I found the most universal metaphor for divinity is light. You know, East, West, indigenous, it's everywhere, Celtic, African for sure, and now that we know what we know about light. In the Christian tradition, John: 1 says, "Christ is the light in all things." And now we know from physics that photons, or light waves, exist in every atom in the universe, Einstein said he wanted to do nothing his whole life but study light—we've learned that it's both particle and wave. So what I throw out there is the idea that the Christ, or the Buddha Nature, is the wave, light as wave, that's in all things. And that is actually the ocean that's sustaining what you're calling the individual waves that are temporary. But Jesus as an individual, just like Buddha as an individual, as an historical figure, or you and I as historical figures, we are the particle So light is both wave and particle, and, in a way, I hear you saying that the truth is both wave and particle, or the Dharmakaya, or the divinity, or the absolute...

TSOMO: No, I would actually say that I've been saying that emptiness is more like darkness—luminosity being light. So there's both light and darkness.

MATT: Well, that too. And that's true.

TSOMO: The Godhead is more like darkness, then.

MATT: And light depends on darkness, and darkness depends on light.

TSOMO: Exactly, the two sides of the coin.

MATT: They're dancing together. They don't stand alone.

TSOMO: That's it.

MATT: Or at least light doesn't stand alone.

TSOMO: I just wanted to bring that part of the coin in.

MATT: Right. It's almost more maybe a four-sided coin we're dealing with. I don't know. But anyway, I've been playing with this for a long time, that the Christ is the wave in all of us, or the Buddha Nature, and that the individuality, the particle, has a history, but it's certainly not the whole picture. It draws on the power of the ocean, like that individual wave does. So I don't know if you're going with that, those metaphors.

TSOMO: I would have to play with it a little bit because the emptiness factor, as opposed to light, that interplay I could work with. So, the emptiness and the luminosity interplay, if you can work with that, the particles and the waves then, I could see, still in the luminosity department, is how I'm interpreting it. And then the darkness/emptiness out of which they both come, I'd still be missing that factor if we didn't include it.

MATT: Right. I think we should include it. Just like waves have a darkness, too. The ocean has a deep darkness to it. But I think probably light does, too, in what we're learning about light.

TSOMO: Yeah, there's antimatter and the anti-light, and the dark stars, and that sort of thing. And there's more of it in the universe than they thought, they're saying now. So maybe this is something that you can all take home and contemplate overnight. That might be, actually, an interesting thing to do is to, now that we've had this more full discussion and you've gone once through the peeling of the onion of the self. Again, it's not about ignoring the self or throwing it away. It's about letting go of our tight grip on the self, the identification with the self. *Ego* means "I," right, in Latin? So, it's the identification with self that brings us a lot of suffering and trouble.

So you might just sit for a few minutes tonight and peel the onion a bit and, hopefully, then, come to what you've just been talking about. Because you'll have opened things up a little bit, opened up the fixation to the point of being able to see the wave through all the particles, and even behind the particles and the waves, somehow, subtly you can see through the veil a little bit to the emptiness. Just have a felt sense of it.

STUDENT: *What's the leading intent? That you're letting go of your life and all of that? What's the leading intention?*

TSOMO: The intention, when I'm speaking of this exercise, is in letting go of identifying as "me." Because after all, at the end of our life, that particular wave in the ocean is going to go down again. Right? So there are a lot of problems with identifying with "me." We have to defend ourselves when we feel attacked. We have to provide for ourselves. We have to puff ourselves up. It's exhausting serving the ego. So if we can let go of it a little bit by penetrating to "Really, what am I?" We're using insight to do that. So to exercise our insight in this way, and just slow down and really see who is this thinker thinking up all these thoughts, then perhaps we'll be able to perceive the level that you're speaking of.

STUDENT: *I was just going to say, something that helps me sometimes in that kind of exercise is like a teacher of mine once said to me, "Show me your self. Just where is it exactly? Point to it." So then he just said to me, "So if you can't point to what your self is, what's left? What is there if you can't point to your self?" And that really brought me to basically everything else. So it's a way to kind of just settle into that which is not "the self" that we can't point to.*

TSOMO: Um hum, um hum.

STUDENT: *So it's a lovely explanation. So we do that? What is our assignment? What do you want us to do?*

TSOMO: To do the exercise of peeling away the onion as we did before, you know, the dying rehearsal.

STUDENT: *Got it.*

MATT: We don't have to lie in a coffin to do this, or is it recommended that you just—?

TSOMO: People have done it. People have done it. It's been very profound for them, actually, but not necessary. You don't have to rent any coffins between now and when the stores close. And when you get to that place of "aah" as we spoke of in the beginning, hopefully, then, the exercise that you're speaking of will come more easily and clearly from that place. Does that sound good to you?

MATT: All sounds good to me.

STUDENT: *And what was the exercise that…Sorry, I missed…*

MATT: You mean about the particle and the wave. Yeah. To see, to experience yourself as both particle and wave. As an individual with your own history, and your own presence, and your own temporality, and as part of a bigger wave, the Christ wave, or the Buddha wave, whatever name you want to put on it. In Western language, then, that is to experience both Jesus as teacher and the Cosmic Christ, because the Cosmic Christ is more like a wave. It's a presence, a big ocean, in which we swim. Yeah. And I think, again, in Western thought, there's too much emphasis on Jesus and not enough on the wave.

TSOMO: I'd like to end now with dedicating the merit of this endeavor, all the different mini-endeavors that we did all day long today, to all beings eventually, hopefully sooner rather than later, attaining permanent happiness: enlightenment. Thank you for coming.

MATT: Thank you, everybody. [*Applause*]

Introduction

Day 2

MATT: Morning, everybody. Welcome back.

AUDIENCE: *Good morning.*

MATT: I'm looking forward to today. I hope you are.

TSOMO: So, as we did yesterday, let's give rise to bodhicitta, the heart-mind of awakening. And just take a moment to remember that all sentient beings want to be happy, nobody wants to suffer, and most beings don't have the chance that we do to sit here like this and contemplate these things and move ourselves toward enlightenment. But we have this opportunity, and everyone here is taking this opportunity, so let's just remember that we're kind of on the front lines for everyone as we sit here today.

[Silence for several moments]

MATT: Okay, so I thought I'd lead you in two modest-sized practices from the Christian tradition, and then later in the day we'll have some more as well. One thing I want to do is to have you sing the song that we chanted yesterday, and we'll do that in a circle. And with the body movement I think that it's especially powerful in tapping into the morphic resonance and the field of the Christ. And this is what all ritual does really; I think we explained, if you will, or at least helped to understand in terms of Rupert Sheldrake's research on morphic resonance, that his theory is that memory, especially group memory, is in the fields, just like our radios pick up radio waves and TV accepts images, so we are attuned. When we get attuned, we pick up the images of our ancestors, the memories of our ancestors. And Rabbi Zalman Schacter-Shalomi says all of Jewish liturgy can be summarized in one word, which is "remember." *Zicher* is the Arabic word for "remember." And at Jesus's last supper, he said, "Do this in memory of me." So the whole thing about memory, how do we tap into the power of the memory of our ancestors?

C: PRACTICE—*Christian Chant*

MATT: In the middle of the night I woke up thinking about this one question that came from this corner, the man in black, yesterday, about what are the Christian practices? And one thing I'd say is that it's our responsibility to bring them back and to refashion them for our times. But also, they are in the collective memory as well, so worship is one such practice, of course. So, what I'd like to do is begin with a chant. Today's scholarship on the historical Jesus proposes that about 15 to 20 percent of the words in the Gospels attributed to Jesus were really his. The other 80 to 85 percent were made up by a very excited and creative community who put the words in his mouth, which I think is a wonderful thing. They didn't bother distinguishing between his words and theirs. That shows passion. Where has all the creativity gone? That's what I wonder. But I'm going to stick to the words we know were his. And there's one very famous line of his that is really the essence of all of his preaching, and that line you've probably heard as "The kingdom of God is within you," or "The kingdom of God is among you." In the Greek, the word used can mean both "inside" and "among," so I think that's very important.

What we're going to chant this morning—we're going to split the group in half. Right down the middle. Essentially, this side's going to sing, "The kingdom of God is within me," and this side is essentially going to be chanting, "The queendom of God is among us." Because that's another problem—that in English, and Latin, and these other languages, the gender gets much more specific than in Aramaic. So that's what I want to try with you, this chant, and this is important stuff in terms of getting into the essence of Jesus's teaching. Because you must understand, he was no dummy. His mentor had been John the Baptist, with whom he spent five years in the desert eating locusts and chocolate-covered ants, got his neck cut off. He knew every time he used the word *kingdom* he was taking on the Roman Empire. He knew that. So it's very political stuff and it's very spiritual stuff. And, of course, the Roman Empire caught up with him, but he was pretty clever, and it took them three and a half years, so he was on the lam his whole adult life.

Let's together, then, begin. Together, let's go with the traditional translation, although it's not accurate: "The kingdom of God is within me." And then I'll give you a signal and this group goes into, "The kingdom of God is within me." And this group shifts into, "The queendom of God is among us." Okay? And we carry it as a chant. So again, just sit straight with feet on the floor and we'll all call in the breath, which is spirit at work. Let's begin with silence. [*Silence for several moments*]

Now, it may mean, it may be possible that the kingdom of God motif is very parallel to the enlightenment motif in the East. It might be interesting to talk about that sometime, but that may be something very parallel. Okay. [*Matt starts to sing.*]

The kingdom of God is within me. [*Repeated over and over by all.*]

MATT: This side.

The queendom of God is among us. [*Repeated over and over by half the group*]

MATT: Now shift.

[*Singing fades out, then silence for several moments*]

MATT: Feel the silence, the grace?

D: PRACTICE—*Aboon d'bwashmaya Chant*

MATT: Again, it's exciting to recover Jesus's language and realize how truly mystical he was, and cosmic. It's all been lost in the translation, practically. When you memorize it for nineteen centuries and say, "These are his words: 'Our Father, who art in heaven,'" you're really selling the whole power of it short. This is why stirring it all up with new translations from the original dialect has real potential. Yes. And this book, *Prayers of the Cosmos*, by Klotz, he was on my faculty for years. Actually, I wrote the foreword to this book. And he's written several books since, carrying on his translations of Jesus's words, out of the Aramaic, and getting much more fresh language, images.

The words were Aramaic. And you want to know how to spell them out? [*Matt writes on chalkboard.*] Now, remember the words yesterday: "ah-boon-de-bwash-my-ya, ah-boon-de-bwash-my-ya"? Notice that the "ahb" sound is also the "abba" sound that we chanted yesterday the name for father. So "abu-in-jib-wash-my-ya," "g" apostrophe.

This can be translated, "Oh birther/father/mother, the cosmos, all that moves in light, or source of sound, radiant one, we shine within us, outside us, even darkness shines when we remember, or that all the breathing life of all, creator of the shimmering sound that touches us." "Wash-my-ya"—it's very onomatopoetic. It's "shimmering sound." It's also light and so forth.

Now I'm going to invite you to stand, and create a circle around our space in the back, and then come around here, and all hold hands.

Great. Okay. Now, remember the words yesterday: "ah-boon-de-bwash-my-ya, ah-boon-de-bwash-my-ya"? Let's say that again.

[*Everyone speaks*.] Ah-boon-de-bwash-my-ya, ah-boon-de-bwash-my-ya.

Okay. And this time we'll sing it, and with a bit of body gestures to it. So, "Ah-boon-de-bwash-my-ya, ah-boon-de-bwash-my-ya." And then to the left. The idea is, first of all, the bow is opening the heart chakra. And then you kind of go like a crescent moon. You're moving your energy into the community, into the circle. So you're opening up first, and then you're sending your energy into, around the circle, and receiving, too. That's the good thing about karma, isn't it? You give and you receive.

STUDENT: *Are we stepping to the right?*

MATT: We're going to the right for two of the chants, and then we do the same to the left. Okay. So, it's like this. [*Matt sings and demonstrates.*]

Ah-boon-de-bwash-my-ya. [*Repeated twice by all*]

MATT: Left.

Ah-boon-de-bwash-my-ya. [*Repeated twice by all*]

MATT: Okay? Get it? And don't hold back. Let, let the breath go. That's the fun thing about chanting, you can't make a mistake. You're never on the wrong note and you don't need a perfect pitch for a voice to chant. Okay, ready? [*Everyone sings and dances.*]

Ah-boon-de-bwash-my-ya. [*Repeated by all*]

MATT: Women only sing.

Ah-boon-de-bwash-my-ya. *[Repeated several times]*

MATT: Men only.

Ah-boon-de-bwash-my-ya. *[Repeated several times]*

MATT: Together, and this will be our last.

Ah-boon-de-bwash-my-ya. *[Repeated several times, then silence for a few moments]*

MATT: Anyone have anything they want to report about their experience with this or the previous chant?

STUDENT 1: *I feel a pulse.*

MATT: You feel a pulse?

STUDENT 1: *More in the hands. It's still kind of there.*

STUDENT 2: *Very little mental activity.*

MATT: Very little. That's a good thing.

STUDENT 2: *So, unified.*

MATT: Uh huh.

OTHER STUDENTS: *"Peace." "Connection." "Happiness, fun."*

MATT: Ha-ha. Well, those are Jesus's real words. And I know the very first time I did this, I had an experience that Christ showed up. Ha-ha. Yeah, it was really amazing. Not to underestimate, even though there's been a lot of sitting on our traditions and a lot of spiritual laziness in the churches, for example, don't think there's not a tiger to be unleashed. But this time in history, especially, whatever traditions we come from, all of them have to be reignited, I think, and discovered, and there are means to do this like never before. And Christianity is no exception. Or at least it doesn't have to be. Thank you.

STUDENT: *Matthew, could you put the Aramaic on the board, or the English version of it?*

MATT: The English version? You mean the translation?

STUDENT: *The words we were actually saying.*

STUDENT: *Just a question. Do you sense in all of the scholarship that you've unearthed that there was actually a developmental path in Christianity that paralleled in some way to the developmental path that I sense—I don't really understand fully by any means—in Vajrayana Buddhism? Just as a subset of that question, is there some sense that there was a teacher and a student, you know, mentor/mentee, or lama, teacher/student relationship where the "mindstream," some equivalent of that, is being monitored and cultivated by the teacher in a very particular way?*

MATT: That's a really interesting question. The religious orders, you see, each one had their own perspective. So the Benedictines are extremely influential. And Benedict and his sister, Scholastica—it's very interesting, there was a gender balance right from the start in that order. Unlike the Jesuits: There have never been women and never will be women in the Jesuits because it's very, very male. Saint Ignatius, the founder, was a soldier, so the Jesuits have their flavor. It's very intellectual. It's very modern, because he was a genius, but at the beginning of the modern era; Benedict was back in the fifth century. So it's very agrarian. But the Benedictine tradition did keep scholarship alive during the Dark Ages when things were rough and Europe was very, very cold. They had to deal with that, and the growing season was very short, and so forth, so they had a lot going against them. And the Barbarians kept invading. The Benedictine tradition, in fact, is very creation centered. And his rule is very liberal. I'd call it that—very open, but beautiful stuff in it. For example, he said, "When there's a real important issue to discuss, the first one who should speak should be the youngest one in the community, because the Holy Spirit usually works with the youngest." That's pretty revolutionary.

There are these many movements in Christianity—it's just like Buddhism. You have the Eastern Orthodox tradition, which is very different from the Western Church. Then you have the Celtic tradition, which is so much the creation-centered tradition, but they kept getting condemned by the Southern Europeans, Augustine and—what's his name—Jerome went after Pelagius, who was a Scotsman, a Celt, and burned all his books. So, you know, you have these dramas going on wherever there are human beings, but different. Then the Desert Fathers, who preceded Benedict, were out as hermits. I think what started the Desert Fathers was when Christianity married the Roman Empire and took it over. Then it was, you had to become a Christian soldier and go out and kill people in the name of the Empire. And the first generation of what we call *Desert Fathers*, I think, were young men who said, "This is not compatible with my faith." They went out to the desert, AWOL, where they couldn't be recruited. All our pictures have them with long, white beards—well, that was 50 years later. There's a lot of politics and a lot of human history going on here. That's one thing I love; it's so rich.

There's a book done on Mary Magdalene this year by Bruce Chilton, a wonderful book, very short, excellent, because he sticks with the biblical facts. It's not about hallucinating about her role in France, but what comes out of that book is how incredibly diverse Christianity was in the first generation: Peter was fighting with James, who was Jesus's brother; and James was in charge of the Jerusalem Church, which was the place to be, although dangerous; and Paul was fighting with Peter and James, and everybody; and Mary was fighting with Peter, Mary Magdalene— there were all these battles going on. But again, you know, Jesus was not "ST," you know. He was definitely intuitive. He did not leave a legal order behind him. And we've underestimated how truly diverse Christianity was from the get-go. And then, you have the language thing; the very first, Hebrew speakers. But then Paul comes down as both Hebrew and Greek, the hermeneutics, the culture and everything, every which way.

I'm just saying that of all these orders that I've spoken of, the Dominican order, along with Francis in the thirteenth century, had a very different take. The monks became very successful financially because they were on the land, they were essentially farmers, and the feudal system was a land-based economy. So eventually, they owned more land than almost anybody, which created resentment and also fatness on their part. They hired laypeople to do their dirty work for them, and this was really against Benedict's principles. Then Bernard came along in the twelfth century and tried to reform the Benedictines. But then Francis said, "Now we've got to leave this whole thing and join that new movement of the cities," in the twelfth and thirteenth centuries. And then Dominic added, he added in the intellectual life of the universities, which were being birthed from Scholasticism and from Islam. The Dominicans were keen on the intellectual spiritual life.

STUDENT: *I think, though, what I'm getting from your response is that you don't necessarily mention there was a developmental path, or a developmental set of practices that led you…*

MATT: No, there was. For example, Aquinas. He was put in a Benedictine monastery when he was six, because his parents knew he was a genius and wanted him to take over Monte Cassino and be the abbot and raise the family's fortune. He left when he was 16. So for 10 years he absorbed the wisdom of the Benedictine tradition; then he left, he wandered to Naples. The university had just opened up, and Aristotle was being taught, even though the pope had forbidden anyone to teach Aristotle. An Irish scholar was teaching Aristotle right under the pope's nose, and Aquinas was totally turned on by science and Aristotle and the Dominicans who were there. He joined the Dominicans. His mother had him kidnapped, dragged back to the family castle where they tried to end his vocation, brought a prostitute into his cell and everything. He was there for a year. Finally, his sister released him. It's great drama. But then he ended up in Paris with the Dominicans. They didn't let his mother at him again. They learned a lesson.

He brought what was best from the Benedictine tradition, the chanting of the Psalms, the wisdom literature of Israel, which is what the Benedictine spirituality is about. But then he added all the new stuff. So there's a definite continuity here, but it's evolving. There's definite evolution with culture, with history. We could go through every order like that and kind of point out what they were about. And each one had its shadow side, or got used, and lost its spirit at times.

TSOMO: Since there is such interest in this, and not too much knowledge about the Vajrayana lineage and how these things had been handed down and even how they contribute to enlightenment, I think maybe I should respond a little bit. I'm going to start with Guru Rinpoche, because covering 2,500 years is a long time. So, when Guru Rinpoche brought Buddhism to Tibet, he was himself in an enlightened state, and he had had these things handed down and taught to him—had studied in forest groves. These lineages were handed down, not only on paper—actually that was the least of it—but the practices were taught in secret. They were sometimes referred to as *empowerments* or *transmissions*, which were given in a ceremony. And someone who was a lineage holder then would give a mind-to-mind transmission and certain pointing-out instructions and so on that they had been taught from their master and had transferred to them in a ceremonial way, and in a way that is really impossible for us to understand until we've experienced it. So it's difficult for me to explain. But the result is that it opens your mind to a particular cycle of teachings which that person is the lineage holder for, which then allows you to take them in in a much more profound way—not just intellectually, not just in the frontal lobes, but actually in the being that manages the brain, if you will. I think that's the best way I can describe it. And so through taking in sacred substances, and again, the mind-to-mind transmission—there's even the vase or the body empowerment on many different levels and from one chakra to the next—these are transferred.

These things have been held in an unbroken lineage since Guru Rinpoche, and I'm just going to go back that far. When he came to Tibet, he gave these empowerments and transmissions and teachings, uttering the words in a ceremonial fashion so that his students could even take in the words in a different way, in a deeper way, and then taught the practices that we keep referring to—and I really can't teach you all today. He taught all of that to his 25 heart students, and then there were nine close-heart students. All of this was written down by Yeshe Tsogyal, who was his consort. Many of these lineages, he realized, were not meant for that time, but had to be saved for the future—different times and places—and these were called *treasures*. These treasures were hidden. He went all over Tibet and hid them inside of cliffs and at the bottom of a poisonous lake—there are just all these different stories. There are sky *termas* that were just in space—*terma* means "treasure." Then the treasure revealer, known as *tertön*—*tön* meaning "revealed"—the tertön was predicted; he wrote volumes predicting very specifically the names, times, and places of the treasure revealers. And the people who came before them, much like John the Baptist came before Jesus, who had sort of paved the way and told the treasure revealer, "I've had a dream, I've had a vision," or whatever, "and it's time for you to reveal this treasure, and you're the one." And every time we go back—now we know historically who revealed what treasure when—and we still have the written documents, and it matches.

I just want to add that his predictions were pretty accurate. We were trying to reconstruct it at lunch yesterday, Guru Rinpoche's prediction about the Dharma coming to the West. He said that when the iron bird flies and the iron horse runs on wheels, and then there was some reference to the Chinese coming, and that many Tibetans would be scattered all over the earth, and the Dharma would come to the land of the red man. That was just one of his predictions. These lineages, again, have been handed down from master to student in exactly the way that they were intended, and new ones revealed that were meant for different times and places since the 800s, when all these treasures were being hidden. The teachings of the four basic stages of the path were complete in each one of these treasure cycles of teachings.

The lama who I studied with, and still do, Gochen Tulku Rinpoche, and who, I think I've mentioned before, carries several lineages because they've been conferred on him. One of them is Longchen Nyingtik, which is a fairly well-known cycle of teachings in the Nyingma lineage. He also carries a very rare one. He's the only qualified lineage holder today of a much more recently revealed treasure. And the master who revealed that—there are all sorts of amazing stories about the miraculous things he did as he was revealing this treasure from the bottom of a poison lake. But, anyway, he transferred that on to Pegyal Lingpa, in Bhutan, who then conferred it onto my teacher. So that's a very, very direct lineage, which we can trace right back to Guru Rinpoche through this treasure revealer. This kind of thing really interested me because, in the interests of really wanting to change my mind and train my mind, I was having trouble finding an unbroken lineage like that in Judaism.

I happen to live on a Native American Indian reservation and there are lineages which were handed down in a similar way, very carefully and ceremonially, and over a long period of training from one medicine person to another. And I know enough about that, because I'm friends with a medicine person who comes from a family lineage. And it's just heartbreaking to hear him talk about how their lineages also, almost all of them, have been broken. He doesn't yet have anyone he can begin to hand this down to in the proper way.

STUDENT: *What is the responsibility of a lineage holder? Because I'm a martial artist and deal with lineages. The teachings of enlightenment in Buddhism, and the teachings of martial arts, say that if you can hurt somebody, there is a responsibility not to give it out.*

TSOMO: That's right.

STUDENT: *Well, what about the responsibility? Okay, so you have the lineage of how to enlighten people and how to get to the next planes of thought. What is your responsibility? Like, are you supposed to hold it back and not say anything to anybody, or are you supposed to spread it out, or is there a concept of, like, because somebody does hold it, it's part of the "I" that's "we" that's "I" that's circulating the world?*

TSOMO: Well, if someone reaches the state of Buddhahood, then no lineage is secret from them because nothing is separate from them. But short of that, we might have to be a little more particular. Some lamas did begin sort of spreading out dzogchen when they came to the U.S. They realized that a lot of people could understand conceptually what they were talking about. So they began talking about things that had been normally revealed much later in the development of that student. They thought, "They understand, so we'll just give these teachings," and it turned out very badly. So once again, they were much more careful and slow in revealing these things to the people who were appropriate and who had gone through the appropriate empowerments.

It can also throw them, themselves, mentally off, off track. A lot of times they think they know, but they really don't because they haven't developed themselves fully. That can be a terrible problem; they become resistant to the real teachings, and later on they still think they know from before, and actually they've been mistaken all along. I don't know if that makes any sense, but I can't be more specific than that. It can also throw them.

STUDENT: *I just had a question about the oral transmission. Is there anything in the Christian tradition that similarly values the direct person-to-person—out of necessity, prior to print and that kind of thing, that's what occurred—but is there anything in the teachings directly coming down from Christ that emphasizes a similar kind of direct oral transmission? Some kinds of information that couldn't really be done through print, like mind-to-mind, chakra-to-chakra, that kind of thing?*

MATT: Well, there's Jesus himself, who's not literary, so he didn't write anything, and so all of his teaching was oral transmission. He had these people around him, not just the 12 that we know about, but a lot of women, such as Mary Magdalene, who were taking in the teachings. Then the stories were told a second generation, in the Gospels and so forth. And then they were tweaked, depending on the political situation and the personality. Now, the Gospel of Thomas, which really probably precedes the Gospels in age, is a series of aphorisms and sayings, many of them authentic from Jesus, not all. That's another source. Remember, Jesus didn't live that long—around 30—so he got his messages across pretty succinctly or tried to. It's an interesting story how these got developed and how they got altered in the Gospels, and Paul comes along. And, of course, Paul never met Jesus, but he had a Christ experience. He met the people who did meet Jesus. He certainly was in dialogue with them, and they found him quite overpowering, overbearing, and they kept saying, "Go west, go west, and send money back to Jerusalem, here." He thought that would be a good deal, so he did go west, and he did raise money and sent it back there for the poor.

Like Tsomo has talked about, it was practice. It wasn't just what's in a book. The early church practice was a practice of community support, and sharing common goods, the rich and the poor, because there were commoners from many classes, especially the poor, but the upper classes, too. And a lot of women were in leadership. A lot of those practices were covered up by the dominant power that took it over, which was quite male oriented. But there have always been these movements to reform or get back to the original message. And then in the monasteries there is spiritual direction, and there's one-on-one for sure. The whole point in the monasteries was, also, to reach the laypeople. It was meant to be horizontal, not just monks in a monastery getting high and getting enlightenment, but certainly serving the people. When they were healthy, they were doing that. When they weren't, they weren't.

STUDENT: *But it doesn't sound like in the, let's say the monastic trainings, at least, there is that same kind of lineage transmission where it's restricted to kind of an oral experience.*

MATT: That's true. It was not restricted to an oral experience. Benedict himself was literate, and he wrote his rule. So they had a rule to be a guidepost, but that wasn't the whole thing. It was not about obeying laws. It was about abbot relationship to the brothers. And *abbot* really means "father," so it's very much a father-son kind of relationship. The women, it was mother-daughter kind of relationship. And again, the democratizing of—Dominic and Francis were in the twelfth century—there were these democratic commune movements. They democratized the vow of obedience. It was no longer about father-son. That's not the Dominican spirit at all. It is about group decision-making, and fraternity, and sorority, too, when the women came along. It was a definite shift. Now, then with Ignatius, it became very vertical. They're called Master General, et cetera, so it's much more ordered.

Each of these movements had its flavor. But they also had their transmissions, for sure, both oral and in writing, but also in liturgy. The practices—I mean, this was not a head trip. My training as a Dominican, we got up at four or five in the morning, we'd meditate for an hour, we'd say the Rosary for another half-hour, you have Mass, we have silence. There's all this training that goes on 24 hours a day, really. When it was healthy, it includes all the chakras, and some, at least in my tradition, the intellectual yoga as well.

TSOMO: I think maybe I should just clarify what's meant by oral transmission, because there are two different functions. One being what the Tibetans call *Trika*, literally sort of "leading along," the master explaining to the students the meaning of the scriptures or the practices, and bringing in historical commentary and so on. It's often translated as "commentary." There are books that are just commentary, not the actual treasures, but commentary perhaps on the treasures or on the practices, but which were part of the treasures. But the oral transmissions that I think you're referring to, and I was referring to, are the actual uttering of the words that were directly revealed from these termas, these treasures, by the lineage holder. And because he's already sort of sounding that note, then by entrainment—entrainment being like if you sound a tuning fork and you sort of hold up the, the damper on the piano, that note will naturally sound when you sound the tuning fork, right? So by entrainment, then, these words are uttered and go deeply into the student in a different kind of way. These transmissions that I'm speaking of, there are all kinds of very specific techniques that are used to cause the chakras also to harmonize with what the master is putting out. So there's another kind of a level of transmission beyond mentoring and teaching in the normal sense that we understand it in the West.

STUDENT: *I'd like to speak to that. The first time I went to an empowerment was 1987, and it was Penor Rinpoche.*

TSOMO: Yes, who is the holder of the Palyul lineage. Yeah.

STUDENT: *And he's extremely powerful. I had never been to anything like that before, so I just came and I sat down and I just kind of looked at him, because I'm, you know, psychic and clairvoyant, so I just kept looking and looking and looking, and I never could find any distortion whatsoever. So I submitted, which is a big deal for me, completely submitted. And I found out later that's the secret refuge vow. But during the* *empowerment, the energy coming from him, the direct transmission of the energy, was so powerful, and it was so palpable to me that I was sitting like this. And I could see the monks over there all looking and pointing and laughing, because I was like this. It took me like an hour to just stop resisting and kind of very gradually let that energy move through me, and relax, and not be afraid of it. But it was so potent and so powerful. I was really amazed. And it's always that way.*

TSOMO: Yeah, with a genuine master like him, he's really quite powerful.

MATT: There are stories about Eckhart that way, too, when he preached. And remember, he was not preaching to his Dominicans, he was preaching to people, ordinary people, especially the Beguine Movement. The Beguines took his sermons down. Even in some of his sermons he says, "Quit laughing." So there's this incredible interplay going on, and even today when I take people to his sermons, which is what one of those books there is about, it's 36 of his sermons, people have these experiences all the time reading Eckhart, eight centuries after he delivered these sermons. Imagine what it was like on the spot. So there is this tradition, and preaching at its best was an effort to do that, to transmit something much more than just intellectual doctrine. And you get it in someone like Eckhart. Even today you read Eckhart and you flip. It's amazing. I know, because I've been teaching him for 25 years, and people have these experiences, even now. So I do think there are real parallels because the motto of the Dominicans was "To share the fruits of your contemplation." It wasn't to teach doctrine. It's "share the fruits of your contemplation." Well, that is the integration of the spiritual soul and the mind, and that was the goal. And when it was done well, there was a transmission going on.

TSOMO: Just to draw as clear a parallel as I can, in the collection of sermons, how many sermons are in the larger book? Thirty-six of them?

MATT: Thirty-six.

TSOMO: Which I have read.

MATT: Which you read.

TSOMO: I studied.

MATT: You suffered through.

Tsomo: No, no, no, it was inspiring. I would say the parallel would still be with the Trika, the commentary. I should see if I can find translations of some of the commentaries for you so you can see, also inspiring and helping people to really see the nature of reality. So I think that would be the parallel that I would see between the two.

Matt: You know, Hildegard of Bingen slept very little, and she got these transmissions. And from it she wrote the first opera of the West. She wrote 75 songs, she wrote 10 books, and she painted 35 paintings. We have all of those treasures. Definitely there are problems in the West. And she wasn't burdened by being a priest. and therefore it wasn't as politicized. Because she was a woman, I think there was a purity there. It was not co-opted by the system like Francis of Assisi. He was obviously receiving all kinds of transmissions, but his order was taken away from him, really, and, in a way, made into an arm for the Church hierarchy to do something with. So, in some ways, I think, the women may be a more faithful place to look for transmission in Christianity, because their work was less diluted by political manipulating—those whose works were able to be preserved.

I'd like to move on to some other topics now. Where are we in our little thing today?

Tsomo: Well, I think you were going to respond to Ricard. Of course, the timing might be adjusted.

Matt: I think, I think instead I'll just turn to some Eckhart. Not the part you were going to cover today, but some things from yesterday that we didn't look at, that and probably the Buddhist approach, too. Okay?

Tsomo: Okay.

Matt: So page 17 in *Meditations with Eckhart*. I wonder if this is a fresh way of talking about impermanence when he says, "Now God creates all things, but does not stop creating. God forever creates and forever begins to create, and creatures are always being created and in the process of beginning to be created." Notice how very different this is from a fundamentalist worldview that is so set on asking the question, "When did creation begin?" Is that 6,000 years ago, or is it 14 billion years ago? But Eckhart's whole perspective is that creation is always going on. And I think that may be another way of talking about impermanence, and even maybe reincarnation, because things are always in the beginning of being created, he's saying. And it, for me, it introduces just a new way of looking at ourselves—that nothing is done. Everything's here, but nothing's done. We're always in the beginning, he says. We're always in the beginning. So I throw that out as a possible parallel with some Buddhist insight.

Then on page 22, I alluded yesterday—the question came up about theism—to panentheism, and you can see how thoroughly Eckhart is a panentheist when he says, "God created all things in such a way that they are not outside the God-self, as ignorant people falsely imagine." It's ignorance to think that God's there someplace and we're here. Pure ignorance. "Rather, all creatures flow out, but nevertheless remain within God. God created all things this way, not that they might stand outside of God, or alongside God, or beyond God, they might come into God, receive God, dwell in God. For this reason everything that is is bathed in God, enveloped by God, who is around about us all enveloping us." The imagery, of course, is very maternal, and he's saying we're all in God and God is in us. That's very, very clear panentheism, and it shifts everything. It shifts everything. It is definitely a movement away from theism, and, in fact, it relates to the chant we did this morning: "The kingdom of God is within you and among you." Jesus, too, was panentheistic. This is not Jesus talking, but the Christ in John's Gospel, "I am the vine and you are the branches, and the Father and I dwell in you and you dwell in us"—that's Christological panentheism.

So, this is very important to shift from theism, which is so linear—it's subject/object, really—to panentheism, which is inter-subjective: we in the Divine and the Divine in us.

Tsomo: Well, that metaphor of the ocean that I keep using, it's in Eckhart as well.

Matt: It's in Eckhart, yes.

Tsomo: And I was very comfortable because it was just like I was hearing in the teachings that I had received in Buddhism. The ocean and the waves constantly making new waves, and the waves are a part of the ocean. How could they be separate?

Matt: Exactly. In both Hebrew and Arabic, the word for "compassion" comes from the word for "womb." And Eckhart knew that. I don't know if you know the Arabic, but that's in that one sermon. It's full of the fetal waters and fetal images, that we are in God and God is in us. And he ends the sermon in the most amazing way, saying, "What is the human soul?" He said, "Well, no one can know what the human soul is. It's too vast. It's as infinite as God is. You need supernatural knowledge to know what the human soul is." "Oh," he said, "We know a little bit about the soul, about the powers that go up to work, but we don't know the human soul." Then he says—this is his last sentence in the sermon—"The human soul is where God works compassion." And he ends right there. I think he fainted, and everyone in the church fainted. I think that may have been his last sermon because it's so mature.

The soul is where God works compassion and, therefore, where you become a worker of compassion, the *via transformativa*. You get used as an agent of compassion. But notice what he's saying. Until you have tasted this compassion and are an agent of compassion, you don't have a soul yet. That's what he's saying. It's shocking. That just because you're born with a soul doesn't mean you've got a soul, meaning you're born with a vegetable soul and a mineral soul, but do you yet have a human soul? That's the issue of compassion for Eckhart, which is the human divine soul, if you will, because from the Jewish tradition, which Eckhart knew very well, compassion is the divine attribute. And Jesus says, "Be you compassionate as your Creator." And having us compassionate, he's calling his followers to their divinity. Eckhart got all of that.

CHAPTER 6

God Without Why

MATT: On page 30 here, Eckhart says, "This I know: the only way to live is to live like the rose, which lives without a why." Without a "why." Without a purpose. "The rose lives in order to be a rose." He says, "You can ask life itself over a period of a thousand years the following question: 'Why are you alive, life? Why are you alive?' And still, the only response you would receive would be, 'I live so that I may live.' Why does this happen? Because life rises from its own foundation"—I'm thinking of the ocean—"and rises out of itself. Therefore, life lives without a reason. Life lives for itself. What is life? Life is a kind of boiling over in which a thing wells up within itself, floods itself, overflows, pouring itself into all of its parts, until finally it spills over, boiling and overflowing into something external as well." Whoa, very orgasmic, very erotic language here—wisdom literature is always erotic in the Bible and beyond.

But living without a why, working without a why, you work to work. And he says, "Most people look on God like they do a cow for the amount of cheese and milk you can get from God." But, no, our relationship to God should be without a why. This is very important to Eckhart, and I think it's very important to Buddhist spirituality as well.

We brought forth, Tsomo did, and then I brought some more of his "*Via Negativa*" teachings, but just a couple more. In one of his sermons—it's been called his "Sermon on the Mount"—"letting your will be free, letting your knowledge be free, and let go of all having." Erich Fromm, in one of his last books, *To Have or to Be*, [paraphrasing], said that Eckhart critiqued the "having" neurosis better than anyone has ever written. It's that ser-mon, in particular, where he comes to the fore. It's a very strong sermon, and it's about returning to our "unborn self".[8] That's how you become free. In your unborn self, you do not worry about having something, or about thinking something, or about willing something. His point is you can return to that unborn self, that pre-state of existence anytime you want. That's what meditation is. That's what a return to the source is.

Tsomo: Well, that corresponds exactly to what I was talking about yes-terday. Pre-Samsara we didn't need anything, when we were the whole ocean, right? We didn't will anything. We didn't need anything, we didn't think anything—well, we already knew, we didn't have to think up any-thing. We already knew everything because we were not separate from it.

Matt: That's exactly what I finished talking about.

Tsomo: Yeah.

Matt: Eckhart says that's when we dwelled in the Godhead. Because for him, we all came from, come from, the Godhead. It's only when we're born that we enter history and with it encounter God. The God of history and creation, you see. Then when you come around, life is a circle, you return to the Godhead. And as he says, "No one will have missed me." In another words, there's no judgment at the end. No one says, "What have you been doing, Brother Eckhart?" because he says no one will have missed me. Because in the Godhead there's such unity that you're not comparing yourself to each other and judging each other.

Tsomo: I wonder if he, in that passage, is saying, "You never actually departed, you just didn't know it, that you hadn't departed."

Matt: Well, that's there, too, because in that passage he's saying that we can return to this awareness of our oneness.

Tsomo: I mean, how do we get out of the ocean?

Matt: Um hum. Yeah.

---

8. Matthew Fox, *Passion for Creation: The Earth-Honoring Spirituality of Meister Eckhart* (Rochester, Vt: Inner Traditions, 2000), 217 [Formerly *Breakthrough: Meister Eckhart's Creation Spirituality in New Translation*]

Tsomo: We never really left the ocean. We just got a little bit distracted.

Matt: That's about how the God side of divinity and the Godhead side relate—while you're in this life, it's, there's a lot going on, as you know.

Tsomo: Well, yeah. You're caught in the movie, but meanwhile there's the whole theater.

Matt: That's right.

Student: *Yesterday, you made the distinction between the God and the Godhead, and I can't remember what you said. Would you talk about that again?*

Matt: Okay. Again, it's in sermon 3[9] of Eckhart. This one, the "Passion for Creation," really goes into it in a big way. But essentially, a God is a God of history and of creation, of liberation, redemption. God acts in those ways. The Godhead does not act. The Godhead is pre-action. It's about being. So it's about mystery, not history. And it's about being "not-action," and it's more feminine. God is more masculine. Again, archetypally speaking. And again, in Western religion, we've been very underdeveloped in teaching about the Godhead, or practicing the Godhead. How do you practice being with the Godhead, and what Eckhart talks about, this return? And that, of course, is the return to the source. So meditation practices of many kinds, including the arts. Like someone asked yesterday, "Well, what about Western practices?" Don't ever forget that in the West, art is, at its best, a spiritual practice. It's not just producing an object, and certainly not about fame, and ego, and getting famous. It is about entering into the divine creative heart. Whether you're making music or art of your life, or gardening, or creativity of any kind, writing, you are entering into a sacred process. It is a spiritual practice to do that if you bring your heart to it, and your intention, and the effort of purification, and finding real truth.

Aquinas says that "the proper objects of the heart are truth and justice". No, this is not Cartesian. Truth is not up here for Aquinas. And that's Jewish, too—yeah, in Judaism, too, the place of the intellect is the heart, not the brain. Aquinas has that, too. We tend to read things through a Cartesian mindset, because we were taught from Descartes that

---

9. Ibid., 76-82.

truth is in the brain, that that's what our ancestors thought, but it's not what they thought at all. Another yoga, another spiritual practice is the West, is study. Again, this is very Jewish; if you study Torah, bring your heart to it, that is prayer. That is absolutely explicit in the Benedictine tradition and in the Dominican tradition for sure: that to study, if you intend it to be prayer, it will be prayer. This has tremendous implications for science. And I think it's one reason that science has broken out in the West as strongly as it has; however, it became secularized. It became cut off from spiritual practice, and it became co-opted by governments with their agendas, and corporations. But for the scientists, it has to return to the search for wisdom and truth as being a heart search. Calons with a heard search.

CHAPTER 7

Images of God

MATT: I think that part of Western spiritual practice—and certainly the East, too, certainly Buddhism—is very profound in its intellectual developments. I'm sure it sees that, too, as part of its spiritual journey and heritage. The great minds and hearts that Tsomo refers to carry these. Well, so does Aquinas, and so does Eckhart, and these great minds. I'll close with one passage from Aquinas that is so stunning, because it was one of your questions yesterday about images of God. Now, here in my book on Aquinas[10], I translated whole books of his that have never been in English, German, or French before, including his most mystical work, never before translated, which was his first book written when he was 28 years old. It's the *Commentary on Denis the Areopogite*. It is about this question that came up yesterday about images of God, and it's stunning. It's just stunning. And this is what he says, and these are just images from the Bible.

He says, "Even the very ones who were experienced concerning divinity, such as the apostles and prophets, praise God as the cause of all things from the many things that are caused. They praise God as good." And then he gives a quote, Luke 18. "As beautiful" ("The Song of the Psalms"), "as wise, as beloved as God of Gods" (this is Psalm 50), "as holy of holies, as eternal as the cause of the ages, as a bestower of life, as wisdom, as mind, as intellect, as reason, as the knower, as king of kings, as the ancient of days, as without age and unchanging, as justice, as magnitude

---

10. Matthew Fox, *Sheer Joy: Conversations with Thomas Aquinas on Creation Spirituality* (Tarcher Perigree, 2003)

exceeding all things, God is in the light breeze. They say God is even in minds and hearts, in spirits, in bodies, in heaven, on earth, at the same time in the same place, involved in the world, above the world, super-celestial, above the heavens, super-substantial, the sun, the constellations, the star, the fire, the water, the air, the dew, the cloud, the stone, the rock, and all the other beings attributed to God as cause." That means every being in the universe is a name for God. That's what he's saying. "And the Divine One is none of these beings, insofar as God surpasses all things." And talk about opening up your mind, and opening up the Church's language. Every being in the universe is an image of God, a name of God, and not.

The *via positiva* is finding God in every being, every being revealing itself to you: every whale, and every rock, and every force. And the *via negativa* is about realizing that God has no name. Is beyond all names. But now this is just one spiritual and intellectual genius of the West who has been totally distorted, not even had his stuff translated. He's been used as a weapon for centuries to beat up people in the name of ortho-doxy. And that's just one facet of his brilliance. So, I want to say that we, the West, has such a rich history around questions like, "What about names for God?" and we've been sleeping on them. One of my favorite practices is from Sufism: the 99 most beautiful names for God that you recite on a rosary. Just the other day I sat down and shut my eyes and I said, "I wonder if, as a Christian, I can come up with 99 names." And it's like three in the morning. Two hours later, I had a 149 names for God, and they're still growing, you see. We can do these things, too. Not only can we, we have to do them. That's the whole point. You've got to wake up this ecclesial cadaver called the Church. Give it a kick and see if there's any life in it. Maybe it's not worth waking up. Maybe there is no life in it, but we've got to do that today. That's what I'm writing about in the *New Reformation* book. That's the *via transformativa*. We're not get-ting what we deserve, and our young people aren't getting it from our inheritance.

Jung himself said [paraphrasing], "We Westerners cannot be pirates thieving wisdom from foreign shores as if our own culture was an error outlived." He's demanding that we look at our Judaism, our Christianity, our whatever it is, and find what's worthwhile to pass on to our kids. I did a retreat in upstate New York a year or two ago. It's conservative country, and it's Friday night—150 people or so. I asked what traditions were they from. About 100 were Catholic. Okay. "And how many of you are practicing?" About 60 out of 100. "And how many of your children are practicing?" Zero. Zero. This is conservative, Republican, upstate New York. Zero Catholic children were practicing. That's how it is. So what are we doing about it as elders, and as parents and grandparents? Well, we'd better do some of our homework. We'd better start reading Eckhart, and reading Aquinas, and getting the right texts, and the right translations, and reading Julian, and reading Hildegard, and finding out what the hell was Jesus trying to teach, and who got it more or less right so we can find some lineage here.

TSOMO: Actually, the Dalai Lama has said a similar thing when people have asked him. I was in the audience when somebody asked, "What religion should I practice?" he asked the Dalai Lama. And he said, "Well, for me, I have to say I am confirmed Buddhist. Ha, ha, ha, ha, ha." And everybody laughed. Then he went on and said, really, whatever religion you come from can have a lot of juice for you. You should start there, and look there, to see is this going to be a good spiritual path for you. If that's not the case, then you don't have to be chained to it, and you can study another religion. But, yeah that's a question of choice. And I think it's great that we have this balance here. Because you went deep into your tradition and found the juice, and I went into my tradition and didn't really find some of the things that I was looking for to really pursue the path of enlightenment. Jung also said—because I studied Jung in my counseling psychology degree—he said those archetypes that come from your own culture and the tradition from that culture are going to be naturally attached to very deep parts of your unconscious, so you can then use those to very good effect. I wanted to try and find that from my tradition, and just wasn't really able to. So I ended up moving to...

MATT: Well, don't apologize. We're very glad that you made the trip. And you can speak good English with us, too.

TSOMO: Well, yeah. What I found was that there were enough deeply archetypal, from the collective unconscious, universal archetypal things from Tibetan Buddhism. My connection with my teacher was such, I think from maybe lifetimes ago, that I was fortunate enough that I was able to find it accessible. And I do speak English, and I can make it more accessible to Americans. Because I'm an American, and I've studied psychology, and have some understanding of the mind and how it works and some bridges that work for me, I can share with Westerners. So I think we make a good balance in this department beside the other ones.

MATT: Oh, absolutely, and that you're a woman, and that you're a mother. You bring all this to it. It's very special to have a vocation like yours, but we all know that a lot of Westerners can't learn Tibetan and sit at the feet of some of the wonderful people you're able to.

TSOMO: That's why I've been starting to write books. I probably should mention that I'm in the process of finishing the manuscript of a book called *Tibetan Buddhism: Why Bother?* published title: *Why Is the Dalai Lama Always Smiling?* It's an introduction and reference guide for people who want to explore Tibetan Buddhism.

STUDENT: *Why the title "Why Bother?"*

TSOMO: Because Westerners don't know why we should bother with Tibetan Buddhism. Is there a reason? And it isn't for everybody. I found that when I was teaching it for seven years on a weekly basis, a whole bunch of people would be intrigued, because that was the title of the course, by the way. And like 80 people would show up. And then it would go down to about 45 people and stay steady at that for a while, because I wasn't expecting that it was going to hit the spot for everybody. And then it would dwindle down a bit, from there, and by that time I had graduated that batch, and then I would start another one. But I don't expect it is for everybody, and I don't think any one path is. I just feel that this is something—because of the archetypal nature of these images and the practices—that does seem to work on Westerners. I was my teacher's guinea pig, Western guinea pig, and he sort of went, "Well, let's see how *Tsa Lung* works on this Westerner." So I did the official hundred-day Tsa Lung retreat and, by gosh, you know, it works the same. I have chakras, too, and energy channels and all that stuff. So it pretty much did transfer over.

MATT: Again, I think the practices are so universal, and so helpful, and so needed today. As a species we have to do something about our reptilian brain, and I think that's what meditation practice is doing.

Tsomo: Yeah. And also we can take some of these things and bring them to our own traditions. For example, the woman who wrote *Cave in the Snow*, Tenzin Palmo, went to Assisi after her 12 years in a cave in Ladakh. She was British and completely learned Tibetan, and learned the practices, and was amazingly accomplished. The book is just about her life. It's very interesting and fun to read and inspiring. She spent 12 years in the cave, and then what to do next, she got thrown out by the Indian government. So she found herself in Assisi, and the nuns at a convent nearby invited her to come and share her methods. She was very careful about it, and just talked in general, and said, "Well, we all experience the divine." And they said, "No, no, no! We want to know some practices." They were actually interested in learning the practices just so that they could be better nuns, Catholic nuns. So they had a wonderful sharing.

Matt: And Francis prayed all the time in the caves. He loved caves. Brilliant. It's a very good place to pray, in caves. Not church, but caves.

Tsomo: Another universal.

Matt: Yeah, another universal. Yes.

CHAPTER 8

Spiritual Music

STUDENT: *I have a question for you. Buddhism doesn't have much music, but Christianity really does, sacred music. I don't go to church, but every Sunday morning I listen to sacred music for two hours every week. But all that sacred music has nothing to do with a Godhead. It has to do not only with God, but with the one bad day that Jesus had. You know, the Mass, we are miserable sinners. The music is fantastic, but the message is not about the Godhead. Do you know any music about the Godhead in the Christian tradition?*

MATT: Well, that's interesting. Sure. Gregorian chant is very rich, and it's not all about that negative message by any stretch of the imagination And Hildegard of Bingen—I think I'll play a little bit of her opera before the day's out, because she is one of our prophets. She wrote 75 songs, and many of them are about Mary as a green shoot, and about wisdom, and many themes other than sin.

STUDENT: *Wow.*

MATT: Now we have a real musical scholar here. I'm sure he can speak to more, but there is a tradition that is about the glory of creation. Right now I'm thinking of Haydn. A lot of Haydn's work and so forth. Do you want to answer that briefly? Well, Mozart, I mean, you know.

STUDENT: *These men and women who were composers, let's say post-Bach, because Bach really codified Western music, and it's completely based on the Christian church. So the Trinity is embedded and encoded in all of the music that we listen to. How do you like them apples?*

QUESTIONER: *Actually I like them apples.*

STUDENT: *Brainwashing. But many of the great composers found themselves leaving the Church and writing outside of the Church, but yet they were writing with the same intervals that were approved by the Church and the Synods I think in 700 maybe, approximately. I'm not sure about the exact year when they started approving what intervals were allowed to be, and not be, the scales that we have—*

TSOMO: Well, the plagal cadence is in all of the classical composers' music, yeah.

STUDENT: *Exactly. All of the music.*

ANOTHER STUDENT: *I don't mean to push the point too far, but what strikes me is that all kinds of fairly modern musicians, when they started to write religious music, it's fantastic. I [inaudible] and it's really so much better than anything else he wrote. Now, I thought it was because perhaps that was beautiful even though the words still deal with Jesus's bad day, but still.*

STUDENT: *There was a rebellion, so, you know he wasn't modern. He's pretty old hat now. When you said "modern," I was thinking more of some of the things that are being written today. Well, I'm thinking of Bernstein's Mass actually right now. It's a response to a Church that lost its spirit. It lost contact with its spirit, and so in a way the Church atrophied. Composers began to write outside of the structure of the Church and tried to revivify and connect with the actual living spirit. So, unfortunately, you can't look too much at church music, except really mid- to late-twentieth century when some composers began to respond to the Church, like Bernstein with his Mass, where he took the form of a Mass and he brought the life back into it again. And I know it's a piece that Matt likes, and Tsomo, all three of us really love. But it was a response. It was literally a response, a talking back to the Church. When he wrote it, which was in 1971, it was to open the Kennedy Center in Washington, commissioned by Jackie Kennedy, and that's one of our big cultural centers in this country, as we all know. It was actually banned by the Vatican, and there were certain places in the United States, like St. Louis, for example, forbidden to play that kind of music.*

    Bernstein died in 1990. He was my mentor, so I knew him quite well. And it was heartbreaking for him. He was sort of like Matt, you know, a revolutionary. He was always fighting, so he sort of took pride in the fact that it was banned by the Vatican. He had no way of knowing that in 2000, the big Jubilee celebrations in Rome, that the Vatican would stage the performance of Bernstein's Mass, and that there's this extraordinary video of it. It's really an interesting dance that happens with musicians and the Church. That they leave the Church. Bernstein, of course, was a Jew, but as Matt points out, Judaism and Christianity are so inextricably linked, you really can't separate them. So Bernstein, this Jew, writes this Mass, but he doesn't call it A Mass; he calls it Mass: A Piece for Singers and Dancers, because it's not actually "a Mass." So that's just a little glimpse. Deeply inspiring. Beethoven, if you read anything about him, or Mendelssohn and Schubert, or…

MATT: Mozart.

STUDENT: *Mozart, my God!*

MATT: There's a difference between, you talk about religious music, the old Church music, and spiritual music, or sacred music—the word you used, which is a very nice word. Mozart wasn't a real good practicing Catholic, but he was a Catholic and, I think, he got the basic messages of life and love and suffering and redemption, and it's all in his music.

STUDENT: *Well, I know. This is what I listen to every week. But if the words are not about the Godhead, well, what are…*

MATT: The Godhead is beyond words, and it's…

STUDENT: *It's alleluia.*

MATT: Yeah, alleluia.

TSOMO: Or just "aah."

MATT: But, really, music that takes you into stillness, into peace, into darkness, into repose, that's all Godhead music. It doesn't have to say, "Now-you-are-en-ter-ing-the-God-head." No. Godhead is the experience of unity, of origin, of source, of beauty. Aquinas says, "God is the most beautiful being in the universe, and all beings participate in the beauty of God." Therefore, every experience of beauty we have, including your listening to music on Sunday mornings, is an experience of God/Godhead. And whether you see experiences as God or Godhead probably depends on you and your spiritual journey.

STUDENT: *It's the words that get me…*

MATT: Words get in the way. God is beyond words.

STUDENT: *That's why I like listening in a foreign language, because I don't know what they're saying.*

MATT: That's true. And that's where Gregorian chant is helpful, too, because it's in Latin, and most people don't know Latin. And so you're just getting the message without getting the words. No left brain. Anyway, where are we in our...?

TSOMO: Well, now I want to have us return to the experience of tonglen, the practice of sending and receiving, because yesterday was really an introduction to it, and it's hard to really experience it by just experiencing the introduction. So, hopefully, today, now that you're a little more familiar with it, you can deepen with the practice and really have the experience on a deeper level. This is something that people do all of their lives, so you're never really beyond doing tonglen. It's just a wonderful compassion practice, and you can always continue to expand and expand your capacity. As you can see, it's, the practice stretches infinitely.

Let's begin with getting comfortable, and the back reasonably straight, and turning off computers. Isn't that terrible, they announce when they're being turned off. Today, the only slight difference is that we're going to begin by breathing out the joy and happiness that we want for that person that we're imagining, and then breathing in. Since it's cyclical, it doesn't end up making any difference really, but we are going to begin with the exhalation of the bright, sparkling cloud, and then the inhalation of the dark cloud. I would like everyone to try, if they didn't yesterday, beginning with themselves, and I'm going to actually talk you through that part. If people are anxious to get on to doing it with another, that's going to come next anyway.

So. Let's begin. And for me it helps with the visualizing if I close my eyes, but it's not necessary. There are different ways of imagining yourself when you're doing this sending and receiving. One way might be to have yourself in front of you. With visualization, we can do that. Or one way that I happen to like is to imagine a small version of myself, maybe even my child self inside my heart, and so surrounded by my heart. And when I breathe out the joy that I wish for that little one, the bright, sparkling cloud of white surrounds and suffuses that little one. And then when I breathe in the suffering, the dark cloud, actually I draw that into the surrounding walls of my heart. So those are two different ways that you can visualize this first part, which is not so traditional, but really helpful for modern people, I've discovered.

So, let's begin with sending and then receiving for ourselves. We begin by breathing natural but fairly sustained breath out, exhalation, sending joy and happiness to that little one either in front of you or in your heart. And when you inhale, really pick a specific suffering that you have. What's your biggest suffering right now? It could be physical, it could be emotional, it could be many different things, but pick one. And be with yourself in this way for a minute.

[*Silence*]

Really be courageous in picking the thing that you're suffering from. Maybe you're feeling misunderstood, or lonely, or betrayed, but pick that one thing.

[*Silence*]

And keep breathing those waves of joy and see them soaking into that little one, who you do love, and breathing in that dark cloud of suffering that you don't want them to have. You want to take that from them.

[*Silence*]

Remember to keep the breaths even between the out-breath and the in-breath.

[*Silence*]

So the sending and the receiving are equally strong.

[*Silence*]

And now imagine someone you are already very sympathetic with who may be suffering from a similar thing. Imagine them in front of you, and imagine sending them joy, the relief of that suffering, the opposite of whatever that suffering is, and permanent happiness as the bright clouds roll forth and envelop and soak into them. See their face changing, . . . their whole being brightening, and then you draw in their suffering.

[*Silence*]

Perhaps you can think of another person who you also feel sympathy for. Maybe they're suffering from something similar, too, and so send and receive with them.

[*Silence*]

Continue to think of more people, maybe one by one. Maybe you're starting to think of groups of people who suffer a similar kind of thing. And, of course, you don't want them to suffer. You want them to be happy, just like the others you've been doing this for. So you do tonglen for them.

[*Silence*]

So more and more faces are popping up, all surrounding you, and you're drawing in their suffering, and then their faces are brightening as the clouds of joy are coming toward them and sinking into them.

[*Silence*]

We can think of whole classes of beings with a similar suffering: many different kinds, but similar. And we care for them, too. We want them all to be happy.

[*Silence*]

For some of you, you might want to challenge yourself and even imagine somebody who you don't feel very sympathetic with. Somebody you're maybe uncomfortable with, or you're angry at, or you feel some enmity towards, and you might just see if you can find the place in yourself that wants them to be happy, too. And you might do tonglen for them, if you feel ready. Otherwise, you can continue with the expanding the circle as we've done.

[*Silence*]

So continue the sending and receiving just a bit longer.

[*Silence*]

And if you feel a need to expand completely out, imagine all sentient beings, who at one time or another, past, present or future, have experienced or will experience a similar suffering, and send and receive a few more breaths.

[*Silence*]

And then finish your session.

[*Silence*]

I just ask you to stop for a minute and notice your present state, the state of your being. People have done this practice in laboratories, and there have been some amazing readings that were like nothing the scientists had ever seen before with people doing this and other similar practices. Not only while they were doing the practices, although then the readings were really astronomical, but even in between when they were at rest. These people who had done this for many years, their brain functions had actually changed. They were putting out high-frequency gamma rays at a higher rate than everyone else who hadn't been doing these practices for years. So the scientists concluded that there were exercises we could do for the mind that changed the shape of the mind just as there are exercises for the physical body that change the shape of the body. I think we can all feel this right now, the effects. And, of course, this is the kind of habit of mind that we'd rather have more of, and if we do this regularly, why wouldn't that happen? It makes sense.

Now if you can find your temporary spiritual community, the people you were with yesterday, please get up and sit with them and share your experiences.

You guys want to report?

STUDENT: *Well, one of us reported that she felt more relaxed with fewer words and felt at the end, "I'm part of all beings," and that she found it easiest actually to do this with the most people in mind, and it had the most profound act of healing. So she said, "I relate more to the universal level, and it became a continuous stream of joy and suffering, not just in and out, but up and down through the top of my head with an image of divinity," in her mind. It tended to kind of speed up this in and out of suffering and joy and resting in the lap of the Divine Mother. And she felt that taking in the suffering of others neutralizes the suffering within herself. So she was the most articulate. Another person in our group was in quite a speechless mode afterward, and I think that's also a good place to be. Another person felt that it was not as easy today as it was yesterday. It started with herself, because she found her own suffering grabbing, so she felt herself drifting off to another subject.*

And as for myself, I found yesterday I misunderstood the instructions, perhaps. I thought we were supposed to send it out, the suffering with our breath, and then when we breathed in, breathe in joy, and that was really hard. But these instructions for to-day—breathing out joy to others—was a heck of a lot easier.

TSOMO: I bet.

STUDENT: *The other thing was that starting with myself, I was able to kind of get a snapshot of how I felt about suffering and how I felt about joy, and then I could map it onto other people more easily. The image that I had of the joy that I was mapping onto other people was of a beautiful end of day I saw down in West Texas recently, of the sun when it just goes down, and no clouds in the sky, but this beautiful glow, and so that was very helpful for me.*

TSOMO: Thank you. This is rich. I wish we had more time for every-body's sharings, but if I do the math right, we're going to need only two to three minutes per group, or we're going to run out of time for lunch. So we'll have to keep an eye on the clock. Sorry. You guys want to share?

STUDENT: *I think we all had a different experience today, but some of us felt still the challenge of focusing on the self, and particularly in, in breathing out the happiness to the self. Visualizing the suffering self was not as difficult as visualizing the self being transformed by that sparkling cloud. I was able to get up to a group level, because I'm part of a group that has a lot of ego focus on suffering, and so I could do that. But I still couldn't get to all sentient beings. That's a problem I have. My mind would need to be more disciplined to really be a conduit for transforming it. So even as a practice that felt a bit risky.*

TSOMO: Well, it's pushing an envelope, and this is pretty early on in the practice. It could take a while to get to all sentient beings. And that's okay. Just think of that king with one orange, right?

STUDENT: *Pretty close to the last thing was dealing with our emotions. I think people were moved to a more emotional experience, a deeper experience.*

TSOMO: Good. Good. Yeah. And I just want to say, I don't know exactly what the problem was with doing it for oneself, but people often do have problems with that. A common theme I've heard is that we often don't feel as though we really quite deserve it. There's some programming that you've talked about that is unfortunate, that you're trying to correct, and the original sin stuff, and whatever it is, that we just kind of don't know whether we quite should allow that to happen. So I think giving ourselves permission and surrendering to that, accepting that joy, is actually very challenging after programming since birth. So that could be a possible reason.

STUDENT: *One of us, who has done this practice before, said something very interesting, right in line with what you were saying, that she had done this practice in the past, but had never really done it on herself. And it felt so good that she did that for longer than she was meant to. We had someone who said that it was easier to do the exhale, the joyous part. Which led to an ongoing conversation yesterday, about the difference between taking in pain and taking on pain. There were a couple of us who can't reconcile themselves completely with this meditation technique because they feel it has to do with taking on pain. And when we had a discussion, my experience with this was that I had a hard time going from the pain to the joy. Because like they said, I felt like I had to hold my breath for 20 minutes before I came through the pain, because really feeling that, it was too heavy to be able to go from there to joy. So we talked a little bit about, and it was helpful to hear images of alchemy and churning, or ways of filtering that would be inside of oneself to be able to transform that into joy.*

STUDENT: *I think tonglen doesn't work for folks who are of the mindset that everyone's got their own karma to work out. And I respect another's suffering. It might be their path. I can hold them with deep compassion, but not taking anything away or giving them anything, because they have the ability to do that themselves. And knowing that they have that ability themselves, for me, is different than taking or giving.*

TSOMO: So then does the next group want to report?

STUDENT: *We all had different experiences, but one, he was able to focus more on himself today than he was yesterday, to draw upon the suffering of another to find himself and focus on his own pain. Our entire group didn't get beyond ourself and the next person. That's as far as we, each of us, really got. And for me, I had a lot of resistance doing the meditation today, and I needed to work on myself and use that as an antidote to the resistance.*

TSOMO: Um hum, um hum. I think that was a wise choice to do that, and I'm glad you were able to. And, you know, this is the second time ever for a lot of you here. I think it's good to go slowly with it. That makes sense to me. So the group back there?

STUDENT: *I think ours, a different experience for all—everyone has their own experience. Some people were more successful today than yesterday, and I felt more calm today, and I think we have a sense that it was a more calming experience than it was yesterday. And the thought of it being a cycle was an important aspect to that, because what you're taking on you're not keeping, and you can let go of it.*

STUDENT: *I think our group would kind of echo a lot of things that have been said. That just in terms of process, depending on what the exercise was, it took different amounts of time to kind of get there, sort of work your way into it, and one person at a time, but once you get there, actually, you didn't want to come back out. And so the end of the exercise was kind of an intrusion.*

TSOMO: Sorry.

STUDENT: *Everybody seemed to have a different handle on the imagery, which was kind of interesting. So some people were meditating on the names, you know, like a written name as opposed to a face, and other people, the face worked for them, but the face maybe didn't change expression. There was a comment about filtering, which I thought was interesting, because, at least in my case, I was working with the idea of dark clouds and light clouds. And I actually thought I needed to stop and hold the breath, and I almost would switch gears, because otherwise the cloud would come out. It would have come in gray or go out gray. Also we had different effectiveness, if you will, between working on an individual, or working on a smaller group, or even the idea of all sentient beings, whether that was something that people could get their arms around or not. And different people—different kind of targets, if you will—worked differently for different people. I thought it was a really interesting exercise, in particular, keeping the prior exercise from yesterday, and then to see how each little bit of that experience was quite different for even among just the three of us. So it's a very rich exercise to be working with.*

TSOMO: Imagine doing this, even for five, 10 minutes a day, over a long period of time, how the practice might grow. Then if you add the fact that you wouldn't just be doing this practice, you would be doing it with what's sometimes referred to as calm-abiding or Shamatha practice on either side of that, so that you get almost like a dovetailing effect between this visualization and the rousing of bodhicitta, and it's really more active—you're in a different gear than when you're just doing the calm-abiding meditation that we referred to a bit yesterday, which cultivates the ability to place the mind on something and have it stay there. Again, that's something that they've tested in the laboratories. And people who have done that for many years had a capacity that the scientists had never seen the likes of before, and didn't think that human beings at all had the capability of doing. But we do, and it can be the foundation, as you were so articulately saying, it's the foundation then for any practice, because you're able to calm the waters enough and steady things enough to actually be able to place your mind on a practice and do it more effectively. This group.

STUDENT: *Okay. With this group, the first thing that came out was how useful it was to be talked through a visualization. A couple of people talked about how that was very helpful, having a person talk them through the visualization.*

TSOMO: I'm including a CD with my book for that reason. Everybody says that. Yeah.

STUDENT: *In terms of extending out versus yesterday, yesterday people talked about how it was more difficult to extend out yesterday. Today, still difficult, but better—some people talked about being able to extend out to the room, to the people in this room. One person talked about being able to extend out to different groups that they knew, like different social groups that they were involved in. Another person was able to extend out to people with a specific affliction, and to visualize lots of people with that specific affliction. Everyone in the group focused on emotional suffering rather than physical suffering, so emotional and mental suffering. Yesterday, I think there was a person that focused on physical suffering, while today everybody focused on mental and emotional suffering.*

The most interesting thing, I thought, was going to the people that we had problems with. And we got the two extremes of that. We had a person saying that they visualized that person and found themselves labeling, and really had to kind of just leave the situation, that it wasn't useful at that point. Another person said that this was great. It was like being able to take people who I found really irritable and give them a showering of blessings, and would like to do that to start with. I found that really the most useful part of the meditation. In general we talked about the calming influence of the meditation. One person talked about the experience of having clouds around them inside the visualization. That was very calming. Another person talked about how getting out of your meditation, the room seemed brighter and calmer, and like there had been a little bit of Windex on the windshield. And so, so it was good.

Tsomo: Great.

Matt: I was especially grateful for the invitation to deal with your enemies also. I'm glad this group mentioned it, because no one else did, but I found that very refreshing. And trying to get behind the suffering of those who bring suffering toward us. And the whole principle that everyone's suffering, and we're acting it out in our special neurotic ways.

Tsomo: Yeah, and we're trying to pursue happiness, and yet we make more suffering for ourselves. We just don't know what else to do.

Matt: Yeah. Ways out. Eckhart says, "We sink eternally from letting go to letting go into the One." So some ways, you can see this whole exercise is a letting go of, with form, with direction.

Tsomo: Well, yeah. And I'm thinking of the *via transformativa* as well.

Matt: Oh sure. Exactly…Absolutely. It's also *via creativa* because you're bringing in active imagination.

Tsomo: Yes.

CHAPTER 9

Via Positiva

MATT: I'd like to make one other comment if I can. The issue about how difficult it was to shower yourself with happy clouds. You know, that's the whole issue of the *via positiva*. I've been teaching for 30 years that *the via positiva* for Westerners is more difficult to get than any of the other three paths. Far more difficult than the *via negativa*. We love to wallow in our woe, in our sinfulness, and anything that depresses us. We don't take time for the *via positiva*. And I think, in some ways, the Buddhists are so good at the *via negativa*, they kind of want to leap in because you've got all these tools. But I also think there's a presumption, maybe in Tibet, that life is rosier, you see. That, in other words, there is a *via positiva* that's kind of taken for granted maybe when you live up in the mountains, and the air is clear, and the colors are wild and all. But I'm just saying I think part of it's what has been called "the guilts" that we carry as Westerners. I thought that as Catholics we got a lot of guilt until I started talking to Jewish people. And, you know, basically, "Mirror, mirror, on the wall, who's carrying the most guilt of all?"

TSOMO: In one couple, the wife was Italian and Catholic, and the husband was Jewish. He said, "We have a great relationship. She gave me shame, I gave her guilt."

MATT: So again, I believe that really came out. I really think it takes practice to appreciate the *via positiva* then, and not just practice, but a healthy theology that you are an image of God. Of course we're all imperfect images of God. Every beautiful tree is imperfect, too, if you go up close. It's got dead branches, and dead ends, and scars. That's how it is. So part of the neurosis is this perfectionism thing, too, which is sick, but is part of, I think, the original sin and baggage that we carry. So, for me, that brought that back, and the whole thing of when Jesus says, "Love others as you love yourself," he's presuming that we've got a *via positiva* going for us, and that someone has loved us enough in our being so that we learn those lessons early. And we can't take that for granted. So I do want to put that out there that we do need to work on the *via positiva*, and how it applies to us.

Another thing is a lot of people here, I'm sure, serve others. Many of you are teachers, or nurses, or therapists, or, and parents. Many people who serve others shortchange their own needs, and it kind of goes with the territory. Once again, I say, pay attention to your own needs. Again, Eckhart: "Compassion begins at home with one's own soul and one's own body." And some of us get into almost a compulsive service treadmill so that we think all our loving is about giving to others. And it's just not accurate. And that's where I think time for meditation is appropriate, to pay attention to yourself and your own needs.

TSOMO: Um hum. That's why I think a lot of burnout comes in the helping professions.

MATT: Exactly.

TSOMO: And what you were saying about East and West—in Tibet, although there is a lot of suffering, it's not an easy life in old Tibet by any means, there's a lot of suffering involved, they did seem to have *via positiva* down pretty well though, so they didn't have doing tonglen for yourself as part of their tradition. They didn't really need it. Those who had been in prison and tortured in recent years—a bunch of Westerners, just across the border in Dharamsala, were all set to help the new refugees coming over with trauma. And they had trouble finding any. And I think it's be-cause they had a very different way of dealing with the suffering they were experiencing. They figured, "In some lifetime many eons ago, I planted a karmic seed and now it's ripened. Now I just need to live through the con-sequence, the results of that." They didn't think, "I'm terrible, I'm guilty, I deserve this." They just didn't go there. So they were able to discharge that. Trauma is actually an overwhelm, it's an overcharge of the system that gets lodged in there and isn't able to be discharged. I think there's something in this question of worthiness, or something, that causes us not to be able to discharge.

The interesting thing is, when I went to Taiwan recently and taught this, the people there were leading a modern life, and had had modern parenting, and so on, even though it's a Buddhist country, basically. So I didn't know whether I should do this part. Did this apply to them? But I just had them try it on for size, and many of them really responded to it. So I wonder if it is a modern problem. They're also not practicing regularly, not going to their temples regularly—Buddhism is for weddings and funerals. There's some practice going on, and some Sangha going on, but really not so much these days.

MATT: I love that question. Is it a modern problem? Yes. I think joy is a modern problem. I remember years ago, it was the year I was silenced by the Vatican, I went to Latin America, and I spent a week in the Amazon with people working within the rain forest and the Indians there. And this Jesuit priest, young man, came up to me and he said, "I have a real problem." He said, "I'm living on this island with this tribe, and their whole life is built around the monkey. And it's beautiful and all this, but I have one problem." He said, "I don't know what I'm doing there. I don't know what I have to teach them." I said, "Well, what are they teaching you?" And immediately he said, "*La joie*." He said, "They experience more joy in a day than I have experienced in my whole life." And, you know, that's it. These are pre-modern people, and they know that life is about joy and the rest is details. With us, life is about guilt, and proving that you have a right to be here, and legitimizing your existence, and pleasing a vengeful God.

TSOMO: And separating work from play.

MATT: And separating work from play—everything from play. So I think you're absolutely right. I think there's more. There's more joy when there isn't the burdens of the modern agenda. And I think moving the post-modern consciousness, bringing joy back, bringing play back, is a requisite for our survival: bringing the *via positiva* back, savoring, savoring. Not dashing, but savoring. Not dashing around, but savoring. Can we learn that again?

Tsomo: Actually, what I found interesting as I got to know about the Tibetan culture and religion is that they were one country that remained indigenous and yet had the written word, both. And when Buddhism came to Tibet, there wasn't a conquering army that brought it. And I wonder if maybe that makes for a healthier combination. I don't know. That allowed for such an amazing configuration.

Matt: That is very interesting to have writing, and yet indigenous.

Tsomo: Yes.

Matt: That's very special.

Tsomo: Yes, it is very interesting how that worked.

Student: *If you think of how many times there's been an invading army, back and forth across Asia and Europe.*

Matt: And you're from Poland, so you know what you're talking about.

Student: *Oh yeah, oh yeah, that's true. And look at people that are experiencing that today—Darfur, Iraq—the amount of trauma that's taking place. I did a study when I was in college about how many generations it takes to heal a huge trauma in the family system. And from what I could gather, it took a minimum of five generations with intervention.*

Matt: Whoa.

Student: *So if you have a culture that is isolated and does not have this constant invasion, conquering, and all that goes with that, then you don't have anything to recover from. And all their practices and belief systems can really take root and flower, whereas most of the world gets traumatized.*

Matt: That is very interesting.

Tsomo: It's fascinating.

Matt: And, of course, they are protected because they're up in the mountains, too.

Tsomo: That's right.

Matt: It's a little hard to bring an army up there.

Tsomo: They couldn't be invaded. And the Mongols and they made a deal that the Mongols would do the defending and the army, and the

Tibetans were good at religion, so they did that for the Mongols. They had this deal going for a long time.

MATT: Well, in some ways the Hopi, too, because they were up on the plateau. They were protected from a certain amount of the colonizing, and they kept their traditions more alive as a result.

TSOMO: Yeah, that's true.

STUDENT: *Around 1680, I think, they threw the invaders out.*

TSOMO: Well, we do finally have to go to lunch. So let's just remember to dedicate the virtue, the merit of this to all beings who are suffering, and we'd like for them to be happy, and we would like for them to be permanently happy, which means enlightenment in my tradition. So that's our inspiration.

[After lunch]

MATT: I thought we'd begin this afternoon with a little different energy around the importance of the *via transformativa* and the *via creativa*, because Tsomo will be dealing with these topics this afternoon, and I'm happy to also. I want to take just a few minutes about what you're going to see. This is a DVD, and it was created by one of our members here, Professor PITT back there. Because Professor PITT and I are involved in a *transformativa* effort to reinvent education, a modest task, and for the inner city with high school kids. So my most recent book is called *The A.W.E. Project: Reinventing Education, Reinventing the Human*[11]. And A.W.E. stands for "ancestral wisdom education." I end the book talking about the 10 seeds to balance the three arcs. And PITT has put each of these ten seeds to a four-minute, hip-hop video piece, because he is a filmmaker as well as a rapper artist, and they're also inside. One of them is especially pertinent to our entire two days together, and that is the seed called *contemplation* or *meditation*. So that's what you're going to see in a minute, his version of contemplation/meditation all put to hip-hop music and video.

I'm excited about it for a lot of reasons, the number one being the language of young people today. I've shown this a lot all over the country, and one older guy came up to me at one place and he said, "I can't imagine a young

---

11. Matthew Fox, *The A.W.E. Project: Reinventing Education, Reinventing the Human* (CopperHouse, 2006)

person today seeing that and not getting interested in meditation." So you see, we're making work for our friend here, is what we're doing. She has nothing else to do but teach teenagers meditation. But another time I showed it in Idaho, and this suburban mother came up and she said, "My kids are listening to that, but I hate the message, but what you're doing here is so great I can hardly wait to take this home to so and so." So we got a lot of exciting responses. It's not that the kids are dumb, it's that we're dumb, I think, to continue to persevere in providing forms of education that are not working, especially this generation, which is very creative and has new languages like rap, hip-hop, and video. We should be speaking in their language. So I think it's exciting that PITT talks about meditation in languages that are new. So, if you can turn the lights off, we'll have a little experience beyond both Buddhism and Christianity. Insofar as it's a different language. I'm kidding, of course.

[*Plays DVD*]

MATT: ...this old white-haired guy...So...[*Applause*] PITT on meditation. Today's language. Let's get a little feedback. What did you think of it?

STUDENT: *Oh, it's fabulous, fantastic.*

MATT: Enjoy it?

STUDENT: *Oh yeah.*

MATT: Speaking a new language, isn't it? But what I like about it, it's not Meditation 101. He's talking about impermanence. He's talking about nothingness. You know, he's taking us places.

STUDENT: *Letting go of attachment.*

MATT: Letting go. Exactly.

TSOMO: Yeah.

MATT: And I have to confess that most films I've seen on meditation are really hard to watch. You're usually watching someone sit there. But this—the images and the archetypes and the connection to the ocean, and the water in the body, and all that, and it keeps moving, and that's why it's very appealing. We've had responses—like we got a letter from a woman in Manhattan. She said, "I teach in the toughest school in the city." And she said, "I showed this film, and I've never seen the students quiet before in my life." And we've had people take this film to prisons and so forth. There are 10 of these—this is just one—on cosmology, creativity, compassion, chaos, courage, character and chakra development, celebration or ritual, and community. I think that's nine, close to it. So that's part of our little effort at *via transformativa*. The new languages that are creative, into pitching ancient wisdom, such as we've been sharing these two days. So we hope to get more work out of, out of PITT as we move along.

MATT: So I think our plan now is, what, that I will teach for a little bit, and then you're going to teach? Is that what we have on our schedule?

TSOMO: That's what we have, I think.

STUDENT: *Throw that out.*

MATT: What's that?

STUDENT: *Throw out the paper. We never stick with it anyway.*

TSOMO: Oh, believe me, this is the revised version.

MATT: The very revised version.

TSOMO: As-of-a-few-minutes-ago version.

STUDENT: *It's a creative process.*

TSOMO: Yeah, creative timing, not just spelling.

CHAPTER 10

Via Creativa

MATT: Here's the dream that Eckhart had, on page 71[12], he says, "I once had a dream. I dreamt even though I'm a man, I was pregnant, pregnant with nothingness, and out of the nothingness God was born." So this is certainly, I think, very Buddhist: the affirmation we've been talking about, about that ocean standing for nothingness and the fertility of emptiness, the generativity that we're all capable of. And notice what he's saying to men—hey, men, we get pregnant, too. We just don't show on the outside. It's a pregnancy of our imaginations, and we have to honor more our creativity because it's our creativity that gets us in our biggest trouble as a species on the one hand, and it's also our creativity that can get us out. About all we have going for us is our creativity as a species. But notice what he's saying: Out of this nothingness, out of this pregnancy, God was born. And see, that is his Cosmic Christ theology. In one of his sermons at Christmas, he said, "What good is it to me if Mary gave birth to the son of God 1,400 years ago, and I don't give birth to the son of God in my own time, and in my own person, and in my own culture?" And then he said, "We are all meant to be mothers of God."

Again, this has something to do with this God language thing. If you think of God as having been here for all eternity, and knowing everything, and omnipotent, and judging everything, and up in the sky, you're

---

12. Matthew Fox, *Passion for Creations: The Earth-Honoring Spirituality of Meister Eckhart* (Rochester VT: Inner Traditions, 2000 [formerly *Breakthrough: Meister Eckhart's Creation Spirituality in New Translation*]

in trouble. But notice this, he says, "Divinity is always yearning to be born." Yearning to be born. And for him, then, yes, Mary gave birth to the Christ, but so do we. She didn't do it all. She's just an archetype, or a model, and we're all supposed to be giving birth to the Buddha Nature, put it that way, in our lifetimes, and in our work, and in all our relations. So creativity, the *via creativa*, holds a very, very powerful place in these four paths for Eckhart and for this tradition. In another place he compares our creativity to the story of the Annunciation. He says, "The Holy Spirit came over Mary. So too the Holy Spirit comes over us when we are pregnant with ideas." And gives birth, you see. So again, he's not isolating some religious event, Christmas and things all about Mary and the baby Jesus, sentimentalizing it. No. It's an archetype. It's what all of us are called to do.

Now, Aquinas, who came just before him, has a great line on that. He says, "The same spirit that hovered over the waters of the beginning of creation, hovers over the mind of the artist at work." Beautiful.

Tsomo: Well, isn't that the same as the Greek idea of the Muse, or similar?

Matt: It's similar, but it's bigger—you know, this spirit that starts the world out of chaos in Genesis 1...

Tsomo: Well, of course, yeah, but in that act of creation of a piece of music, or something like that.

Matt: Yes, yes. From that point of view, yes.

Tsomo: It's a small example of it. Yeah.

Matt: I would almost compare the Muse more to, like the role of angels. Whereas Aquinas and Eckhart are talking about the work of God, the creator, who is creating still through us, hovering over our minds and bringing forth new creation, you know.

Tsomo: And I was saying yesterday that the Dharmakaya was like this pregnant emptiness that is constantly flashing forth all form.

Matt: Exactly. And that's one reason I landed on this dream he had about him being pregnant with nothingness itself. And again, then, the positive side to nothingness, you know—nothingness can be a shattering experience, it can be a falling apart of things, but it's not all negative. It's also just what you said, and what Eckhart is saying; it is the source of generativity, of something really new. If we don't pass through nothingness, we're not bringing something new into the world. We're just shuffling the deck, the chairs on the deck. We have to go through this radical letting go, this radical tasting of the void, tasting of the ashes, the dark night of the soul.

CHAPTER 11

Via Negativa

MATT: And the dark night of the soul, I know Rabbi Heschel used to say we shouldn't just talk about the *dark night of the soul,* but the dark night of society. But I talked today about the dark night of our species, because I think, as a *species*, we are in a collective dark night today because we're facing things that are really serious, and time's running out, and we can't be fooling ourselves.

So the mystics have lessons for us. What do you do in the dark night? Well, first of all, don't go shopping, even though that's what you've been told to do. Don't drink, don't take a drug, and don't get addicted to television. What is there to do then? You travel. It's a journey and it's a school. The dark night is a school for learning the most important things in life, because this is what the mystics really teach us about the dark night. The dark night is the purification of our longing, the purification of our longing. Now how important is that? Think about it. What is our species really longing for? That's the question of our time. What are we really longing for? And how can we purify that longing so we're not being distracted by consumer addictions and all the ideologies that are reigning in our time from all kinds of fascist and fundamentalist movements: political, religious, and everything else? And this is where meditation comes in to find that centering, that purifying, what our heart's are really looking for.

That's the school that we're all invited to today. And it's so important because it's precisely in going to that school that we grow up spiritually, that we move into the next level of our evolution as a species. Because we're going to make this or fail, I think, as a species. It's that kind of thing. We're in this together. No continent is exempt, no religion, no race, no class. We're in this together. And I think it's very important to people to name what "this" is, and I say it is a collective dark night of our species. It's not the end of the world. It's not all bad news. It's the vestibule to a tremendous breakthrough, to a breaking up, to a growing up, to moving, really moving.

There's this wonderful passage from Hafiz, the fourteenth-century Sufi mystic. He says, "Sometimes God wants to do us a great favor: turn us upside-down and shake all the nonsense out. But almost everyone I know, when they find God in such a playful, drunken mood, quickly pack their bags and hightail it out of town." So the temptation at a time of *via negativa*, of dark night of the soul, or being turned upside-down, is to pack our bags and get out of town. That's a natural response, that's the reptilian brain; it's action-reaction-survival. But the point is that it takes a spiritual warrior in you to stick around, not pack your bags and hightail it out of town. Stick around for what God is trying to teach us, like turning everything upside-down to shake all the nonsense out. I think that's the moment in which we find ourselves today.

And this is why the mystics, East and West, are so important to us, because they teach us the courage to stick around. *Courage* from two French words: "a large heart." How to enlarge your heart even in the midst of turmoil, chaos, upset, melting of our institutions, churches that are not working for us, education that is not working for us, media that is working mostly against us, blah, blah, blah, getting ahold of your soul and purifying our longing.

CHAPTER 12

Via Transformativa

MATT: Let me jump to just a few thoughts in the "*Via Transformativa.*" Eckhart says, "A person works in the stable. That person has a breakthrough. What do they do? They return to the stable." Now, breakthrough, again, is the realization that you and God are one. That's what it means for Eckhart: the realization that you and God are one. So he's saying that just because you undergo a spiritual transformation does not mean you have to quit everything. It means you're a different person now. You go back with a different attitude. It doesn't mean you can't quit your job, but I love that image he uses of the stable. You know, a stable is a place with a lot of horse flies and horses' asses. And a lot of us work in places like that, you know. And he's saying you don't have to escape all the manure of life. You go back with a different attitude to life, a different viewpoint. You were talking about the windshield getting cleaned, and that's what he's talking about.

And he says that spirituality is, "not about running away from the world." He says—let me find the quote for this, it's really nice—"Rather, we must learn an inner solitude." He says, "Spirituality is not to be learned by flight from the world, running away from things, by turning solitary, growing apart from the world. Rather, we must learn an inner solitude. Wherever or with whomsoever we may be, we must learn to penetrate things and find God there." Penetrate the news, penetrate what's going on. So this is his "in the world" spirituality. It is our responsibility to find our inner solitude and carry it with us wherever we go. And, of course, he was fighting the battle of the Middle Ages about monks who were ensconced in their monasteries. And he was arguing that, no, you can be in the world and be carrying your monastic heart, if you will, your contemplative heart with you. And more than ever, I think, that is required in our time.

When the late Bede Griffiths was dying, this wonderful monk who lived over 50 years in an ashram in India, said to me, "I think the future," he said, "of monasticism is with laypeople." And I see great figures, like Thich Nhat Hanh and the Dalai Lama, who've had the privilege, really, of being trained in their monastic disciplines, but are so much in the world sharing this with us "in the world" people. They've managed to distill. I think that's the kind of time we're living in, when we have to distill the wisdom of our teachers and ancestors, our lineages, to make it practical for everybody.

One way I think of it is the whole move from the Age of Pisces, which is dualistic, two fish swimming in opposite directions, to the Age of Aquarius that we're now in. In the Age of Pisces, you knew who was a monk and you knew who wasn't. Today, we don't, which is great. We're all called to be monks, because to be a monk is to carry solitude. *Monk* comes from the word *monos, solitude*: "learning how to carry solitude." And that's how you calm the reptilian brain. Reptiles are solitudinous animals. They're not real good at bonding. They like to lie alone in the sun, those crocodiles. And our crocodile brain needs attention at this time, every one of ours, every human being's crocodile brain. And I see that as the Buddha's genius—of putting a leash in the crocodile brain, on the crocodile's brain.

The point is that it's finding solitude. And when you can find solitude, then you've calmed that reptilian brain. And then your mammal brain, which is the compassion brain, can come forward. The mammal brain has been underdeveloped in our societies of late. That's what compassion is, then; it's really putting the mammal brain into gear. Why is it that every single spiritual teacher of worth that I've studied, and by that I mean the world's traditions, whether Isaiah, or Jesus, or Mohammed, or Buddha, or Lao Tzu, or Chief Seattle, and all of them, they're all talking about compassion. The Dalai Lama says, "You can do away with all religion, but you can't do away with compassion. Compassion is my religion" he says.

So it's about compassion. That's the *via transformativa*. But to get there you do have to go through, I think, these other paths. You have to go into joy and fall in love with life. You have to go into the darkness, the letting go, and the suffering, but also the silence and the solitude. And you have to gather up your creativity. Gather it up because this is what you're going to put into motion and compassion. Compassion isn't just about sitting around feeling sorry or empathy for one another. It is about becoming the hands of God. That's how Heschel talks about it: God depends on us for compassion to happen. So we need hands that are skillful, that have some craft to them, that can make some changes in the way we're doing business, the way we're doing education, religion, worship, our parenting, grandparenting, citizenship, driving cars, et cetera, et cetera.

So that's how I see Eckhart speaking to us today. And not just Eckhart but this other tradition represented here. For me, it's interesting, because I was going to ask you the question, "What is enlightenment?" and just at the end of the morning you said for you that enlightenment was beyond words.

TSOMO: Well, no. Enlightenment is actually a pretty specific definition. There's that point of no return, that I think I mentioned yesterday, when we've cleaned the windshield enough and actually taken away the windshield altogether—in other words, purified the obscurations of karma, and the habits of mind, that have piled up over the eons of incarnations of various kinds. When we've cleared all of those away and brought forward our Buddha Nature, also a 100 percent, then we cross the line of no return so that all of these appearances that arise from emptiness all the time, constantly, these waves on the ocean, we never make the mistake again of seeing a wave and saying, "That's me," and identify with that one single wave. We finally are able to stay as the whole ocean, including the waves, the whole enchilada. So once we've crossed that line of no return, then we've reached full Buddhahood. And that's a very particular state that is pretty unusual, but eventually the Buddha said we all get there. As the Dalai Lama said, "Sooner or later we all reach enlightenment. Better it be sooner."

MATT: Okay. Well, that would be an interesting discussion for another time, because for me, my goal would be more. But there's an overlap. It is about compassion. For me it's compassion, but I think there's real overlap, because compassion is about the acting out of our interdependence, of our being part of the ocean, and not just an independent wave.

Tsomo: That's right, you can't reach full Buddhahood without the compassionate desire for Buddhahood not only for yourself, but for all beings, and all kinds of compassion that comes with thinking in those terms, that's it's not just for me.

Matt: Yeah. Okay. Well?

Tsomo: I think we're on to my responses to Eckhart, and continuing on at a blazing speed through all of this.

CHAPTER 13

Pregnant Emptiness

Tsomo: I actually picked up on a similar place to start. On page 79[13] of the Eckhart: "This birth takes place in darkness, and not only is the son of the heavenly creator born in this darkness, but you too are born there as a child of the same heavenly creator and none other. And the creator extends this same power to you out of the divine maternity bed." This is not a vacuum we're talking about in this pregnant emptiness. I think we've been clear about that. Not only is there this all-knowing, because if you're not separate from anything, how could there be anything you wouldn't know? You're in touch with everything. You're all-powerful. The whole ocean is, of course, all-powerful and continues to make these appearances, these waves. And also all-loving, because, again, there's nothing that's separate from this all-encompassing awareness that we're talking about. And there is the quality of awareness itself. All of these Buddha qualities, then, we carry within ourselves because we're not separate from the ocean. The waves are made of the same water of the ocean, and it's just one phenomenon. So I think this is speaking to that, very poetically.

And then, in this "eternally giving birth" idea, it also reminds me of a wonderful concept in Tibetan Buddhism, in Vajrayana, of spontaneous presence. And this is not something that only Tibetans experience. I've seen in a lot of Eckhart's writings that clearly he had a direct perception

---

13. Matthew Fox, *Passion for Creations: The Earth-Honoring Spirituality of Meister Eckhart* (Rochester VT: Inner Traditions, 2000 [formerly *Breakthrough: Meister Eckhart's Creation Spirituality in New Translation*]

of this spontaneous presence. I don't know if you can get a sense of what I mean by that, but in moments when you've been in some sort of epiphany or a transcendent experience, there is this quality of presence, and it's constantly new. It's constantly fresh, eternally fresh and new. So this term *spontaneous presence*, I think, evokes that presence that probably many of us in this room have experienced at one time or another.

STUDENT: *When you say "spontaneous presence," presence like you're talking about the present moment where everything opens up into just the feeling of spaciousness, and everything is new?*

TSOMO: Well, within that, there is a presence. You know, it's like "somebody's there" kind of thing. It's not somebody we can actually see in a physical form, but the sense that somebody's there. It's presence within that timeless quality of being.

MATT: Could you say it's just—searching for a synonym—intimacy? An experience of an intimate presence?

TSOMO: For me, it is. Yeah. How can I say? I think, yeah, in the experience of intimacy we must feel spontaneous presence, and probably then attach it to a particular person.

MATT: No, no. That's not what I meant.

TSOMO: I'm flipping it around.

MATT: Oh, you're flipping it around.

TSOMO: Yeah, yeah, yeah.

MATT: Well, you did understand what I meant?

TSOMO: If you take the person away, and then you're just feeling that presence, perhaps it is an intimate moment in a certain way, even though there's not actually another person there. Yeah, so I just had to kind of flip it around for a second.

So sticking with this theme of this giving birth and so on, this gets, I think, more into more human acts of creation. On page 82, "Why is it that some people do not bear fruit? It is because they're so busy clinging to their egotistical attachments, and so afraid of letting go and letting be, that they have no trust either in God or in themselves. Love cannot distrust. It can only await the good trustfully. No person could ever trust God too much. Nothing people ever do is as appropriate as great trust in God. With such trust, God never fails to accomplish great things."

So whenever I think of my own life and myself, anything I've done that's been some kind of huge creative act, I've had to get out of the way to a certain extent. I've almost felt as though there's this tide coming in, and it's coming through me, and there's some interplay with it that I do as a creative being, as a human being. And humans are uniquely creative. I agree with you when you said that. So that this creative act happens, in part, because I do get my machinations of my mind a bit out of the way, and allow this tide to come in and move with it. And that allows great things to happen.

I experienced that as a therapist, for example. I would just start each session in silence, and feel in, to get a sense of what wanted to happen before anybody opened their mouths. And it was amazing, because if I kept just sort of allowing and watching for what already was trying to come, even before we spoke, I found those were the best sessions, and it was the most helpful to the person. It was the most creative way of doing the therapy.

STUDENT: *Something I wanted to ask you, and I sort of have a hard time articulating it, Maybe I can frame this. About a week ago I heard someone who said that he spoke to this Indian guru, who described exactly the same thing, that this sort of ineffable oneness that we talk about, that it became creator, not only because of this sort of prodigious overabundance, but because it was lonely. And then in order to experience itself, it had to be other than it was. So the independent manifested reality is love. She said if that's true, then why is there evil? And the guru said, "It thickens the plot." And he thought, well, now, great. You know, the Holocaust, the bubonic plague thickens the plot. That's not a very good answer. And you ask someone who's studied Western philosophy, secular philosophy, even post-modern, there's even some theosophist who talks about metaphysical violence, which is interesting intellectually, and it sort of makes sense, but not spiritually very nourishing. So this is something I struggle with. I did my graduate studies in France, and my thesis was called "Thinking in Violence." Actually, I studied with somebody who appreciated my sort of disenchantment with Western philosophy. But anyway, so the question is, I'm not exactly asking you why is there evil, I mean, although, if you've got the answer...*

MATT: You need a bumper sticker.

STUDENT: *How do you reconcile this trust? I mean, faith as trust with evil? And not evil that's incidental, but that seems to be woven into the very fabric of being.*

MATT: Who are you asking? Both of us?

STUDENT: *I'd love to hear from both of you.*

MATT: Well, first of all, I do define faith as trust. That is the meaning of faith. It's not primarily about doctrines, dogmas, et cetera. It is about trust. And the word for it in the Gospels, *pisteuo* in Greek, means "to trust." And, you know, I did do a book on evil called *Sins of the Spirit, Blessings of the Flesh: Lessons for Transforming Evil in Soul and Society.*[14] I did a lot of reading for that about evil and, frankly, the best book I read, and I read a lot, was by Erich Fromm, *The Anatomy of Human Destructiveness*[15]—powerful, brilliant book. He has one sentence in there that I think summarizes the whole thing. He says [paraphrasing], "Necrophilia grows when biophilia is stunted". Necrophilia grows when biophilia is stunted. So *necrophilia* is his kind of working synonym for evil, if you will. The love of death in all of its expressions. I'm sure, probably Buddhism has 84,000 names of love of death. But I love this sentence because it names things, and it also shows the medicine.

"Necrophilia grows when biophilia is stunted," so biophilia, the love of life, the *via positiva*. When that is stunted, all kinds of misshapen desires get born.

STUDENT: *Can I say something here? As I told you, I was raised Catholic. I was very devout when I was younger, and I was this, but I loved that tradition. I think that's one of the reasons your work has been so gratifying, just to come back to this tradition that I grew up in. And I find it actually is spiritual. It's not against spirituality. And I've read that, but that is really about human sinfulness.*

MATT: Ah ha, ah ha.

STUDENT: *It doesn't speak to sort of cosmic...*

---

14. Matthew Fox (author), Deepak Chopra (foreword), *Sins of the Spirit, Blessings of the Flesh: Lessons for Transforming Evil in Soul and Society."* (Harmony, 1999)
15. Erich Fromm, *The Anatomy of Human Destructiveness* (Henry Holt & Company, Inc, 1992)

MATT: No, but I want to speak to that because you used the word, you were quoting someone about violence, was it? And see, what we now know is that chaos is integral to everything in nature, and all the good things we appreciate, chaos is part of it. The chaos of weather systems, the chaos of the continents ripping apart, the chaos of the volcanoes that is now beautiful Hawaii, the chaos of the original fireball, of the galaxies of the supernovas that gave birth to the stars and everything. What we now know is that chaos is a habit of the universe. And this is why in the old days they worshiped the Goddess of Chaos, because she's a goddess, because all birth is chaotic.

I was lecturing this year with this fellow who's written this wonderful book on chaos. In fact, he's one of the founders of chaos theory, Ralph Abraham. His book, wonderful book, *Chaos, Gaia, Eros*[16]. And afterwards this woman came up. "I'm a midwife" she said. "Nothing's more chaotic than birth." But look what comes out of it, you know? And then it struck me why. And, of course, his whole thesis is right when patriarchy took over, we, they, killed the Goddess of Chaos and turned chaos into evil. And so you have the myths shifting. You have Marduk now killing Tiamat. You have Saint Michael killing the dragon. The patriarchal mind felt it was their job to kill chaos. And that's religious orthodoxy. And then he says, "Science took over from religion in the seventeenth century." He said, "We're the test of true orthodoxy, so we'll now do this." And so science itself took on that role of killing the Goddess of Chaos until the 1960s when literally the computer invented in this backyard in Silicon Valley rediscovered the importance of chaos.

So chaos is not evil. Chaos is disturbing. He says this thing being turned upside-down and all this nonsense—it feels evil to us, because it hurts. We're not in control, but it's not evil. It's built into all creative processes. So I just don't buy that violence is evil. Violence is difficult. It's disturbing. By violence, I'm talking about the violence of super-nature, mega-nature as you say. But look around us. The laws of the universe in

---

16. Ralph H. Abraham. *Chaos, Gaia, Eros: A Chaos Pioneer Uncovers the Three Great Streams of History* (Epigraph Publishing, 2011)

clude this amazing—that's the miracle of it all—that out of chaos comes order, that out of chaos comes beauty, out of chaos comes astounding beings, and that's the universe we live in. Now maybe there's another one where everything's serene all the time.

Tsomo: I just have completely different forms of reference. In Tibetan Buddhism, it's not a question of chaos versus order regarding evil. That wouldn't come into the question of evil. But when I was describing the fellow who got off track in his thinking, and then began acting with evil intent, and filling Samsara with hell beings, he was powerfully evil in his intent. So in that sense, the Tibetans believe that there is evil. There's evil intent, there's negative intent, and it tends to come along with intent that is out for number one. That can be little evils that we all do every day, and then great big ones like this fellow I was talking about. But even in the case of him, eventually, the bodhisattvas came to everyone's aid, including his, and were able to help him—they kind of did the turning upside-down shaking. One of them actually came up through him and "roto-rooted" inside of him. And by the time he came up through the crown of his head, this being suddenly realized that he had been acting from a negative, selfish intent in a very huge and powerful way, and was filled with remorse, and then turned his prodigious powers to benefit beings.

Student: *Just to give you an idea of what I'm still struggling with, a good example would be, being from Louisiana, I'm trying to deal with Hurricane Katrina. I, what I'm hearing is that on some level, there's a karmic reality to that, that it's not by chance, but there's terrible destruction that took place. I find that very hard somehow. It's about trust in the cosmos, and at the same time digesting that experience. And not just for me, but I taught high school for a couple of years, and that's where some of this cynicism comes from. It's the sense that the universe is not a place that one can trust.*

Matt: But, you know, let's look at the facts of Katrina. You know, the facts that we destroyed...

Student: *It's not a natural disaster.*

Matt: It's not a natural disaster, but nature had developed to absorb that kind of thing, and then the whole global warming thing. It is related to Katrina. So that's human.

TSOMO: Yeah, it's human-made, and whether it's coming from nature itself, or human beings interacting with nature, or human beings on human beings, still, for me, I can have faith in pure reality and its ability to create pure appearance. And the beings who have been wandering around lost in Samsara and being their own writers and producers of this movie—I don't have faith in them. Those are the ones who made Katrina happen, in my opinion, and who are experiencing it. And maybe the ones experiencing it had done something similar in the past. Who knows which eon, and it happened to ripen for them then. So that's how I can reconcile it, myself.

STUDENT: *I don't have a question. It's a kind of a response to her question in just how I deal with the exact same question. One Buddhist saying is that we have to have faith that every act in the universe is to bring us happiness. So it's like, well, something bad is happening, it is still to bring forth happiness. But another way that that's helped me out, if you know the, you know, the Bugs Bunny cartoon of the coyote and the sheepdog? There's a coyote and a sheepdog that all they do all day is fight over protecting the sheep. And one is always getting the other. And it's a constant battle, and they're really doing a lot of damage to each other. But at the end of the day, an alarm clock goes off, and it's five o'clock, and they go, "Oops, job's over. Hey, how's it going, Bob?" You know what I'm saying? And that's how I see, that's how I see demons and angels. They're on the same side.*

TSOMO: Like lawyers in court.

STUDENT: *They have their differences. They have a job to do. Most of the times that we have epiphanies it's because a good demon did something seriously deep to us that then pushed us to the angel. So I've had to come to a point of not growing attachment to hate for the demons because they're always going to be there. They have a job as well. That's the balance. You can even go higher, in my mind, go as far as to say that angels and demons every couple of centuries change places just to keep life exciting. But the point is, it leans toward happiness. I am who I am today because of all the struggles that I went through that pushed me to the angels, and then the angels carried me so far until I got lazy, and then the demon came in and kicked me in the ass and made me go back to the angel.*

TSOMO: We could go on and on just for a whole weekend talking about the question of evil. But I just want to get back and maybe go with one more quote to respond to, and then we've got yet more to do before our time is completely up. So let me read this quote from Eckhart. "The divine countenance is capable of maddening and driving all souls out of their senses with longing for it. When it does this, by its very divine nature, it is thereby drawing all things to itself. Every creature, whether it knows it or not, seeks repose." When I read this, I thought of the five facets of primordial wisdom, one of them being—well, let me start back from that and say the five poisonous, neurotic emotions. If we were to group all those eighty-four thousand of them into five categories, one of them was the desire/clinging one. And you were talking about this earlier, in reference to purification of our longing, that catalogs are called *wish books*. So when we sit and look in a catalog, we're following our bliss, following our longing, in a pretty occluded way at that point.

But if we were truly to stay on it, and this is the Vajrayana way of working with these neurotic emotions—when I truly looked at my desire to smoke cigarettes, for example, I really went deeply into it with a friend who sat and dialogued with me. And we went quite deeply. What I found was that I wanted to take something in, that I felt so separate that I just needed to feel something going in. And my lungs are around my heart, right? And you notice where I'm pointing to when I say, "Take something in." So I wanted to breathe this in. I only smoked, at the time, three cigarettes a day, but I had to smoke those three. I was a slave to those three cigarettes. When I traveled, I had to make sure I had enough of them to take with me, because my brand I couldn't always get. And if they dried out that wasn't good, so I had a little thing, the little piece of tissue paper that was damp inside. I was a slave to these things. I wanted to be free of them, and I couldn't be until I really kept on it with following this longing and coming to the essence of it. This was really a Vajrayana process that I was doing before I even knew that that was a Vajrayana process.

What I came to was this wanting to take in from the universe that we've been talking about, this understanding, really knowing and feeling that we're not separate from creation. I was feeling very separated, and obviously was laboring under many kalpas of feeling separated, and reaching for a quick cure and taking refuge in a cigarette, instead of taking refuge in the Three Jewels—the Buddha, the Dharma, and the Sangha—that could actually lead me to what I was trying to get to. If I followed that longing enough, I got to the point where I could come to profound places in Buddhist practice. It was when I studied with Gochen Tulku Rinpoche, when I studied deeply with him and I began doing these practices, I was breathing in these visualizations of Kuntuzangpo and Kuntuzangmo and so on, and it was so satisfying that I actually stopped smoking, for lack of interest if you can believe it. Nicotine is a very addictive physical substance, but I honestly forgot to smoke. I was more surprised than anybody.

The wisdom we get to, if we follow desire and we follow our longing, is discerning wisdom. Along the way we come upon one of the four joys, which is the joy of bliss. So longing brings us to bliss, and we come to that aspect of primordial wisdom, or timeless awareness, that we could call discerning wisdom, because the longing knows. The longing is an unerring compass. We can use it as that.

I could go on and on, but we're running so short of time. We wanted to have time for the closing processes, and I would like to give up any other time that I would spend playing with these wonderful poetic utterances of Meister Eckhart. I'd like to ask everybody to once again be in their groups of four, this time to have a chance to digest the rich banquet that we've all had for this weekend.

The questions that I'd like you to bring to your group are, first of all, what were the gems of this experience that you'd like to carry forward? Because all of you, I can see, are on a spiritual path. The next question: What are you already practicing that's working for you? And then, right on the heels of that, I would ask, what would you change, or add, or somehow augment after this experience or this little—what would you call this—a tasting banquet? And what resources of support do you have in your spiritual work, going forward? What do you see that you have? Then, just the last thing would be, of this little mini-Sangha experience that you've tasted now, hopefully, what would you want to bring into your life from that? Or where is it already in place?

Then I'm hoping that there is a little bit of time for everybody to, or some people to, speak something significant from these ruminations. So please get together with your little Sanghas.

[*Groups meet*]

We thought that we could start by having everybody not necessarily reporting for everybody from their groups, but just sort of popcorn style,

if anybody has something they wanted to share, something important
from these questions that they mulled over in digesting the experience.
This is really, hopefully, to help you begin the digestion process, which we
assume will go on for a long time to come after this experience. So anyone
have any gems they want to share? Yeah.

STUDENT: *Years ago I heard the Eckhart quote that "if the only prayer you say in your
entire life is, 'Thank you,' that would suffice." Eckhart's name stuck in my head, but
this is the first time I've actually dealt with Eckhart in any solid, meaty kind of way,
other than that one aphorism. And it's been a great experience, a great opening and I'm
going to set some of these to music.*

MATT: Great, great. Eckhart deserves it. Have fun. Great. Just to pause
on that, I've said many times, there are only two languages for mysticism:
One is art, and the other is silence. So it's just altogether organic. A musician would be moved to music, or a painter to painting, or a filmmaker to
filmmaking, a poet to poetry. I really think, again, our culture thoroughly
undervalues the role of art, and art is the language for our mystical experiences, our experiences of awe and of grief, the heights and the depths of
nothingness. So I'm glad to hear this, but I'm not surprised.

TSOMO: Yeah.

STUDENT: *Our group sort of underscored the value of this little four-person Sangha, and
this room that we sort of consider a Sangha, and sort of took us a little bit to bring that into
our practice, whether that's in the morning shower, or formally sitting, or nighttime, but . . .*

MATT: You're going to have four in your shower? Wow! Did I get it right?
No, no, no. What did I miss? What did you miss?

STUDENT: *I'm at a loss for words.*

TSOMO: Wait a minute. Was that Freudian hearing?

MATT: I don't know. I apologize if I interrupted you. Left you speechless.

STUDENT: *You did.*

STUDENT: *I wanted to add, though, one of the things that Aubrey talked a lot about
was the value of the opportunity to practice while we were here. That it gave us a beginning point for us, for all of us, a new beginning, a first beginning to have actually
experienced the practice of meditation.*

STUDENT: *Something we talked about in this group was some really new musical metaphors we can take with us back out in terms of jam sessions. You know, like the ocean metaphor, metaphorical waves, and the Jesus having one bad day. It's a good metaphor. It's great.*

TSOMO: Jesus had a really bad day.

STUDENT (*Continuing*): *And the creases in the paper for our karma, or our defects, or sins, or whatever you want to call them is a very useful metaphor.*

STUDENT: *To add to the gems, the notion, the concept of panentheism and joy, the focus on joy, the books. And then two things that you said: The dark night of the soul equals a purification of our longing, and longing brings us to discerning wisdom and then bliss, those two bookends.*

STUDENT: *I think we all decided we wanted to read more of your books, and it's just kind of opened a new window for all of us to look at Christianity really differently. It's nice. It's a blessing.*

MATT: Well, I'm glad to hear that, and it's not about me. These books are really—I let Eckhart speak, and I let Aquinas speak, and Hildegard speak. And unfortunately the Church apparatus has been sitting on these treasures, or distorting them for centuries, and we have to take that back. It's just like we were talking about doctors here. We just can't turn our bodies over to every doctor, and you can't turn your soul over to every theological system. We have these amazing souls in our inheritance, and let's let them speak to us and see what happens. I think something wonderful can be born. And this is where Buddhism and certainly my tradition totally agree that the Buddha Nature is presence, the Christ Nature is presence; there's work to do. You know, we've got to study. We do have to study, and we have to do the meditation, the inner work, too. It's not just going to drop out of the sky. And unfortunately what we're calling *church* at this moment in history is not giving us the meat and the substance of our lineage, of our heritage. We'd better start doing it ourselves. So I'm very glad to hear that.

TSOMO: Yeah.

STUDENT: *Also, for me, we ignited fire and were looking at Christian mysticism, but you were talking about the importance of just digging one hole, digging one well, and* *all. Now I find myself equally interested in Buddhism and this Christian mysticism, and so how do I dig one well?*

MATT: For me, it's a question, and even using Tsomo's analogy, it's really not about one or two; it's about the depth of the well. But I would say it's important to go down at least a well. But, I think, today, the wells are themselves merging, and there's a certain mixing going on.

TSOMO: My teacher's teacher was Dilgo Khyentse Rinpoche, who was one of the more famous lamas of the Rimé, or ecumenical, movement of Tibet. And I guess the way I would say it is, he dug one well really deeply first, and then, because he had come already to the waters of truth there, he was then very quickly able to get all the way down to water anywhere else he drilled, because he already knew about the water. So it's not quite the either/or that you might think it is. You might want to dig deep with one, and then you can move to another one once you've already gotten to water, and you'll get to water again.

My teacher was in prison with many very accomplished lamas and scholars. And there was this one very highly accomplished lama who asked another lama to give him the transmission for a particular teaching that was in another treasury, a cycle of teachings that he hadn't already entered. Well, once he had the transmission, and then the explanations, in two days he accomplished the practice. He had signs, very clear signs of accomplishment of the practice. Why? Because he already had mastered, he had already dug his well with his own tradition. So then it was going to be very quick and easy for him to really get to the depth of the others. But if we try to go quickly from one well to the other before we've done that one deep one, that's where I think we Americans can run into trouble.

STUDENT: *Yeah, but how deep do we have to go?*

TSOMO: Until you get water.

STUDENT: *Well, I know, but what is water? Does that mean I have to go to a monastery and stay there?*

TSOMO: I don't know that this fellow had been in a monastery. I don't know where, you know, he dug his well. There aren't set places you have to stay in, or certain numbers of years, or anything like that. The question is, have you really gotten to a significant level of enlightenment? You've gotten the juice. Then you have committed, presumably—that's part of the well-digging process—but it's not just the commitment, it's the actual result that I'm speaking of. And I think it's one of those things. You know it when you strike water. Yeah.

STUDENT: *I was struck by how we're talking about, in our own lives, a certain amount of chaos, and life taking you like this and shaking all the nonsense out, and— it's kind of a fractal thing—how it's also happening on the level of our civilization. I'm trying to diagnose what's happening with our civilization and the need for joy. And I was really struck by the Western feelings about our guilt and original sin. It's kind of putting dark glasses over us as far as our feeling about the predominance of good or evil in the world, and how even secular people have been colored by that.*

TSOMO: Yeah. I think that's true. And my sense is that this weekend was a good antidote, in many ways, for that.

STUDENT: *I enjoyed the high quality of what you two are doing, back and forth, and back and forth. I thought this was really great. No smoked-up, no rah-rah thing. Down to business. I appreciated that from both of you.*

TSOMO: Thank you.

STUDENT: *In terms of the wells, to kind of change the metaphor, I kind of see the two traditions, choosing one versus the other, as going through the forest in a way. And when I see the Tibetan Buddhist tradition, in the Buddhist traditions, it's like there's lots of guides to sort of take you through that forest. Whereas on, in the Christian side, you're really on your own, which can be really exciting, but you can get really lost, too. And I'm wondering, you know, how would you resolve that from a Western standpoint?*

MATT: Well, I don't feel I'm on my own. I've gotten help from a lot of people who you told me were dead, but are more alive than a lot of people who think they're alive. And I won't name any names, but I've found Eckhart, and Hildegard, and Aquinas as three guides, plus the wonderful scholarship being done today on the historical Jesus, and finding the prophets in our tradition—and there are so many. Howard Thurman is just incredible; he was the spiritual guide to Martin Luther King. I'm a hunter-gatherer for wisdom voices that are, that have something to teach us, or at least me. I don't think we're bereft at all. And there are a lot of other people who are feeling the sadness of the failure of Western religion, people who want to live in community and want to be nourished. For just a concrete example, I have friends on the East Coast in the Boston area, because I lived there for a year, years ago. And Roman Catholics, Italians and Irish, who are all Unitarian Universalists now, because they can't stand the current fascist leanings of the Vatican. So they've joined the Unitarian way, because the Unitarians have a commitment to social justice, and in all of its expressions, plus they have the mystical tradition, even if they need ex-Catholics to come on board and help teach them what it is.

There's a lot of this shifting going on today. There's a sociologist named Walter Truett Anderson, who teaches at U.C. Berkeley. He's written a good book on post-modern times, and he says, "Today we all belong to so many communities at once that we should write 'e-t-c period' after our names." When the pope fired me, and I became an Anglican, an Episcopalian, in order to reinvent worship, the forms of worship, where you can use dance and all of this, I didn't sign the papers saying I'm out of the Catholic Church. I just did an aikido move and slid over. So I belong to all kinds of communities. And it is your job today as a hunter-gatherer to find communities that work for you. The Unity Church works for a lot of recovering Catholics, because it's not about dogma. It is about meditation and mysticism. They really stress that. I get a lot more invitations to speak in Unity churches than I do in any other tradition. It's a time for hunting, and there are many interfaith ministers who are doing good work today.

And that's the point of the times in which we live. No one religion has all the answers. And what that means is, hey, we've got to step up to the plate—*via creativa*. Start creating. What can you contribute? And I do want to say, I'll put this out there, that at Mills College, in a month or so, there's going to be a gathering of people, and it's open to anyone, who want to discuss Creation Spirituality communities, what I call "un-churches." Because these are people, many of whom have graduated from our programs over the years, who have tried to take it back to their churches, and it hasn't really fit or worked for them. So they realize it's time to create Sanghas of a new kind that are not carrying all the burdens that many of our parishes and congregations are dealing with. I think it will be quite exciting because people are coming from all over North America. Many of them have been really trying to create communities within churches of all kinds, and now outside, and they're trying to brainstorm about doing it differently, post-modern forms of communities.

TSOMO: And now we've pretty much run out of time. We were going to do quick closing remarks. I don't know if you have anything that you wanted to say. And then I was going to close with a chant, because I didn't get to do any chanting.

MATT: Good. Well, I look forward to the chant. I think we've all remarked pretty well. Well, quite remarkable. So I want to thank you all for coming and participating. And I especially want to thank Tsomo for coming all the way from Montana and bringing her wisdom and her lineage here. And it's been fun to return to Stanford and do a little sabotage.

TSOMO: And I also thank you all for coming. This was a wonderful group of people who really are thinking on a high level about this, and really wanting to sink their teeth into it, and care about their spiritual lives to the point of coming here and so seriously pursuing this. It was our hope that, through our dialogue and the traditions, that we hoped to bring through, and through your dialoguing in your small groups and just in the larger group together, that all of this contributed to your pursuing of your spiritual paths, and that you have something to take home and further your pursuit.

E: PRACTICE—*Buddhist Chant*

TSOMO: So with that said, I wanted to lead us in the chant, "Om mani peme hung." Does anyone need for me to write that on the board? I'm going to do it with the Tibetan accent. "Om mani peme hung." So this is a sound formula from Sanskrit that is recited by all Tibetans, even if they don't know what they're saying, or haven't studied anything else, they all know "Om mani peme hung." And this is the archetypal sound formula, the mantra that invokes Chenrezig, or otherwise known as Avalokitesvara. Some people may know him by that name. He's often depicted with a thousand arms. He's one of the great bodhisattvas. And so his only intention is benefiting beings. So this ceaseless compassion that is a very quality of the pregnant emptiness of the Dharmakaya, that comes forward into all creation of all the appearances.

This being decided to stop just short of complete enlightenment and melting into the ocean of oneness in order to have enough personal intent to really focus the bodhicitta, the wish to benefit beings, in incredibly skillful ways. He's depicted with a thousand arms fanning around him with all different implements, because he can appear as a fish, or a dog, or whatever, to benefit fish or dogs or whatever. He has many, many tools through which to benefit beings, and can be many places at once, because he's such a great being. We've talked so much about compassion, I thought let's invoke the presence of compassion through this archetype.

So through the sound, and if you could just imagine this white bodhisattva standing there with this fan of a thousand arms and layers, circles and layers around him, and he's got many heads facing different directions, then hopefully that evokes this being of compassion. And let's invoke compassion into the room.

So I'll have to start obviously, because I know the melody, but please everybody join in as soon as you can.

[*Tsomo starts chant.*] "Om mani peme hung." [*Everyone follows.*]

[*Silence*]

TSOMO: So I hope you can feel the presence of bodhicitta in the room. And in the spirit of bodhicitta, let's dedicate the merit of our efforts this weekend to the peace, happiness, and ultimate enlightenment of all beings.

THE JUNG CENTER
HOUSTON, TEXAS

In February of 2008, Lama Tsomo and Matthew Fox were invited to lead a workshop at the Jung Center in Houston, Texas, as part of the Center's 50-year anniversary celebration. The richness of archetypes in both Matt and Tsomo's spiritual traditions made for perfect symbiosis with Jungian ideas—and this audience.

CHAPTER INDEX

Introduction

Day 1

INTRODUCTION: One thing each of these individuals has in common with the other is certain willingness to risk going outside their comfort zone. One of them, Matthew Fox, has, within institutions, outside of institutions, been particularly able to critique and examine the prevailing presumptions of our culture and our institutions to recognize something terribly amiss in our relationship to nature and what the price of desouling nature really means to us in the long run. The other presenter, Lama Tsomo, is a person who has also stepped outside of the paradigm of her origins as well, to explore the radical otherness of nature, particularly to undertake a dialogue with Eastern culture, Eastern practices. Each one in that regard, I humbly think, is courageous; each one of them has been on a pilgrimage; each one of them now returns to share with each of us what they've seen and learned along the way and how some of these insights might be useful to each of us as we explore the meeting point between two worlds, both inner and outer, of the transformations that go on between them and between our relations with each other and with other cultures as well. So would you welcome, please, Matthew Fox and Lama Tsomo.

MATT: Good evening. Thank you, Jim, for your hospitality and inviting us here, and congratulations on your 50th anniversary. As we were driving over here, I heard the news that this is the most alive and most profound Jung center in the entire United States. So I congratulate Houston for that.

I'd like to just give a little map of where we will be going this evening, and then Tsomo will get going. We'll each take about ten minutes to talk in general about archetypes, because archetypes are the language that we'll try to speak in these two days here, and then we're going to go into the archetype of the Buddha Nature from Tsomo, and I'll be talking about the archetype of the Cosmic Christ from the Western tradition. Then we'll move into the archetype of the Divine Feminine. Again, Tsomo will lead and I will follow. I have with me also a little short DVD of the Black Madonna archetype, which I think is really coming back these days. And then we'll be ready for discussion. And I think—[*to Tsomo*] are you throwing in an exercise in here?—a short experiential piece.

We'll have some experiential work tomorrow, but I will be stressing especially the Sacred Masculine. I've just finished a book on that topic. It comes out this year. And I think it's extremely important at this time when the Divine Feminine is returning that men and the masculine archetype itself also get cleaned off, detoxed, and shaken up. So we'll be doing that in the morning. We'll return to the Divine Feminine tomorrow as well because we'll only have a brief look at it this evening. Also, in the afternoon tomorrow, the Sacred Marriage. And again, we'll intersperse some exercises, both from the West and the East, in our time together tomorrow. And there will be time for discussion on these topics, too. So that, in a nutshell, is our little map.

CHAPTER 1

Working with Archetypes

Tsomo: *Vajrayana* is one of three main branches of Buddhism, and it's the one that went to Tibet. It was the last one to be revealed in Buddhism. *Hinayana* was the first one, and that's quite different; it doesn't make so much use of archetypes. *Mahayana*—also very little use of archetypes. But in Vajrayana, there is a pantheon, a richness of many different archetypes that are used quite deeply in practice and with great efficiency. So for thousands of years, and especially since it came to Tibet in the 800s CE, archetypes have been used in such an efficient way on millions of people. They have been refined and refined, these techniques of working with them, to the point that I was really more and more amazed as I went into these practices deeply. I would spend three months at a time in retreat, doing strict retreat from morning until night, and I've done this for years under the close guidance of a lama, Gochen Tulku Rinpoche.

And as I did these more and more, I came to see how they really were effective and efficient at transforming my mind. I was able to bring a lot of these archetypes to the surface, and to detox. And, really, I have to say that the integration that we all are looking for when we go to Jungian analysis was very much possible. I don't think I could have understood what I was doing in these practices if I hadn't had the Jungian background that I'd had. I have a master's degree in counseling psychology, which emphasized Jungian studies, and I did analysis, over the years, with a couple of different analysts, and studied with another analyst personally—and then, of course, the reading and so on. This allowed me to make the bridge so that I could understand really what these practices were doing.

I think I need to give you the context in which they hold these archetypes. It's huge, of course, because we're really talking about an entirely different worldview. Where I think you and I meet right from the start is that they believe not in original sin, but in original purity.

The way they see reality is that there is this great emptiness out of which all appears, and those appearances actually are not real and solid; they are inherently empty. We're talking about two different sides of one coin. We've got the emptiness side and the manifestation, or appearance, side. And modern scientists are verifying this: If you break things down into atoms and then subatomic particles and so on, it gets to the point where they actually found these "items" that were smaller than atoms; they couldn't decide if they should call them waves of light or if they were actual particles. So they refer to them as *wavicles*. This is true. Scientists who wanted to prove that they were waves could do it every time and replicate it. Scientists who wanted to prove they were particles could replicate their experiments anywhere, showing that they were particles. So we're finally getting to the point where we also have to really look at how matter comes to be.

And the understanding that the Buddha had is that there's this ocean of one great awareness. This is not a vacuum. When I say "emptiness," I'm not speaking of a vacuum; I'm speaking of this emptiness that has ultimate power to produce everything that then appears. So the appearances aren't not real; they do appear, yet they are inherently empty. This is a conundrum that we can't easily understand. I'll explain a little bit why we have so much trouble understanding it.

So we've got these two sides of a coin—there's emptiness, and there's *luminosity* as it's sometimes called, this shining forth—and the best way I can talk about it is like waves on an ocean. This ocean, of course, by its nature produces waves, and they're constantly ever changing, so it's very creative. Now what happens when one wave gets mixed up and thinks, "I'm separate from the whole ocean, I'm separate from all the other waves, I'm just me"? This is the ego attachment that you have maybe heard about from the East. It's the first act of delusion, it's the first time that we fall off track because—and it leads to a slippery slope—because once this one wave decides, "Oh,

I'm me, and then there's all the rest of the ocean and everybody else, all the other waves," now it's a very different story. Before, we had no needs because, you know, "I and all"—there's no confusion about it, there's one great awareness, and the waves are really part of the ocean. You can't really separate them. I have no needs if I'm just part of the whole ocean. But if I'm just one wave and I have to protect myself, and I have all these needs because this one wave, of course, now has to worry about gathering all the things it needs—then it's a very different story.

So delusion, also known as *ignorance*, leads to desire, clinging, attachment. The first thing we cling to is our identity: "Oh, I'm me, this one wave." No matter how much trouble that causes us, we cling desperately to it because we're afraid we'll just disappear otherwise; in the act of death we think we're going to just disappear. That's how it feels.

Yet what can happen is we can once again restore our consciousness to the whole ocean.

So the ignorance leads to desire and aversion; we're very busy gathering things to ourselves, and we want to push away other things. We want happiness; we want to push away suffering. If you stop and think about it, every action and thought of ours, almost, so many of them are about pursuing happiness and pushing away suffering.

The Buddha went on his journey in the first place because he could see that everybody wanted to be happy. Nobody wanted to suffer, and yet for some reason we're all miserable so often.

In order to restore the original state, we need to clear away the confusion that has built up since beginningless time when we first fell off track. It's like our windshields are splattered with these misunderstandings that then continue through time and habits of mind over lifetimes. And karma—the weight of karma, the acts that we've committed that leave their trace on our soul—that also occludes, shadows, and colors the windshield and leaves its mark. So when we look through our lens, through our windshield, what we see is not actually the perfect reality that is. You just would not believe how different the true reality is, the pure three *Kayas*, as opposed to what we're seeing right now. So what we need to do is clear that windshield away so that we can see reality as it really is.

The other thing we need to do is to bring forth our Buddha Nature. I said before that we're originally pure because we're just waves on the ocean, and the whole ocean is pure. The only thing that's impure is these confusions that we have in front of our eyes. The Buddha set out many, many methods to help us to clear away the occlusions on the windshield, the *obscurations* as they're called, and to bring forth our internal, true, inherent Buddha Nature.

Getting back to the three Kayas, I mentioned that there's emptiness and luminosity. In the luminosity—or sort of manifestation end of things, the form realm of things—there's another category that's a more fully manifested form. When emptiness is first coming into manifestation, it goes through the *Sambhogakaya*, which means "body of complete enjoyment" in Sanskrit. I just want to give you a little bit of a feel for the first archetypes we come to that are the five wisdoms. The wisdom that is part of the *Dharmakaya*—of course, it's all-knowing—this wisdom divides into five different qualities of primordial wisdom.

The moment we move our focus from the unity of the Dharmakaya to the five wisdoms, we're no longer in Dharmakaya territory; we're speaking of the Sambhogakaya. The wisdom of the Dharmakaya now is like a five-faceted jewel. Wisdom divides into five aspects: the wisdom of basic space, discerning wisdom, mirror-like wisdom, the wisdom of equality, and all-accomplishing wisdom. Now that we're in the area of archetype, the one state of Buddhahood is divided into the same five facets, so that there are five *Dhyani* Buddhas. And each of them represents one of the five wisdoms.

These five Buddhas that are the lords of the five Buddha families, their names are Vairocana, Amitabha, Akshobhya, Ratnasambhava, and Amoghasiddhi, respectively. They each have their own purelands, their Buddhafields, and their consciousness pervades the universe. Since the universe is seen as being holographic, where wouldn't all five of them be? They're all within all of us as well. They and their respective wisdoms are principles of reality. They're each associated with qualities of being, colors, directions, and countless other things. They weave together in ever more complex forms to create all that appears. Because they're not separate from anything, they feel the suffering of all the lost beings just as if it were their own, for it is. Their ultimate compassion that is ceaseless and endless weaves together all that appears.

Of course, because of our warped and splattered lenses, we can't see all this as it really is. We only see our own deluded dream. Not only do things appear in a very warped way, we can only see things on the channel that we're fixated on, and we've lost the channel changer. This is quite a catch-22 then, isn't it? To make matters worse, our habit of seeing in this deluded way is entrenched from eons in seeing in this way. How could there be any hope of finding our way out of this dream?

Well, this was what the Buddha was faced with, and he did find methods to work with us and start with us where we are. We have the five senses. We have the tendency to be driven by archetypes. I'm glad I'm among friends and I can just say that, by the way, and you know what I mean. We have minds that are very busy following discursive thoughts, so in Vajrayana all of those things, and even the passions, the emotions, are used as the grist for the mill of awakening. They're actually used in the techniques. And our subtle energy channels are used. And so on.

I'm going to talk about the five basic categories of afflictive emotion that lead right to the five wisdoms once they're purified through these methods.

Ignorance goes to the wisdom of basic space, which I mentioned before—that's the Buddha family. Desire—once we peel away the layers of drama, we come to discerning wisdom that's actually at the heart of that emotion, and that's the Lotus family. Aversion or aggression—again, once we peel away and get to the true, pure essence, that sharpness of anger becomes actually mirror-like wisdom. So it's that quality that's the essence, and that's the *Vajra* family. Then two subcategories of this last aversion/ aggression category. Pride, in its essence, is equalizing wisdom, which is the Jewel family. Once we stop identifying with the ego, and there's just this sort of generalized pride, then it's identified with the whole universe, then it's equalizing wisdom, that all is equalized on an exalted level. And the last one is jealousy, which is actually at its heart all-accomplishing wisdom, and that's the family of Enlightened Activity.

When I first began studying Jungian studies, I was told that we can't perceive the archetypes directly; we've lost the channel changer to the Sambhogakaya level. But through these techniques, slowly, slowly, it's more and more possible to experience these archetypes, to bring them to the surface rather than having them driving us from the unconscious. Integration is possible, and purifying our vision is possible.

MATT: I was struck by what Tsomo said about how we get out of the dream, out of the illusion. For me that is the real value of archetypes in general, that they wake us up. They rock us. And with different cultural moments, different archetypes rise. They rise in our own dreams. They rise in our own psyches, in our own needs, and in those around us. I think, for example, what we'll be talking about very shortly—the return of the goddess today, the return of the Divine Feminine—is an archetype that was surely overdue after three or four hundred years of excessive patriarchy. And the archetype we'll be talking about tomorrow—the return of the Sacred Masculine—is overdue for the same reason. For me, archetypes contain a lot of energy. They are like the prophetic unconscious.

As Rabbi Heschel says, the work of the prophet is to interfere. I think archetypes arise to interfere and to set us on different courses, different directions. Now, Jung himself said this. He said [parphrasing], "An archetype will reappear in a new form to redress imbalances in society at a particular time when it is needed." That's certainly my experience of archetype: that they're very active, they're very energetic, and they're not neutral. I would say that a good artist is a fisher of archetypes. And I deliberately use the word *fisher* because fishing means going down and bringing up from the depths and bringing up from the mystery, from the unclear and the unknown and the unorganized and the chaos of what is deep. Whether one is an artist, a musician, or a dramatist, a novelist, a painter, a ritualist, I think that authentic art is stirring the depths like that and bringing up archetypes. And these are the brow chakra, where we bring together the right and left hemisphere of our brain, and with the third eye.

Meister Eckhart says, "The eye with which I see God is the same eye with which God sees me." So being hit between the eyes is a God experience. And of course part of the shake-up of archetypes, too, is just what do we mean by "God"? And can we come up with better names than "God," especially if the name "God" is carrying a lot of unnecessary baggage. Meister Eckhart once said, "I pray God to rid me of God." It's one of the more profound prayers that I've ever heard uttered by a Christian. And I think we're going through that as a species and as a culture at this moment in history. So even the God archetype has to wake up and shake us up and be shaken up. As I say, an archetype rocks us.

Now, there's a wonderful passage in Marion Woodman, I think it's Marion Woodman[17], that names this power in a wonderful way, and I want to share that with you. She says that an archetype is bodily, it stirs the sounds, the words, the breath, and [paraphrasing], "its language is bound in the bodily source in the mother's body. Language has rhythm, breaths, and sounds." She thinks that archetypes affect the cells of our bodies and take us back to that immediate presence that we had as children and even in the womb. And she says [paraphrasing], "An archetype is an energy field like a magnet onto which we project images. If metaphorically speaking the complex is carrying 1,000 volts of energy, at its core the archetype carries 100,000 volts." So that says it, with a great image, that archetypes essentially are not neutral. They are like hundred-thousand-volt experiences.

With that in mind then, with that awareness, we realize that, given the reality of our species today, that on the course we are traveling, we are not sustainable. We are not sustainable. We have to look around and say, using Tsomo's tradition, how do we wake up from this dream? How do we really move profoundly? And tapping into archetypes, and then acting on that, is a profound way to be moved. I sat down with a very renowned scientist from Stanford a year and a half ago, and I'll never forget a sentence that came out of his mouth. He said, "We are the first species that can choose not to go extinct." Four and a half billion years on this planet, and we are the first species to come along that can choose not to go extinct. "But," he said, "of course, we haven't chosen that yet." So there we come down to the nose, you know, how do you wake people up? How do we move from not choosing to wallowing in what Tsomo named as addiction and comfort and all of it into that era of being and acting that is actually going to sustain our species and the species who are being dragged down with us at this time? I think that archetypal shifting is one such very important practice. And I like very much how you spoke about, in your tradition, that there's a practice of playing with the archetypes themselves.

---

17. Marion Woodman, *Addiction to Perfection: The Still Unravished Bride: A Psychological Study (Studies in Jungian Psychology by Jungian Analysts)* (Inner City Books, 1997)

CHAPTER 2

Cosmic Christ Archetype

MATT: So now we're going to turn to the archetype of the Buddha Nature. Okay, followed by the Cosmic Christ, which is very parallel.

TSOMO: Yes. What if we start with the Cosmic Christ? You're on a roll, so . . .

MATT: Am I on a roll? You want to start that way? Well, okay. It's just that I was really glad to hear about the Buddha Nature because I've been telling Westerners, "Hey, if you don't get the Cosmic Christ, call it the Buddha Nature. It's the same thing." And of course that's so true, you know. As we rub elbows more and more with the global spiritual traditions, the more I learn how much we have in common.

The Dalai Lama says the number one obstacle to interfaith is a bad relationship with one's own faith tradition. And I propose that most Christians don't have a clue about their faith tradition. What they have is a lot of literal pieces pulled from the Bible or pulled from papal encyclicals, and it doesn't add up to the magic of the story. How this fisherman, or gatherer of fishermen, this peasant—we know he was a peasant—from Galilee ended up stirring history two thousand years ago is an astounding story. And, as I say, so rich are the archetypes in Christianity that not even the Church has been able to kill it. It's tried mightily, it's tried mightily, but it can't kill it because it is an absolute field of profound archetypes. And let me be concrete.

In December I did a public dialogue with Rabbi Michael Lerner on Hanukkah and Christmas. There were many Jewish people there, and Michael spoke first. I wanted to speak about Christmas, but without offending anybody, so I went back to the stories about Christmas. And they are stories. This is not the historical Jesus stuff; no one was there. They're stories of the Cosmic Christ because the Cosmic Christ is about the experience, the breakthrough of the Divine, the light. You use the word *light*. It is about the light in all beings that is the Divine presence in all beings. So every atom, we now know, has photons, light waves, and that's the Cosmic Christ. John: 1 says, "Christ is the light is all things." Pretty simple.

I gathered 12 or 15 archetypes just from the Christmas stories. Archetypes like the child, the Divine Child, in all of us, being born in all of us. The manger, the simplicity of it—to experience the Divine in you, you have to get back to your simplicity, back to the manger, back to your pure origins, or what I call *original blessing*, original purity. We have to make that journey back, and it will include the animals gathering around the manger because the animals are there. As Thomas Merton, the Catholic monk, said, "Every non-two-legged creature is a saint." Remember that the next time you're about to swat a mosquito. So the holiness of animals, the lack of pretension: Bears are busy being bears, and whales are busy being whales. It's only humans who go wandering off from being human. And that's why we need the Buddhas and the Isaiahs and the Jesuses and the Mohammeds to wake us up and shake us up and begin a return for us.

So the Christ is the light, the Cosmic Christ is the light in all things. Interestingly, Tsomo talked about light as wave and particle. And actually that, to me, just fits perfectly with this tradition that Jesus is a particle. You are a particle. You have your history, you have your DNA, you have your days on Earth. Buddha, the historical Buddha, was a particle, too. But Buddha set off something, and we call that the *living Buddha* perhaps. And in the West, we may call it the *living Christ*, or the *spirit of Christ*, or the *resurrected Christ*—same concept. Jesus is one thing, but what he unleashed is something else. One thing he unleashed was that the early writers of the Christian texts, they put all these words into Jesus's mouth. They got so excited they just stuffed his mouth with their words. They were brilliant words. But they didn't come from Jesus. They put them in his mouth because there was this fire ignited. We call it *Pentecost* in the West, but a fire was ignited in the social imagination, or to put it in Jungian terms, the archetype was ablaze.

The Cosmic Christ is intimate to each of us, and yet it is also the vastness. In the passages from Wisdom literature, which is Cosmic Christ, and is cosmic wisdom in Israel, they talk about how "wisdom holds everything together in the heavens and on the earth". That's the pattern that holds everything together, the pattern that connects. That is the Christ. That is the Christ Nature, that's the Cosmic Christ, or that's the Buddha Nature. The name you give it is not what's important. It is the relationship that matters, that we see not just our individual particle stories, and as you were saying, not just that individual wave, but the cosmic wave. And of course science is just flooding us today with its discovery of the vastness of this wave. No generation has known what we know today, that there are hundreds of billions of galaxies.[18] Newton thought that there was one galaxy. One galaxy! And he thought the stars were the biggest thing around. He didn't have a clue about supernovas or the billions of galaxies. Everyone in this room is a lot smarter than Newton, but how this shakes up our religious consciousness, you see. Now the Cosmic Christ takes on depth, breadth, hugeness.

The Christ is not just the light in all beings, it is also the wounds in all beings. And that's very important, that the Christ got crucified. The Christ is being crucified today when the rain forests are being destroyed, or the polar bears, or the soil, or the ozone. The Christ is being crucified all over again, and that's very important, and it's very Buddhist—the awareness of the suffering. To name the suffering with archetype, with language, with metaphors that stir, so the ecological collapse in which our species not only finds itself, but in fact is in great part responsible, this is a moment for the return of the Cosmic Christ or the Buddha Nature. We have to rediscover it in the depths of our hearts, souls, and ultimately our institutions, that original purity, the beauty of this planet, the beauty that is being destroyed when a species disappears. And today, one fourth of mammals on the planet are in the process of disappearing. And when a species disappears, it disappears forever. An extinction is an extinction. So that's why we're at this critical moment in history when these archetypes of vast power are re-emerging: the Cosmic Christ and the Buddha Nature.

17. Two summers ago, several years after this dialog, we learned the universe is two trillion galaxies large, each with hundreds of billions of stars.

CHAPTER 3

The Buddha Nature

TSOMO: First I just want to respond a little bit to all these things that got kindled in me from your fiery . . .

MATT: Ah, good.

TSOMO: In the Buddhist view, to have a human birth is a very rare and precious thing, and it's also a high-risk venture. Of all the beings that there are in the universe, most of them are in realms that we can't perceive, though the Buddha was able to perceive since his consciousness was the whole ocean of reality. And if we have been incarnating and reincarnating since beginningless time, then we have been mosquitoes, germs, fish, dogs, and lots of other beings that I won't even bother naming because you guys probably haven't heard of them. And remember, we've lost the channel changer so we can't change to those channels and see them. So in the Buddhist view I don't know that animals would really be saints; if we think about it, in the lifetimes that we were animals, we didn't have the capacity for self-reflection and the choice that you speak of. This is both wonderful and terrible. It's true that the family dog seems like more of a saint than the family, but while one is incarnated as a dog, one is also much less capable of the self-reflection required to reach enlightenment, to do the things I was talking about before, to clear away the obscurations to our vision of reality and to bring forth our Buddha Nature.

So it's a high-risk game, but it's also a powerfully positive one if done right. And that's why we need the Buddha Nature and the

Cosmic Christ to come forward in these incarnations that people can see. Remember, we don't have the channel changer, so the Cosmic Christ is all around us; we're bathing in it and we *are* it, too. We just forgot. We're also Buddha Nature, and we forgot. And the Buddha was so moved by watching the churning of beings by the billions and billions, countless beings in so many worlds and realms of reality, churning for countless lifetimes around and around, running after the things they want, pushing away the things they don't want, and causing more misery for themselves in the process, planting seeds that then they reap. And I think there's something about sowing and reaping in your tradition.

MATT: Karma.

TSOMO: Yeah, they have the karma that they talk about in the East, and of course it's very similar. So the Buddha was deeply moved by seeing all of this suffering. In one sense it's needless because these beings are already the Buddha; it's all one great pure mind filled with what is called, in our tradition, *spontaneous presence*, which I think corresponds with some of what you were talking about. This luminosity is pouring forth from the emptiness, and all of the three Kayas are actually pure and beautiful and perfect, but we can't see it that way.

This is why the lama is so important in my tradition of Vajrayana Buddhism, because the lama of course also is essentially Buddha Nature, as are we, but he's far less occluded. He or she has done specific practices and often, as in the case of my root lama, for lifetimes, so that I'm able to perceive the Buddha Nature more easily in my contact with him. Because I don't have the channel changer, it's hard for me to look at these depictions of the archetypes and have the same experience. It's through the lama that we can experience the Buddha Nature of the various deities. Of course, there's really only one Buddha Nature; it just has many, many faces. There are a hundred peaceful and wrathful deities that we meet in the *bardo* right after we die. They're all deities, they're all perfect Buddhas, and they all have slightly different qualities. Some of them are wrathful, even though they're pure Buddhas and they're only acting out of compassion, but sometimes we don't listen to the peaceful means, so the wrathful deities then come. First, we experience one after another of the peaceful deities, then we experience one after another of the wrathful deities, and then our journey goes on.

So, the way my lama described it was it's like you have a perfect lamp, and the light bulb works. If you want to turn it on, you're going to have to plug it into the wall. The wall plug connects you to the power company, some great source of power. So when we do these practices, or we think of these deities, we connect to them through the lama we've met, who actually personifies them for us. So that's our archetypal image that hopefully holds the luminosity and so on, and then is like the wall plug that connects us to the full power source. Whether or not the practice works actually depends entirely on how well we can get past ourselves, connect, through the wall plug of the lama, and then be open to the pure, unlimited power and compassion of these enlightened beings, or Buddha Mind, Buddha Nature.

In practice then, let me give you an example. There's a famous master and student. Tilopa was the master, and Naropa was the student. And Naropa left his very nice life as a scholar behind and went tromping off in the wilds with this wild and crazy yogi named Tilopa. He followed him around, and learned and learned from him, and was deeply devoted to him. Well, he had been doing one deity practice and the deity was, of course, this very powerful and enlightened being. And one day as they were sort of going along, this being appears above and in front of him in the sky, and they can both see it. It's just really manifesting there. And, of course, Naropa was astonished. And Tilopa said, "Quick, who will you prostrate to?" And, of course, Naropa immediately prostrated to this deity he finally was seeing. Tilopa said, "Wrong," and he vanished. Naropa had to search for him for years in the wilds, camping out everywhere, until he finally could find him again. That was the wrong answer. He needed to prostrate to his guru, who was the gateway through which he could experience the deity.

So the lama is seen as the gathering of all the Buddhas in that way, and any of the deities that we spend time with and evoke and invoke, they all, at their essence, are Buddha Nature. Now we always project this image in Vajrayana meditation and relate to it, have this whole experience, and then dissolve it back in. That's always the way it goes. And this is to help the mind in years of experience to understand that we have all of the deities and perfect Buddha Nature within us. We just don't see it, so we have to have this whole drama go on until we can finally get it eventually: "Oh, that's me, too. It's all this, even me."

MATT: So that sense of immanence. It's rediscovery of the sense of immanence, of finding the Divine within, and our own Buddha Nature within, and how it connects to the external world, to others, which is, I suppose, the path of compassion.

TSOMO: Yes, this is getting into ultimate truth and relative truth. Once we come to ultimate truth, then there's ultimate compassion because there's no separation.

MATT: So the Buddha Nature in me is responding to the Buddha Nature in you out of empathy and out of joy, in your suffering and in your joy.

TSOMO: All of these waves on the ocean, this creation, is referred to as "the play" of Buddha Mind.

MATT: Yeah. That's nice. Yeah. That's interesting, too, because I alluded to the Cosmic Christ really coming from Israel's sense of cosmic wisdom. And in the Jewish scriptures Wisdom "plays" in the universe. She plays, and out of this play is born creation itself. And, of course, Jung said [paraphrasing], "There's no creativity without play." So the whole process of the Buddha Nature, and the Cosmic Christ, it's not about a noun. It's not about something sitting there. It's about the unfolding of creativity itself. It's the unfolding of the universe—both our perception of it, but what we bring to it in this lifetime, as you would say, in this incarnation. So, and this is in a language, again, of the early Christians about a new creation, you know. Creation is constantly being made new by this, this newness in the new forms that the Buddha Nature or the Cosmic Christ takes on.

TSOMO: Yeah, so the waves are never the same twice.

MATT: There you go.

TSOMO: The pattern of the waves on the ocean, never the same twice. So . . .

MATT: . . . boredom is not possible.

TSOMO: Not if we're paying attention.

MATT: We've eliminated the word *boredom* from our vocabulary if you're paying attention to the extent that you're paying attention; to the extent that you're awake. And this is what Jesus meant by saying "the kingdom and queendom of God are, is, among you". Not will be, not has been, *but is there*. But are we seeing it in the Gospel of Thomas, it says that the kingdom is spread across the world, but you don't see it. Very Buddhist idea.

TSOMO: Yeah, well, where isn't it actually?

MATT: Exactly. Where isn't it?

TSOMO: And where isn't this or that archetype? I think then we were going to move to the Divine Feminine, and you gave me a great segue. Thank you.

MATT: Oh great. I love to do that.

CHAPTER 4

The Great Mother

TSOMO: So I'm going to speak of the Yum Chenmo, Great Mother. This is the best we can do for evoking something that's really beyond thoughts, beyond words, and beyond concepts because this is the great emptiness out of which all of the Buddhas come. She's the mother of all the Buddhas, and she's known as Prajnaparamita, Perfect Wisdom. She's beyond time. She's completely pure. In this context that we're speaking of, she's beyond form. So everything issues from her—and this is why she is the mother of all the Buddhas, of course. As I said before, luminosity emerges from emptiness, so then we have to see the emptiness as the Great Mother. This emptiness is, again, not a vacuum; it's this pregnant emptiness that's constantly issuing forth all form, thought forms. Archetypes are forms, too, and, of course, the forms that we know of as solid forms.

She has been depicted over time because we're fixated in this form level and we need something to evoke for us that sense of this Great Mother of all. In this country we are finally going to have a pilgrimage site where people can come and experience this. There's the Garden of One Thousand Buddhas that Gochen Tulku Rinpoche, my teacher, has decided to create. He said, "Why should we have all of the relics and all of the pilgrimage sites in Asia? Let's have something in America where people can come and be inspired." And the understanding that they have is that through sacred architecture, through archetypal forms, we can actually have the seeds of enlightenment planted within us. And not just we humans, but the animals passing by—the bugs that land on her and fly by, the wind blowing past her—because there are relics inside of her and the whole statue was produced in a very particular way. It's over twenty-five feet tall. It's quite large. And then around her are the thousand Buddhas of this eon in the shape of a wheel, a *Dharma* wheel, with spokes, and they're all along the spokes. They're only about this high, so you get the sense of the great emptiness out of which these thousand Buddhas come. And, of course, there will be flowers and trees and places to walk. The statue is there, and we're slowly but surely making these thousand Buddhas, and we'll eventually then set all that into place.

I want to mention something called the "overtone series" in music. This is a law of physics that within a note on the piano, let's say, it isn't just the note that we hear, but there are overtones. The string isn't just sort of bowing this way and that way as it vibrates. There's actually quite a complex mathematical formula for figuring out how it's dividing into many subdivisions of vibration. And each human's voice has a different map of overtones, which are strongest and weakest, so that we can actually distinguish a person just as accurately through their voice imprint, if we get the overtones, as we can through fingerprints.

Let's say we hit C down near the base of the piano; then C an octave higher naturally would sound if we take the dampers off. It naturally just begins to vibrate in sympathy. The next note is G, which is a perfect fifth, and that was used a lot in Gregorian chants—a lot of octaves and fifths. So then we get the next C, then we get E. Now C, G, and E, if anybody knows music, are your basic major chord, and that is the basis of Western music—after Gregorian chants, they added the third interval.

Like that, Prajnaparamita, the Great Mother, as she then manifests into form, there's a higher octave of that. The next octave up, the next overtone up, would be Green Tara, whom we see in the center of this *thangka*. So she is associated with many of those qualities as well. She's also the Savioress, and we'll go much more into this tomorrow and have an experience with her. If you go to higher overtones of her, then you get the Twenty-One Taras that you see around her of all different colors. And they're different, holding different implements, and they can be both peaceful and wrathful, and are quite powerful, and have different qualities. So people will pray to different ones in order to evoke those qualities and invoke the power of that archetype in their lives.

A: PRACTICE—*Buddhist Aah Chant*

So now I just wanted to give us a short experience, hopefully of the fundamental, but this is, of course, a high hope since we're all lost in *Samsara*. I'm sorry about that. So we will use sound to do this. The original sound out of which all others come is the sound that babies first make, which is "aah." So we will just sit and say this for a few times, or chant this, and hopefully that'll bring back our memories of home.

[*Everyone chants together.*] "Aah . . ."

TSOMO: Now silence.

[*silence*]

TSOMO: So, hopefully, you had just a glimpse in a moment between thoughts—maybe a glimpse of Prajnaparamita, Yum Chenmo.

MATT: I think it's so interesting that so many Divine names around the world have that sound in them. When you think about it: Yahweh, Buddha, Krishna, Abba, which was Jesus's favorite name for God . . .

TSOMO: It means father.

MATT: . . . Allah, you know, so it's interesting that you say that's the first sound of the baby. It's the return to our origins just to chant those sounds. And, of course, "ma," which is a Hindu way of invoking the Divine Mother.

So when I think of the Divine Feminine and the Divine Mother, what Tsomo has been talking about, the idea of the Great Mother being the great emptiness from which all things flow, well, there is a parallel teaching in the West, and that is the idea of the Godhead. The person who's spoken the most richly about the Godhead is Meister Eckhart, fourteenth-century Dominican mystic. He spoke Latin and German, and in his languages, *Godhead* is feminine. *Gotheit* in German and *Deitas* in Latin. Both feminine. So "God" was *Got*, masculine, in German. And *Deus*, "God" in Latin, was masculine. The Godhead has been totally ignored for centuries. I doubt if any seminarian in North America has ever heard three sentences about the Godhead.

But this goes with the banishing of the Great Mother and of the Divine Feminine. We have to bring the balance back. And Eckhart is brilliant in his laying out of the Godhead, but it's so close to what you're talking about. He says God is about history; Godhead is about mystery. That all things emerged from the Godhead is precisely the Christian teaching. And we return to the Godhead. God is about history, and that's why we're talking a lot about God because we're always messed up by history, and we're messing up making history. The whole salvation history in Western religion since Augustine has banished the Godhead. Because the image I have of the Godhead when I meditate on it is a great big, Cosmic Mama, with the universe on her lap, you see. It's about being, not doing. God is about acting says, says Eckhart, but Godhead is about being. All mysticism is about being; it's about a return to the level of being. And then our action comes from our being. In the East, they may say the action comes from non-action. Which is to say, I think, in Western terms, from being— from the Godhead.

But Eckhart has this brilliant sermon, it's his third sermon in, in my book on, that has 36 of Eckhart's sermons called, it was originally called *Breakthrough*, now it's called something about . . . What is it? *Passion for Earth . . . ?*

Tsomo: *Passion for Creation.*

Matt: That's it, thank you. Something like that. Thank you very much.

Tsomo: He made me read it.

MATT: [*Chuckles*] It's about how we flow out from the Godhead, and then we return to the Godhead not only when we die, but when we meditate. Along the way, we can return to the Godhead at any moment we want, we choose. That's when you get refreshed and that's why you feel young again. As Eckhart says, "I'm younger today than I was yesterday. If I'm not younger tomorrow than I am today, I'll be ashamed of myself." To return to God is to become young again. He says that's why the Bible begins with the words "In the beginning," the Hebrew Bible, Genesis. And then in John's Gospel in the Christian gospels, "In the beginning." Because, he says, God is always in the beginning, God is always in the beginning. God is *novissimus*—the youngest being in the universe. And to return to that youthfulness is precisely what refreshment is.

Now, that's one dimension of the Divine Feminine in the West, the Godhead. And there are many. But another one, in two sentences, very briefly, is of course the return of Gaia, the return of Mother Earth—our growing awareness of Mother Earth, and what she's suffering today. As I say, the Goddess has returned, and she's pissed. And of course you brought this out, too, the fierceness of the Divine Feminine. The Divine Feminine is not just about being sweet and motherly all the time; it's also about being fierce, fierce. Kali with the skulls around her neck. There's a fierceness to the Divine Feminine. Robert Bly has a brilliant passage on that in his dialogues with Miriam Woodman. He says, you go to the biggest shopping mall in America, which is outside St. Paul, where he lives in Minnesota, and they have a Snoopy there that's—talk about twenty-five-foot statues— it's a fifty-foot statue or something, this huge idol. He says they shouldn't have Snoopy there; they should have Kali with the skulls around her neck. Because the religion of consumerism, the idolatry of consumerism, is eating us up. And that's the first side of the Divine Feminine, the Divine Mother. And I think he's 100 percent right about that. We have to start naming what the religion of consumerism is doing to our souls, and those of our children. To say nothing of our entire economic system and why it's so unjust, not only in our country, but around the world.

The third example of the Divine Feminine archetype is that of the Black Madonna. I've written a solid article; you can go to my web page. It's there for free, matthewfox.org, on the Black Madonna. But I just want to point out a few things. She's coming back, and she's coming back with power today. All kinds of people I'm meeting are having dreams or encounters with the Black Madonna. Because the Black Madonna is also the Brown Madonna of Guadalupe. Our Lady of Guadalupe is the Black Madonna traditionally, and Pele, and so forth. And of course the Black Madonna is found in so many places: Czechoslovakia, Russia, Poland, Germany.

TSOMO: If I could just jump in here and say that my lama went to Hawaii, and when he heard about Pele, he said, "Oh, in our scriptures, Palden Lhamo," who's one of the great deities. She is a protectoress and blue and fierce, and has many of the qualities of Pele. It's exactly what they wrote about, and he thinks it's the same archetype.

MATT: There you go. There's so many dimensions to the Black Madonna archetype. I named 12 in my article, but just to point out a couple, one is, of course, darkness. And when you think about it, the call to darkness is a call to depth. Meister Eckhart says, "The ground of your soul is dark." The ground of the soul is dark. We're afraid of the dark, the enlightenment has left us all in the light. We can flip a switch and we can live oblivious of the dark. To return to the dark, the depths, the mystery of your own soul is. the work of the Black Madonna. The depths of land are dark, the soil down there: It's dark. The depths of the ocean are dark. The depths of the sky are dark. I've talked to cosmonauts and astronauts, and they had these mystical experiences going out into space. And the reason was, they told me, the silence and the darkness. And I sat down and figured it out: It took 42 million dollars to turn these jet pilot fighters into mystics. There must be a cheaper way. I think Buddha's developed some other ways, and so did Jesus and some others over the years. But the point is that the darkness is so much a part of living deeply.

The opposite is living on the surface—superficially, externally. This is a common archetype in all mystical writing about the inner person: that the Christ is within, the Buddha is within, not on the surface someplace. So the honoring of the darkness, even the whole issue of racism comes up here. You know, that the Divine is found in the dark. And, of course, now we're finding that even those of us with white skin, we all come from Africa.

What I'd like to do is show you a few of her images from around the world, and there's some nice music with it, too. The fact that, of course, in our own country people of color are rapidly outnumbering Caucasians is also, I think, part of the return of the Black Madonna. It's a scandal how little Christians know about the Black Madonna. When I first met the Black Madonna, I never heard of her. I come from Wisconsin. I was studying in France and wandered into Chartres Cathedral and saw this statue. And I just stared and stared, and I said, "This is amazing. What is this? No one told me about this." I turned to a French woman who was at Chartres. I said, "What is this?" "Oh," she said, "that's centuries of candle wax that have turned the statue black." And I looked at her and I looked at the statue, I looked at her and I looked at the statue, and I said, "I don't think so. There are other statues here that aren't black." So this French person—and, of course, France is where the Black Madonna's been most alive in Western culture—she was totally out of touch with her own tradition. She didn't have a clue. She thought it was about ashes and candles, so it's a scandal. It's what the Dalai Lama says: "The number one obstacle to interfaith is a bad relationship to your own faith tradition."

[*Music starts for images.*]

MATT: The Black Madonna holds, she celebrates. She also grieves. She is also a trickster at times. And, of course, she comes from Africa. Isis, the oldest shrine in the West of the Black Madonna, is third century, it's in Sicily—a hop, skip, and jump from Africa.

Isis is often pictured with the Divine Son on her lap. So this adaptation in Christianity, especially medieval Christianity, is very striking.

[*Music stops.*]

TSOMO: Wisdom being in the heart of the Black Madonna, that really struck me, because in Vajrayana practices, when we do a *sadhana* to a particular deity, we invoke first the pledge being. But then we do a second invoking of the wisdom being, which is in our heart. We imagine ourselves as the pledge being, and then there's the wisdom being in our hearts. And so it looks like that. It's very interesting.

MATT: Yeah. The sacred heart of the Great Mother.

TSOMO: And the honorific word for heart and mind is the same word.

MATT: Boy, Descartes took us a great distance from that, didn't he? We separated the two.

TSOMO: Yeah. I actually told this Tibetan nun who is a friend of mine that Westerners believe that the mind is in the brain, and she looked at me and she said, "Really?" And I said, "Yeah, we really think so." And she kind of laughed, embarrassedly.

MATT: Yeah, embarrassed for us.

TSOMO: "Do you really think that?" She's thinking, "These natives."

MATT: In Judaism, the mind is in the heart. And Thomas Aquinas said the proper objects of the heart are truth and justice. So we've not always felt that. Again, that's Descartes, that's the modern era, that we've shoved the mind into the head. But the truth is that our spiritual course, in Jewish tradition, and our deepest Christian thinkers like Aquinas, they put the mind in the heart. That's what wisdom is, you see? That's why what we have in the West today is lots of knowledge and no wisdom. And that's part of the return to the Divine Feminine, wisdom around the world is feminine, and certainly in the Scriptures: Hokhma in the Jewish tradition, and Sophia in the tradition of the Cosmic Christ. And now the latest scholarship on the historical Jesus says that he comes from the Wisdom tradition of Israel. So all that is the feminist tradition. But, of course, for three or four hundred years we tried to pretend there wasn't such a thing because we were so busy creating a patriarchal culture.

TSOMO: And we separated ourselves from our own bodies in the process; mind over matter, matter, matter.

MATT: Exactly, exactly. Yes, sir. We are at the point now of discussion, right?

TSOMO: Yes, absolutely.

MATT: Great.

STUDENT: *If truth and luminosity was synonymous, and the Black Madonna had the third eye and was in herself luminous, why is she depicted black?*

MATT: Well, I'd say, first of all she comes from Africa, and as I said, black is luminous, you know. Luminosity through darkness.

TSOMO: It's the source of luminosity.

MATT: And the source of luminosity. That's right. Light comes from darkness.

TSOMO: I just might mention that the dark-colored depiction of the primordial Buddha, it's always a deep, deep black-blue because he's just barely showing his form, because he's actually coming from a place of emptiness.

MATT: So what is formless is black, is dark.

TSOMO: This deep emptiness. Exactly.

MATT: Remember Jung said this—and I realize I'm in a Jung house here—one of his most important observations. He said [paraphrasing], "Ignatius of Loyola had no *via negativa*." Now, what he's really saying is that the entire modern era had no *via negativa*. What is the *via negativa*? It is the experience of the Divine darkness, the divinity of the dark. And it literally means "the negative way." But it's not just about suffering. It's about darkness. You go into the darkness to find connections. For example: a sweat lodge. How many people here have been in a sweat lodge? A sweat lodge is dark, right? And there's a communion experience in there. In fact, it's a return to the womb. The womb is dark. We were all there for nine months. Things were pretty good for us. So, we begin in the dark. We were luminous, but we were in the dark—and not just luminous, but numinous. That's what the teaching of the Cosmic Christ is about, that we all radiate the numinosity of the Divine. But don't think that that means you're running around with neon lights on you. You radiate beauty and luminosity and numinosity in the dark as well as in the light.

TSOMO: [*To a questioner*] Yes.

STUDENT: *What do you mean by going into "the dark"?*

MATT: [*To Tsomo*] I'm sure your tradition has a lot to say about this. Do you want me to go first? Going into the darkness can mean going into silence. You see, darkness is not just the absence of light; it's the absence of distraction. Really, what you were talking about earlier tonight: all the tantalizing, titillating distractions. Silence is a darkness because it's an absence of images. Of course, suffering is a darkness. We can be in the dark night of the soul, for example. And, in fact, I believe our species today is in a collective dark night. We don't know the way. We don't know what's happening next. We're on new territory today. Just the eco-crisis itself is something profoundly new, really, and it's immense chaos.

Chaos is another experience of darkness. Today's science is finally back on board with ancient wisdom that chaos is integral to birth, it's integral to creativity, and it's integral to all of nature's processes and to creation itself. So we have to learn not to be afraid of chaos, but to ride the waves of chaos. So I fully agree; darkness itself is an archetype, but, as so many, it's so rich, and there are many, many expressions or forms that it takes. And, of course, just literally being the dark. As I say, like in a sweat lodge, everything shifts because we're not operating with our eyes, which need light. So in the dark, your skin, your tactile senses become more important, your hearing becomes more important.

You see, the modern era was all about light, because it was all about the printing press, and you can't read in the dark. This is why we call it the "enlightenment." We have to balance the light with the dark. Look how nature is. Nature doesn't run just on light. That's why it turns off the lights at night, but we keep them on with electricity and neon lights and everything. Darkness is about meditation. I think meditation takes you into the dark because it stops the input.

Tsomo: Actually, there is a tradition in Tibet of the dark retreat, and people usually only can do it for about a week. It's very intensive. They build a special dark retreat hut, and they go in there, and there is absolutely no light—none whatsoever. And what people find is that in the absence of images to be able to see, there's no reference, and of course it is quiet, then they're thrown back on their own minds, and it becomes very clear that their minds are producing everything. It's a very short path to high levels of enlightenment, and it's also really scary because you encounter your own demons, your own deities. It's like going into the bardo without dying.

Matt: That's really interesting. And you're in there alone, are you?

Tsomo: Yeah.

MATT: So there's no talking either, right?

TSOMO: None whatsoever. It's completely silent.

STUDENT: *No other body either, no other energy.*

TSOMO: No other body unless a mouse gets in.

MATT: That reminds me of a vision quest I did with the Native Americans years ago, where you're up all night outdoors in the darkness. The night I was doing it, it was raining, so it was very dark. But what happened was, the whole forest became illuminated. It was an amazing experience; alone in the dark, and all of a sudden the leaves started taking on the forms of animal spirits and so forth, and it was amazing. I think that happens in these huts.

TSOMO: Oh yeah, there's quite a show. You can see quite a lot.

MATT: Exactly. Better turn off the lights to really see the show.

TSOMO: It is clearly, that is obviously, the display of your own mind. Normally it isn't so obvious.

MATT: Well, that's not what my native teacher told me. No. What he said was all those beings that came lived on this land at one time. Now that, in your language, would be reincarnation. And he said, "They are reappearing to support you." He said, "Human beings will not always support your courage and theology, but the animals are supporting you." So he said these were real spirits returning. I saw bears, I saw snakes, I saw dinosaurs—it was amazing. And he said, "Well, all these lived here at one time, and this is their home."

TSOMO: Well, yes, and it's like the way I had to answer one student who said, "Okay, these deities, you know, that's all very great, and they're very powerful and everything, but are they really real?" And my answer, the only one I could think of, was to say, "They're as real as you are."

MATT: Which is quite relative in Buddhist language.

TSOMO: Yes, because we're all apparitions, actually. So the animals, the first time around, while they were incarnating, were also apparitions with empty nature.

MATT: Although if you met one and he was hungry, it would be more than an apparition.

TSOMO: I'd be searching like crazy for the channel changer, but I wouldn't find it! That's the problem.

I just want to mention one thing that I think is important to all of this discussion, which is the understanding of the two truths in Buddhism. There's ultimate truth, which I've spoken of—true reality, which is this ocean of oneness that's throwing up all these waves of apparitions, appearances in the play of that and so on. That's what the Buddha saw. But then there's relative reality, which is the one where I think I'm me and I think there's a bear chasing me, and I think I die when he comes and eats me. You can't fall to one side or the other and just say there's only this emptiness, and this other is just apparitions, and we don't have to pay attention to it, and so karma doesn't really exist either, and we can do whatever we want. People have fallen into that mistake. But the truth is that we can't fall to the side of relative reality—"relative" because to a fish, water is something very different than it is to us, for example. So the unchanging true reality of ultimate truth, we can't fall to just that side or just relative reality, but rather it's this ongoing *koan* of seeing both: seeing emptiness and luminosity all at the same time, and seeing relative and ultimate truth all at the same time. This is what we strive for in our meditation practices. I just wanted to mention that as we talk about Buddha Nature and so on.

MATT: Is that a little bit like seeing the particle and the wave?

TSOMO: A little bit like that. And the emptiness in between. In between the proton and electron, there's the same proportional distance as between the sun and the planets. So there's a lot of space in between what we think are particles.

MATT: Other comments or questions? Yes.

STUDENT: *I don't understand a problematic thing for me. The Gospel of John saying of Jesus being the only way to God—that was made manifested differently when you were talking about the student and the master. When you were talking of that tale, it did a flip for me so that for those of that tradition, that is true. I was wondering if you could comment on John's saying the way to truth and the light, against the nuancing of the story of the master and the student.*

MATT: Well, again, those are not words from Jesus. Jesus did not talk like that. Those came from a late community, John's Gospel being very late, 90 to 100 AD, which really means 70 years, probably, after Jesus died. So that's a long time. But it's the Christ talking. The Christ, you see, is in all of us. So for the Christ to say, or the Buddha Nature to say, "I am the way, the life, and the truth" is very interesting. It kind of conjures up responsibility. "I am the living bread." How are you living bread? "I am the door." How are you a door? "I am resurrection of life." How are you resurrection of life? How are *you* resurrection of life? "I am the living truth." Okay, how are you living truth? So it's turned back onto every being. Every being is a door to God. That's what's being said.

The fundamentalists don't have a clue about this because by nature, fundamentalism is literalist. By nature, archetypes are universal. That's why once you get the archetypal awareness, and it's especially important in the Bible Belt to spread this, you've undone a certain form of Christianity. You haven't undone the real depths of Christianity, because the real depths do come through in language like that; Meister Eckhart, who was a Dominican preacher and theologian, he just naturally talks about this all the time, that we are other Christs. Christ did not take incarnation only in Jesus, but takes incarnation in every being. Therefore, every being, what's being said is, "I am the way." Yeah: Every being is a way to the Father or to the Mother.

TSOMO: Yes.

STUDENT: *Hi. I have real problems with your story of the lama and the student. What rings in my head is, "If you meet the Buddha on the road, kill him." When we project that kind of authenticity and authority on another being, to me, it's a huge hindrance to needing the Divine. It's huge. It just drives me nuts to even hear you say it.*

TSOMO: Well, we go through stages of development on the way to enlightenment. At this point, most of us aren't already enlightened, and so we can't see that divinity all the time. So, for those of us who take this particular Vajrayana path that I'm speaking of, they find that it's easier if, on the channel that they're stuck on, there's somebody who they can project their own Buddha Nature onto for a while. And eventually the teacher then gives it back to them when they're ready.

STUDENT: *Like a good psychotherapist.*

TSOMO: There's some similarities. They're quite aware that we're projecting our Buddha Nature onto the lama, and that eventually we take it back. And this is why, in all of those practices that I was speaking of, we project the deity out, we have this drama happen, and then we take it back in and rest in oneness again, because the recognition of the truth of what you're saying is actually there from the beginning. It's just a way of pursuing the path.

MATT: I think that's an important answer, although I would also add, you know, don't get too upset. It's just a story. And stories are all metaphor and they're slippery. Just don't take it literally. Then you're getting fundamentalist on us, and that's what's scary. Don't take it literally.

But I'll also say, I'm struck by how you used the word *projection* and how important that is, you know. Falling in love is a projection. We fall in love, and as you say, then neat things happen. But eventually it kind of comes back, maybe.

TSOMO: We hope.

MATT: And then it goes into deeper love. And I kind of think of falling in love is like being on a springboard, but love is the water itself, you know. Something happens in those early stages, as you say. At the same time—now I will say this as a Westerner, of course. You're a Westerner, too, but that's what's so interesting about Tsomo; she's Jewish, but she speaks fluent Tibetan. But, I do think that, especially for Westerners, gurus can be very dangerous. It's scary because a lot of crazy things have happened. And not just gurus, but even popes.

TSOMO: Or the Reverend Jim Jones.

MATT: Well, there you go. Projections are always scary. And I know one Jungian analyst, a beautiful man, John Giannini—some of you may know him. He says, in listening to people's stories, dreams—he's an older guy now—for 50 years, he says, "I'm convinced. The number one addiction is addiction to our parents." And of course, *pope* means "parent"; it means "papa." It can be a very scary and dangerous thing. So, you know—talk about archetype.

TSOMO: The word "lama" actually means . . . well, *ma*, of course, means "mother," and *la* means "superior"—so kind of like "mother superior."

MATT: That's really scary.

TSOMO: I'm sorry.

MATT: We can do better than that. I think we can reconstruct a little Buddhism here.

TSOMO: "Superior mother"?

MATT: I know we can do better than that.

TSOMO: "Exalted mother"?

MATT: How about "big mother"?

TSOMO: No, Yum Chenmo, no, no. Exalted mother, maybe.

MATT: Exalted—that's a little better.

STUDENT: *[to Matt] At one point in one of your books, you talk about original sin not really being part of Jewish theology.*

MATT: Right.

STUDENT: *It comes from Genesis, but was turned . . .*

MATT: No. It doesn't come from Genesis at all. It comes from Saint Augustine, fourth century AD, please. That's the point, but go ahead. It's not in the Bible. Jesus never heard of it.

STUDENT: *Don't they distort it that way?*

MATT: No. Augustine's the one who really distorts it. Augustine mistranslates Paul to teach us original sin. I only gradually came to this realization, and it was when I was teaching in a women's college years ago in the early 1970s, that this Jewish woman, who was middle-aged, came up to me after one class we had, and she said, "What's this thing about original sin that all these young women are talking about?" And I said, "Well, you knew about original sin." "No"—and she's Jewish—she said. "I never heard of original sin. I never heard a rabbi talk about it. I've never heard a word about it." That's when I did some research.

The truth is that the Fall is one thing—the story, the Fall—but that's not original sin. And not only do Jews not believe in original sin, or Buddhists, neither do Native Americans, or Eastern Christians. Eastern Orthodox Christians tell me, "We can't believe you guys canonized Saint Augustine. We can't believe it." So it was Augustine's neurosis, and, of course, he actually identifies it with sexuality.

TSOMO: Sure.

MATT: He needed a *good* therapist early, and it would have changed the whole history of Western religion if he had gotten one. So where were you Jungians when you were needed? Or even Freud would have done it.

TSOMO: I was going to say, maybe he needed Freud.

MATT: So that's the point. And it's so interesting now. The response of the Vatican, this present pope when he was chief inquisitor when my book [*Original Blessing*][19] came out, they went ballistic. Original blessing? Arrgh! Well, first of all, this pope did his doctorate on Saint Augustine, and it shows. Our religious tradition that begins with original sin is anthropocentric, because sin is a human thing, and above all it's leaving out the beauty and the glory and the original purity we're all born in.

It's a major shift, and that's why the Vatican overreacted to my book, because they realize this pulls the rug out from under a lot of guilt, which is what keeps the money rolling. They're afraid they're going to lose their jobs. They don't realize that we need teachers, we need spiritual directors, and they could get some work there if they had learned something about all this.

TSOMO: Well, then they'd have to do spirituality, though.

MATT: Then they'd have to do that. They'd have to practice some.

TSOMO: I think we all, on the one hand, would be so much happier if we woke up, but also we kind of like to just stay asleep.

MATT: Especially if we're making a good living at it.

TSOMO: Again, that's that category of emotions called *desire*. And if you don't get what you want, then the anger tends to come.

---

19. Matthew Fox, *Original Blessing*: (Bear & Co. 1983)

A simple example was my daughter who was maybe two and a half or something like that, and was in one of her first experiences playing with another kid. They both desired the same block. Well, guess what happened next when he grabbed ahold of the block first: She pulled his hair. I was so embarrassed. But there was ignorance, of course, and then desire, and then aggression. It's a slippery slope. [*To a student*] Yes.

STUDENT: *This is just a comment that I've made for your reaction, but you were talking earlier about light and dark. Most of the images that you produced of darkness were fairly grim or harrowing in some way. It was as if we were talking about dark in contrast to light. But in the spirit of non-duality, I just put forth the idea that within darkness there is the inner illumination. We talked about darkness and silence. Our society fears both of those things. CNN, Fox News, twenty-four-hour chatter all the time is to keep at bay the depth and illumination of the light that's in the silence and in the darkness. And I just put that forward for your consideration now and also for what might take place tomorrow.*

TSOMO: Do you want to start?

MATT: Go ahead.

TSOMO: I had mentioned in the beginning that darkness and emptiness and luminosity, the darkness and the light, were two sides of one coin. This is something that we have trouble wrapping our minds around, and this is why I tend to use the metaphor of the ocean, because we can understand that you can't separate the waves from the ocean, or the ocean from the waves. Likewise, another image that they often use is the sun and its rays. You know, you can talk about the sun and its rays, but actually you can't separate them. They're one phenomenon.

MATT: I'll be honest with you. I don't agree that we said darkness was all about "harrowing."

TSOMO: I didn't hear that, yeah.

MATT: I don't agree at all. I talked about the astronauts who had their first mystical experience out in the darkness of space. I talked about the darkness of the sweat lodge. So I just don't agree. It's interesting that you heard that, though.

STUDENT: *No, I didn't hear that it was only about that, but I was hearing, kind of as the discussion progressed, that there was, you know, a more frightening experience, darkness as having all these associations. I think of the isolation tanks; they used to have them around. I used to love to experience that. And then that enclosure in that moonlight solitude was restorative, as you said.*

MATT: Absolutely. But I do want to say this about the dark night of the soul. To boil down what the mystics tell us about the dark night of the soul, what's really going on here, what they're telling us is that this is a school: that we learn something in the darkness that we don't learn anywhere else. They're saying that the dark night of the soul is the purification of our longing. Today we are in a collective dark night of our species. And I say, "Hmm. Are we on a path to purify our longing? What does it really mean to be a human being?" Because if we don't start purifying, we're going to be done as a species. The odds are not in our favor that we're going to survive on the paths we're on. So we have to come down to these radical questions. What does it mean to purify the longings of a human being?

And, again, I see this as both painful and enlightening or illuminative, you see—that by going through this school of the dark night, individually and collectively, you learn things. You learn about compassion. You learn about your own suffering so that you come out of it then much more aware of the suffering of others. You learn the universality of suffering. No one suffers alone. No one grieves alone. The Black Madonna is often grieving. She's not alone; she's an archetype. She's giving us all permission to grieve, and we have to start grieving today. How many people here have had authentic grieving rituals and ceremonies in their lives? When we do our Cosmic Mass, which is my effort to kind of bring new form to worship, we always have a grieving part. And invariably people come up afterwards, and they'll say things like, "The grieving was a high point for me. I grieve alone in my bedroom. No one has ever invited me to grieve in a group before." We have so much to grieve today with the disappearance of these species. There's so much to grieve, and we do so much of it alone.

So the dark night is not something to be afraid of so much. It is a school. It's a school of compassion, but above all, I think, a purification of longing. Longing takes us right into the heart. Longing is something the heart does, and to purify that, to make it strong so we don't wilt under the weight of the losses that we're all going through today, and that we go through also just as individuals, the betrayals of life and everything else, the suffering that the Buddhists name so bluntly.

TSOMO: And in Vajrayana we actually use those strong feelings that come up of anger, or painful longing, and grieving, when we're in retreat, or sitting in practice. We actually plow those into the practice. I've done this myself and found that not only did I survive the experience of letting myself go ahead and despair, but actually the support of these archetypes was there for me. I let myself fall through the floor, and discovered I was caught by the whole universe.

MATT: That's beautifully put. Father Bede Griffiths said [paraphrasing], "Despair is a yoga, that many people do not experience transcendence, God, or spirit until they go through despair."

TSOMO: Jung says that all the neuroses are actually our efforts to step around the pit of despair, just kind of tiptoe around it. And so if we keep indulging those tiptoeing-arounds, we never get the chance to do the free-fall and then be caught by the whole universe.

STUDENT: *A couple of observations. One, if anyone has not experienced total dark-ness, one way to do that, it happened years ago, I was on a trip that was going through a set of caverns, underground caves, and at one point they just got all of us to be quiet and then turned off the lights. That is such a total darkness, underground with no light around, and there was a sense in which it was oppressing almost. But I think that op-pressiveness was really about all the possibility that was in that darkness. And my sec-ond observation is Dom Hélder Câmara, who was a bishop, and died not too long ago, wrote a poem he called "A Symphony of Two Worlds."[20] And in that he talks about the Nativity experience, the birth of Jesus, happening in the middle of the night. And he says, "Christ, you were born in the middle of the night because midnight is pregnant with the dawn." And that, for me, gives a kind of a positive way to look at darkness, that darkness is not a terrifying thing. It is infinite possibility. It is the possibility of creation, of becoming, of newness.*

STUDENT: *The vast majority of us in this room are white-skinned. Would you care to comment on that in light of our discussion?*

---

20. Dom Helder Camara, *The Symphony of Two Worlds* (English Translator Joseph Gallagher) (Pastoral Press 1984)

TSOMO: As a person who has found themselves a bridge between Tibetan culture and American culture, my sitting here in this room with a bunch of light-skinned Americans, it's interesting. Because I know Tibetan and English, I found myself translating back and forth, and the interesting thing is that I can't just translate the words. First of all, the words aren't like two sides of an equation. *This* doesn't always exactly mean *that*, and there are words in Tibetan that there aren't any words for in English and vice versa. But beyond that, I find that I have to build the receptors on one side or another to even understand the concepts and take them in and do something with them. So I guess that would be my simple response. [*To student*] And you have one question there?

STUDENT: *Yeah. Isn't the Madonna a symbol for the archetype, and don't we have other symbols of that same archetype? In different cultures?*

TSOMO: An archetypal image, and, of course, everybody has . . .

STUDENT: *So it's not like the Black Madonna is the original archetype or the beginning of the archetypal whatever. We have different archetypes in different cultures.*

TSOMO: Yeah.

MATT: Well, of course. But this particular symbol, which awakens the archetype, is returning with special force today. And it is cross-cultural; that's the point. It's African, it's Sicilian, it's French, it's Russian, et cetera, and, with Guadalupe, it's also Mesoamerican. This is where the riches of culture are so valuable to us; there's no one way to spread the balm of healing and rejoicing again. There are so many ways. And we are living at this moment in history when all the cultures are mingling; "mixing" is my verb for post-modernism. That's when we talk about the DJ who mixes and the VJ who mixes. We're all mixing today. And there's so much to draw from the wisdom of the East, of the indigenous, of African, of Western, and Caucasian. It's just a glorious moment to be alive if you—*if* you—want to be alive. Otherwise, we go hiding and dropping bombs; we go to war with those who represent other ways of doing life.

TSOMO: Yeah. Fighting to stay asleep.

MATT: Fighting to stay asleep. Listen, I think our time is up for the evening. Thank you all for your participation and we look forward to tomorrow.

TSOMO: And thank you for hosting us here in Houston.

Day 2

Day 2

MATT: Just a little map of what we're about today. We'll begin with a little exercise together that I will lead. Then we'll spend an hour on the recovery of the Sacred Masculine, and Tsomo will respond from her masculine side, a 10-minute response. We will have a break and, at some point, we're going to return to the subject of the Sacred Feminine, because we only had so much time last night for that. Tsomo will lead with that, and I'll give a brief response from my feminine side. Then after lunch we want to take up the subject of the Sacred Marriage. And there will be, of course, discussion time this morning and discussion time this afternoon, and there'll be some practices along the way. Okay?

TSOMO: Actually, a large part of your experience of the feminine today will be a practice that I'll explain and walk you through.

MATT: Great. So I thought we'd begin with a couple of chants. Last night, we chanted the "aah," and then we mentioned how so many Divine names do this "aah."

So why don't we do it this way? Let's just begin with an "aah," and you can pick any note you want to start with. Just keep the breath moving. And then I will throw in some Divine names, and I ask you then to shift to these names. So we're going to move from "aah" to various Divine names, and just bring in the Divine wisdom, knowing, as the Hindus say, that God has millions of names, or as Thomas Aquinas said, "Every being in the universe is a name for God…and none are." That covers the whole gamut: everything and nothing. So we can all be at home with this. Okay.

[*Everyone chants "Aah."*]

[*Everyone chants "Adonai."*]

[*Everyone chants "Allah."*]

[*Everyone chants "Buddha."*]

[*Everyone chants "Tara."*]

[*Everyone chants "Abba."*]

[*Everyone chants "Gaia."*]

[*Everyone chants "Krishna."*]

[*Everyone chants "Yahweh."*]

[*Everyone chants "Aah."*]

[*Silence*]

MATT: Thank you. Are you up for one more chant? Okay, one thing that I've been working with lately is chants from the Christian tradition. One of the problems in Christianity is that our scholars, especially in the modern era, right up to today, are very good at exercising their left brains, employing the exact words of Jesus and all this stuff. But the Bible is much more than a sourcebook for analyzing. You can chant. And chanting the Bible is a totally different experience from reading it, thinking about it, analyzing it, taking it apart. So what we're going to do is chant a line that we know is authentic from the historical Jesus, and that is the line "The kingdom of God is within you, the queendom of God is among you," because his phrase means both of those things; it's not just about *within*, it's about *among*. In fact, in the Gospel of Thomas, he says the kingdom of God is spread around the earth, which is certainly an "among" consciousness.

This is what we're going to do. We'll split the room in half. This half will chant, "The kingdom of God is within me." So let's say that together. [*Everyone in that half says, "The kingdom of God is within me."*] This half will chant, "The queendom of God is among us." [*Everyone in that half says, "The queendom of God is among us."*]

Okay, let's begin with this group, and then you'll get going. Then I'll signal you to come in, and when they come in, you keep it going. Okay? So . . .

[*Half the group chants along with Matt: "The kingdom of God is within me."*]

[*The other half of the group chants simultaneously: "The queendom of God is among us."*]

[*Silence*]

MATT: Breathe in the silence that we've raised. All authentic prayer raises silence. Then the silence becomes a food for our day together, our nurturing. So take yourself now and wash yourself with the silence that we've brought into the room here from the depths of our hearts. Wash yourself three times. Eat, drink the silence. Meister Eckhart says, "Nothing in all creation is so like God as silence." Thank you.

I think that exercises like this have tremendous potential, especially for Christians who are, well, Protestants, who are maturated in the modern consciousness, to move from text to sound. Chanting is very different from singing. You don't have to have a super voice, any note works, and you don't need light on. You do it in the dark. And it affects, literally, the skin and the cells of the body. We have to get back to these pre-modern ways of praying.

And the potential: I have a whole list of chants, including the Christ chants like, "I have come that you may have life and have it in abundance." I did this with a group of ministers at Vancouver School of Theology, about 200 or so, a year ago, at the end of a session, and the next day 90 percent said they were up all night. It's new for Protestants, especially, to know that we can chant the Bible, not just read it, study it, think about it, and quote it *ad nauseam*. There's power in this.

CHAPTER 5

Sacred Masculine

MATT: Now it's my pleasure to move to the topic that I've written this new book on that's out, called *The Hidden Spirituality of Men: Ten Metaphors for Recovering the Sacred Masculine.*[21] I think that's the subtitle. You know how subtitles are. I wanted to just briefly just run through those 10 metaphors, 10 archetypes, but zero in on one, or maybe two, if I can sneak it in.

So, very briefly, the first archetype we're dealing with is Father Sky. And it's so important—we must remember that the Newtonian world, the modern age, locked down Father Sky. We were told the sky is inert and dead: "Get over it." I think this has everything to do with the rise of violence in our culture. We've always been aggressive—that's part of being sons and daughters of apes—but the extent to which we've exploded our aggression into violence has a lot to do with men not having a place to put their vastness. The vastness of the sky, we were told for 300 years, had nothing to receive us. It was nothing but mechanical, dead, inert, mechanical parts out there.

Now, with today's cosmology, everything has shifted. I can't recommend enough the book *The View from the Center of the Universe*[22]. How many of you know that book? Joel Primack and Nancy Abrams. A contemporary cosmologist, Joel worked at NASA; he's worked on the biggest computer

21. Matthew Fox, *The Hidden Spirituality of Men: Ten Metaphors to Awaken the Sacred Masculine.* (New World Library, 2008)
22. Joel R. Primack and Nancy Ellen Abrams, *The View from the Center of the Universe* (Riverhead Books, 2007)

in the world, which is oriented to the stars—a wonderful book. They have a one-hour DVD as well, which is a nice summary of their work. It's the latest knowledge we have of the universe, and it's absolutely stunning what they're talking about there. If I have time later I'll go into it, but I have to move along.

That's Father Sky. It's opening up, is my point. That is huge for men. It's huge. There's no telling the implications of our recovering a relationship to Father Sky. And when I say men, the masculine, I'm talking about women, too. I'm talking about your husbands and your brothers and your lovers and your sons and grandsons and your father and grandfather, but I'm also talking about you. You know that because you're Jungians, and that's part of your recovery, too, because women, too, have been damaged by a toxic masculinity. The proof of that is they allow their sons to go to off to war to kill other women's sons, and that's pretty ridiculous, as Pablo Casals said years ago. He learned that from his mother.

Okay, second archetype, and this is one we're really going to squat on in some length, is the Green Man. I'm going to run on and then return to the Green Man.

A third archetype is a retelling of the Icarus/Daedalus story. I think that the way we've told that story is very ageist. We blame it on Icarus: "Oh, this young man, typical, he didn't obey his father," blah, blah, blah. Well, I did some research, and Daedalus was no saint. He killed his nephew out of jealousy. So this is not just about disobedience of the elders, not at all. It's about miscommunication between generations. If Daedalus had rapped the message, "Don't fly too close to the sun because your wax will melt," maybe something healthier might have happened for his son. So that's Icarus/Daedalus. It raises an issue of intergenerational wisdom and intergenerational communication.

Another archetype I play with is the Blue Man. Swami Muktananda had this tremendous mystical experience, the greatest one of his life, where he saw a pearl, a blue pearl, that turned into a blue man, and it just changed his life totally. He overcame his fear of death, and all kinds of consciousness and creativity exploded for him. Well, interestingly enough, Hildegard of Bingen, Western mystic, had a vision of the Blue Man.

When I put her vision up against his, it's amazing what they both have to say. Hildegard says the Blue Man is the healing Christ in all of us. For her, too, it is about creativity, it's about consciousness.

Another archetype is the Spiritual Warrior. Again, knowing the difference between soldier and warrior, which our culture does not know, but any spiritual tradition worth its salt does know. Very important that men get the difference between being a soldier and being a warrior. I have a wonderful chapter on that. I think it is chapter 18; the last chapter in my book, *One River, Many Wells*[23], is on the Spiritual Warrior.

Another archetype is the Hunter-Gatherer. And, of course, this is more than an archetype. This is in our DNA. We are all hunter-gatherers. And one of the questions I raise is, "How are we hunting-gathering today?" Ninety percent of our time on Earth, our species has been hunting-gathering. How have we translated that today in positive and negative ways? Is hunting-gathering about the shopping mall? Getting the best sales? Is that what we've done with hunting-gathering, or is it about hunting for the truth of our place in the universe, or the truth of the wonders of our body, or how we can heal, how we can overcome divisions? So I think that's a very important archetype.

And another one Meister Eckhart talks about is God's "paternal heart". So the Fatherly Heart is a chapter and a metaphor—the whole fatherhood thing. Just the other day I was lecturing someplace and a woman came up. She said she was present for her first grandchild, and her son-in-law—his first child—said, "Never in my life have I fallen in love so fast and so totally," as receiving his first baby from the womb.

And finally, the Grandfatherly Heart: the whole role of eldership. I think those are 10—I don't have my list here—so it's pretty close.

STUDENT: *Eight.*

MATT: Eight? Uh-oh. I left some out. I got it someplace else. Don't worry about it. I'll bring them up later in the day. I'm sorry. I thought I remembered them all, but that's how it is.

Okay, let's turn now to a really big one in our time: the Green Man. And it so relates to the Black Madonna of last night, because the last

---

23. Matthew Fox, *One River, Many Wells: Wisdom Springing from Global Faiths* (TarcherPerigee, 2004)

time the goddess returned to Western culture was the twelfth century. And the last time the Black Madonna came through in a heavy way was the twelfth century. And the last time the Green Man came through in a heavy way was the twelfth century. My mentor, Père Chenu, a wonderful French Dominican, said that [paraphrasing] "the only renaissance that worked in the West was the twelfth-century renaissance," because it was grass roots, it was women, it was the young, it was freed serfs, unlike the sixteenth-century Renaissance, which was top-down, aristocratic. He feels it was not authentic.

But, in any case, what happened in the twelfth century blew the lid off of Western culture. That's when we invented universities, so we reinvented education. University was the place to go to find your place in the universe. And the goddess, Wisdom, reigned over the university, both arts and science. It also reinvented religion. The cathedral—*cathedra* means "throne"—was a place where the goddess sat in the middle of the city, because, in the twelfth century, culture moved from country, feudal country, land-based and monastic, to the cities, which were flooded with young serfs, freed serfs, who just fled the system. And, of course, all of Europe is warming up. It all happened because of climate change, the movement from the dark feudal ages to the renaissance of the twelfth and thirteenth centuries. So much changed, but the goddess led the way.

The Green Man is, among other things, a naming of the goddess within the male. The goddess's return is not just, as we know, about women, and Green Man is one way of knowing that. It is a recognition that men, too, carry the goddess within. And the goddess represents creativity, the immanence of Divine creativity in all beings.

I'm going to show you a DVD of the Green Man, and you'll realize that at this time the Green Man just burst onto the scene. Now, remember, the Green Man is a pagan and ancient archetype, but here it entered Christianity in a very big way. For example, at Chartres Cathedral, where, of course, the Black Madonna is very important, and the feminine is so important, there're over—I had the number once, I don't remember—I think it's over 130 images of the Divine Mother at Chartres Cathedral, where there are over 40 pictures, or statues, or carvings, of the Green Man.

And yet I'll tell you this. This fellow, he's an Englishman who has spent his whole life being a docent at Chartres Cathedral, and I met him in the

1960s when I was studying in Paris, and I've been back a few years ago—he's still there, he's quite old now—I've never heard him once talk about the Green Man. He stands in front of the Green Man, and he doesn't talk about it. Why? Because it's not in his theological perspective at all. His theology is Fall/Redemption. He doesn't know creation theology. He doesn't know the Cosmic Christ either. It's really interesting. He's standing there in front of this amazing temple and doesn't know half of it, because he can't see it. It's that perception that Tsomo was talking about last night.

What this is, then, is a gathering of the Green Man images from many French cathedrals, but a few German, and some English cathedrals. Again, this is an experiential thing just to enter into this image. I will talk over it some because there are very important lessons in these images about the Green Man, and what it's going to mean to us today. It might be good if we could turn the lights off, too.

STUDENT: *Are these DVDs from the images you used for the Cosmic Mass?*

MATT: Yes. They're from a classic book called *The Green Man*, by Clive Hicks, an English photographer, and William Anderson, an English poet[24]. They're both deceased now, but they gave me permission to take their slides, which are from the book, and to do with them what I want. And this is what I want to do with them: show them at a Jungian center in Houston.

[*Music starts.*] So you'll see the mouth plays a tremendous role—the fifth chakra. The fifth chakra is very important. It's about our generativity. We're giving birth to trees, to leaves, to plants. You'll notice each of these is a different personality and a different age. The young are represented. The middle-aged and old men are represented. And sometimes you'll find—this is a German one—the figures look kind of cross-eyed. That's the artist's way of depicting introspection.

The Green Man is about our relationship to the plants, the oldest of the living creatures. The Native Americans say the plants are the wisest of all the creatures because they invented photosynthesis. Where would we

---

24. William Anderson (author), Clive Hicks (photographer), *Green Man: The Archetype of Our Oneness with the Earth* (HarperCollins, 1991)

be without it? They're eating the sun, which, of course, is another connection with Father Sky. The Green Man connects us to Father Sky. All these archetypes interconnect, because we're eating the sun, we're eating the cosmos every morning. Here's an elderly Green Man. But it's also honoring our sexuality. It's saying something very positive about sexuality. The beard and the mustache represent our generativity, our coming of age.

The whole idea of the fifth chakra is so important with indigenous people for preliterate cultures. The oral tradition that what comes out of your mouth is between your heart chakra and your mind chakra, so that's wisdom. Wisdom is gathering heart and mind together, and, notice, that's what should be coming out of our mouths, not lies and not illusion. Now this fellow is obviously quite bug-eyed. He's had an experience of awe and wonder.

It is all about our intimate relationship with nature, and, of course, that is why it's so significant today at this time of eco-crisis and eco-collapse that we relearn. As I quoted Jung last night, archetypes return at critical moments in history for reasons. Now this is a Green Woman, which is very important. About 10 percent of the Green Men are Green Women. This is at Norwich, where Julian of Norwich is from. So again, not to get literal about anything. I've learned after 67 years, that everything important in life is a metaphor, and literalism kills it. Whether you're talking about life, spirit, God, sexuality, love—it's all a metaphor.

STUDENT: *Where is this from?*

MATT: This one? Which cathedral? I'd have to look it up. I think it looks kind of British to me. So this might be Norwich also, but I'd have to look it up. It could be French.

It's interesting this one says something about the crown chakra, too. Doesn't it? It's about the wreath of all of our light. Now you know where this is from. This is from Germany. You don't want to meet this Green Man in a dark alley. This is the warrior side. There's a fierceness to the Green Man. There's an articulation of certain plants like the sacred oak that goes with the Green Man, and plants that heal, healing plants. So there's a very, there's a sophisticated herbology connected to many of these Green Men as well.

It's interesting at this time in history there was no homophobia. The book by John Boswell on homosexuality and tolerance in the Middle Ages shows this. Homosexuality, homosexual literature, was taught in the first generation at the University of Paris, and there was no condemnation. The abbots, in fact, the bishop who built Chartres was homosexual, and there was a recognition of diversity. This is why it was such a rich and diverse renaissance. That window on non-homophobia lasted for about a 125 years in Western Christianity.

Now, Hildegard of Bingen, who lived in this time, calls Christ a Green Man. In fact, she builds her entire theology on *viriditas*, a word she made up, which means in Latin "greening power." She says, "The only sin in life is drying up." She wrote abbots and bishops and said, "You're drying up. Do what you can to stay wet and green and moist and juicy." So she was thoroughly swimming in the Green Man consciousness, thoroughly. She built a theology on it, for God's sake. And then the Church forgot it for about 700 years. Until I translated her, she had hardly been in English at all.

This is one of those where at first you think, "This guy needs glasses," but what they're really saying is he's being introspective, and the point is that introspection, going within, is an important part of being a Green Man or a Green Woman, to get grounded, to connect to your deepest DNA, if you will, and your spiritual paths.

So it's a celebration of fertility.

Now this is a dying Green Man. Very interesting, I think, of the mask of death, the leaves returning to the earth. It's a whole statement on dying. When you get in touch with your Green Man, you're also more at home with dying—that's why Easter comes in spring, right? Because it is the plants that renew. They are the lesson of resurrection or reincarnation. And we are them because we're eating them, and even animals are also plants because, of course, there'd be no other animals either without the plants.

So, that's a little journey through the Green Man. Let's take a few minutes to respond. What experiences did you have with the Green Man here? What comes through for you? [*To student*] Yes.

STUDENT: *Hi. I'm just sitting here going, "Wow." I just—Did you see the movie about the—?*

MATT: I can't hear you. Can you speak louder?

STUDENT: *Did you see the movie? [Student describes movie about a character who turns into a green man—most of the student's comments are inaudible.]*

MATT: Wonderful. Well, you see, that's very important, the tree of life. The Green Man is also about the Tree of Life and the Cosmic Tree. Again, this is where the Green Man relates to Father Sky because it's about our place in the universe. The Cosmic Tree is about the centering of our place in the universe. That's a wonderful connection. Also, the phallus represents the Tree of Life. In many of these cathedrals there is the whole Tree of Jesse portrayed in the stained glass window, and it rises from a phallus. It's an honoring of our sexuality, which, of course, is not familiar to most Christians, and yet it's there.

In fact, Clive Hicks, who climbed all over these cathedrals—he's the photographer in this team here that did the Green Man book—he told me that on the top of Chartres Cathedral—you have to climb up there— there is a statue of a man masturbating. Now, I think that's very interesting because you have temples not just in India, in Hinduism, but also in Islam, temples in Africa, that honor the sexual organs for what they are, which is part of the theophany, the mystical powers of the universe, and they do relate us to the Divine. We have a book in the Bible, the Song of Songs, which does the same thing, although the Church has spent 2,000 years trying to clean that book up, but has not succeeded, because you talk to any Jew and they'll tell you what it's about. As a rabbi told me, "On the Sabbath you're supposed to do two things: read the Song of Songs, and make love." And that's the tradition. So my point is that it's interesting they had to hide it on the roof, but they did it. They put it in a Christian temple, a statue of the fact that sexuality is part of the ongoing creativity of God and spirit. [*To student*] Yes, sir.

STUDENT: *Is the Incredible Hulk thing here in any way?*

MATT: Well, I don't know. I suppose maybe as a distortion. Maybe it does, and he's green, too, isn't he? Yeah. Now don't ask about the Jolly Green Giant. I will not answer that. We want to go deeply. [*To student*] Yes, sir.

STUDENT: *In the twelfth century, the people that were going to that cathedral and they had seen all these Green Men, would they have known what that meant?*

MATT: Of course. At least psychically they would. They would *get* the archetypes. It's only our culture that's so left-brained that we have to, "This symbol stands for." That's what I meant last night about indigenous people and pre-modern people. They know what a mask is saying. They say, "This mask is about fear. This mask is about terror. If you wear this mask, you don't have to go to war in Iraq when you feel terror." You know, get over our literalism. We all have this in us. This is what it means to be human. I'm sure Tsomo can talk on and on about what all these images mean to Tibetans. I don't think they have PhDs in symbolism. They get it, and part of our post-modern time is to return to our pre-modern wisdom, which is, "Whoa—" responding, like I said yesterday, to archetypes that can shake us up. [*To student*] Yes.

STUDENT: *The cathedral that's just outside of Edinburgh that was made famous by The DaVinci Code. I can't remember the name of it; I've been there like a few times. It's very, it's a very, very feminine cathedral. It's a very comforting place. Right in the center of it, on a long wall is Green Man.*

MATT: Oh, how interesting.

STUDENT: *A cathedral filled with lots of plants and nature symbols and flowers. And it's just beautiful. But there's the Green Man.*

MATT: That's great. And you remember it. Of course, that's Celtic. See, the Celts never lost the Cosmic Christ, unlike the Augustinian tradition in the Western church. They always kept the Cosmic Christ alive, and the Green Man stands for our relationship to cosmos and Earth processes and Mother Earth. It's also about our relationship with "the Mother," with the Mother Earth. Yeah. That's neat, though.

STUDENT: *This summer I spent about 10 days in, at Wells—Wells, England—at a cathedral there, and I noticed how much incorporated the Green Man, the Madonna, the rose, the angels. But when tours were given, it was good and bad. It was: the Green Man clearly carries the negative, the devil.*

MATT: Creepy.

STUDENT: *Yes. And yet, on a mantel, all four being represented—unity, all one.*

MATT: Well, there you go. The shadow, the dumping on true masculinity. And what do we give them instead? That the man is here . . . to what? Play the stock market to the end, and play the golf course to the end, and all this. That's the point. When you miss authentic archetypes, what are we substituting instead?

Let me get down to my main point here. At this moment in history, there's no question in my mind that the top three moral issues of our time are ecological crisis, ecological crisis, and ecological crisis. Because you can talk about anything else, but if humans don't have healthy water, healthy food, healthy soil, healthy bodies, healthy babies, healthy minds, and healthy animals and other beings to delight our hearts and souls and move us, it's over. It's over. It may take a while, but it's over.

Now, at this time then, what the Green Man is really about, why he's returning, it's about finding authentic warriorhood. Men are here to defend the earth. That's why we're here. We're not here to make the latest version of a car, or latest war weapons, et cetera, et cetera. There's a clarity here in the Green Man archetype and why it's returning. The Green Man is strong. The Green Man is a warrior, a warrior on behalf of the earth. That is what the Green Man is telling us today: the role of the man, whether as father, as teacher, as preacher, as counselor, as husband. In all our work, in all our relations, the Green Man archetype, which is about love—wisdom combined with knowledge has to imbue it. It brings forth the powerful energy.

It's a wonderful way for men to clean their act up, to clean up our act. As I said last night, we have to detox. We have to undo a good amount of the images of masculinity that we've been taking in for several hundred years. And while each of these 10 that I name has something to offer, I think the Green Man is the obvious one for our time.

He also honors intelligence. You know, it is about our minds and our heads, as well as our heart. So it's not that we have to become anti-intellectual. And again, to me, this is the biggest problem in fundamentalism. The Vatican's version today—the Catholic Church, the last 25 years—has dumbed down its tradition totally. This present pope silenced 108 theologians, of which I am just one. I was told by a professor at a Catholic university in Paris when I went and did my doctorate, she said, "Theology's been dead here for 15 years. The last pope killed it. There's no theology going on worth the name in Europe." She said, "What you're doing with scientists and all this, this is just astounding because no one's doing this in Europe. We're not allowed to under Catholic auspices."

And the dumbing-down of Protestantism by fundamentalists is a scandal. This is why I went to Wittenberg a few years ago and pounded theses on the door. The Catholic Church is corrupt at the top at this time, but the Protestants are sleeping and have allowed fundamentalists to hijack the names Jesus, Christ, and even God. It's anti-intellectualism. It's the fear of not using our minds, and not standing up, and not saying "This makes no sense." Now, of course, there are wonderful things happening in the Jesus Seminar, and the scholarship, and Marcus Borg, and all these good theologians, but my point is that it's been too long coming. So this is part of the Green Man, too. The sacred tree—and, of course, the *bodhi* tree under which Buddha had his enlightenment—this is part, too, of what's involved in this archetype. The sacred tree grows within, and it brings us to the center of the universe, the axis of the universe.

So, those are a few thoughts on the Green Man. Before I close now, I'd like to say a few words more about Father Sky because it is so important and it's so exciting. Just as the Green Man archetype speaks so profoundly to so many needs today around the ecological crisis, and men finding who we really are, we are all warriors on behalf of Earth. Now that, that doesn't mean we do it the same way. One thing I love is how unique each personality is. Notice that there's young and old: The young and the old all have to be warriors, spiritual warriors today for the earth.

I want to share with you some of the work of Joel Primack and Nancy Abrams and their brilliant book, *The View From the Center of the Universe*[25]. This is the latest cosmology. What we've learned the last five years from Hubble Telescope, they say, just surpasses everything else we've known about the universe. They bring it together, and they put it in metaphor, in archetype. In fact, they talk about the metaphors themselves. Just as we talked last night about the power of archetype, they talk about how these new metaphors from the universe itself can change everything.

Here is the key: what they call the Goldilocks Principle. What the modern age left us thinking was that we humans were just an accident in the history of the universe, which, of course, totally dumbs down our responsibility. It takes away our responsibility, and it also takes away meaning in your life. "Oh, we just happened. Okay, so give me another beer. Let's make money. Let's go shopping." That's what's happened.

---

25. Joel R. Primack and Nancy Ellen Abrams, *The View from the Center of the Universe* (Riverhead Books, 2007)

Science itself was part of the problem in the desacralizing of our lives. But this is why they are so excited, and these are scientists. Actually, Nancy herself is a lawyer and an artist, and her husband—they're husband and wife—Joel, is an astrophysicist, but she's very articulate and very brilliant, and being an artist is very interesting: the metaphor of all this science. So they wrote the book together, they do their workshops together, and so on. From the Goldilocks Principle, what we have found is this—and they do this beautiful picture of the Europus—as human beings we're in the middle of size in the universe. The big things that constitute half the universe above us, if you will, are bigger than us. But the small microbes and all constitute the other half. We're square in the middle, just like Goldilocks. You know, this bed was too soft, this bed is too hard, this one's just right. That's point number one. Another point is that we have the size brains to look at the universe. Whereas if we were much larger physically, if we were as big as elephants, we could not have brains that could study the history of the universe; our brains would be too taken up just surviving on the planet; that we are the exact size for our intelligence to examine the universe. Furthermore, we've come at the right time in terms of the history of the earth. Earth is going to survive for about nine to 10 billion years; then it's going to be swallowed up. We're at four-and-a-half billion years, and we're right in the middle, or very close to the middle time in the history of the Earth. It's taken 14 billion years to give birth to a species like ours. It's the right size with the right intelligence, to arrive at the right time.

Furthermore, in the history of the universe—which is at roughly 14 billion years old, 13.7 billion million years old—we've come at the time when we can still pick up the sounds of the original fireball, which we've done, and the radiation, the color of it, the heat, the light, but also we can still see the galaxies expanding and going away from us. Before long, we're not going to be able to see the galaxies expanding and going away from us. We've arrived at just this moment in history. They go through many sets of Goldilocks Principles, and that's where they got the title of the book, *The View from the Center of the Universe*. We are special. We're not special like we thought we were before Copernicus, when we thought we were the center of the universe. No, that's gone for sure. But we're special because we can view the universe with our minds, our intelligence, our creativity and technology, and in terms of the history of this planet and the universe, we are set at an amazing moment.

In addition, they talk about the cosmic gift to the earth. This is Father Sky stuff right here. "Twenty-five percent of the extra-solar planets astronomers have found so far are hot Jupiter's natural gas balls." They cannot in any way produce what we have here on Earth. "Jupiter has been an ally in assisting Earth. Jupiter's gravity has protected Earth from being hit by comets. Like the big brother, Jupiter has protected us. We're so fortunate that we're in this galaxy with Jupiter. Without Jupiter we would have been done a long time ago from comet after comet. The distance of Earth from the sun is just right: where closer to the sun, water would evaporate and be lost; where further from the sun, water would be permanently frozen." Which is, of course, the case in all the other planets, one or the other, in our solar system.

"Thanks to the [relatively] thin crust and abundance of surface water on Earth, geological activity is alive and well." Plate tectonics moves continents, resulting in volcanoes and so forth—absolutely essential for the life that's going on on the earth. If Earth were steady, entirely steady, there would be no diversity of life on the earth." As they say, "It is imperfect." The universe itself is very imperfect, and it's imperfection that makes the abundance of creativity possible. Another way of saying that is, chaos is integral to the processes of creativity and the earth and the solar system that feeds us so magnificently.

And then the moon. The moon, which is created from the Earth itself with a crash, how fortuitous was that? The moon stabilizes the rotation of the Earth and our climate, and it's unusually large compared to other moons and other planets that we know. The largeness of the moon tilts the Earth just the right amount so that we have the seasons. Without the moon we would not have the seasons. And without the seasons, would we have green? Would we have a greening place? Furthermore, every time there's a full moon or a new moon, the entire North American continent rises six inches. That tells you a little bit about the power of the moon. The moon is amazing.

These are just a few of their findings. They say, "If space time had been perfectly smooth, there would be no galaxies, no stars, no planets, no life; just a thick soup of particles. Life could only have evolved in an imperfect universe." So those are just a few notes about Father Sky. Father Sky has never been more alive, folks. Now, the ancients know this. I've been with the Aboriginals in Australia a few years ago, and I'll never forget. This Aboriginal friend, it was a starry night, and he said, "In our tradition we don't call those stars. We say those are the campfires of our ancestors." The campfires, the ancestors, are up there looking down on Earth, "What's cooking on Earth?" This is what they tell their children: that there's a relationship. There's campfires with the ancestors in the sky. We, for 400 years, under modern science and modern consciousness, have been telling our children, "Don't even look. It's dead. It's inert." You see? But now what's happening with this new science is just the opposite. Not only are we looking, we're building special telescopes to look. It's more exciting. There's more life going on there.

You have to understand, until 1968 we never applied the principles of evolution to the universe itself. This is new stuff for our species, but no generation has said or suspected that the universe was hundreds of billions of galaxies large—and that's only this universe—each with hundreds of billions of stars. So don't tell me that Father Sky is exhausted, worn out, or indifferent. Father Sky is feeding us daily. That's what all our food is. I had oatmeal this morning. I ate the sun in the form of oatmeal. And I drank orange juice. I drank the sun in the form of juice, thanks to photosynthesis, thanks to the plant world.

This is the kind of stuff that can stir up authentic masculine energy. And we need it desperately, because just like the Church has allowed Jesus and Christ to be hijacked, I say that Jerry Falwell is to Jesus what Osama bin Laden is to Mohammed. Men have allowed—not consciously, but it has happened to men and to women—we have had our masculinity hijacked, not by warrior archetypes, but by soldier archetypes, by military-industrial-prison-media complexes that are serving profound psychological needs in the male, because, yes, the male is set up for aggression, and the male is set up for shame. And until we deal honestly with those, and I do deal with them in my book, especially under the chapter of Hunter-Gatherer, because that's, that's where it comes clear. Our hunter-gatherers, many of them, were cannibals. We don't like to talk about that. We'd rather think the hunter-gatherers were saints. But there was this other thing going on, and we have to put that on the table. This is our DNA.

So how *do* we deal with aggression in our culture? How do you deal with the shame of having twin towers collapse and 3,700 people killed? Do you go to war in Iraq? Is that an appropriate response? These are real issues, and it does come back to our understanding of our masculinity. And so these are a few of my thoughts. [*Lots of laughing from students*] Why are they laughing? Why are you laughing? I'm, I'm not embarrassed, but why is that funny? I like laughter, but I'm just not real clear. I'm smiling; I'm smiling at your smiles, I guess.

TSOMO: It was more than a few, maybe, thoughts.

MATT: It was more than a few?

TSOMO: Yeah, maybe, well not just—You sort of—"It's just a few of my thoughts." Something about the contrast.

MATT: Okay.

TSOMO: Let me start by just responding from my masculine side, which is what we had in the program, and then we're going to open it up and dialogue with everyone.

I was especially struck by the Green Man because, being raised in this patriarchal society and wanting to be successful in this society, and also just in my personal family, I identified, as it happened, more with my father. I sort of had him more as my model for how to be in this world than I did my mother. It's just, you know, some of us are closer to one than the other. As a result, I made some of the same mistakes that Marion Woodman talks about in *Addiction to Perfection*, that a lot of her female clients suffered from. My animus was alive and well, and developing a lot, but in some cases, not in a healthy way. In some cases it was a healthy way. It was just able to come out.

I would like to announce to you—this is maybe the first time I've ever announced it publicly—that the first day of kindergarten I was elected president of the tomboy club. So I'm card-carrying. And also in that kindergarten, I managed somehow or another to be wrestling with a couple of boys at the same time. They were pretty tough guys, and I ended up somehow on top of both of them at once. I came home and I announced to my dad very proudly that I was third-toughest of the boys and first-toughest of the girls.

So I relate that, if I try to go a little bit more profoundly with that, with the Hunter-Gatherer that you hark back to, because 90 percent of our time that's what we've been and what we've done. The role of the woman was to be more the hub of the family. Even when she ventured from the cave, she was gathering the berries and nuts with her kids. And when the men came back from hunting, they were really integrated into the family in some ways through the woman. The woman was telling what had happened at home and still very much at the center of the activity there. The women were doing a lot of nurturing and connecting. I would say those are the key job description requirements.

And for men, there was aggressiveness. Men had to gear up a lot in an aggressive kind of way to be able to hunt. In reading about how the Native Americans hunted buffalo, this is a very dangerous occupation and not to be taken lightly. So they geared themselves up with ceremony beforehand and then went out, and only the youngest, strongest could do this. There was a lot of skill involved as well. They would together hunt the buffalo. Now, they had to have enough of the ability to connect to be able to win against the buffalo, because the buffalo were actually stronger. But the other job that men had was to defend the family, and this also requires a certain aggressive kind of power.

So getting back to me and school, I really enjoyed sports. And it was difficult for me in those times to be able to really pursue sports, because that was something the boys did. And so I would wrestle with my brother and climb trees, and do what I could. Finally in high school, a few of us girls who could actually play volleyball for real, not just stand and giggle, got to play with some of the boys, and I just had a blast. I really got to let that come out. And so much healthier to let it come out in that way than in, I think, what happens so often with girls when they're in junior high and high school, with the sniping and the aggressive social climbing. There's a kind of aggressiveness, a pointed kind of aggressiveness, that I think is masculine, but toxic. And it was very painful for all of us girls who had been through that.

Those are some ways that the Green Man has been a healing presence for me to think of. I just want to mention, interestingly enough, I'm going to be speaking about Tara, and she's the central figure in that thangka there, and she's green. It just so happens. Fertility has been very important to me, and to have it be connected to the Green Man . . . When I was living from a garden for twelve years, it just so happened that my then-husband had been studying the Green Man. He was a carpenter and working with wood, and working with wood in many ways; he was also a woodsman, a forester. That was his job. I was busy growing plants. And because I hadn't been so close to my mother, to go to "the mother" in that way was so healing for me. But I think it was also healing to be involved, at least somewhat, with the Green Man archetype. You know, the *dryad*, which is the spirit of the tree, is depicted in this same way.

The other thing I loved that you brought was just wonder at the aliveness of the universe. I talked a little bit last night about how that is, that this emptiness is not a void, but it's actually one great awareness. It's ultimate *bodhicitta*, awakened heart, because, of course, there's no separation. So how could we not feel the suffering of other beings just as if we'd stubbed our own toe? And if somebody else is starving, then we're in pain, too. So, if we have ultimate bodhicitta, once we're coming from this one awareness, then that's quite natural.

In my experiences in meditation, and at first only very, very rarely, before I studied Tibetan Buddhism, I would have these moments, epiphanies, where I experienced spontaneous presence that actually was underlying everything, and flowing through and suffusing everything. The power of it was astonishing. I was just in awe. I thought to myself, "I need to have a way to be able to recall this any time." At first I kind of could, just from the memory of it, but I wanted to be able to sort of change channels, and be able to go to *that* channel and feel that spontaneous presence all the time.

I think that indigenous people, in their original state, are quite familiar with that and live with that much more than we do. They've spoken of it, actually, as our minds being kind of deadened and dull and gray. There have actually been some brain studies where the indigenous people tend to be in alpha state where they are more open to this spontaneous presence. And we're more in the beta state all the time, which is good for office work, and assembly line work, but not so much for being human in the universe. So I love that you brought that.

MATT: [*To students*] We invite your response, discussion, questions . . .

STUDENT: *First of all, the Green Man really touched me with awe. Thank you very much. The richness of it, the growth, the generativity. On the other hand, I was kind of amazed. First of all, I thought Green Man was something you had made up in harvesting environmentalism, "Oh, I'd better be green man," you know. I had never seen it, heard it before, so this is astonishingly new to me. But I was thinking when I was looking at the growth and the vegetational Jesus, "I am Divine, you are the branches," but I always looked at it more in terms of the anima, you know, in terms of the feminine rather than the masculine, because women carry life within them for nine months and men are just there at the beginning, you know. So that affected me emotionally. Number 2, when I worked in New York, I took the subway from Connecticut to New York and watched these guys, executives running with their briefcases, very . . . and competitional . . . I don't know what you call them: the warrior, hunter, gatherer. Where does man, the human being, fit in terms of driving to work and competing?*

MATT: Well, I think you've named something there. It is the playing out of the hunter energy. And part of it is really what Tsomo talked about, putting food on the table. So that's, that's part of it, but, but we can take competition and aggression obviously far too far, and greed. If it feeds greed, then, of course, this is really how Tsomo began yesterday with the illusions that we live out of. If you tap into the greed dimension, then you're in deep trouble. Then you destroy the earth. It's exactly what we're doing, you see. So it has to be tamed. It has to be domesticated in a way. We have to learn as a species, and we have learned at different times in history. Buddha taught us and Jesus taught us some of this, and all kinds of teachers have. And the Goddess tradition dealt with this. They learned to deal with aggression.

For example, there's a tradition among the Inuit tribes in the North Pole that when a war is about to break out between tribes, they hold a poetry contest. They get the best poet from each tribe, and they make up a jury of members of both tribes. They go at it for a week with their poetry. At the end of the week, the jury votes for the best poet and that tribe wins the war. It's what William James wrote about almost a hundred years ago, we need a moral equivalent for war. And, of course, Tsomo touched on sport, but art is a way to steer aggression and violence into something that serves the community. So what you're talking about, how, how aggressive capitalism has become, how it seizes the soul, and how if it's just narrow, just about the bottom line, then it, of course, it is literally destroying the forests and the plants and so forth—the planets. Well, this planet, yes.

This is why we need traditions and spiritual disciplines that calm that reptilian brain and allow the mammal brain, which is our kinship brain, to flourish. And that is the compassion that Tsomo, Buddha, and Jesus, and the Jewish tradition talk about. All traditions do—a lot, you know. In the Koran the most frequently used name for divinity is God the Compassionate: Allah the Compassionate One.

STUDENT: *I've had the opportunity to be part of the military side of our country right now as a minister. And as you were speaking today about the reappearance or the re-emerging of this warrior archetype. I really see the struggle around that within our military right now. Number 1, in Iraq and Afghanistan—it's a real struggle in this area in particular. If you listen on the news, you'll hear it. The word now is not soldiers: We have wounded warriors. And we now have WTUs, which are "warriors in transition units" that have now been created. The military has created the WTU to care for these wounded warriors and their families. In the medical centers, where I have the opportunity to serve, we are really trying grapple with this archetype in a way that we might be unaware of, because we truly are trying to be attendant to, and listen to, and struggle with how do we nurture, how do we . . . What do we do with it, this? What is it we're doing with the wounded warrior?*

MATT: Again, I think our society has badly served us by confusing warrior and soldier. My awareness of this happened a few years ago. In our doctoral program we had a Native American who told us this story. When he came back from the Vietnam War, his elders said to him, "You've been a soldier. Now we're going to make you a warrior." I said, "How long was the training?" Four years of training. So notice the difference. Four years of intense training to move from being a soldier to a warrior. What's the difference? A soldier's given a gun and told, "Kill or be killed." It's a very specific duty. It's very clear what the job is. I asked him, "What was the training?" "First off," he said, "they taught me to play the flute, and I mastered it. I played the flute, and they called the whole gathering of the entire tribe. It was like a recital one night. And I played for the whole tribe. And at the end of the evening each elder came up with a knife and took a chunk out of my flute. At the end of the evening I had no flute." I said, "Now that's interesting." I said, "Meister Eckhart says the soul grows by subtraction, not by addition." He said, "What Indian said that?" I said, "That was Meister Eckhart." "Well," he said, "that was my whole training. For four years they taught me something, took it away, taught me something, took it away". See, that's not the training a soldier gets.

Now, the warrior does his or her inner work. That's the difference: the inner work. The best writing I know about the spiritual warrior is Hafiz, the Muslim/Sufi mystic, came after, right after Rumi, fourteenth century. I could actually read you one of his brief poems of this if you wanted. It's just brilliant about how soldiers are falling in excruciating pain, but this is in my book, *One River, Many Wells.*

STUDENT: *I think you're exactly right. They go over as soldiers with the training you're talking about. They come back as warriors, but they come back as wounded warriors.*

MATT: That's right. A lot of that we call post-traumatic syndrome and so forth, but their hearts have been wrecked. Here's Hafiz [paraphrasing]: "It is a naïve person who thinks we're not engaged in a fierce battle." Now, I want to mention this, too. When it comes to mass maleness and masculinity, we don't have just an issue with aggression and violence and all that; that's one-ended. We also have an issue today with softness, that a lot of men who were raised under the Women's Movement just kind of backed off and said, "Oh, I'm supposed to be sweet all the time. I'm supposed to be more ladylike." That's an issue because it's one reason, I think, we've not stood up to the fundamentalists, for example. "Oh, it's not nice. Women don't do that, and men don't do that." That's why recovering the authentic masculine is so important.

What is the authentic use of our aggression? And like you said, to defend the family. That's not the same as nurturing the family. Nurturing is important. Defending is another thing. It takes other skills to take on the tigers and the lions. But just how he puts it: "It's a naïve person who thinks we're not engaged in a fierce battle." Liberals think there's not really a fierce battle sometimes, and that's not true. There are fierce battles. "For I see and hear brave foot soldiers all around me going mad, falling on the ground in excruciating pain." That's real. That's what soldiers do. "But you could become a victorious horse person and carry your heart through this world like a life-giving sun, but only if you and God become sweet lovers." So the difference between a soldier and a warrior is that the warrior is a lover. And the warrior deals with the ghosts of his past that are trying to break the jeweled vision in the heart—and also the ghosts of the future, which is, of course, all fears about the future.

So this is where we all need warriorhood today. There's a lot to be afraid of in our world today: The ecological crisis is one thing, terrorism is another, and bad politicians is another. So we all have to develop this strength in us—men and women alike. It's based on mysticism. It's based on our relationship with the beloved. And that's why the theology is so important. If your images of God are images of a general, and not of a beloved, then, of course, that just encourages the armor, the armor that stands for maleness as opposed to the depth of the personhood that spiritual experience is about.

Tsomo: This is what I loved about your talking about the first dose of medicine that was given to this Navajo, was it? A Native American soldier turning to warrior was playing the flute—the phallic symbolism is obvious. And so it's turning to something beautiful. It's making something beautiful: beautiful music. And love, of course, is involved in that. And then they even took away that symbol. It keeps throwing it back; then it has to go to a deeper and deeper, more and more universal level.

Student: *I just had this thought of Joan of Arc. And the coming together. And her being a spiritual warrior, and her love, and guided so much by her love.*

Matt: And her courage.

Tsomo: And her courage.

Matt: My friend Anita Roddick—founded Body Shop—died this year, and I was asked to lead her memorial service in England, and there were 2,000 people there by invitation only. But I talked about her—and I told her to her face when I was with her many times—I called her the Joan of Arc of business, because she took on an all-masculine world and really brought healthy values to it. For example, she started a school for an MBA program in England where they study not just accounting of the bottom line, which is one thing which they study, but accounting of ecology: What is our company doing for, around ecology? And accounting of community: What is it doing to give back business to the community? She really shifted, but she had to be a warrior. And yet she played the game; she was a successful businesswoman. Body Shop was everywhere, and they sold it a few years ago for 660 million dollars, though they only cleared 60 million, but that's not bad. I think there are contemporary Joan of Arcs. We don't just have to look back to the ancient days. I think she was one.

A lot of women who stepped up in becoming clergy, or becoming business people, or becoming therapists and so forth in our day are carrying this healthy masculine energy, but not, I hope, ridding themselves of the healthy feminine. And that's what's special, to bring this into our culture. That's where I see the marriage of the Green Man and the Black Madonna. I'll talk more about that this afternoon, I guess. [*To student*] Yes.

STUDENT: *Is the Black Madonna kind of like a little Green Man in black?*

MATT: I'll leave you to meditate on that. I hear that there is a church here in this city to the Black Madonna in a Black community, which is really neat and very special, because it's rare. The Black Madonna has been kept a secret. That's what I mean by saying that archetypes have to come out of the closet at this time and shake us all up. And remember, Isis was always pictured with a headdress that included a rattle. And that's because part of the Isis, or the Black Madonna, is to rattle us, to rattle our institutions, to shake it all up, to bring new consciousness and perception into a culture. That's one more reason, I think, why the Black Madonna has a lot to say to us today. She's a prophet, she interferes, she rattles us; she's making other demands around our attitude toward darkness, toward blackness, toward compassion, toward a lot of things. [*To student*] Yes.

STUDENT: *I don't hesitate to tell this, and I hope it's not too personal, but I didn't know I was coming to hear you until just last night, but I had had in the last two weeks two visions. One, now, I recognize as the Black Madonna, a very personal one, and then I saw the Green Man. I had studied Jung years ago. My Green Man came out of the river and he had a beautiful green jumpsuit on with water falling, and he had black skin. This Green Man was flat with a strange kind of suit on—a lot of squares in the suit. His head is a flat map of the world with all different colors of mountains and what have you. And . . .*

MATT: Are you painting this?

STUDENT: *I can't yet. But, yeah, I would like to be able to.*

MATT: When you say flat, is it like a gingerbread man?

STUDENT: *Yes!*

MATT: Well, you can eat him. I love gingerbread men. I don't know about you. I love gingerbread men.

STUDENT: *Thomas Friedman wrote that book,* The World Is Flat.

MATT: Thanks for sharing that. That is personal, but it's also communal because we can identify with stories like that. That's beautiful, but I'm struck that you had visions recently of both the Black Madonna and the Green Man.

STUDENT: *I do that.*

MATT: Wow. You do that. Okay. Maybe the Blue Man will be next.

STUDENT: *Haven't heard of him. But, yeah, I'd like that.*

TSOMO: When you were mentioning about the rattle, I was just thinking about some of the wrathful protectresses who are enlightened deities, and they're wearing a garland of skulls, which rattle, of course, as they dance and move. Their intention is to help us to awaken and to relieve us from suffering, but their style is ferocious. They're very serious.

STUDENT: *You have a bunch of teenagers, you know, with these baggy pants hanging way down, and they're just dying to be initiated into manhood. What can be done?*

MATT: That's a very important question: the question of initiation, the rites of passage. As we all know, our rites of passage are so weak at this time. I remember a number of years ago we had Malidoma Somé come and speak in my program when I was at Holy Names College. The pope hadn't kicked me out of there yet. He's the spiritual teacher from West Africa whose whole emphasis is on rites of passage, because he missed his, because the Jesuits had kidnapped him when he was six years old and taken him off to a seminary. When he escaped, when he was 16, he went back to his village. He had not been through the rite of passage, and he said, "I was impossible to live with. I was angry all the time." So then they finally helped him do it, but he was, 18 and the others were 13, and it was pretty important to him.

When he finished talking, I asked the group—there were about 60 students—"How many of you went through either a bar mitzvah experience or a confirmation experience?" Everyone raised their hand but one. "How many of you remember that as a significant transformation or moment in your life?" Every hand went down but one. That taught me that we have these things in our attics, you know. Our religious attics have something which was meant to be a rite of passage. In fact, it's interesting, even if you go to the silly catechisms about confirmation, essentially they use the word *soldier*. They're trying to say "warrior," but they use "soldier for Christ." It's as scary as can be, especially if you're Jewish or Iraqi. The point is that there's a memory there that has been totally emasculated.

So your question is right on. I'm working now with—and thanks to the help of some philanthropists, who I will not name—with an African-American rapper. We've developed an after-school program, which is now becoming an inner-school program for inner-city kids, the toughest ones. We're teaching them a meditation through the marriage of heaven and Earth, which is a practice that Professor PITT, this 31-year-old rapper. He's been doing these practices, bodily practices. And this is very important for young men, that they learn what we call martial arts. He doesn't use that word. He uses the word *healing arts*. This literally saved his life as a young man. He's been developing them ever since, going to masters of tai chi and others, *Qigong* and others, to learn these ways of calming the reptilian brain.

We're also using film and rap because he's a filmmaker. Nancy Abrams and Joel Primack, the scientists, came to our program with these inner-city kids and taught the new cosmology to them for a few classes. So we put the new cosmology into rap and filmmaking. In the process, they're learning how to make film, which is, of course, a wonderful new art form: Thanks to the new technology, anyone can make film if you've got this basic technology and a Mac. And we're doing the spiritual practices with the body. We've linked up with a charter school, so it's actually accredited. So that's what we're trying to do.

And for me, as a white guy who doesn't come from the streets, like PITT does, who comes from academia in many ways, it's so amazing to hear these kids' stories. And that's what we're trying to do, change education. I think the problem isn't the kids. The problem is the adults who think education is working.

I was lecturing in Napa a few months ago, and this woman came up and she said, "I'm a teacher. I'm a great teacher. I love teaching, and I'm quitting. And every good teacher I know is quitting, because of this No Child Left Behind bullshit. We did not become teachers to give an eternal amount of tests to kids. This is not what learning is about, you see." My most recent book is on this, *The A.W. E. Project: Reinventing Education, Reinventing the Human.* And PITT has taken 10 of my thoughts there and put them into five-minute rap videos. So that's what we're trying to do. It's the Icarus/Daedalus story I'm telling you about. When there's a crunch in the education budget, out goes theater, out goes music, out goes art. You know that. And, of course, there's no cosmology taught there, and yet this is what the kids want to know. I've worked with people in South Central L.A. "No, I don't know any group in America who are more interested in cosmology than inner-city kids. They're not getting it in church, they're not getting it in the media, they're not getting it in school." So for me, all of this is about initiation. Let's initiate this new generation into the new cosmology, and into those arts that humanity has developed, every religious tradition has developed, that calm the reptilian brain. Because, obviously, for these kids every day is a survival day, they are tapping into the reptilian brain very readily, and they have to know that we have a mammal brain, too. That's the compassion brain and the kinship brain.

And what I've learned is these kids—just to hear their stories. Like one of them has not come to class the last few weeks because he was stabbed very severely, and he, he's still healing. Another didn't come last week because he was hit by a gun, and had stitches all over his head; he says he'll be well enough to come next week. A young man was thrown out of his house by his family with all of his belongings out on the street. He's 17. A young woman found last week she's pregnant, and she's 16 or 17. Et cetera. Every day is drama in these people's lives, and we just can't do education the way we've been doing it.

This post-modern generation—this is not just for inner-city kids. A scientist at Stanford told me, when he heard about what we were doing, "You know, my son graduated from Palo Alto High School, it's one of these privileged high schools, last year. He hated it. I hated it. What you're doing is not just about inner-city kids." (This is a very famous scientist.) "We have to reinvent education across the board." And that's right. We're—the Dalai Lama says, "Education is in crisis the world over." And it's because our species is in crisis. We can't do education in a postmodern time that is modern in its form.

The language of rap and video is very powerful. I have one of PITT's four-minute videos with me that is about meditation. And when you see meditation explained in rap, it's a whole new thing, and you realize, "Hey, the young can carry this." The others don't have to do all the work. We just have to supply them with the stories and some content. For me, this is all about initiation.

STUDENT: *Will you show us the video?*

MATT: Wow, that's nice to hear. Yeah, I'd be glad to show it to you. It's only four minutes. In the afternoon, when we're finished with the proceedings.

CHAPTER 6

Sacred Feminine, Part I

MATT: Okay, I think it's time now to move on to the Sacred, move *back* to the Sacred Feminine: Sacred Feminine continued.

TSOMO: All right. So what's being handed out is your own personal picture of Tara. She's the green figure in the middle of the thangka here that's hanging on the wall, and her mantra, which is the sound formula that invokes her presence, is written in both Tibetan and then Anglicized letters. The Tibetan letters are considered to have power just in their very form. The Sanskrit of the mantra is a language that has never been commonly used in everyday life. It was only for spiritual purposes.

And in the biorhythms of the universe—how can I say this?—the spiritual air is thinner or thicker with delusion at different times, so that there will be arcs, where it's very easy for us to see reality as it really is, and then it goes down, and then it goes up again. And there are small blips in between, kind of like biorhythms that we know about. The whole universe, of course, is in waves, so this is another waveform. And at this time you may not be shocked to know that we've been going on a long downslide. These dark times were talked about in the prophecies by Guru Rinpoche, who brought Buddhism to Tibet in the 800s CE. He gave a lot of specific predictions, including global warming and how the mountains in Tibet would look as the snows, the glaciers, that were thousands and thousands of years old, would melt. And indeed they're looking like that now. He predicted SARS, he predicted AIDS, he even predicted the shape of the organisms for AIDS and SARS. So it's kind of interesting to think that these biorhythms were understood by the Buddha and then by Guru Rinpoche, who also reached full enlightenment.

He also wrote many cycles of teachings that could take us from here to liberation, and then hid them in various places throughout Tibet. He predicted the name and the place of the person who would reveal this particular treasure, and at what time, and that particular treasure, and he gave specifics. And many of these treasures have been discovered. The practice we're going to do today, or at least be introduced to today, is from one of these treasures. The treasure revealer was Tsasum Lingpa. This is a particular lineage within the Vajrayana tradition, and it's a practice to Tara. We'll be doing that in just a minute.

I just wanted to say, in listening to you, Matt, talking about the healing of the toxicity of the masculine, I think that there is a lot of toxic feminine, which feminists are a little afraid to talk about, because the feminine has been considered so terrible for so long. We're still fighting against the writing of *The Witch Hammer*. What?

MATT: That was written by not one, but two Dominicans. That's the shadow side.

TSOMO: You didn't have to say that.

MATT: I know.

TSOMO: When you were talking about the greed, the immeasurable, unimaginable greed that is driving this society, some of it is a greed for power, and I think pride. That can be sort of a masculine version of the motivation. But I think there's also overwhelming desire. This longing is a very real and powerful longing, which is very mixed up about what we're longing for. And isn't it interesting that, as I mentioned last night, desire is the confused, neurotic, emotional version of the true essence of that which is discerning wisdom? So if we just keep asking ourselves the question, "What is it I really long for?" Is it really to have this item from this store? Is it really about eating chocolate? Or is it really about so many of the things that we keep longing for? Even our lover: We long for our lover, but as many of us in this audience know, we've projected our own animus, which is the doorway to our spirit. We've projected that huge, powerful part of ourselves on another person, and then when they walk out of the room we feel bereft, and we have this unbearable longing—in the first throes of love, anyway.

STUDENT: *Could you repeat that? Desire is the confused emotional . . .*

TSOMO: Sort of outer crust of the true essence, which is one of the five aspects of primordial wisdom, and this one is discerning wisdom.

So, there is, I think, a case where it's toxic feminine, and so there needs to be healing of that, and working with an archetype such as Green Tara is very healing. I'm just going to tell a personal story of mine. Because my relationship with my mother was difficult, I didn't receive a lot of the nurturing that I felt I needed. And, of course, there was this other longing that is beyond this lifetime; it's about having wandered in millions of lifetimes, since beginningless time, and wanting to come back home to the great ocean of awareness, which is also a feminine archetype: *the* mother of archetypes, if you will, Yum Chenmo, the Great Mother.

So I found myself somehow in the country growing my own food. We were vegetarians. And we had goats for milk, and I made cheese and yogurt, and we had a huge garden; then I put up the vegetables and made my own bread, and this kind of thing. With very little effort, I was getting all of the food for my family. And I was a mother by giving birth to three kids and nurturing them. This was really a healing time for me. I did this for eleven years, so it was a significant part of my life; it was the beginning of my adult life. I left that experience a very different person, able to appreciate my own feminine and beauty, and so on and so forth, and was on the road to even healing my relationship with my mother. I was unable to say goodbye to my garden when I left. It was just too much for me, and I didn't know how to do it. I could have used a ritual then. I didn't know how to work with the feminine after that, when I then moved to the city, but at least I brought some of that with me.

Many years later, when I was taking my training in psychology, we were practicing some techniques on each other, and somebody was practicing the technique on me—I was being the client—and it suddenly just came bubbling up. My grief at missing the garden was so profound that I just was a mess. I was completely undone. I was just a puddle of tears for days after that. And I finally came to realize, "Why is this so huge for

me?" It's because I never said goodbye to my garden and found a way to
. . . you know, when that fellow's flute was taken away, you have to find
your way to the greater thing. When I didn't have the perfect mother,
which none of us does anyway, so we all have pain about that, I went to
something greater—Mother Earth—and was nurtured by her. And then
I didn't have that garden anymore. By the way, I've always had small
gardens since then, even in the city, and I now live in the country again
and have a bigger garden. But now I don't depend on it for that so much
because I've gone to something even greater. I keep growing beneath
it and to a greater presence of "the mother" and able to really connect
with it.

C: PRACTICE—*Green Tara*—*Venerable Mother*

Tsomo: The purpose of the practice that I'm going to teach today is to bring us into a strong connection with the Great Mother, as I mentioned last night: Yum Chenmo, the Great Mother, Prajnaparamita, the great ocean, the ocean of emptiness, awareness, out of which all appearances arise. And we're all appearances; I just thought I should inform you. We don't believe it, but actually it's true.

Anyway, this is like a fundamental. I was giving the metaphor of a musical note. If we sound a musical note and then divide it, if we can analyze it through scientific methods, there are sub-sounds within that actual note. How many people know anything about music, can read music? Okay. So from that fundamental note, and I don't think I can do this with these microphones, if I make a note, I can filter it out with my mouth: the overtones. You can do this on a piano if you lift the damper. If you play a low C, the high C will resonate if you hold it down to raise the damper because that string on the lower C is not only vibrating in one arc, it's vibrating in half. So that's twice as fast then. And it's vibrating half and half and half again, and so on. So, you get twice as fast as middle C, and then you come to G. That's the next note within that fundamental. And then you get to the next C, then you get to E. So C–E–G is the basic tonic major chord. So I wish I could demonstrate for you, but we don't have the right sound setup for that because it has to be very quiet to hear those overtones. But a person could learn to filter those out, and I learned that from a musician and composer who taught me that.

In that same way, Yum Chenmo then, on the next octave up, the first overtone, is Green Tara. And because Yum Chenmo is beyond form and concept, and we're stuck on this channel, which is all about form and concept, unfortunately—and pretty confused form and concept—it's very difficult for us to relate to Yum Chenmo. But my teacher has tried to do something to alleviate that, and through sacred architecture has built this huge statue that's in Montana at our center. It's Ewam, and you can look it up online at ewam.org and learn about some of the deep meaning of Prajnaparamita as well as this Buddha Garden. She's quite large. She's, as I said, 25 feet tall, and out of her come all of the Buddhas. So there will be a thousand Buddhas about this tall in a *dharma* wheel around her with flowers and trees and places to sit. The statue is built, and the central figure is built, and we're constructing the other statues.

The next octave up is Green Tara, and this is the practice we're going to be working with today. Within the practice we sing the praises to the Twenty-One Taras, which are then the next overtones that you get within that fundamental note. So they have all sorts of different qualities that issue from the Green Tara. With no further ado, I'm going to just take us through this practice. And the reason I'm doing this is that I think if you could understand how the Tibetans work so skillfully with archetypes to evoke them from within ourselves, and invoke them from the universe, to sound that note of that particular archetype, I think it's quite enriching. And it's such a pleasure to share this with people who have been so interested in the work of archetypes, because of the Jungian background. I, because of my Jungian background, found it much easier as a Westerner to relate to these practices and understand what the intent was and what they were doing. Because of my Jungian background, I'm so thankful to that because that was my bridge.

If we think of the universe as holographic, then the Tara Principle suffuses everything. Where is that principle not? Where would that archetype not be? And, of course, why would it not be within us? We are a hologram of all of the archetypes. This is why, at death, Tibetan Buddhists believe, that all the hundred peaceful and wrathful deities appear. We contain all of them within us, *but* they're all murky in the background, and sometimes causing a whole lot of mischief because of it, especially in their toxic forms.

We include all the five senses as well as the thinking mind, the tendency of the mind to follow thoughts. We include all of those in the practice. We take all of what we are, what we work with, as we are now, and put it on the path to enlightenment. Even our passionate emotions are folded into this so that they're actually empowering this endeavor to pursue enlightenment. It's very different from other Buddhist paths, such as Hinayana, where you're really trying to keep yourself from all of these afflictive emotions that spatter our windshields and keep us from seeing reality as it is. In this case, we're actually taking the emotions and, in Vajrayana, as I said, with desire, seeing to the essence of it, peeling away the layers of the onion so that we can see, we can come to discerning wisdom. So there's an example of skillfully starting with where we are and getting us to where we want to be.

So, with body, speech, and mind, and all the five senses, as well as the capacity of thinking, we address this practice. We prepare the shrine, and there're all sorts of symbolic things on the shrine, which, again, even us foolish left-brain-driven people don't consciously understand, but our unconscious in our right brain seem to register just fine. Westerners have had success with these practices, and this Westerner has hugely benefited from them. So, apparently, they're universal enough, even without a lot of explanation. The lamas do get a little impatient with the Westerners' questions: "What does this mean? What does that mean?" You just do it.

So we prepare the shrine, and then as we sit down, we always begin any session with making sure that our motivation is coming from only two purposes: enlightenment for self, and enlightenment for others. Enlightenment for self is not just to get ourselves out of Samsara and into a place of always being happy, but we don't want to leave everybody else suffering when we go. If we're drowning in Samsara, we're not going to be very good at saving anybody. But if we become enlightened ourselves, then we can do a lot of good at liberating everyone. So those are the motivations that come from bodhicitta. *Bodhicitta* is translated sometimes as "awakened heart."

We begin by invoking Guru Rinpoche—who, remember, hid this treasure, this teaching, this practice, many, many years ago—through the Seven Line Prayer. The sounds invoke his presence. Then we pray to the lineage lamas who brought this down to us today, including our own root lama. Gochen Tulku Rinpoche, who is the lama of Ewam, is the only qualified lineage holder for this particular lineage in the world today. We then invoke all of these lineage lamas so that we are now connected in line. Remember I was mentioning last night about the practice being like a lamp. And until you plug the lamp into the power source, the lamp doesn't light up. This practice won't light up until we connect ourselves, our mind to their minds, so that the fullness of spontaneous presence comes through. Before even doing this practice, one usually goes for an empowerment with the lama. I have had the empowerment, the Tara empowerment, of this lineage from Gochen Tulku Rinpoche. That then plants the seed. It opens the mind then to this lineage and this avenue to Tara and to enlightenment.

So we've now invoked the, all of the lineage lamas, and Guru Rinpoche and so on, and now we set up the visualizations. So then the liturgy goes like this. [*Tsomo reads from the practice text.*]

"In the sky in front of me appears the Accomplished Transcendent Conqueress, inseparable from my lama."

Remember the lama's doorway to this, and his enlightened mind is no different from hers, because there's only one enlightened mind.

"Kye! From the mandala of the hand of the protector Amitabha."

Amitabha is the bu-, gu-, the Buddha of Limitless Light, and that's the discerning wisdom, wis-, one of the five wisdoms that I was mentioning earlier. So, "From the mandala of the hand of the protector Amitabha, whence arose from the eye of the Lord of the World, Avalokitesvara,"

He is one of the great Bodhisattvas, and from one of his tears came Tara. That's one of the stories of Tara.

"The Swift Mother, the source of an ocean of *Dakinis*, twenty-one emanations of the Conqueror's compassion, the Glorious Swift Mother, the activity of all victorious ones, to my lama, lord protector, inseparable from all enlightened ones, I prostrate and pray that you bestow blessings and empowerment."

Prostration is taking the brain and the thinking mind, and really the ego, the smaller mind, and bowing it down to the ground, literally touching the ground, before greater mind. Some of the Jungians might think of self, but I think it's perhaps even beyond that.

Then the next stage, now that we've set up the imagery, so we're engaging eyesight, we're going to engage the body and the smell even. There's Tara incense that you can burn that evokes Tara. Now we take refuge, because she's presented here before us. We're consciously deciding to unplug from taking refuge in shopping, and even our friends and family, and all the things of Samsara that eventually, one way or another, let us down, because there're just things of Samsara. We're now plugging into something beyond Samsara; that's one of the purposes of refuge. It's also just consciously setting one's foot on the path of enlightenment. And we want to keep renewing that on a regular basis. So there's refuge, and this is combined with the stage of bodhicitta, which, again, is giving rise to awakened heart. Knowing that all beings are suffering, we want to help all beings. That's got to be our motivation. So the liturgy continues.

"*Namo!* To the Venerable Mother, the essence of the ocean of refuge, I go for refuge until I reach the heart of enlightenment. May all sentient beings drowning in the ocean of suffering accomplish the state of the Mother Arya Tara."

Then we make offerings. There's the Seven Branch Offering and so on. Now there's more invoking. We begin with "OM AAH HUNG." If you say "OM," "AAH," and "HUNG," you find that they resonate in these three chakras, respectively. We might just stop for a minute and see if that's true.

STUDENT: *Which chakras? Can you just point to them?*

TSOMO: Okay.

[*Everyone sounds out "OM."*]

TSOMO: Can you feel that vibrating up there?

[*Everyone sounds out "AAH," then "HUNG."*]

TSOMO: So you see that's very real. These are sound formulas from Sanskrit. So we begin with "OM AAH HUNG."

"In the completely pure realm of Yulokod, Array of Turquoise Leaves," That's her pureland. This is her palace within the pureland. I won't go into all the symbolism, but there's a huge amount of symbolism in this mandala. These four lines here are the four walls of the palace, and the four gates are in the center of each of those. And the symbolism continues. There's a wall of fire protection, and within that, the blue line just inside of that striped line, is actually like chainmail of *vajras*, which are completely surrounding within the firewall. The palace is within that. She's in the Land of Turquoise Leaves and she's sitting resplendent, as you can see, in this picture. Her left hand is up in protection. Her right hand is giving out the signs of accomplishment—both the more common *siddhis*, of flying through the air and that sort of thing, but also, the ultimate *siddhis* of enlightenment.

"In the completely pure realm of Yulokod, Array of Turquoise Leaves, in the center of an ocean filled with clouds of Samantabhadra's offerings,"

Samantabhadra is the primordial Buddha.

"TAM."

That's this syllable. It looks like this. And again, there's actual power to call Tara just within the form of it, but also in the sound, "TAM."

"Instantly, upon recollection, I appear as the perfect form of Mother Arya Tara. Clearly in the three places, forehead, throat, and heart, appear three vajra letters, OM, AAH, and HUNG. From the heart, light rays radiate to all the victorious ones"

That's all the enlightened ones.

"and their heirs,"

the Bodhisattvas,

"invoking the form of Arya Tara. With twenty-one emanated goddesses, who, dancing in delight, appear real and perfectly clear to my senses."

Now that they're here in front of us. First of all, we had to be to an exalted level even to truly invoke this presence, so now we invoke it. We evoked it before with the seed syllable, and then from that we instantly appear. This helps us to get out of the habit of thinking we have to be born, born, and reborn. We're born as Tara, who's a being of light, and instantly. We've invoked Tara in front of us, and she appears real and perfectly clear, and yet she's not substantial. She doesn't have kidneys and blood and all that sort of thing. She's a body of light.

Now we make these offerings to her.

"OM AAH HUNG."

"Together with an ocean and clouds of real and imagined offerings, I offer the mandala of my body, enjoyments, and collection of virtue."

We do this hand *mudra* of offering out, like this, which I won't try to teach you today. It's difficult. But just involving the kinesthetic sense.

"May I and all beings gather the accumulations and purify obscurations. From now until the heart of enlightenment is reached, may we never be separated from the compassion of the Exalted Mother."

We chant the 21 names of the Twenty-One Taras. Then we go back and do the offering again. We chant her name, her 21 names, two times altogether, and then go back and do the offerings, because now we're offering to them, go back and do the names three more times, make the offerings again, then seven times, then we proceed on.

"Kye! From the mandala of the hand of protector Amitabha, whence arose from the eye of the Lord of the World, Avalokitesvara, the Swift Mother, the source of an ocean of Dakinis, 21 emanations of the Conqueror's compassion, the Glorious Swift Mother, the activity of all victorious ones, to my lama, lord protector, inseparable from all enlightened ones, I prostrate and pray that you bestow blessings and empowerment. From the exalted teacher's three places . . ."

The teacher as Tara.

"From her three places, white, red, blue, and yellow light rays radiate sequentially. They dissolve into my four places."

So there are now four chakras involved, including the one below the navel.

"Arya Tara joyfully dissolves into light, and then into myself."

In these empowerments, all of the toxicity and obscurations of these chakras then are completely purified, and the Buddha Nature in each of those particular facets of it comes fully forth. There are hand mudras with this. Again, as we say,

"dissolve into my four places, and I obtain the four empowerments. Arya Tara joyfully dissolves into light, and then into myself."

As we do these hand motions, then, we truly imagine the joining of the inner and outer Tara. And then we say,

"I appear clearly as the Accomplished Transcendent Conqueress. Look upon the Absolute Noble Mother, the unity of lucidity and emptiness."

Here we have the accomplishment of the Exalted Marriage, or the Sacred Marriage of lucidity and emptiness. Remember, that's what everything is: emptiness and then the luminosity, the appearance that comes from that emptiness. It's one ocean. She has mastered that, and we are that mastery now in the form of Tara.

Now I'd like to switch to the other. Here is the mantra that we'll now say. We've now manifested Tara to a great extent, but we're going to even strengthen it. The Tibetan has the form that, that invokes her presence, and the sounds I wrote out in English. "OM TARE TUTTARE TURE SVAHA." So let's say that slowly.

[*Everyone recites the mantra together.*] "OM TARE TUTTARE TURE SVAHA."

Let's say that, maybe, one or two more times.

[*Everyone recites the mantra three times.*] "OM TARE TUTTARE TURE SVAHA."

In order to master this, often people will recite this mantra one million times so that they really spend time with this. I knew of one lama—he's a great Rinpoche, one of the greater ones of this time—who, when he was accomplishing a practice, would never count a mantra unless he was so moved with strong feeling that he had tears in his eyes, or had goose bumps all over his body. If we then can imagine ourselves in the Realm of Turquoise Leaves, we are now Tara ourselves. We've evoked that, invoked it. This is now the presence of Tara. As we say this mantra, we imagine it going around clockwise inside of our hearts. In the very center of it is the seed syllable, "TAM."

We're going to recite this with a lovely musical chanting of it. The melody is the traditional chant melody; there's some flute with it. And Ani Tsering Wangmo sings this. She is an accomplished Tara practitioner. She's devoted many, many years of her life to Tara, and has had amazing experiences in retreat, doing Tara practice. She's singing this and truly embodying Tara as she sings it. We'll do some with her, and then after a short time, we'll turn the recording off and maybe just continue a little bit ourselves.

So remember, we are Tara [*Music starts.*] in this mandala, the Land of Turquoise Leaves.

[*Everyone chants with the recording.*]

The letters are green and the light rays go out from these green letters. The light rays are green, and they touch all enlightened beings who appear as Tara. And the light rays come back into us so that we're on this Tara wavelength, sounding this Tara note.

[*Everyone chants with the recording.*]

So bring your longing for the Great Mother.

[*Everyone chants with the recording.*]

As we bask in this presence, we just say the mantra slow, quietly, or just even making the shape with our mouths to ourselves. It's said quite rapidly once you're used to it. But just take your time with it right now and say it to yourself a few more times.

[*Everyone recites "OM TARE TUTTARE TURE SVAHA" quietly.*]

Again, basking in the Tara presence.

[*Everyone recites "OM TARE TUTTARE TURE SVAHA" quietly.*]

The light rays also go out to all sentient beings, liberating them from suffering and bringing them to bliss, everlasting bliss.

[*Everyone recites "OM TARE TUTTARE TURE SVAHA" quietly.*]

Tara has her right foot out—she leaves her left foot in because of self-mastery, and her right foot out to be instantly available to all of us who call on her. She is beloved by Tibetans because she can be called on in times of need for protection, for clearing away obstacles, and also for manifesting the things that we need. So now that we've brought her presence so clearly into the room and into ourselves, and this room is her pureland now. We ask her for any of those things: protection, clearing away obstacles, or manifesting things that we need. OM TARE TUTTARE TURE SVAHA, OM TARE TUTTARE TURE SVAHA. And truly ask for specific things.

[*Everyone recites "OM TARE TUTTARE TURE SVAHA" quietly.*]

And then, because we've come to the end of the practice, and in case there were any imperfections mentally or in any other way in the practice, we say the 100-syllable mantra of Vajrasattva, who is the archetype of clearing away any imperfections and toxicity. So we recite that, and then we confess before the Exalted Mother.

"Ho! Before the Exalted Mother, I confess the mass of my impurity and faults."

In confession, in Tibetan, the word *shakpa* means "to reveal." If you crack open a seed husk and reveal the seed, it's no longer viable. So the karmic seeds that we planted, because of confession, are no longer viable. This is the thought there. So.

"I confess the mass of my impurity and faults. With my completely pure three doors,"

That's body, speech, and mind.

"I enter the path of timeless awareness."

This is the primordial wisdom that I was talking about.

"I dedicate the assembly of virtue of the three times"

Past, present, and future.

"Within basic space. May I quickly attain the state of the unity of the Noble Mother. Until enlightenment is reached, may there be the auspiciousness of never being separated from the compassionate protection of my lama, Venerable Mother!"

CHAPTER 7

Sacred Feminine, Part II

TSOMO: Then there's more dedication and aspirational prayers. So that's the complete practice.

I hope you've had a little bit of an experience of the feminine. This helps me when I don't get to get out in the garden enough. So did you want to respond, then, as a man?

MATT: Yeah, I was supposed to take a few minutes to respond as a man. I was struck toward the end when you were talking about the repetition of the seed syllable in the heart and all that. By what I experienced as a young man with the litany to the Blessed Virgin Mary in the Catholic Church, it is a mantra, of course, because you have these beautiful phrases like "mystical rose," "tower of ivory." And then you say, "Pray for us. Pray for us." So the "Pray for us" part is a repetition thing. It's a mantra. And I always found these extremely ecstatic. I would soar. It was an invocation of the Divine Feminine for sure, but it had some wonderful imagination to it. The imagery there was very rich.

And I was struck when you talked about the seed in the heart. You know, it does take me back to the Green Man, which is all about seeds. Plants are all about seeds, and it is about planting the Divine seed in the heart, and working from the heart. From there through the fifth chakra, but also calling down, calling down the sixth chakra as well, so it goes out of the mouth.

I was struck by the mandala painting you had there. As you were describing it, it was kind of déjà vu again for, for me: Hildegard's mandalas. So many of them are of the same kind, ilk. There are many, many layers to it, and there's a lot going on in these mandalas. And yet there is the order that a mandala provides: the centering device. So I was certainly resonating with a, a lot of your imagery there.

As a man, for myself, discovering the feminine, how did that happen for me, really? Interestingly, somewhat parallel to you, but the reverse: I was closer to my mother than my father. I was told, in my twenties, that a week, or a few weeks, after I was born, my dad said to my mother—I was the fourth child in four years—he said, "You're going to have to raise this guy. He's too sensitive for me." Which is interesting, because it shows how sensitive my father was, that he would know that. So I was closer to my mother. But my mother was a very strong woman—a lot of animus in my mother. Well, my father was, too. He was Scorpio and she was Taurus, so they had some good fights.

Tsomo: Those are both fixed signs.

Matt: But they stayed together. What's that?

Tsomo: They're both fixed signs.

Matt: Fixed?

Tsomo: Fixed.

Matt: Oh, stubborn.

Tsomo: So nobody's going to move.

Matt: Yeah. That's how it was. Here's one of my favorite stories. My mother was half-Jewish and half-English, and was raised Episcopalian. My father was Irish Catholic, and, of course, they had a mixed marriage. But after a couple years, my mom made a decision on her own that you can't have a mixed religion. So she took lessons secretly—never told my father that. Of course, they would go to Mass on Sunday together, but my mom would never go to Communion. So this one Mass, my mom gets up to go to Communion with my father. And my father looks at her, "What the hell are you doing?" So in the middle of the church aisle, they're having a fight, while people are going to Communion. You see, that, for us as a family, is archetypal of my parents. You know, it's each stubborn, each doing their thing and, but working it out.

So my exposure to the feminine was never wimpy. My father was Republican, my mother was anything but, so we used to say, "Why do you bother to vote? You cancel each other out every time. You ought to stay home and save it." I think, for me personally, that's very important, that I've never identified the feminine with wimpiness or passivity.

In the 1950s, when I was a teenager, I would go to Saturday Mass. I would go to Mass also during the week, because I had a paper route and got up early when it was dark, and it was easy to drop into church at the end of it and then go home. I realized I was really drawn to Saturday Masses, because in the Saturday Masses they had the Wisdom literature from the Wisdom books of the Jewish scriptures. I couldn't articulate what it was that was happening to me, but there were profound mystical experiences for me in hearing the passages like "Before the creation of the world, I was there. I walk the vaults of the sky and I walk the sands of the deep." It just totally spoke to my male heart, because what I was getting as a teenager was cars and football—and I liked football; my father was a football coach and I was a good athlete and all that—but I knew something was missing. And I got it from the feminine scriptures, about which now scholars are saying, "Oh, by the way, this was the stuff that Jesus knew. He comes from the Wisdom tradition." So, he, too, had a very strong feminine dimension, not a wimpy feminine dimension.

I find this in the echoes of what you were saying about Tara and the necklaces of death and the toxic feminine. I think the toxic feminine is the Barbie doll, among other things. You could make a litany of the toxic feminine. There's a lot of it, and I appreciate you naming it, because it's true. Especially as a man, and during the time, during my generation of women's liberation and women's awakening, it's not my task to tell women what's the shadow of being women. That's for women to bring out. And women have to do that. Just as, as a man, you know, I'm trying to talk about how we can do better as males.

And, so, those are a few responses I have. I love the whole thing of the Green Tara. And it just so links up to this whole archetype of the Green Man. And she's in all of us. As you say, she's in us men as well. For me, being whole, being a person, being a human being, is about finding that balance. Jung can call it *animus* and *anima*, but I find that language a little—I don't know—a little weighty, a little tired. I think we can come up with more colorful names. Maybe it is the Green Tara and the Green Man, for example. Or maybe it is the Black Madonna and the Green Man. But in any case, too, and we'll be getting more into this this afternoon, this is that Sacred Marriage. This is coming to the sense of balance. It's yin and yang. And our culture's not been good at that. We have had a patriarchy, and that patriarchy has wounded men and women, and culture itself, and religion, God knows. So we are quite bereft. We're longing. I think we're longing for some healthy marriages, some healthy sense of the sacred.

I had a dream a number of years ago that was so unusual because it was so clear. There was one sentence, and it just affected me. It said, "There's nothing wrong with the human race today except for one thing—that you've lost the sense of the sacred." That was it. The sense of the sacred, where is it? And it's not going to be found by just shouting patriarchal slogans. As Jesus said, "Not everyone who invokes my name gets it. Not all who say, 'Lord, Lord' shall experience the kingdom."

I love the, the sophistication and the subtlety of so much here. It's using all the senses and the sounds and all that.

TSOMO: And, of course, there's way more than I could mention.

MATT: Well, of course there is. We're, we are an amazing species. We are capable of such subtlety just in sound alone, as you say, just in sound alone. It's very inspiring, I think. It pumps you up to know that there have been scholars and sages and practitioners, East and West, over the centuries. Thomas Aquinas says, "There's never been a culture without prophets." Prophets come through all cultures. It's inspiring to know that this is a communal treasure that we inherit. This is the lineage. These are the ancestors, and they've not been doing nothing. That story you told about a monk or a guru who chants a mantra a million times is like, "Whoa." I mean, so that's what you do in your free time? You go chant. You don't have to go turn on that TV at all. You just chant mantras a few hundred times. Try it. See what cooks.

TSOMO: I've chanted a mantra a million times.

MATT: Ah ha. Wow!

TSOMO: A lot of practitioners have done that. You are changed by the end of spending that much time with the archetype.

MATT: Yeah, of course. And the mantra of Rosary in the West, which, of course, comes from Islam, and through Spain, which is where Islam was so strong. The myth is it came through Saint Dominic. But the point is, that, too, is a mantra that said over and over again has an effect on numbing—I call it "numbing"—the left brain so that the mystical brain can kind of soar.

So those are a few responses I have. I went to public high school. When I was considering joining the Dominicans, I went to visit them in Dubuque, Iowa, where they had a monastery and a training center. And what most drew me in was the sense of community, but also the aesthetic of hearing them chant, and they were chanting in Latin. It just moved me. It got to my heart. And, for me, that is the feminine side of community in a way: the aesthetic. We can't live without the aesthetic. The Tibetans are so good at it. Catholicism, at its best, is good at it, or was good at it. The Gregorian chant—that's not owned by anybody. It's brilliant. Of course, it comes from the synagogue. We know that. It comes from the synagogue.

You see, the modern era threw out aesthetics. Descartes has a whole philosophy, but no philosophy of aesthetics. Beauty is not in our moral vocabulary. This is part of a post-modern era, that we have to recapture our idea of God as beauty. Aquinas was pre-modern. He says, "God is the most beautiful being in the universe, and all beings participate in the Divine beauty." So every experience we have of beauty, whether it's visual, musical, silence, the ancestral truth, whatever it is, this is Tara appearing, this is divinity appearing, this is God appearing. And we have to get back to that. That's one big dimension in which we've lost the sense of the sacred.

I met a Greek Orthodox theologian who said, "In our tradition, the bottom line in a moral act is this: Is what I'm doing, is what we are doing, beautiful or not?" There you go. That's bringing the aesthetic to center stage, which is where it belongs. Again, I honor Buddhism for having so many practices that do that. I'm thinking right now of the sand paintings. And so much of Native American, too, is, the test is beauty.

Tsomo: I'm just thinking of what you said about the bottom line being beauty. I don't know how many of you know this, but the king of Bhutan has talked specifically about gross national happiness because he's very aware that just going by gross national product, the bottom line in the way that we've done it, has produced the opposite. And so he's become rather famous for that: this tiny little country. And it's Buddhist, by the way. It's the only Buddhist kingdom, I think, left in the world, actually.

Matt: Really?

Tsomo: Yeah. That's what they claim, but then I wonder about Thailand. So, anyway, they practice Vajrayana in Bhutan, as well as Tibet. Now we'd like to open this up to all of you. I would love to hear your responses. I threw a lot at you, to throw that practice at you today, from nowhere, and I'd love to hear your experience.

Student: *Well, I do have a question that—I noticed that she has marks in her hands and her feet, and like pictures of, of the crucified Christ. They're very beautiful.*

Tsomo: Actually, if I'm not mistaken, those are eyes.

Student: *Eyes?*

Tsomo: Yeah, and one of the Twenty-One Taras is White Tara. She's quite a popular one, too. And she has eyes on these chakras, because of being so awake.

Student: *I've been doing my own work with moving into the feminine divine. And it's progressing, but last night when you, Matt, showed the Black Madonna, I couldn't get, I could not have, the sense of the archetype as a physical experience. I could not physically relate to her, really, because I've seen too many pictures of the Mary who's been hijacked by the negative parts of Christianity, of the Mother, the Madonna. But this is a beautiful person here. This is very appealing to me. So thank you for that. I, I don't have the words for that, but thank you for that.*

Tsomo: Yeah. I think we, as Westerners, can be very susceptible to Tara. [*to student*] Yeah.

Student: *Would it be helpful to anybody but me for you to talk about the Turquoise Leaves?*

Another Student: *I'd love you to.*

TSOMO: Gosh, just in the sense that in this pureland, the colors are more vibrant and more varied than we see in our flawed vision now. And by the way, of course, the Land of Turquoise Leaves is not another address. It's not another location. It's right here and everywhere. Her palace is surrounded by this Land of Turquoise Leaves, and the beings there all have the appearance of Tara. And again, this is just the Tara archetype playing itself out in form, but on the archetypal level, the Sambhogakaya, that I was speaking of last night. Anyone want to speak of their experience?

STUDENT: *Again, the sense of the feminine. When I was in the seminary, we had Mary shrines the month of May, those sentimental Irish hymns of "This Day O Beautiful Mother." So that touched me very much, plus the music. On the other hand, around the time of the Vatican Council, liberal theologians were kind of attacking what they called Mariolatry, and it was like there was too much Mary. Well, in a patriarchal church, there can never be too much Mary. And, in fact, we all once fought with the dogma of the Assumption that it was a great idea, in fact, because the Catholic Church has caught the fact that the feminine is part of the Divine. That sense of the feminine through hymns, through music, but, although it was there, it was always combated by the other side: the power, the superiors, the bishops, the popes, and everything. So for me, personally, it's always been a struggle between the feminine. Not a marriage, you know—kind of an internal fight.*

MATT: Well, you see, one thing about Catholicism is that it's pre-modern, so it has a goddess. And that is the point of Black Madonna, but Mary in general. Whereas Protestantism almost consciously threw out the goddess because the modern era did. And Protestantism is contemporary with the, with the modern era. So there is at least a memory. Like the stories I told about the passages from Wisdom literature that were rolled in on Saturday, because Saturday was always dedicated to Mary. So, at least Catholicism has a memory. But you also have to say, though, there's a great distortion. When patriarchy takes Mary, or takes the feminine, it doesn't treat it appropriately a lot of the time. For example, putting it on a pedestal, or establishing the virgin versus the whore archetype. So there's a distortion. There's a toxic Mary. And that's, I think, what these theologians were fighting in talking about Mariolatry, because you'll find in fascist states there's often a devotion to Mary. And you have to critique that. Is this the authentic Lady of justice and compassion, or is this a sick use of the feminine principle to reinforce control over?

STUDENT: *This is Mary?*

MATT: Yeah. I'll give this concrete example. It's not extreme, but, when I was working on Hildegard, I was at a conference in Portland, I think it was, on the Divine Feminine, and I was invited. It was all women speakers but me, because I had Hildegard slides. So I showed Hildegard slides and talked about her, and all this. And I'll never forget. This woman came up afterward, and she said, "I am going to run home. I have three teenage daughters." She said, "I've never heard of this lady." She said, "I'm Catholic, you know. Mary's great, but she didn't do all that much. This lady, she's a healer, a scientist. She wrote ten books. She was a genius musician and a painter. And I," she said, "I'm running home to tell my daughters about this, because they don't know anything about the rich feminine in the Christian tradition. They only know about Mary, and Mary as interpreted by a patriarchy, can be one great big fat projection." I've never forgotten that moment, because this lady was really ready to roll with Hildegard.

I don't have daughters, and I thought about it a long time, and I said, "Wow," you know, "raising daughters without a healthy feminine model is, is a very dangerous thing to do." And, of course, it's dangerous to raise boys without both healthy masculine and healthy feminine models. And we're flooded with a media of unhealthy . . .

TSOMO: I came to the same conclusion, which is why I wrote the book *The Princess Who Wept Pearls*, which is a collection of feminine fairy tales and interpretations so that the parents can understand what they're a little bit about, what they're actually giving through the symbolism to their kids. And the stories are also included. I found that I had to go to premodern times, really pre-Christian times, to find these stories.

STUDENT: *What's the name of the book?*

TSOMO: *The Princess Who Wept Pearls*, but it's not in print right now. Sorry. Are there any other comments on the experience, or questions that arise from it, or is it beyond articulation? [*To student*] Yeah.

STUDENT: *I would just love to chant the mantra longer with the melody line. It's beautiful, only I've never heard the, the "HA."*

TSOMO: It's "SO HA." She trails off at the "HA." She did say it, but she sort of trailed off with it. [*To student*] Yes.

STUDENT: *This is a subjective experience, experiencing the two of you, Tsomo and Matthew. It goes to the same place, and I just want to articulate that. I'm enjoying both of you, and you take me there in a different way. And I think that that might be the feminine.*

[*Applause*]

MATT: Thank you. I think that's a good note to end on.

CHAPTER 8

Sacred Masculine & Divine Feminine

MATT: This afternoon we're going to wrestle with the issue of Sacred Marriage. And this is actually how my, my forthcoming book on the Sacred Masculine ends: It ends with not one chapter, but two chapters on Sacred Marriage. So I'm going to share with you some of those ideas. I'm scheduled for 20 minutes. And then Tsomo has 20 minutes on the topic. Then, then discussion.

Obviously I'm very interested in Sacred Marriage, because once women find their dignity, and their beauty, and their womanhood, and men find theirs, then there's a new equality. It's not working, to the extent that women have developed their consciousness quite profoundly the last 40 years, and men are still kind of wandering off into the desert alone We need to bring more equality to this discussion of the Divine Feminine and the Sacred Masculine. Both have been exiled, but I think, frankly, women are on the faster track than men right now, and I'm concerned about that, and it shows. It shows in the eyes of Dick Cheney, among other places, without naming any names.

I'm struck by a statement by Jung, which I quote in here, that has to be said in a Jung house. No, actually, it's not a statement *by* Jung, it's a statement *about* Jung. I have a friend; you may have read some of his books, John Conger. Have you heard of him? He a bioenergetics guy. He's grounded in Reikian therapy, but also Jung. He considerers himself a Jungian and a Reikian, and he's very much into the body. He's in his seventies. When he was 61, he took up Korean martial arts with his sons, who were teenagers, and got a black belt in it. So he's a very interesting guy. He's an Episcopalian priest, by the way—very bright, very intelligent. And I was doing this book, and I said, "Well, what's your take on the Sacred Marriage according to Jung?" And this is what he said, and I loved it. This may offend some of you, but I love it because it made sense to me. He said, and I quote, "Every time I read Jung on this subject, I find him totally confused and confusing." That's my experience exactly.

So this opened it up so that I could do this myself. This is why I have two chapters. I don't talk about the Sacred Marriage: I talk about Sacred Marriages. It's a plural thing. Once we find the needed balance between yin and yang, we will have multiple marriages that need to take place. What I'm doing in my precious 20 minutes is to name a few of these marriages that have to happen, and now. We don't have time to waste as a species whatsoever.

Obviously, a first step for men is to recognize the Sacred Feminine in women and in themselves and not resist it. Like, for example, the Vatican. The Vatican still forbids priests to use the female pronoun at the altar. That is so retro. But, of course, when the present pope condemned me, whenever it was, 15 years ago, they had 10 objections to my work. The first was that I'm a feminist theologian. I did not know that was a declared heresy. The second was that I called God "Mother." You see, this is a Rorschach test on the Catholic Church at its top at this time. The third was that I called God "Child," even though I demonstrated all these medieval mystics called God "Mother." Even the Bible does, but not often enough. So you realize the resistance of patriarchy to women being themselves is fierce. It's still going on. The first step, obviously, to any Sacred Marriage is that men have to get over their terror.

And let me tell you this. I feel I've finally come to an analysis of fundamentalism. What the Vatican, the Taliban, and Pat Robertson all have in common is a fear of the feminine. And I know what this comes from. It comes from Chaos: the Goddess of Chaos. The Goddess of Chaos was honored during the goddess period, and chaos is integral to life and birth and everything else. But when patriarchy took over, we changed our myths, and pretty soon Marduk was killing Tiamat, because the notion now, the myth now, was that chaos has to be killed and controlled by the masculine energy. That's what really shifted there. Then religion took over, and, of course, chaos in religion is heresy. Then in the seventeenth century, scientists said, "We're objective. We're the objective ones. You believers move aside. We'll, we'll handle this chaos thing." And science, in its compulsion to control, tried to do exactly that until the 1960s, when a post-modern invention, called the computer, proved to scientists that chaos is integral to all the natural processes we know.

I've had a pleasure of doing dialogues with one of the mathematicians who was behind that discovery of chaos theory, Ralph Abraham. And I'll never forget. We did a dialogue, and this woman came up afterwards. She said, "I'm too shy to talk publicly. But I'm a midwife. And nothing's messier, nothing's more chaotic than birth. And there's blood all over the place. But," as she said, "look at the being that comes out of it." And then it really clicked for me. This is why, in the goddess period, chaos was honored. Because everyone—any artist—knows that chaos is integral to giving birth. And every mother knows that. And fathers are beginning to learn it, too. So I think it's very important that we have to stand up to the forces of misogyny in ourselves, in culture. There'll never be a marriage if you can't at least admit that we're equals. And that's first.

Okay. The first Sacred Marriage, then, is that of Father Sky and Mother Earth. We've talked about both these last two, two days, but just to remind you, Mother Earth is, is, is a, a springboard for poetry. Thomas Berry is one of the great prophetic ecological prophets of our time. And this is one passage that he has, and he's done his scientific homework, and a lot of other homework [paraphrasing].

"As humans we are born of the earth, nourished by the earth, healed by the earth. The natural world tells us, 'I will feed you. I will clothe you. I will shelter you. I will heal you. Or you do not so devour me or use me, that you destroy my capacity to mediate the Divine and the human. For I offer you a communion with the Divine. I offer you gifts that you can exchange with each other in the vastness of the sea, in the snow-covered mountains, in the rivers flowing through the valleys, in the serenity of the landscape, in the foreboding of the great storms that sweep over the land. In all these experiences I offer you inspiration.' It is clear what the Earth offers us, but what do we offer the Earth in return?"

That's a spiritual node of the ecological moment we're in. Are we just taking, or are we giving?

And David Suzuki, in talking about Gaia, has a poem that Homer wrote to Gaia.

> *Mother Earth*
> *The mother of us all,*
> *the oldest of all,*
> *hard,*
> > *splendid as rock*
> *Whatever there is that is of the land*
> > *it is she*
> > *who nourishes it,*
> *It is the Earth*
> > *that I sing*

The Father Sky we talked about this morning marrying Mother Earth; that is a great thing. And in many ways, the Green Man is an archetype of that, because there's no plants without the sky and the earth. The trees, deep in their roots in Mother Earth, and they reach for the sky, and their leaves are constantly dancing in the act of photosynthesis. The Blue Man archetype, too, is about sky. It's about consciousness, expansive consciousness, truly being integrated into our hearts and into our minds. Those are a couple of examples of that marriage. I go through Saint Francis's wonderful poem of Mother Earth, and Jesus's name is not mentioned once. But it's a poem of the Cosmic Christ, or the Buddha Nature, found in the flowers, the rivers, the sun, the moon, and so forth. So this is in our collective unconscious for sure.

A second marriage, a Sacred Marriage needed today is that of the Green Man and the Black Madonna. We talked about both here, so I don't want to dwell on this at great length, but think about that. Play with it. That's what archetypes are for, you know. I think any intelligent idea is to play with. That's what an intellectual life is. An intellectual is one who plays with ideas. And don't think playing with ideas isn't absolutely important. I always tell my students, "All Karl Marx did his whole life was hang out in libraries. He was a lousy father, a lousy husband. He came up with a few ideas, and he dictated twentieth-century history." Our culture underestimates the power of ideas, totally. It overestimates the power of advertising, underestimates the power of ideas, or, if you will, uses ideas in perverse ways. But the idea of Black Madonna marrying Green Man, try it on for size. Play with it. Play with it.

Another Sacred Marriage is yin-yang. This is, of course, an ancient Chinese symbol, but as one of the ancient sayings says, "Yang is like man, yin is like woman. Yang wouldn't grow without yin, yin couldn't give birth without yang. Yin is born and begins at summer solstice, yang is born and begins at winter solstice." Interesting at Christmas time and winter solstice. "Yin and yang," [paraphrasing], says Richard Hooker, "represent all the opposite principles one finds in the universe. Each of these opposites produces the other. Heaven creates the ideas of things under yang. The Earth produces in material forms under yin, and vice versa." So the, the Sacred Marriage of yin and yang in its broadest sense.

Now interestingly, the Gospel of Thomas, which is recognized as one of the earliest Christian writings that they've really uncovered in our century and the past century, has Jesus saying the following:

"When, and if you make all twos into one, if you make the side you show like the side you hide, and the side inside like the side outside, and your higher side like your lower one, with the result that you make the man and woman in you as one, so that there's nothing more to become either male or female, when you find what really sees, eyes in the place of your physical eye, and you find what really grasps and stands and walks, when you make your self image the original image of humanity, then you will be entering the original guiding power of the king and queendom of the Holy One."

That is one translation from the Aramaic of the Gospel of Thomas. It is a beautiful, ancient way of talking about the yin-yang out of the Western tradition. That the kingdom depends, the kingdom's arrival, our awareness, as Tsomo talked about the first night, our perception depends on this marriage going on in our soul. And like any marriage, it's bumpy, and it's not a noun; it's a verb. You have to come up with your Divine Feminine and Divine Masculine every day. It wouldn't matter what moods we're in, and what the circumstances. Every marriage is a verb and not a noun. It's never accomplished. It's an ongoing procreative process.

Interestingly, the Celtic tradition has rituals of the marriage, ancient rituals of the marriage of the land, which is understood to be the feminine, with the King, who's supposed to be ruling, looking over, guiding the community. They have these ancient rituals. And as she said, "The feminine is understood as a ground of being," these ancient rituals. So the feminine is older, you might say, but the men come along and they have their role. But they have to ritualize. It is the Earth itself that is anointing the King to rule with justice. Without these sacred ceremonies, the Celts could not believe that their society was being held together in a sacred and effective way. So this is one more example of yin-yang out of the Western tradition: the Celtic ceremonies that she writes about.

Now, other additional Sacred Marriages that are arising today, one of them is a marriage between gay and straight. When gays and straights together, can work together, you have a very powerful and creative society. As I alluded to this morning, the twelfth-century renaissance, when that happened, it was the most creative moment in Western history. At that time, homophobia was not on the table. A very significant lesson there, because, obviously I'm continually amazed at what science is telling us about homosexuality.

And, of course, the Vatican and other fundamentalists . . . You know, this pope, the present pope, wrote three diatribes against homosexuals and never quoted science once. And yet, the past pope approved of all these things. This is a Galileo case of our time. He removed the condemnation of Galileo after 400 years. We all held our breath for that. And when he did, John Paul II, he said, "There are lessons to learn here." Religions can learn something from science. Well, then their head is in the sand again about homosexuality, because science has spoken. Eight to 10 percent of any given human population anywhere is going to be gay or lesbian. Furthermore, we counted 464 other species with homosexual populations. So, get over it. It's natural. It's a minority, but it's natural.

It was a wonderful thing that happened a few weeks ago. Gays in Italy protested the pope's visit to a university. He had to turn around and go home. It was great. As gays assert their personhood, as they're doing all over the world, and they've been getting marriages in Spain and everything, this is a major shift. It's a beautiful thing. I'm talking about the marriage of gay and straight, you see, not about getting literally married, but about, "Hey, let's pool our wisdom instead of beating up at each other and forcing our kids and others to hide in closets, or play games, and then say,

'Oh look how perverse our lifestyle is.'" Yeah, well, when they're not allowed to be publicly in love, why wouldn't they have to hide? As I say, my Bible says, "God is love." It does not say God is heterosexual love. Answer that the next time you run into one of your fundamentalist homophobes. And by the way, the idea that the Bible says homosexuality is a—what is it, a perversion, or what's the word they like to use?

STUDENT: *Abomination.*

MATT: Abomination, yeah. Remember, the Bible also says that eating shrimp is an abomination. So check it out. The Bible can't be taken too literally too often.

Another marriage that's happening is that of human and Divine. This is a recovery of mysticism. Everything that Tsomo has learned and found and, and traveled to experience from the Eastern mystical tradition that she has found so real, this is happening. Many people of our generation have taken journeys East, or someplace, to find the mysticism. My whole pitch has actually been from Jung. I keep quoting Jung. He says [paraphrasing] that "We Westerners cannot be pirates, thieving wisdom from foreign shores, as if our own culture was an error outlived." Now, I'm not at all saying that you're thieving wisdom. You're not. But his general point is this: We've got to find this stuff in our own cultural DNA. And that's what I've spent my, my life trying to do. We have Eckharts, we have Hildegards, we have Aquinas as a mystic. We have these greats. And Jesus as a mystic. We have great mystics, but we have to demand of our religious traditions that we bring them forth. And demand of ourselves. You can't pass it off on the pope or a bishop, you know. We have to find our mystical lives again. That's a huge thing, but it's so within our grasp. It's so needed. This is post-modern. I find this younger generation is profoundly mystical. This is why they're not in church anymore.

Then the marriage of Protestant and Catholic. Both of them, as we know them, are dead. Paul Tillich wrote an essay in the late 1940s stating the end of the Protestant era. Well, believe me, if you haven't noticed, we're at the end of the Roman Catholic era, too. I did a retreat in upstate New York a couple of years ago. It's conservative country. It's Republican. A hundred and fifty people there when we started Friday night. "What traditions do you come from?" About a 100 were Catholic. "So how many of you are practicing?" About 60 were practicing. "How many of your children are practicing?" Zero! Zero Catholic parents in upstate, conservative New York had children practicing Catholicism. That's what the pedophile crisis, among other things, has done. And the dumbing-down of the Church by Cardinal Ratzinger by condemning every theologian that had anything to say. Let's not be silly about this. The forms of Christianity called Protestant and Catholic are done. Great. Third millennium—it's time to give birth to new forms: new forms of worship, new forms of community, and to draw whatever the treasure is from the house that's burning down that we used to call *church*. And don't think we're the first generation to do this. Whenever there's been reformation in Christian history, people have returned to the source. And today, thanks to scholarship, we have whole new juice about the historical Jesus and the Cosmic Christ in our real mystical tradition. There's no excuse to be intellectually lazy and not pursue that.

Another marriage going on is lay and monastic. You look around the world, some of the greatest spiritual teachers in the world, the Dalai Lama, Thich Nhat Hanh, most are refugees from their monasteries. Not that they don't return in a while, but the point is that they realize that the future lies not in monasticism. Father Bede Griffiths told me this just before he died. He said, "The future of monasticism is not with monks, it's with lay people." This dualism, that we're lay people, and you're monks, and you do all the praying for us—Eckhart once said that someone came up to him and said, "Pray for me." And Eckhart said, "Why do you ask me to pray for you? Pray for yourself. I'm not a professional prayer." So that's the point. I think we have to melt this Piscean division between monasticism and lay. We all have a spiritual life that needs nurturing.

What's so wonderful about the Thich Nhat Hanhs of our time is that they are boiling down the essence, the distillation of meditation, and of years of practice, what we can carry like troubadours lightly as we move through our very busy lives. And, of course, even science is on board now. I have a good friend who is a scientist. And she's convinced that what we can now do with the brain—and this is far more than biofeedback—she thinks in a few years we'll be able to shortcut the process of meditation with the help of technology. That we will all be unleashing the, if you will, the monastic view of the world, with some help there.

Another marriage is East and West. That's what we've been doing this weekend with Tsomo from Tibet, and myself from the West. And this is happening everywhere. Of course, it's about rubbing elbows, but it's more than that. Several years ago I was invited to do a workshop in Santa Monica, and they put me up on the weekend in a Buddhist home on the ocean. It was very beautiful. And they said, "Well, now, you're alone here at night, but in the morning they're going to come in and probably do some chanting." I said, "Well, cool. Do it." And they did. At five in the morning this group comes in and starts chanting in the living room. It was a glorious thing to wake up to. But I had a dream that night. And I dreamed about Jesus and Buddha, and I realized something. The Buddha died about 84. He had lived all of life. He had been a father and a husband, and a prince, and he died serenely. Jesus got himself killed at about 30, you know. And, hey, we need both of these. We need holy patience and serenity, and we need holy impatience.

The West represents that prophetic dimension of breaking through history to stand up for justice. Gandhi said, "I learned to say, 'No' from the West." That's the prophetic dimension, that "no" dimension. Humans need that, but we also need the Eastern sense of "yes" and it yielding to the cycles of life and of incarnation. I think we're all limping if we're either all Eastern or all Western. We need both. We need holy patience and holy impatience. That's why East and West are coming together, I think, because we need the whole enchilada, because we're in a situation of survival as a species, and it's critical.

When I had translated Hildegard for the first time and I shared it in class, and just this first part, I'll never forget it. I was in Chicago. This guy stood up and said, "I spent the last 15 years on an Indian reservation. My spiritual director was a shaman. And that woman you just read sounds exactly like my spiritual director." Hildegard has more in common with Native American than she does with Cardinal Ratzinger. So figure that out, and your soul does, too. Your soul does, too. Frederick Turner's brilliant book on Native American history says that for the Native American, religion is "Aboriginal mother love." Aboriginal mother love, that's everything we've been talking about this weekend in terms of the Sacred Feminine.

And another marriage is what Daniel Pink calls L-directed thinking and R-directed thinking: right hemisphere of the brain with left hemisphere. He has a very interesting thesis. In summary, it is that we moved from farming to industrial age, and that took a certain kind of brain to work in the factories, or even to work in the mines; and then we're in this white-collar age, the computer age, and that takes a different framework, but it's left brain. "Now," [paraphrasing] he says, "what we need to survive is a whole new way of thinking. It's the R-brain way of thinking." He says, "Creativity is much more important today." And he says even if you look at the jobs that are available, like nurses' jobs, and entertainment and creativity, this is mostly right-brain work, he says, the empathy that's needed. But it's a balance. The nurse, of course, has to know her science, too. It's a wonderful book. I highly recommend it—*A Whole New Mind*[26], he calls it. It's really a wonderful way of naming that particular Sacred Marriage.

So, my time is probably up. Oh, I've got to mention this marriage: young and old. This takes us back a bit to Icarus and Daedalus that I mentioned this morning, but it is so important. We need intergenerational wisdom. And let me stress "inter," because there is wisdom among young, and you know that from children and grandchildren, and there is wisdom, hopefully, among the old. But like never before, we have to marry these, and they have been separated. There's been this huge divorce in our culture. We lock each group up with its own group. We have to get the old off the golf courses and integrate them more with the youngest generation. Now, the middle-aged, they're busy running society and trying to survive. So I'm talking about this special innate wedding between the grandfather/grandmother elders and the youngest generation. That needs to be pumped up. It needs to be pumped up rapidly, this marriage of the old and the young, because we're not going to carry a new culture without that marriage really happening.

For me, this is where this little four-minute video I have comes in, too, the new languages of rap and filmmaking. As you know, your children or grandchildren are much more adept at technology and computers than we are, at least most of us. So they have whole new ways of telling stories, but it is the elders' role to help relay what the content and substance can

---

26. Daniel Pink, *A Whole New Mind: Why Right-Brainers Will Rule the Future*. (Riverhead Books, 2006)

be. So if I still have five minutes in my thing, if we could show this and I'll get it over, and then I'll shut up. Okay? If we could have the lights, maybe.

This is Professor PITT, this 31-year-old filmmaker-rapper who was saved by martial arts when he was 10, learning kung fu. And now he and I have hooked up to create this Y.E.L.L.A.W.E. Program. And he's taken what I call the "10 Cs" to balance the three Rs, the 10 Cs of education being cosmology, creativity, community, chaos, cosmology, and ceremony, and critical thinking, and so forth. So he's put each of these to a rap film, and it's inside my book on education, *The A.W.E. Project*[27]. We can show you one. This is a contemplation one. This one is on meditation.

[*Video starts.*]

[*Video ends.*]

MATT: That's it.

STUDENT: *Where can we order that?*

MATT: That's inside my book *The A.W.E. Project*. It comes with that in the back of it. There's nine others like that around each of the nine Cs. My book is called *The A.W.E. Project: Reinventing Education, Reinventing the Human*. A-W-E, it stands for awe, reinventing education with awe, A-W-E, but also it stands for Ancestral Wisdom Education. And PITT and I are doing this program called Y.E.L.L.A.W.E., Youth and Elder Learning Laboratory for Ancestral Wisdom Education, where we're trying to do a modest thing, and that is reinvent education using the 10 Cs, including meditation—contemplation or meditation. We're working with inner-city kids after school, and shortly in school as well, because I feel education has to be reinvented from the inside out.

We're in denial. We're too busy making money or playing the golf courses to give a damn about the younger generation. It's a scandal. It's going to kill us. Humans need education, and when a whole generation is not getting it, when their school is prison, you're really asking for something. And, of course, part of this is our system. We have now an industrial-military-prison complex. All kinds of people are making money off of prisons, and that's one reason

27. Matthew Fox, *The A.W.E. Project: Reinventing Education, Reinventing the Human* (CopperHouse, 2006)

that's driving this horrible situation. So we all have to stand up about the subject of education, and that's what PITT and I are trying to do here.

I was glad you liked it—you clapped—because I find great hope in this. The young have whole new languages, and this one's being ignored in education: their creativity. There's no room for it. They're too busy taking exams so they can go to schools that are going to make them rapacious destroyers of the Earth. Thomas Berry says [paraphrasing], "Most of the destruction of the Earth is happening at the hands of people with PhDs." So there you have it. It's the old Celtic saying, "Don't give up a loaded gun to a young man who has not first learned to dance." You know, that a PhD is a loaded gun, and if we haven't tempered it with wisdom, we're asking for it. And that's what we're getting: the destruction that knowledge alone can accomplish. We have to marry that with wisdom, everything Tsomo and I have been talking about this weekend. And what that will mean will be different forms of education, and different ways of honoring our young people.

And the whole question raised earlier about initiation ceremonies. You see, many of them have not been taken through an adult initiation. So they don't have the responsibility of the adult, and yet they're in this in-between place, and they're longing. They're searching and longing for something. A study was done at UCLA, I think a year ago, which is, of course, a prestigious school. Something like 85 percent of the students said, undergraduates, that there was too little spirituality at the university and in their program. That's what they're longing for. This is a postmodern generation, and like pre-moderns, they want to see the world as a whole. They want a spiritual relationship to all their relations. And you're not getting it in the modern university.

Tsomo: I'm so glad to hear about this UCLA study because it verifies what I've experienced in speaking with young people in school. I talked to them about my observation that the classroom, whatever subject it is, is meaning-free. And then after school they go to the mall. It's also meaning-free. They go home, they watch TV: meaning-free. And when I say these things, they're nodding their heads like crazy and they're saying, "Yes, we long for meaning, and we're not getting it anywhere, anywhere: not in school, not at home." No, not when they go out with their friends, nowhere. They're really lost. So I love your bringing the marriage of the elder and the youth. One of the relationships, one of the marriages, I was going to speak of was the root lama and the student, because it's very similar. But I'm getting ahead of myself.

MATT: So is it your time now?

TSOMO: It is, but I wanted to first start with some other aspects of it. We have very little time left now, but I'll just go through some aspects of marriage that I've thought of, and that come from Buddhism as well. I wanted to uncover this thangka now because you can see there is a Sacred Marriage, a sacred union, happening here.

This is Vajradhara, who is the primordial Buddha, but in Sambhogakaya form. In the very most ultimate and pure level, the dharmakaya level, they're shown here, and I don't know how many of you can see this, but he's a deep blue and she's white, and they're completely without any gems and jewelry, or even any clothing. So it's complete naked awareness in its masculine and feminine aspects. The primordial Buddha in the dharmakaya form is called Samantabhadra, and she is Samantabhadri; so, the masculine and feminine primordial Buddha. And here they are wearing the ornaments that display their deity-ship, you could say, on the archetypal level. There are rainbow lights of all different colors of all the Buddha families that I mentioned were the five aspects of primordial wisdom. Each has its own color. They're radiating those. They, themselves, have rainbow bodies. They're not, as I said before, bodies that are just bags of organs and blood. And they're inside of a *tigle*, which is this sphere of mind. I don't know how else to say it: Buddha mind.

So I wanted to just show an image of that so that, while you look at that, you can think of some of the things they associate which, with each one of those figures. So he is the *yab*, and she is the *yum*. I should mention that they're actually in sexual union. And at one point in a lot of the practices, we imagine them above us. And from their point of union, wisdom nectar comes down. Amrita comes down and bestows the four empowerments on us, cleansing us completely of all of our imperfections and the karma we've carried since beginningless time, and bringing forth our Buddha Nature. So he is the yab, and she is the yum. She, as I have said before, represents emptiness; he, luminosity, or appearance. So really, just really imagine those. I hope you guys can see through me. I don't have a body of light. I'm sorry.

I should mention actually that the rainbow body, which has been attained by many Tibetans, was also attained by a Westerner. He was practicing in India, and this Tibetan master happened to be sharing the house. This guy was up, always in retreat, on the second floor, and this master was on the first floor. And they just called him *sahib*, because they'd heard the Indians referring to English people as *sahib*. So they just called him the sahib. One day this Tibetan fellow, who had been practicing, noticed rainbows, rainbow lights, coming out of the windows of the room above. He and everybody else were sort of startled—they all saw it. They went upstairs and there was nothing there but the guy's nails and hair and his clothes. And there were rainbows coming out of his clothes. That happened in the twentieth century, and it was a Westerner. So, there's hope for us.

Then, also, you can imagine her as emptiness, he as bliss; she as emptiness, he as compassion; wisdom—she is wisdom, he as compassion. There are many different ways we can play with this. She is wisdom; he is skillful means. It's one thing to have wisdom, and it's another thing to actually manifest something with skillful means.

It's probably not necessary to mention, but I will, that in Tibet, a lot of men imagine themselves as Tara. In the preliminary practices, and often in the practices to transfer one's body to the pureland at the time of death—we practice this and make a habit during life, and then at the moment of death, we can do that, according to Tibetans—in those practices, we see the Sacred Marriage above us, and we imagine ourselves, quite often, as Vajrayogini, who is obviously female, but many men will practice that they are Vajrayogini. Then again, as a woman, I've imagined myself to be Vajrasattva, who's male, and Guru Rinpoche, who's male, and so on. So we don't take all these things literally, and we imagine ourselves often in union with a consort. And so if I'm Vajrasattva, I may be male in union with Nyema Karmo, who's female, for example.

It loosens us up from attachment to our sexual preference, or our sexual manifestation in this body, and it completely understands that we need to bring forth the pure masculine and feminine. We need to unify them in a healthy way. So in some of these practices, as I was saying, we'll be Vajrayogini, whether we're man or woman, and imagine this perfect union above us, and eventually, then, join with that, so there's a complete union and a complete melting away of this idea of separation.

This idea of separation, this idea that we are . . . Well, *ego* means "I" in Latin. And it's a funny thing, but according to the Tibetans, that sort of started a row of dominoes that led to the mess we call *Samsara*. And if we wanted to undo the dominoes and go back to our original state, or finish the journey back to our original state, however you want to look at it, we need to loosen up and let go of this sense of being a separate self. So all of the practices are arranged to help us to let go of that sense of separation, and to begin to open our minds and let the Buddha Nature come forth, and open up our identification with the whole ocean, not just this one wave.

Maybe I'll go into this next thing. If we can take our projections off of our father and mother, there's one, because there're just sentient beings. How can they compare to this? They can't, but of course they're more easily accessible. That addiction to our parents that you were speaking of, is because we don't have anything else to rely on. So, as faulty as they are, we keep trying to rely on them. And they keep letting us down, because they're just sentient beings, too. We rely on, often, our own earthly family, marriage, and that often lets us down. Nature abhors a vacuum, though, so if we just stop relying on that and have nothing else, what are we to do? That doesn't work for us. We're not going to do that.

Even within our own body, there are masculine and feminine energies flowing through it. The Buddhists believe that from the father we receive the white energy, and the mother, the red energy. And these come together, and they're flowing through our bodies through energy channels. And in the advanced practices in Tibetan Buddhism, we actually work directly with the channels and the energies and create the sacred union within our bodies. It's believed that the mind rides on the energies, and the energies are guided by the channels. So in working with these energies and the channels, we can actually enact this inner union. And when we do, it's known as *great bliss*. And it's renowned for being quite a blissful practice, and very, very powerful. It's also powerful for undoing the karma that's splattering our windshields so that we can't see, and helping to bring forth our Buddha Nature.

I just wanted to speak a little bit about my own experience in retreat. I was doing the mandala offering retreat, which is traditionally done in the preliminary practices. I did this for a month from five in the morning until nine o'clock at night only with meal breaks. So it was very intensive. And the image that I happened to be doing all this offering to was very similar to this, except she happened to be white. It was from another lineage, so there was that variation. So I was sitting there offering and offering and offering, and after about a week, they were so real to me as I was sitting and basking in their blessings and offering out, and this kind of thing was going on, that I would be distracted sometimes, of course, because my mind gets distracted sometimes, and I would come back and they were still there. And then I remember, for some reason or another, I had to reorient in the room. Now I was going to have to project them on the other wall, and I thought, "Oh, I hope this works." And then I went, "Oh yeah, oh yeah. Where are they?" So, of course, they were just fine on the other wall. There they were.

This was all really very real for me, and I was basking in these offerings and receiving the blessings and so on. By the way, I think receiving blessings might be like getting infected with Buddha mind. I have this little idea about that. So anyway, after about a week, I got a disturbing—or I think I got a visit—from somebody I was dating at the time. And I realized that basically he was kind of sort of wanting to break up with me, and I thought, "You know, actually, this hasn't worked for me either." So I called him back after he left, and I said, "You know, I just want to break up altogether."

In the intensity of retreat—which is a very particular alchemical experience where you're in the crucible, and then you really turn up the heat with these practices, and you put all these images in there with your mind—you have a very intense experience. Anything you drop in there is going to be intensified. So you can imagine the intensity with which I experienced this, and I thought, "You know, clinging to relationship, even one that doesn't work, is my way of stepping around that pit of despair that I think we all are busy stepping around all the time, that Jung was referring to as being actually the root, the basis, of all neurosis, that stepping around the pit of despair." So I thought, "You know what? I'm not going to step around it anymore. I'm going to let myself just go." And so, with the support of these beings, and the support of this practice, in that alchemical vessel, I went ahead and sunk into this pit of despair of feeling like I was just going to vanish altogether.

I was still doing the practice and praying and everything, and actually applying all of these huge emotions that were flaming up inside. It was like a wildfire going on. So I'm sitting there, actually physically offering semiprecious stones and precious spices and things on a silver platter, and doing this again and again and again. By the end of it, at the end of the month, I offered 108,000 times. So as I'm saying the recitation and I'm visualizing and I'm doing this, the tears are pouring down, because I'm just shaken to my roots, really wondering if I'm going to exist somehow. I really was letting myself go into the longing completely, because it wasn't about this guy who I didn't even, you know, have a good relationship with. It was about something much more, and I knew that, and I just was letting myself really go for it. The tears are really pouring down, and I'm realizing, "I've taken refuge in relationship, in people's praise, in my parents, and all kinds of things that never have worked really. They might work for a time, but they never work ultimately and permanently. I think I'm just finished taking refuge in all of these things."

Here I am, really, then, taking refuge in these beings who are beyond Samsara, these principles of reality that are beyond Samsara. They are aware, and they are capable of love: as a matter of fact, huge, perfect love; huge, perfect compassion. They know and see me completely and perfectly, and they love me. I thought of them as the original father and mother, the primordial Buddha in masculine and feminine form. And so, in this whole process, I unplugged from the usual things I was plugged in for refuge, and plugged into this, which is difficult to tune into. It takes a lot of time and a lot of work, at least 108,000 recitations. And it's because we have to build a relationship now with these cosmic parents, you might say. But I was able to do it in that moment of extremes. And I think it sometimes takes extremes for us to do such an extreme and radical thing.

This changed me completely and forever. I, to this day, I'm not the same. I finished my recitations for that day, my sessions. I went to sleep that night actually kind of not knowing if I would wake up and be there in the morning. And I was. I think it was because I fell through the bottom, and discovered what real bottom was. Real bottom is this great dark emptiness that we've been talking about, that I'm a part of. Where would I go, exactly, if I go away? What's "away," anyway? I think it's a wonderful blessing to discover the real bottom like that, and fall through, and be held by the whole universe. But, I have to say, at the time, because I've been through a few of these, when I was still crying and all in the midst of it, I thought, "I'm going to have another, transformational experience, and I'm going to tell people later how grateful I was to have it." And it only made me madder at the time. And here I am telling you this.

I wanted to also talk a little bit about some of their ideas associating the impure aspects of primordial wisdom with women and men. Women are more associated with desire, which, again, if you get to its essence, is discerning wisdom; men with aversion or anger, or aggression, or however you want to call it, which is mirror-like wisdom—that sharp, clear seeing. I think of needs that we all have as humans, and I put them into two basic realms that often we think are mutually exclusive: autonomy and connection. When I work with men and women, the men say, "You know, I think connection is wonderful, but I want to be sure and have autonomy." And the women tend to say, "You know, I really need autonomy, but for sure I've got to have connection." There's something very interesting in that. We really want lots of both, and I don't believe they're mutually exclusive. I absolutely believe we can have lots and lots of both.

The problem is that we have unskillful and perverted versions of both of those. The perverted version of autonomy, in my observation, is isolation. There are times we feel we need to isolate, but then, of course, we don't have connection and we're lonely. Isolation is not really a great place to be. Autonomy is great. Isolation feels terrible after a while. With connection, there can also be the overrunning of boundaries. We've all felt that when somebody's been overbearing and just gone across our boundaries. We can't have that. We need the integrity of our shape. So, in an effort to preserve our autonomy, we run for isolation. And people often go back and forth between the two and think, "Well, maybe if I just had half isolation and half overrunning of boundaries, I'll be sort of okay." But that's not what we want. We want lots of autonomy and lots of connection. So there's another Sacred Marriage, in my opinion, in human relationships.

Another one that I was mentioning before was that of the mentor and the student, the root lama and the student. This is a huge and numinous relationship in the East. And I think it takes a lot of the weight off of marriage. In the story of Tristan and Isolde, it's a tragedy because there's this huge romantic love, and the numinosity is put on a human being who, then, you're supposed to live with. I think in modern times we have a lot of divorce because we're projecting the goddess or the god on the person that we're sharing the bathroom with, and who we're trying to raise kids with, and pay bills with. In the tradition of courtly love, where they originally brought this idea of romantic love from the Middle East through the troubadours into Europe, this was done with somebody you weren't actually married to. They had arranged marriages. So you could project that on somebody and live out this whole beautiful dance with it, and write the poetry, and do the music, and, have this experience as a way of bringing it forth from within yourself. But once we had love marriages, as I think somebody mentioned, then we were actually trying to set up housekeeping with the god or the goddess, and for some reason that doesn't work so well.

So, if we were to find the right places for it, such as the goddess or the god, and continued that drama that we need to continue, breathing it in and remembering, "Oh yes, that's within me, too," then we're free to have a human relationship with our human spouse, of whichever sex, and human relationships with our family, and we don't put so much of the weight of the numinosity onto our human relationships. I think it would be very healthy for us all.

So I think I could stop here. And then were we going to have some back and forth?

MATT: Well, it's already 3:30. We got started late and everything. So why don't we just open it up? Okay?

TSOMO: Okay. Yeah.

MATT: Okay? For our last half hour here. So what are you people thinking about this topic of Sacred Marriages? And how does Tsomo's presentation or mine trigger things?

STUDENT: *One of the things that I thought about last night, and it's coming back to me, is trying to understand the form of the Western religious experience, with God as separate. And when we were talking about autonomy and connection not being mutually exclusive, I had this image come to mind of your traditional Western church, where the pastor or preacher, whatever it is, stands in the front. And the crowd believes* *there's a connectivity going on, between them and God, but what it really is, is the mediated building-up of the person at the front of the church, who took too literally the idea that "connection must come from me. I'm the messenger, I'm the mediator entirely." It just sort of reminded me that in some way it's, to me, a paradox, that you promote autonomy so much, and yet when it comes to our spiritual development in the form of religion, we actually have given up. And I just find that just fascinating. Why do we do that?*

MATT: It's very interesting. You began by saying, God outside, and that's, that's a problem. For me it's a problem. That's theism. And to me that's not panentheism, which is healthy mysticism, as God is within and we are in God. That's like water in the fish, and the fish in the water. To me that's the mystical tradition. So part of my answer to your question is that to the extent that we've wandered from the mystical tradition, then we set up these subject-object relationships, which are inauthentic in themselves, because we are within one another. Even as you say your words "isolation" and "connection."

TSOMO: Autonomy and connection, or isolation and overrunning of boundaries? Which?

MATT: Well, my words for it would be solitude—I mean the positive isolation of solitude—and then community. But solitude is not in opposition to community. There's a dialectic. There's a tension. But community needs solitude, and one in solitude needs community. So there's a real dance that we need to find.

TSOMO: I had a friend who visited Aboriginals, in Australia, who had almost never seen Europeans before. And your isolation-community is reminding me of her experience. She said they were all sitting around the campfire, and one of her European, Caucasian friends decided to just begin to wander off a little bit. And one of the Aboriginals said, "Why are you going away?" and she said, "Well, I just feel I need to be alone for a little bit." And this Aboriginal woman said, "So why do you have to go away to do that?"

MATT: That's nice. Yeah. Yeah.

STUDENT: *Wow!*

TSOMO: Any other questions?

MATT: By changing the forms of worship, we're asking for that kind of relationship. When you put people up front, like at the theater or something, you have people sitting in benches looking at the back of each other's heads, like you're in a theater, you're asking for all kinds of perversion. What we're doing in our Cosmic Masses is there are no benches, and there is no front. There's that altar in the middle, and people are dancing. And the basic messages are coming through the images using post-modern forms: the VJ and DJ and so forth. They come through the images, which are, literally, circular. So you're dancing these images through your body, and through your heart and mind, and it's therefore a totally different experience. I think we've deconstructed this relationship of expert versus everyone else sitting and taking it in. For me, that's a very significant shift. And I've seen the results. The results are very profound. People have literal healings, and also other kinds of healings: spiritual and emotional healings. It allows different energy to come, including the angels, the spirits.

My thesis is that worship has become so boring in the West that even the angels aren't in church anymore. They love to worship, but they're not, they're easily bored. They're bright beings. And you talked about all these bright beings that want to be with us, and want to support us. You know, we have support not just from the two-legged ones, but from the deceased, from the ancestors, from the angels. And do we even let them in to our places of worship? Well, not if we've, we've got a whole text and we've got it locked down, or if there's this ego thing that you're talking about: the ego of the minister, or the personality of the minister. See, when things depend on personality, you're on very, very treacherous ground. So, again, making things more circular, bringing the body in—the body does not lie—and breathing. It's interesting: In many African languages, the word for breath and spirit is also the word for dance. So to dance is to bring breath and spirit in. And think about it. It's kind of hard to dance without breath.

Getting back to these pre-modern ways of praying is very salvific. It's very healing. And we find that all ages love it. I remember an 84-year-old lady out there dancing away. One night she said to me, "I took three buses to get here tonight. By the time I'm dancing, the buses aren't going to be running. I'm going to need a ride home." She said, "I've been waiting 82 years for someone to connect dance with prayer." And yet we've never had a problem with a child or a baby. It's so organic, you don't need a crying room, because they're not bored. The children are more honest. They're crying; the adults wish they could cry in most church services, including ministers. I've been listening to ministers and rabbis for years. They're just as bored as everyone else, but they're stuck in these forms. We're not stuck. That's what creativity means. You break through the form and you redo the form.

TSOMO: The Dalai Lama has really wanted to bring religion outside of the monasteries and into the lives of people, and reforming education so that it's brought to the kids from a young age. It seems to be taking over the whole world, this idea, which I'm thrilled to see. [*To student*] Yes.

STUDENT: *In talking about the pit of despair, you had gone through that, but are, were you aware of the presence of the beings? Were they still . . . ?*

TSOMO: Absolutely. Thank goodness they were there. Yeah.

STUDENT: *Oh. Okay. I was thinking about Mother Teresa's journals that just came out recently. She talks about being totally separated and abandoned by God. I don't even think she was aware of any presence.*

TSOMO: I think that is something that sometimes happens. It just wasn't in my experience in that particular case.

STUDENT: *But you're still feeling the despair.*

TSOMO: Yeah, because it it's still a difficulty to fully connect and feel held by them. And it wasn't until I completely relinquished in a certain way, and surrendered, that I was then able to feel myself being held by these wisdom beings, and by the cosmos, the great emptiness.

MATT: I had a dark-night-of-the-soul experience where I went through this. It wasn't so much despair as grief, I think. But it was totally dark. For many weeks, there was no relief until there began to grow an image. And the image was my falling, ceaselessly falling down a well, a dark well. But the beginning of the breakthrough was, even though I was falling down the well, an image flashed just for a second. An image flashed like that. So it's these beings kind of showing up, but late. And I was reminded of Mechthild of Magdeburg, a thirteenth-century lady, a Beguine, a mystic. She says, "There are times when the light of the lantern goes out, and the memory of the light of the lantern goes out." That was three centuries before John of the Cross talked about the dark night of the soul. So there is darkness without the support of the other beings, but then there's darkness that does include them. But you're right: There could be complete darkness.

TSOMO: The way I would describe it for me is sort of like a trapeze artist when they let go of the one person holding them, and they're just sort of flying through the air hoping that the other person's going to catch them. It was a bit like that. [*To student*] Yeah.

STUDENT: *I'm really interested in the sense of presence. You talk about spontaneous presence sometimes, an all-new presence. Who really categorized that? How do you know that it's something that's beautiful, like a sign and coming to you, or something that you've created through your knowledge of these entities that preexisted in the mind?*

TSOMO: The very first time I experienced it, I didn't quite know what to think. And I was sort of asking myself the same kinds of questions. And I thought, "Well, should I wait until science proves the existence of what I'm experiencing before I let myself admit that this is happening?" It was just such a palpable, real experience for me that there was no denying it. So if we allow ourselves to let go of our usual more academic left-brain way of thinking about these things and just check it out: Is this really happening, or is it not? Sometimes it feels as though it's a presence of a being, but other times it's just spontaneous presence that's suffusing every-thing, including ourselves. It can be either and both.

MATT: Well, I'd like to say this about it. I think Jesus has as good a line as anyone: "By your fruits you will know them." So it's not just what's happening to us biologically, although, obviously, everything humans do is biologically conditioned: Things happen to us biologically, too, or physiologically. But the meat of the question—okay, what do you do with it? How does it make you a different being or a better person? A more compassionate person, or a wiser person? Eckhart has a test, too. He says, "The test of whether I have been given birth to the Christ is whether I see everything more filled with the Divine." To me it's, you might say, the step afterwards. What follows from that licking of the ice cream cone that you did at the fair. Have you become a more, a more, you know, a brilliant-souled person, a more generous person, a more compassionate person?

So I think in some ways we have to turn our back on that, because it is about our being altered if it's authentic, and then being leads to action. Are our actions more . . . ? We can see actions more than we can see being. That's why it's a test, that "by their fruits you will know them." As he says, "A bad tree gives birth to bad fruit." Has your treehood become more healthy, so the fruit you are bearing is more plump and juicy and rich? That is my test.

TSOMO: My teacher says a similar thing. And he warns against people putting too much on moments of experience like the one you were describing. He says they're wonderful and they can often be signposts along the way, but in the changing of the habits of the mind that have been built up for so long, and even the pathways in the brain, it takes a lot of years of action, right action, as well as practice and working with the mind and being self-aware and so on, in order to be able to follow through in everyday life—first of all, to have that as an ongoing experience available to you, and second of all, to be able to produce the fruits of action that are the ones that we want that are in keeping with divine intent.

I also wanted to just mention that the HeartMath Institute has done a lot of studies on the relationship between the heart and the brain. I would say that the mind has the experience, and then the body follows, because the mind manifests the body in the first place. So that's my observation of it.

MATT: [*To student*] I do want to say one thing. You used a phrase that bothered me. You said you work with poets, not mystics. Well, that's so dualistic. Every poet, every authentic poet, is a mystic, I think. And art is the language of mysticism. It's the only language we have to utter our experiences of beauty and breakthrough. So, you know, don't fall into that dualism.

STUDENT: *No, the dualism occurs because I'm afraid of offending anyone in their spiritual condition by saying something that's implied, but it's not a real experience. I feel more comfortable talking about poets, because I'm not saying anything about real religion. It's just a cult of people. And it's not just for poets.*

TSOMO: But it's not labeling it as much. Yeah. As soon as you put labels on it, it can offend somebody. Yeah.

Getting back to what I was going to say, the way I see it, and this is informed by some of the HeartMath stuff, and a lot of the work they've done on the heart and brain and the vagus nerve in between—first of all, they were able, finally, to check the amount of traffic going from the heart to the brain, as opposed to the brain to the heart, and they discovered that, rather than most of the traffic going brain to heart, telling the heart to beat, it was the reverse. There's more traffic going from the heart to the brain, when they measure the normal traffic on the vagus nerve, which is a big nerve, nerve bundle. So you have to take that into account. So I think of the heart as the CPU and the brain as the screen. It might be a way we can think of this in the post-modern era.

Entrainment between the two causes all sorts of wonderful things to happen—healing—the immune system goes up for hours after five minutes of entrainment, for example, and many things like that. I don't know if you know about entrainment, but the fellow who invented clocks found that the clocks with the biggest pendulums could cause all the other clocks in his room to entrain with it until they were all going at the same rhythm. And this happened day after day when he would wind his clocks. The heart is the biggest pendulum in the body, and the waves that it's putting out are 35 times as strong as those of the brain.

So if we bring our awareness to our hearts, then the brain will easily fall into rhythm with the heart. I happened to do biofeedback on this and discovered that any Buddhist practice I did, guess what happened? Right up directly to 100 entrainment, and stayed there until I stopped doing the practice. Now, if I were really good, it would still be going.

Do we want to do any closing comments, or are people wanting to speak still?

MATT: Well, I like the questions myself.

TSOMO: Yeah, okay.

STUDENT: *Let me ask you. I'm not into Buddhism, but I believe the diaphragm separates us from ourselves to some extent, and we are sort of here in a Western culture. But I'm wondering if the center really isn't the solar plexus.*

TSOMO: Mmm hmm. Well, there's neurological material around the gut—when we have a "gut" feeling, knowing something, that's actually real. There's neurological material around the heart as well. So I really think of all three of those. When I really want to make a big decision, I have to run it by all three before I'm sure about it. Absolutely, I'm glad you brought that forward.

STUDENT: *I completely agree with re-education and that there needs to be more spiri-tuality. But how, as a parent, do I get my kids involved in this? I'd like to go to Northern California every weekend and go to your church, but I can't do that.*

MATT: Well, I think it begins with where you are, with dissatisfaction, and you find allies. You start talking it up. Are other people also dissatisfied? You create a movement, and you say, "Hey, we can do better than this. Let's start an un-Godly program for our kids"—whatever you're going to call it, an alternative. You take ideas such as I am presenting, which I think are very authentic today. What the kids can do in making films, do-ing poetry, doing rap, and so forth is amazing today. The key is tapping into their creativity, because I think of the book I did two years ago on creativity. I found that, again, all around the world, all spiritual traditions honor the creative process as a mystical experience. Meister Eckhart, for example, has a brilliant sermon on what he calls the Holy Spirit as a rapid river. When you're in a creative state, the image I have is being on a raft and just being taken along by a force bigger than us.

So I think that our education and our religion, and indeed our cul-ture in general, and certainly our media, has underestimated the power of creativity, and how important it is for healing and for optimism. Otto Rank, who's done such brilliant work on this, says that "pessimism comes from a repression of creativity." So let's look at the opposite of that. Oh! Well, the overcoming of pessimism comes from the flooding of creativity.

So, to build programs. For example, years ago I was approached— and this was 25 years ago; I was living in Chicago—by parents of, of 10-year-old boys who couldn't stand their religion classes. And they came to me and said, "We hear you're kind of different. Would you create a Sunday morning program for our kids?" There were just, like, six kids. And I said, "Well, okay, but I'm going to do it my way." "Do whatever you can do. Our kids hate what they're doing." So for one semester I had them in my basement building catacombs. It was a mess, of course, with papier-mâché, and chicken wire and all. Then when we built it, we sat in there and told stories. In the process they were learning that church is not this million-dollar building on the corner. For 300 years it was hiding from the Empire in catacombs. And then, of course, being 10-year-old boys, they created skeletons and all kinds of spiders and stuff. And I got rocks, and we handed out rocks. We told stories.

Well, 20 years later—and this really happened—20 years later I was lecturing in Chicago. This guy comes up, a young man about 30. He says, "Do you remember me?" "No." He says, "I was in your catacomb class." He said, "It totally changed my life. My whole profession now is," and he brought out this big rock. He said, "I hunt rocks all over the world. I've been in the Himalayas and everything, and then I carve them. And I'm going to give you one." He said, "It began in the catacombs because you handed out these rocks." I was just blown away. Then another guy comes up and says, "Do you remember me?" "No." "I was in your catacomb class. And as a result of that, I'm a painter." So what I learned was we underestimate the vocation, the sacred calling, of our kids to do creative things. Both of these guys were making a living, but doing something they loved, and they got permission to be that kind of male way back when they were 10. It's just because they met a goofy male, you know. And then I think, "Wow, what happened to the other eight kids? Are they in jail or something?" I don't know.

Don't underestimate this dissatisfaction of yours. It's a holy dissatisfaction, so act on it. Gather allies and make, move, you know. And come on up and check out what we're doing, and see how it works, what the dynamics are, and take it back. We're just trying to create a model that others can use; we want to give it away. But I'll ask you something. I don't know why this pops in my head, but are you a drummer at all? Drumming circles are very, very ancient, and very simple to pull off in any neighborhood. And it's multi-aged, and having a, you know, a drumming circle where kids can feel safe can be very viable. Also, of course, poetry. There's a great deal of poetry in these kids, and they need a safe space where they can let it out and share it.

STUDENT: *Decades ago I did that with inner-city New Orleans kids. It was teaching with poetry, and it was fascinating. You know, I could play some music, and get in line, and, and just basically say, not a whole sentence, just half a sentence, everybody finished the sentence. And now collect all of them. Everybody could collect them.*

MATT: Remember, education: Educing—you're bringing the poetry that's in them, out.

STUDENT: *Yes.*

MATT: You're not really teaching them poetry, you're bringing the poetry that's in them out. That's very important to realize what's there. You're bringing their stories out, and there's an affinity there. The African-based languages, like rap, have a beat and a rhythm to them. There's a drum to it already. So you're not laying anything on. Just help bring it out, and bring the parents into it, too. Get them sharing, and celebrating, and laughing, and crying. And you're, you're doing something very valuable. It's not about money. It's not an expense. Like Eckhart says, "The truth does not come from outside in. The truth comes from inside out and passes through in a new form." So our role as adults is to bring the truth that's in the kids, out.

TSOMO: *Educare* means "to lead out" in Latin. And, well, we've come to the end of our time, I'm afraid.

MATT: Speaking of leading out.

TSOMO: Yeah, yeah. Somebody lead us out. So, I've really enjoyed spending this time with you, and the quality of your attention and going into all of these new things and the intelligence that you've brought. We've both talked about this. We've really enjoyed sharing these things with you, and the hospitality of the Jung Center here in Houston. Did you want to say anything?

MATT: Ditto. Thank you. It was good.

[*applause*]

TSOMO: We had planned that I would just conclude with how we always conclude Buddhist practice, which is to dedicate any merit of considering these things, which is a meritorious act, to the enlightenment of all beings. And this is a Tara sort of dedication of merit followed by aspirational prayers.

"Victorious Mother Tara, whatever form you may assume, whatever retinue you may adopt, however long you may manifest, in whichever pureland you may abide, and whatever excellent names you may assume, in exactly the same way, may we become just as you!

"By the power of offering praise and supplicating to you, may there be no illness, poverty, or conflict. May these disturbances be pacified in all directions and wherever we abide. Grant the increase of dharma and auspiciousness!"

Thank you.

MONTANA

In January of 2010, Matthew and Tsomo met at her home in the Rocky Mountains to continue their ongoing dialogue as colleagues and friends—this time with no audience except each other. Untethered by curriculum or agenda, they were free to let the conversation flow wherever it led them.

CHAPTER INDEX

MATT: And Catholicism also has that, you know.

TSOMO: Yes, well, this is why it's a good thing it's from your tradition and mine because, if it were a Lutheran, then they'd have to talk with a Zen person . . .

MATT: [*Laughs*]

TSOMO: . . . because there's not much to work with, you know, with the visuals.

MATT: Lutherans don't get Zen—they have a lot more work to do before they get there.

TSOMO: It's just a strange thing.

TSOMO: I know; I'm just talking about the iconography.

MATT: You see, Eckhart was Catholic, so he had all that stuff . . .

TSOMO: Exactly.

MATT: . . . and yet he was Zen, too; he really had the emptying, too—he had both.

TSOMO: But so does Tibetan Buddhism because Zolchen's just completely, it's just resting in the pure nature.

MATT: Right. And you talk about that a lot, but then to see your chapel so full.

TSOMO: Yeah, because you have to start with that.

MATT: And you go back to it, too. You don't just start and leave it behind; it's a circle.

TSOMO: Every day.

MATT: It's a spiral. We're talking. Are you filming? Oh, that's perfect!

TSOMO: Our best conversations have been off camera so . . . [*Laughs*].

MATT: [*Laughs*] They shouldn't have told us they were filming.

TSOMO: We just need an omnipresent b-roll—my new vocabulary word.

MATT: Yes. I just learned that word in the last 12 hours, too.

CHAPTER 1

Balancing Spirituality Practice

MATT: I like the extremes in Tibetan Buddhism, as you have them in strands of Catholicism. Not just Roman Catholicism, but Eastern, Russian, and so forth, is very elaborate with the candles, and the incense, and of course the music and the robes and . . .

TSOMO: They're further east.

MATT: [*Laughs*] There you go.

TSOMO: I think there's something to that, actually.

MATT: But then the emptying, see, the one has to be emphasized as much as the other; otherwise things get out of balance.

TSOMO: Precisely.

MATT: And I think that's part of what Luther was complaining about, that they had all the whistles, and the colors, and the noises, but none of the spiritual . . .

TSOMO: The empty, essential nature.

MATT: . . . groundedness, yeah—hopefully, the morality that goes with it.

TSOMO: What Tibetan Buddhism is trying to do is take these methods that meet us where we're at right now—and right now, we pay attention to what's coming into our senses. We're fascinated by them and we go out towards them and we make this whole movie. So they have scripted a very precisely created movie to work with the senses and create an experience that sort of ushers us into emptiness.

MATT: Beyond the senses.

TSOMO: Then our job is, at the end, to sit in the emptiness. And there we are.

MATT: And that same theme is played out in John of the Cross, too, in the West. St. John of the Cross is very big on the emptying. Of course he was a prisoner, too, so when you're in a jail and being tortured, by your brothers, because you're trying to reform the order, reform religion, those things happen. So he goes very deeply into this whole thing with the emptying, going beyond the senses. But then he ends up writing the most sensual poetry—in fact it's a parallel to the entire Song of Songs—so it's really about purifying the senses so that you get more out of them in the end. Things become richer, yet you're less dependent on them.

TSOMO: There is a parallel very much in Tibetan Buddhism. One of the stages of the path is *Yidam* practice, or deity practice, and the purpose of it is to purify the senses. So we're meditating on the deity, understanding—being very clear—that this is not a substantial thing, the deity. We don't believe they have organs and that you could actually touch them and reach solid flesh. This is insubstantial because we understand the essential empty nature of the being—and yet it appears.

That's actually true of everything around, but we have this very opaque kind of lens that we've created, that makes reality look like this. But our surroundings in this practice are transformed into the pureland of the deity and the palace of the deity, so our home becomes a palace, and it's purified in that way. Our body becomes the insubstantial light body of the deity. And instead of our friends and coworkers, who we sometimes have arguments with and who sometimes have a pimple on their face or whatever, now that's all purified, and it's the entourage of the deity.

That's done visually in the way I'm describing, but then there's the mantra. That's archetypal sound that is pure in itself and it sort of invokes the pure presence of that particular archetypal facet of wisdom. It works on all these levels, so you work with that to the point where then you are ushered into pure, unelaborate emptiness, just naked emptiness. And all of this then eventually dissolves back into yourself because you've gener-ated—because we have everything, everything's outside and inside, and this kind of thing; that's understood. And so it's all drawn back in, and we sit in emptiness.

MATT: And do you think sitting in emptiness is part of our returning to our origins, and our source? That's a very positive dimension. We come from nothingness; we have to return there periodically, to refresh our-selves and to center ourselves, to ground ourselves.

TSOMO: So you're implying that we've left it?

MATT: We carry it with us but we can ignore it. [*Laughs*] We're really good at ignoring it; it really takes some effort to find it again.

TSOMO: Yeah, we're ignoring it, but it's reality all the time; it's the essen-tial reality anytime. I'm trying to remember if I mentioned to you about the scientist, because the scientists are sort of discovering this too.

MATT: They are indeed.

TSOMO: So one of these scientists, awhile back, really believed it was true because he'd done all these experiments, and he believed his experiments, so towards the end of his life he wore these great big fat boots, because he was afraid he was going to fall through the floor.
MATT: [*Laughs*] And this is a scientist . . .

TSOMO: We're not so solid as we think we are.

MATT: . . . wearing snowshoes.

TSOMO: But of course those are empty, too, but nobody could tell him so.

CHAPTER 2

The Awe of Silence

Tsomo: How would you describe this emptiness?

Matt: Well, if you could describe it, would it be emptiness?

Tsomo: Of course, we're having to fake it with words; all we can do is sort of indicate in the direction . . .

Matt: I think silence is probably the better way to describe it.

Tsomo: Yeah, that would be the 100 percent way to describe it, but . . .

Matt: Eckhart says, "We should quit flapping our gums about God and return to the inner wealth of silence." So I think once you've tasted emptiness, nothingness, and silence, there's not a lot to say—about *that*. Now there's a lot more to say about other things because you've got your energy back. I think all creativity comes out of an encounter with silence. And when you think about what is an experience of awe, for example, it shuts you up.

There's a great story of Job. You know, Job had all these troubles, you know. He's arguing with everybody and, then finally, God reveals himself to Job. And God says, "Were you there when I formed the world? Were you there when the lion was born?" and so forth. And then it says that Job put his hand over his mouth and he shut up. He learned some silence. But with hand over your mouth is a sense of awe. I think all awe renders us silent, and therefore all experiences of awe are this quick trip back to no sound, no word, to nothingness. And that's why they're so valuable, and we have to build our lives, our culture, our education, our spiritual lives, on those profound experiences that take us beyond. For one thing, if you look at it physiologically, it's beyond our left brain. It's our left brain that wants to talk. The right brain is happy to be silent or make music or try another language. That takes you closer to carrying on the journey of awe. I like to see art as humanity's capacity to increase awe in the universe. So, everything we do that's beautiful brings more awe, and therefore more silence.

Tsomo: And purifies vision.

Matt: Purifies vision.

Tsomo: Which brings us back home.

Matt: And purifies the visionary—that is, the artist gets purified in the work.

Tsomo: Hopefully so.

Matt: Hopefully so, yes—not always.

Tsomo: There are some trends these days that . . .

Matt: . . . one can resist.

Tsomo: There's a corollary to the Buddha: The students asked him to describe pure truth, what he saw. And he fell silent.

Matt: Ah ha.

Tsomo: So it's a famous moment in Buddhism as well. Nevertheless, maybe we can sneak a peek at it by saying what it's not.

Matt: Uh huh.

Tsomo: Because one thing it's not is a vacuum, an unknowing vacuum. There's a cognizance about it. There's an awareness about it.

Matt: John of the Cross calls it silent music.

Tsomo: Yeah, that's beautiful.

Matt: It's paradoxical, you know.

Tsomo: Actually, in music, between the notes there's silence. You can't have music without silence.

MATT: There you go: you can't have music without it. Yeah, so it's between the notes. It's allowing the between the notes into us. Whereas our culture, especially now, is so busy with all notes, and no silence.

TSOMO: Yeah, that's right. I talked with this Tibetan doctor, about space being the fifth element; they have the four elements, the fifth being space. And I asked, "So how does that work on a psychological level?" And he said, "If there's no space between thoughts, that is the definition of insanity." And haven't we been coming closer and closer to that?

MATT: Wow, no space between thoughts is the definition of insanity.

TSOMO: That's what he said, yeah.

MATT: That makes sense.

TSOMO: Now that we count in nanoseconds, between thought events, I think we're approaching that.

MATT: So honoring space, honoring emptiness, and of course, in our own lives, finding room and space, creating solitude—even if it means structuring time during the day, or a corner of our room, or a room in the house, or a walk in the woods, whatever it takes. Here's a story I don't know if I've told you before. One of my faculty members, over the years, was a teacher of Tai Chi and Mask Making. And he would go to San Quentin Prison, and would do Tai Chi and Mask Making with the prisoners there, and he said whenever he did it with murderers, people on murderer's row, the same thing happened. People would come up to him after the process, the workshop, and say, "This is the first time in my life that I've experienced stillness."

TSOMO: I'd be interested to see how that compares with the book on violence by—and now I'm trying to remember the psychiatrist's name. He worked in the prisons in Massachusetts, and first he started with one prison, where he was assigned the worst, and he was plumbing the depths of violence, the shadow. And he found that it was actually self-worth that had been completely decimated in the childhood of each of his patients. I think that when we get away from the original source, we forget that, to put it in your terms, we're all made of God—how could we not be, what isn't?

MATT: Another point that comes out when you're talking about the violence of these murders and such is that whole thing about original sin. How much does that ideology encourage the young to feel bad about themselves? Or at least how much does it contribute to self-doubt? And if you also have an abusive parent or guardian, or uncle, or clergyman or something in your picture too, all that just is enough to really beat you down.

TSOMO: This speaks to the Tibetan experience in prison. So many Tibetans were tortured, and they saw people killed, and there was a lot of trauma. At one point, some Western experts in trauma, some psychotherapists, came to the border where Tibetans were escaping, and they thought, "It's a cinch they're going to need trauma work."

The amazing thing was almost no one needed any trauma work. So the Dalai Lama came up with the same answer that my teacher, my lama, came up with, and they hadn't talked to each other. But being Tibetans, they came from the same experience, and my lama had been in prison, and he watched the Chinese who were in prison, because sometimes they did a crime or something and they came into prison, and their experience was very different from the Tibetans', even in the same place. Whereas the Chinese tended to be quite traumatized by it, and many of them killed themselves, the Tibetans, because they had this understanding of being an appearance, coming out of this great emptiness that we've been speaking of, and they didn't have any understanding of original sin, and they did have a belief in karma, they thought, "Well, in some other lifetime—who knows how many thousands of years ago—I must have done something terrible to somebody. And I'm simply living out "you should reap what you sow"—that's karma basically—"so I'm reaping that now, and if I live through this and just let it spend itself—because eventually it will—then some other karma will arise, and I'll be finished with this." And that's what happened, for example in Rinpoche's case; he was then let go.

MATT: Did they also do spiritual practices in prison?

TSOMO: He did; not all the Tibetans did. You know, a lot of them say, *om mani padme hum*, and that's really all they know, but he did spiritual training under a great lama in prison.

MATT: So he took advantage of the situation.

TSOMO: Transformed the experience.

CHAPTER 3

Understanding Compassion

Tsomo: I do want to get back to one other indication about this great emptiness that we're talking about, which is that if this is the place at the bottom of the ocean where everything comes together, the source of all appearance, then it's one great vast awareness. Therefore, any piece of any appearance that is suffering is felt by this whole awareness that underlies everything. So this is seen as ultimate compassion. It doesn't get any more direct than that. It's fully felt: every tiny bit of suffering, of every ant, anything.

Matt: And could you also include every tiny bit of joy?

Tsomo: Absolutely.

Matt: So that compassion is our participation both in the suffering of all beings, and of ourselves, but also in the joy of all beings.

Tsomo: Absolutely.

Matt: When we're in difficult situations, this prison or the analogous kinds of prisons we find ourselves in, it is also very powerful, both to ride the inner connectivity, the compassionate consciousness of shared suffering, but also to ride the compassionate consciousness of shared joy.

Tsomo: Well, the basic state, in our tradition, is that of bliss. When you get to this pure, empty awareness, the true ultimate reality, it's a state of bliss, just as a quality of what it is. The suffering only comes from obscuration and confusion with making this movie, that, then, we suffer within.

MATT: I think I'd go a little further than that; I think suffering is more than a movie. [*Laughs*] I wish it were just a movie.

TSOMO: The suffering isn't. The suffering is real.

MATT: Oh, the suffering is real—okay, we agree on that.

TSOMO: When you sit and watch a movie, you can cry. And that's real crying.

MATT: Yeah, but you're crying over someone else's spilt milk, not over your own.

TSOMO: But then in this movie where I'm identifying as me, I'm crying over my spilt milk. And my crying and my suffering are absolutely real.

MATT: They're real—oh, good, okay.

TSOMO: And I can't say, I wouldn't say, that the appearances are not real.

MATT: Now, this is where I think Christianity is quite strong: that whole idea of the Crucifixion. If you don't turn it into a morbid preoccupation, or an idolatrous thing, what's really being said is, hey, there's something archetypal in suffering, even in unjust suffering, because Jesus's suffering was an unjust act. I think this is why Christianity keeps having such legs in spite of Christians. There are powerful lessons there as there are in Buddhism, that are universal, universal teachings, about human nature and the history not just of humanity, but of the universe itself. Stars suffer, too, and they give birth and they die, we now know. And they go into some form of resurrection or reincarnation.

The Christian teaching says, hey, even when the divinity enters history, in any form whatsoever, divinity's going to suffer, too. So, kind of cool it, you know; you're not alone in your suffering. It's part of the karma, it's part of the story, the journey. And of course Buddhism talks this way, too: the suffering of all beings. And what this does, it objectifies suffering, it takes it away from guilt, and even from karma. We can put too much emphasis on karma, because then I think that builds too much guilt. And with guilt we freeze. And I don't think we come to the next stage beyond suffering, which is creativity. Suffering gives you a chance to turn things around.

TSOMO: No, the Tibetans in this situation were not feeling guilt about the karma because that was another lifetime.

MATT: Uh huh—that's how you deal with that.

TSOMO: And you know that they were just confused and bumbling through some sorrow with their neuroses because that's what we do, and we're trying to wake up and we're not there yet. And so that's what happens. There wasn't a sense of guilt with it. It was just like, well, this is the karma that's arising, and I have all the karma, good and bad.

MATT: What about the role of blame? For example, Tibetans at this time in history, jailed by the Chinese, who are invading their country, or at least what Tibetans say is their country—I won't get into the politics right now—but the point is, your guru in jail, is he also putting some blame or responsibility on the part of the Chinese for putting him in there, for torturing his family, etc., etc.? Where does that come in as part of the karma story?

TSOMO: Well, of course, he had to address that. There he was, and looking at it through his lens, he could see that he was, how shall I say, paying off karma, and they were accruing karma.

MATT: Negative karma. Can karma be negative or positive?

TSOMO: Well, you can acquire what they call "merit"; if you do something positive, then it's merit; usually when you're speaking of karma, you mean the negative kind. He's paying off the negative karma from whatever lifetime, and meanwhile they're accruing some very heavy karma. He's watching them in the act of accruing this karma, and they're sentient beings who are trying to figure it out in life and who are very confused and stumbling around and have not had real guidance. And so they became a source of compassion for him. And that had to be real. It wouldn't work if it weren't real, because he was right in it.

MATT: I think that relates to King, you know.

TSOMO: One other Tibetan was getting tortured a lot, and when the Dalai Lama asked him, "Were you ever afraid?" he said, "Yes, I was. I was afraid I was going to lose my compassion." That's what he was afraid of. And he said the way he was able to keep it was that he looked in the face of his torturer and saw that his torturer was not happy even while he was accruing this karma and doing this.

MATT: To me that's identical to King, talking about facing his jailers and the racists who were trying to kill him and others when he was trying to bring the rights of his people alive. He had to see them as not his enemy but as potentially healed, and able to be healed. And again, that's compassion at work, whether it's East or West.

TSOMO: And from your tradition as well as mine, if we look at it from the point of view of original blessing, or original purity as it's spoken of in Tibetan Buddhism, if that's what we all are in our essence, and it's just covered over, then it makes our job much easier—to be able to look at each sentient being as . . .

MATT: . . . as a Buddha or a Christ, in trouble.

TSOMO: Mmm hmm.

MATT: And it's Jesus saying "love your enemies." And, really, this is what Gandhi picked up on.

TSOMO: And this is how.

MATT: Right, right, and Gandhi picked up on that. And this is how you do it. You go to jail if you have to. And you don't return violence for violence. You get into your capacity for nonviolence, and that spreads. It can spread just as much as violence can spread.

TSOMO: I think these things are infectious.

MATT: That's what happened in King's movement. It spread and it worked. But it was harrowing; I've talked to people who were there. They told me how James Farmer, who was one of the leaders of one of the marches, who was a great big guy, literally ran and hid in a drugstore. Afterwards, when they all gathered, and everyone was very despondent, James Farmer stands up and tells the truth of what he did; he said, "I was so scared, I went and I hid." And instead of berating him or booing him or firing him as their leader, they stood up and clapped, and held him, because the common humanity of fear, in the face of police dogs and police on horses and the bludgeoning and everything, everyone recognized that none of us is a superman . . . or woman.

TSOMO: There are these two kinds of compassion: one is this ultimate compassion that's completely out of the fray, in this ultimate stillness kind of way, but then there's compassion that happens within the drama that you're speaking of.

MATT: The concrete.

TSOMO: Within the world of appearances, there's this emptiness, and then it comes into appearances, and then it just keeps doing that. They speak of it almost like frames of a movie, where it keeps going back into the emptiness and flashing forth, just the way the movie does. And of course we put together the appearances and make a whole story, and we never see the blank part in between. So there are these two kinds of compassion as well.

MATT: And the darkness that individuals go into. Then, King certainly felt in jail at times. Sometimes he was writing great letters from jail, and at times I'm sure he was feeling the torture of being separated from his family and what comes next and all the rest of it. And certainly the same is true with Jesus's life: He continually retreated, getting out in the desert away from all this madding crowd and so forth, and trying to find solitude to balance the action.

TSOMO: Perhaps that's the origin of the Sabbath.

MATT: Yeah, I think it has a lot to do with it. Definitely, definitely.

TSOMO: I myself find that the rhythm of beginning my day with meditation and then within the timing of the year, usually in the sort of introverted time of winter, I go into retreat so that . . .

MATT: There's a mother bear in you?

TSOMO: [*Laughs*] Well, the bears hibernate all winter here.

MATT: Just like you—or vice versa.

TSOMO: And the Buddha and his followers would do three months of retreat during the summer rains, which was sort of an introverted time in that bioregion.

MATT: Monsoons, huh? Makes sense to stay indoors, stay dry.

TSOMO: Well, they were camping. Isn't it amazing to think that there were all these parks and groves and so on that they could go to? India was a much different place back then, where they could live outside. There was a huge entourage.

CHAPTER 4

Understanding Enlightenment and The Feminine Balance

MATT: This talk of compassion is interesting because one of the questions that's come up in our conversations is this enlightenment goal of Buddhism, and the compassion goal of Judaism and Christianity, and how alike are they, really? Because the more I explore it, I think they're really the same thing because compassion is about enlightenment; it's just what you were saying, it's an awareness of our profound interdependence, and it carries us obviously beyond a rugged individual ego or soul or anything else, and yet it's more than just the awareness; it's the acting out, it's the acting out.

TSOMO: And the feeling of it, the felt sense of the connection. In Buddhism, I have to say that when you say the emphasis is of enlightenment, actually it's enlightenment and compassion together. And it's depicted as the male and female in union. One is enlightenment and one is compassion.

MATT: Oh, good—it's like a marriage.

TSOMO: Exactly. And it takes both of them because they feel that if there's too much insight, or wisdom, without the compassion, then you have things like the atom bomb, which is very clever but not very compassionate. Or, on the other side, if you have all this compassion but no wisdom to guide it in its effectiveness, it's actually powerless and it can just fall into sentimentality or just ineffectuality. So we always . . .

MATT: I'm thinking of a political phrase called "compassionate conservatism," that brought us the Iraq war. We don't have to talk about that.

TSOMO: I call it "idiot compassion." We don't want to fall into idiot compassion or this horrific . . .

MATT: . . . or the sentimentalizing of compassion, which is another thing—sentimentality and not compassion.

TSOMO: Yes, that's right.

MATT: Compassion has a hard edge to it. Eckhart says "compassion means justice".

TSOMO: Sentimentality is still about yourself; you're getting off on something.

MATT: On your feelings.

TSOMO: That's right. Your own feelings. In fact, it's not about the other person.

MATT: Your emotions. Exactly, exactly.

TSOMO: It's called "the near enemy of compassion" in Tibetan Buddhism, because it can be mistaken.

MATT: It's pseudo; it's ersatz.

TSOMO: Exactly.

MATT: But it can fill your soul with self-righteousness: "Aren't I good, and aren't I more compassionate than this person?" It's very deceptive.

TSOMO: Well, then, it's still about ego, isn't it?

MATT: There's a great line, a medieval line, *corruptio optimiest pessima*: "the corruption of the best is the worst." To take compassion and corrupt it is a very dangerous thing. That's why compassion has to be critiqued. It has to be understood.

TSOMO: The wisdom has to be applied. If we're to apply the compassion skillfully, we'd better have some wisdom in there, or it's not going to be effectual.

MATT: Okay, so now I'm getting closer to understanding enlightenment. I'm glad we talked about this. So for you, enlightenment is wisdom applied to compassion.

Tsomo: Well, it's wisdom and compassion joined.

Matt: Joined, okay, that's nice.

Tsomo: This has been depicted in many different ways. We can have skillful means and wisdoms, so then the skillful means is the masculine and the wisdom is the feminine. They have lots of different qualities they attach to these figures in union so that, hopefully, you associate all these with this one image. And then of course an image goes very deeply into the brain and into the nervous system and so on . . .

Matt: But it is interesting at least from the West, that wisdom is feminine in the West and so is compassion because compassion comes from the word for "womb," in both Hebrew and Arabic. So the least we can say is this: that we must have the yin energy, the feminine energy, back in place, as a healthy balance to masculine energy, if we're going to recover wisdom, enlightenment, or compassion. And then you back up and say, "Oh, that's what's wrong." That in a patriarchal world, or consciousness, we're missing wisdom, enlightenment, and compassion. And things do get a little out of control that way, out of order, disordered, unbalanced.

Tsomo: Peggy Sanday found that societies that didn't worship a feminine deity were missing certain qualities. They were much more warlike; the women weren't treated well. Where they built their cities depended on this warlike culture, to be able to defend and attack and this kind of thing, and they were just very different, qualitatively, from societies that had a feminine deity.

And then she went around, and while she was speaking, she would just take a little survey and she would just say [paraphrasing], "If I say the word *god*, what are the words you associate with that?" And it was "all powerful," it was "jealous," it was this, that, and the other, "all-knowing." But then when she said. "Now, if I say the word *goddess*, they go, Oh, all-compassionate," and this kind of thing, and they came up with quite a different list of qualities, and yet those weren't represented in a deity and they weren't worshiping . . .

Matt: Let me ask this question: A number of Buddhists don't like to use the word *god*. And, for the same reason, Eckhart didn't like to use it. He wasn't a Buddhist as such, when he said, "I pray God to rid me of God."

That god language can trip you up and hijack you. But it's interesting that you almost sound more at home talking about the deity as goddess. So is Buddhism at home talking about divinity or deity as goddess? So it's not about throwing out the concept of deity, or divinity, or does this vary with different traditions?

Tsomo: The way it's handled in Tibetan Buddhism . . . I used the word *goddess* just now because Peggy Sanday did, and she was working with Westerners.

Matt: Uh huh. But you have many images, too, of the goddesses.

Tsomo: Many of us like to refer to those as *deities*, and we use them for deity practice. But that's quite apart from this great vast emptiness that has no form whatsoever and is the sort of root of all, the source of all.

Matt: It has no name and all names.

Tsomo: Right—that sort of thing; they're epithets.

Matt: The Godhead.

Tsomo: There are epithets, but they can't really be named.

Matt: When you say "deities," you're talking more about what might be translated as angels?

Tsomo: Well, they're archetypal figures, archetypal images, if you will. I think the closest thing we'd have to angels would be *Dakinis*.

Matt: Spirits?

Tsomo: And some of those are also used in deity practice; they're enlightened beings.

CHAPTER 5

Lama Tsomo's Spiritual Journey

MATT: Can I ask you a question?

TSOMO: No.

MATT: About your Buddhism?

TSOMO: Certainly not.

MATT: Good. Then I will.

TSOMO: Of all things, you're going to ask me about Buddhism?

MATT: Paradox. So tell me: As a Westerner, since you were raised very much in North America, what does Buddhism bring to you? Why is Buddhism important to you? At the practical level, you might say.

TSOMO: Well, I was looking for methods, techniques that could help me work with my mind in such a way that I'd be a better, happier person. That was my basic goal, and I started with the Western skillful means, which would be psychology, and found that they were helpful on sort of a basic level of rearranging the furniture in one's unconscious, and you get to wear a headlight while you do it. So that was nice.

But then when I became the first American guinea pig of this lama, I had a chance to study some methods that had been studied for thousands of years. Way before Freud. And they were standing on the shoulders of some Hindu techniques—because he learned those first, right? So as I began road-testing these methods, I found that they were really effective. And, furthermore, that the point wasn't just to rearrange the furniture and then keep rearranging and rearranging, but finally to get out altogether, to open the door of this little tiny cell I was in, and get out. And be in full reality.

I found that those methods were not only able to give me a clue about that, but to show me the door.

MATT: It's interesting that when you said that when you were looking for Western ways, you went to psychology, you didn't go to religion, to Jewish practices, for example.

TSOMO: Because in my temple I didn't find a satisfying source for that wisdom and those methods.

MATT: For what you were looking for.

TSOMO: Yeah, so if I didn't find the methods from that source, and I already knew it, then I had to look elsewhere. Now it could be that—I'm sure—there were some of those methods there that I just didn't know about.

MATT: Yeah, up in the attic of the Jewish tradition, dusty trunks.

TSOMO: Somewhere—I just didn't find it. And the headlamp, you know, and I didn't come upon those and our lineages, you know, a lot of them have been broken because of Hitler. And because of 2,000 years passing since we were conquered and spread to the four directions.

MATT: The diaspora.

TSOMO: The Tibetan diaspora is much more recent, and there are lots and lots of live lineages with lineage-holding lamas who have had the transition not just on paper but been mentored carefully, and had the whispered lineages, the mind-to-mind lineages, mouth-to-ear, that they can trace all the way back to enlightened beings.

MATT: That is special about this time in history, isn't it, that there is as you say a Tibetan diaspora happening because of the politics. It's blessing the rest of the world really by getting out and reaching people like you and many others.

TSOMO: Exactly. And it was predicted by Padmasambhava, who really caused Buddhism to take root in Tibet. He made a lot of predictions which were very specific and very accurate, kind of stunningly so.

MATT: When did he live?

TSOMO: He lived in the 800s, CE. He predicted that Tibet would be conquered and that Tibetans would scatter to all corners of the earth . . .

MATT: I hear they're even coming to Montana.

TSOMO: Yes, they do. His Holiness the Dalai Lama is coming to bless the Buddha garden. Yeah, we're very excited about that—but anyway, in this prediction, just so we could locate it in time, he said, "When the metal horse runs on wheels, and the metal bird flies in the sky, this will be when the Tibetans will be conquered and Buddhism will come to the land of the red man."

MATT: Wow, amazing, "the land of the red man."

TSOMO: So that's one of his quotes, yeah. So here we are.

MATT: That's exciting.

TSOMO: Yeah.

CHAPTER 6

Matthew's Spiritual Journey, Part I

MATT: If I were to turn the question around, to myself—how our stories are different, and how they overlap—I, too, was looking, as a young man in my teenage years, for a deeper Christianity, for the same thing you were looking for, I think: some meaning and practice. What matters, and is this all there is?

TSOMO: Yeah. How is this helping me, really?

MATT: What can I say? I took a chance on joining the Dominican order and exploring it that way because I was impressed by some of the things that I'd experienced, such as reading Aquinas, and knowing there was some intellectual tradition here, and also visiting a Dominican house and hearing the chanting, and seeing the community in action, and because I was from a big family anyway. I found it very aesthetically profound. Especially the chanting, the praying, and then the meditation—there were hours a day of meditation. That appealed to me as something quite different for a 16-year-old male growing up in the 1950s in America. So I went that path, and then it developed into other things, but I kept digging deeper, until, finally, I thought, "Well, I have to go study this thing called *spirituality*, because we're not getting enough"—in my training I felt we weren't. Things were happening to me—I was having experiences—that no priest could guide me on.

I was realizing my generation's was going to be interested in spirituality and not religion. And you've got to have someone here who can guide people and help them, and that's why I went to Europe to study spiritual-ity, and I realized, especially holding my journey up to yours, they're not that different. But I've been probing, and I've had to leave a lot of Chris-tianity behind, to find what nuggets are there, if you will, the treasures that are there. And there are treasures. Meister Eckhart—that's where we first met, really, was over Meister Eckhart—we were teaching a course together, and I was struck by how you were struck. You said you didn't know this was in Christianity. And it took me a lot of hunting to find that and other sources, too, including the mystical side of Aquinas that no one had ever exposed me to. And now the scholars are showing how profoundly mystical Jesus was, how he comes from that wisdom tradition of Israel—so a real lineage, of finding God not just in texts—Jesus was illiterate—but in practice and in nature. And in the turmoil, in the chaos, because he was living in a tremendously chaotic time of the Jewish people trying to survive under the Roman empire, not that different from the Tibetans and the Chinese today. Really, they'd been driven everywhere and taken apart and crucified, and then there were zealots, and "Let's go after the tanks with knives" or something. There was all kinds of craziness going on in the first century, when he showed up or tuned in.

CHAPTER 7

Restoring Mysticism & Wisdom

MATT: It's interesting to talk about, not just our personal choices, in these journeys, but the lineages that we've hooked up with. They have a lot more in common than we've been told.

TSOMO: I recognized in Eckhart's writing not only some understandings of the great emptiness and so on, from Tibetan Buddhism, but from what I was hearing my rabbi talk about when I was a kid, and he was in the kitchen debating with my dad on the existence of God. And his description was more like Eckhart's; I just hadn't seen anything so similar, since then, really. So it was quite an experience for me to have those echoes coming back.

MATT: I think a lot of it in the West is not just failure of our religions; it's failure of our education. Because the Enlightenment, you know, the whole modern consciousness was so excessively left-brained, so much about text, that in Judaism and Christianity, we were embarrassed by our mystical traditions, we buried them. It's kind of like Newton: He had this big trunk of mystical works that he literally kept in a trunk until after his death. He was not just this great scientist, but he was exploring the mystical. But he was embarrassed to mention it.

TSOMO: And we've just now been able to see *The Red Book* of Jung's.

MATT: Oh? Tell me more—about *The Red Book* of Jung's[28].

---

28. Carl Jung (author), Sonu Shamdasani (Editor. Translator), Mark Kyburz (Translator), John Peck (Translator,) *The Red Book* (Philemon, 2009)

TSOMO: Finally the family has now just allowed it to be printed. It's full of mystical stuff and mandalas that he was drawing.

MATT: Well, we knew he was into that.

TSOMO: I know. But they tried to hide as much of it as they could. He was into alchemy, but we really never saw the texts. I knew of an alchemist that wanted to print some of that stuff, that wanted to get his hands on it, and the family threatened him with a lawsuit. He kept that under wraps through his whole life, and even this far after his life, the family was still keeping it under wraps until about two months ago.

MATT: Two months ago, that's exciting—wow, great, I've got to see that. Theodore Roszak has a great line. [Paraphrasing] he says that the Enlightenment held mysticism up for ridicule as the worst offense against science and reason. So when our Western culture took this science/reason trip, then religion got on board because there would be even more ridicule. So we sat on our mystical traditions; both the synagogue did, and the church did. And in the process we distorted mysticism, and in the process many good souls like yourself had to go east; you went east because at least you could get something authentic.

TSOMO: Well, you only had to go as far east as Russia, though, to find Jewish traditions that still had the mysticism and weren't fixated on texts and concepts. And there were lineages and so on.

MATT: And great refugees like Heschel and so on and Marc Chagall and all the other Russian, Jewish, Eastern European refugees. Of course, another way to find it is with the indigenous, what I call the *pre-modern.* They never built their religion on books.

Being here in Montana like we are now, I'm struck with some similarities between the Buddhists and the native, the indigenous, like your flags, the four directions of the flags.

TSOMO: Four different archetypal facets of wisdom, of reality.

MATT: Absolutely. Of course, the four, as Jung points out, is the archetype of the cosmos, it's the quaternity, it's north, south, east, west—but how far is north, how far is south, how far is east, west—well, it's hundreds of billions of galaxies. There's no end; you don't get there.

TSOMO: In Tibetan Buddhism it's five Buddha families in five directions, including center. I think the way I would express it from the Buddhist point of view, the Tibetan Buddhist point of view especially, is that once wisdom is beginning to come into manifestation and begins to divide from one into the many, the next step after the one is these five facets of wisdom, that have colors associated with them and directions, and qualities of wisdom. There's the penetrating, insightful wisdom; there's the blissful, attractive sort of wisdom; there's the all-manifesting wisdom. The five different wisdoms weave themselves into ever more complex forms. So you have this whole tapestry that we call *manifested reality*.

That's what those colors are representing. And we're all weavings of that. But we usually have a leaning in one or another of those Buddha families. We'll have certain qualities that are more prominent. Rinpoche told me a long time ago that my favorite was the lotus family and on the more occluded side, that has to do more with desire and clinging, but on the more enlightened, once you get to the enlightened core of that, it has to do with bliss, which is again an aspect of this great, pure, empty awareness reality that we've been talking about.

MATT: Exactly, exploring our true nature. These many facets of wisdom you were talking about struck me because the latest scholarship on historical Jesus is that he comes out of the wisdom tradition of Israel. So that whole thing, the deepening of our understanding of the wisdom tradition of Israel, was very important at this time because, again, it was banished, partly by patriarchy, because wisdom was feminine, even in Israel. And she didn't have a big role in the last few centuries in either Christianity or Judaism, certainly not in our seminaries and schools.

TSOMO: I didn't hear about the *Shekinah* until New Age Judaism came along.

MATT: There you go, you see; and you were Jewish.

TSOMO: I know.

MATT: And that's my point. I don't know one minister or priest who had a solid course in wisdom literature in their entire seminary training. Now this is beginning to change, especially because women are now teaching in seminaries, and they're bringing it back. But the fact that Jesus himself comes from that lineage is so vital and important to understand this person, and realize that what he was really trying to teach was wisdom. And then there's the other, the layer on that, is the Christ story, Christianity, is that Jesus not only teaches wisdom, in fact he was wisdom incarnate. He lived it, he drank it. And he died for it, if you will, because of it.

A rabbi once told me, "You know, in our tradition, any person who's really living out wisdom we call a son of God. So as a rabbi, I can call Jesus a son of God—not *the* son of God but a son of God—because I do believe that he was one of our better Jewish brothers, and he was living out wisdom." And if that's not a bridge between Judaism and Christianity . . .

TSOMO: Maybe that's what Jesus was saying, what he meant, when he said that.

MATT: Exactly. Maybe he didn't say, "I am here to start an empire, and buttress it with the church." Maybe he didn't say that.

TSOMO: No. He didn't seem so inclined toward institutions.

MATT: Not at all. [*Both laugh*] He was not impressed.

CHAPTER 8

Methods of Spiritual Inquiry

TSOMO: I was intrigued by your describing your journey, your inquiry into some methods that could help you become basically a better, happier person, and your inquiry into meaning, and those kinds of things. What specifically are the methods for training the mind within the traditions that you've inquired into that you've found most helpful?

MATT: Well, in the training I had for nine years I guess it was, nine or 10 years as a Dominican, the things that most impressed me were meditation. It was sitting in silence for an hour in the morning, early in the morning. You were taught various ways you could deal with that silence.

One practice I had that worked for me was to find just one short line, one short phrase from the Bible, and just dwell with that. And dwell and dwell, and then you move from dwelling with it to just being in a space of silence. And just being with, not thinking about, but being with. And that was extremely interesting.

TSOMO: That's what I was talking about where it takes the conceptual mind and, with the hook of concepts, ushers it into.

MATT: You move from discursive to non-discursive, absolutely.

MATT: I remember one line, and I don't even know what book in the Jewish Bible it's from, because it's such a short phrase, but the phrase was, "Son, give me your heart." And I rolled with that probably for weeks, if not months. That was in my novitiate year, which was a year of lots of meditation and discipline. You got up at, I don't know, four in the morning. It was Winona, Minnesota, freezing cold, the snow. First thing you would do is meditate—you were silent, too, until breakfast—so you meditate for an hour, and then you had Mass for an hour, and chanting, you had the chanting of the Psalms, wisdom literature. And that was very profound because, again; just one line from one of the Psalms can be extremely rich. I had a problem with it, and I would tell my superiors that "we race through it; it's like racing to get to the end of the psalm." I said, "that's no way to meditate." Then when spring came and everything was flowering and so beautiful, I would say, "Why don't we go outside and meditate with the trees?" And they said, "Are you crazy?" I said, "Well, maybe I am." It sounded better than being in church and racing through these things.

So I found that useful. And then of course we had the Gregorian chant; it's very beautiful, it comes from the synagogue. As a musical form, it's extremely powerful, reaching many of your chakras. The latest science on Gregorian chant is that, in fact, they had different chants for different diseases, different seasons of the year. If you were having a liver problem, you'd chant this . . . . So it's really sophisticated, much more so than we were really ever aware, or taught. Different modes would heal different psychological states: you're depressed, you're happy—all that. All I knew is that we were singing these chants. I wasn't a real good singer, but there were people in my class who were, and it was just marvelous hearing them sing and joining in. And we'd have these processions singing these songs. And we had the Rosary, which is of course a mantra. We would actually do three Rosaries a day, back to back, in my novitiate training. And, again, that takes you into an altered state.

Tsomo: And you're using an archetype, within that, archetypal visual, archetypal sound.

Matt: Right, and it's also about Mary, so it's about the feminine, the yin. And then there was nature. We'd go outdoors and we would play sports and stuff, and I always loved, I always had mystical experiences playing sports, frankly. Well, my father was a football coach; that may have something to do with it. But there was a balance, and then there was the intellectual side, and to me that was very important, that was one of the things that drew me into the Dominicans to study, and my mind, my questioning mind, was not being famished in the presence of this mystical mind that was developing.

There was silence at meals, and then sometimes someone would read from a book while everyone else was silent. Then there was physical work to do, cleaning the place and all that. And kind of healthy manual labor, working in the yard or something. And then just the community give-and-take, you know, the friendship.

So that went on for nine years with some slight variations. And we got a couple of master's degrees in the process, working on philosophy and theology. All that just appealed to me very much, but I went into such a state that my confessor suggested that I become a full-time hermit. Then I took this trip one summer to a hermit colony on Vancouver Island. It was very powerful and beautiful, and I think I ran on that energy for about 25 years.

At the hermitage you talk to no one, except for a little bit, every other day for an hour or something. But it was just really being in nature, very simple; I literally lived with a candle and a Bible and a mattress on the floor. I can remember taking a bath in the river with a bar of soap. I was about 23 when that happened.

TSOMO: Were there specific practices that you did during that time?

MATT: Well, reading the Bible and chanting. We would have a very simple daily Mass. But it was really on your own, so I was developing some of the practices that were working for me, like taking phrases from the Bible, but journaling, too. But, no. It was not at all heavily directed. In fact it was hardly directed at all.

The people that were there, that's what interested me. There was a fellow who worked as a forest ranger during the year, and what's more monastic than being alone, sitting at the top of a tower, looking for a fire 20 hours a day?

TSOMO: That was my favorite job aspiration for a while, as a kid.

MATT: Really? Well there you are. There were monks from various monasteries who were there. And the head guy was an abbot from Belgium, who Thomas Merton knew very well. And it turned out, when I look back at it, I was actually in the hermitage at the very time Merton won his fight with his abbot, and was allowed to go into hermitage. So that was interesting. I think it was around 1963 or 1964.

So that was very interesting, and of course learning the tradition of the hermetical life in Christian monasticism, which is ancient. Then I returned with a lot of energy, and I started a magazine and other things, but I took that energy and kind of put it into practice. So those are some of the influences I had, the practices I had. The Dominicans started in the thirteenth century, so it really is a 700-year lineage that has had its ups and downs, its good seasons and its bad. But it did give us people like Meister Eckhart and Aquinas in the Middle Ages, but also in our time, great souls like Chenu, my mentor in Paris; and Schillebeeckx, the Dutch Dominican; and Yves Congar, another French Dominican; and some of the significant scholars. And I say, holy men, practitioners . . . yeah.

TSOMO: If I were to ask myself the same question, "What did I find?" the most convincing thing for me, as I explored, first, the spiritual smorgasbord and then eventually Tibetan Buddhism, is the practices themselves and their effectiveness. When I first started studying with Rinpoche, I so much appreciated, as a Jew doing this, that he said, "I'm not giving you a religion so much as I'm giving you, what I'm really giving you, is a series of methods that you can use for training your mind so that you can reach enlightenment."

As a psychotherapist, I could appreciate some of these methods. We would sort of change gears and have different practices that would cultivate different aspects of the mind, and different movements of the mind, and so on. One meditation might be simply calming and making peaceful the mind, which we discussed before. And then another one might be a very penetrating insight into the nature of these things, trying to pierce the veil of illusion, sort of pierce through the movie screen to what's really there. Another one would be compassion meditation, where you use our natural tendency anyway to have dramas go on, and make dramas about the people around us, in *Tonglen*—that meditation, for example. But that's just one example. You've got insight, and you've got *bodhicitta*, and *bodhicitta* means "the mind of awakening." I think of it as being more like the heartfelt sense that we're not separate. We're cultivating that in various

ways. And, again, we can change gears and do that through not just compassion but sympathetic joy, as you were looking for before. There are four
boundless qualities, or immeasurables, as they're sometimes translated.
One is a feeling of love, and wanting people to be happy and not suffer.
Then there's compassion, sympathetic joy, and a really very important
one is equanimity—that we don't just feel a sort of an indifference that's
disguised as equanimity, that's a near enemy of equanimity—it's like,
"Oh, I feel the same about everybody: equally numb."

We start very close in with people we really care about and practice
these feelings and then extend it, as we did with Tonglen. But there are
these other ways of also. giving rise to bodhicitta. And the two purposes
that they always talk about are enlightenment for self and for everybody
else. We don't want to leave everybody else suffering in their confusion.
So those are examples of some of the very basic foundational practices
because if you don't have a calm mind and you haven't begun to peek
through the veil and you haven't given rise to bodhicitta, you're not ready
for the next ones. That's your very foundation, and that's common to all
the lineages of Buddhism, those kinds of practices.

On top of that, you have the *mudras*, or preliminary practices. And
they're called that not because they're considered very pedestrian; they're
actually quite powerful. It's a collection of five practices that again come
at it from different angles, that prepare us for whatever is next. So if we're
going to do a ceremony, we always begin with preliminaries, which are
these five practices. Or even when we're sitting alone in our meditation
room, we begin with the preliminaries and then maybe go on to *sochen*.

We spend a lot of hours—that's where you get 108,000 prostrations,
or 108,000 recitations of this or that, and so on, once again distilling
ourselves and training our mind to become more stable and more supple,
as they call it, through the bodhicitta practices and so on, till we come to
this purifying of our karmic vision that we talked about earlier with the
deity practices. So that's the third grouping. And those we're now ready
for: My mind is now stable enough to pull this off, and we've seen through
things enough and everything, so we can pull this off. And so now, we do
those practices.

There are practices after that that work directly with the channels and
the winds, or *energies*, as they're called, because our mind rides on those.

And karma is sort of shaping the channels and affecting how the chi—you know what chi is—how the chi flows. It's on a subtle, subtle level. So we're working directly with that, and that's pretty strong medicine. This is a "don't do this at home" kind of thing unless you have instruction.

The last level is when it really goes to this pure, empty nature. Again, there are very powerful practices to take you, and lead you, usher you in, and then dump you off in pure, naked experience of reality as it truly is.

MATT: Obviously very sophisticated pathways there.

CHAPTER 9

Matthew's Spiritual Journey, Part II

MATT: Another dimension to my journey was certainly what was going on culturally in the 1960s—so the Civil Rights Movement. My theology studies were in Dubuque, Iowa, and we were restricted to stay where we were. But, nevertheless, King and all that was coming in on radio and television.

TSOMO: That was so close to where I was homesteading . . .

MATT: Really? In Wisconsin?

TSOMO: Yeah. I was at the far end of Wisconsin right near Dubuque, Iowa, just across the Mississippi.

MATT: There you go. Oh, wow, how interesting. Morphic resonance there, huh? And then, of course, the Vietnam War I remember—it may have been my last year before I left Dubuque for Paris, to do my studies in spirituality—this young man came wandering through with a guitar, just kind of showed up at our place, and he was singing Bob Dylan songs, which was totally new to me, and then there was Joan Baez, so I remember being profoundly influenced. After all these years of going through purification and training and everything, and being very spiritually, I don't know what you say, vulnerable, open. And then this whole thing shows up: the Joan Baezes and the Bob Dylans. And it showed up through art, again, through the aesthetic. This wasn't so much a political argument; I could feel the beauty of these justice movements.

So when I was able to go to Paris and study more of our history and our lineage of spirituality in the West, I really had one question: What is the relationship between mystical experiences (of which I'd had a number and about which I didn't talk to anybody; I wanted to talk to some priests, but I couldn't find one in the entire building who could talk back to me about it) and the struggle for justice. And that was my absolutely pressing question that I took with me to Paris, and that question is in every one of my books, including my book on compassion. And then I found these figures like Eckhart and Aquinas, who were very profound spiritually, but very engaged politically. Eckhart was such a feminist in his time, working with the women's movement, in the Middle Ages, whom the pope condemned, 17 times in his lifetime, the very pope who condemned Eckhart. So these weren't people just sitting on the sidelines. And of course Chenu then, my mentor, helped me to understand the connection between the mystical and the prophetic, the social justice and the spirituality, beautifully. And of course I was there in Paris literally when the students brought down DeGaulle's government in 1968. The whole world—not just Berkeley but all over—students, young people, were engaged in this struggle. Thomas Merton pointed this out to me in a letter, because we had some correspondence, how some were going off in the direction of drugs. I remember meeting a young Dutchman about my age, late 20s, in Europe, and I asked him about drugs, and he said, "Well, you know, who needs drugs when you can get high on life?" And for me that said something.

Of course I was also being immersed in the amazing history and culture and art of Paris, and Europe in general. And that was part of my training, too, to see how this impetus to creativity and art and spirituality played out in European culture so much more freely than in America. Because I felt that in America there was very little encouragement of the artist. Whereas in France it was taken for granted. You go to museums, and parents were there with their little kids, and it wasn't about misbehaving; it was turning the kids on to art. I really discovered the poet in me. I had written poetry when I was a kid, but by the time I was a teenager, it didn't seem very important anymore. But it came back in that context of a Latin appreciation of art and it was really an essential dimension to a spiritual journey.

So that whole thing about justice and art was very important. And then when I returned, of course, there was an ecological movement and the gay and lesbian movement. All this really integrated for me and that's why—and when I read Eckhart, who connected compassion directly with justice—that brought it together for me. One of my early books is called *Spirituality Named Compassion.* I think it's kind of Buddhist. [*Laughs*]

TSOMO: It's aspirational bodhicitta and engaged bodhicitta that they talk about. So there I think we meet, our traditions meet.

CHAPTER 10

The Role of Science

MATT: The role of science, too, is something that to me has always been important. How can you study nature if you don't listen to the scientists who spend all their time studying nature? Again, it's my whole tradition because Aquinas put his whole tradition on the line, by bringing Aristotle in through Islam, into Christianity in the thirteenth century, and, in the process, totally threatened the fundamentalists of his day.

TSOMO: So he wasn't participating in the schism, and that freaked them out, I imagine. But there never was a schism for Buddhists, as far as I can tell, against science; they just didn't go through that particular experience. His Holiness the Dalai Lama loves interacting with the scientists because the Buddha insisted that we really make a very clear-eyed, open-eyed inquiry and encourage debate and so on and so forth. And through thought experiment—they didn't have laboratories so much—but it's amazing what they did know. In my early teachings from Rinpoche, he was discussing atoms, which they had a word for, and subatomic theory, and it was sounding like what our scientists had been discovering in the last few decades. And I got all excited, and I said, "Guess what! Our scientists are saying the same things you're saying." And he looked very unimpressed, and he said, "Well, the Buddha lived 2,500 years ago; why should I be impressed? What are you talking about?" [*Both laugh*]

MATT: He didn't know about the divorce in the West.

Tsomo: One of the scientists, coming from a Western point of view, just had to ask His Holiness, "Well, if we disprove one of the tenets of your faith, through science, what are you going to do about it?" This was when they were going to begin this dialogue that has only grown and flourished over the years, and lots of books have come of it and scientific experiments, and contemplative science is now in some universities. But this was way back at the beginning, and His Holiness said, "Well, if you methodically use the scientific method and clearly and definitively disprove that, I have to accept that." And so the guy didn't let it go quite then. He said, "Well, what if we disprove reincarnation?" He said, "I would have to accept that. But you're going to have trouble doing that." [*Both laugh*]

Matt: Hildegard, a century before Aquinas, said, "All science comes from God." And she herself has been given credit for discovering vitamins.

Tsomo: I knew she was my patron saint.

Matt: Yeah, oh, there you go: You take her vitamins. She was out there hunting for the best scientific answers she could get.

Tsomo: And she was a medical doctor.

Matt: She was a healer, definitely. In fact, there's a whole clinic in Switzerland today, run by a German doctor and his American wife, who's also a doctor, and their entire clinic's based on Hildegard's medicine. They've been in business for over 25 years, so obviously something's working— which is really interesting.

Tsomo: It is.

Matt: So, again, the distorted picture we have of Christianity being anti-science, that is only one wing of Christianity; it's the fundamentalists.

Tsomo: It's the loudest one, though.

Matt: Very loud, and also the moneyed ones. So they have their own TV stations, which makes them triply loud. And of course they serve political interests that support them and corporate interests that support them very strongly and make them even louder. But the truth is that there's not always been this division. And Aquinas was a good example; he said, "A mistake about creation results in a mistake about God." So obviously we have to study creation, and that's what scientists do. And he built his entire life's work around Aristotle, who had just been discovered in the West through Islam. And because Aristotle was the best scientist at the time . . .

TSOMO: He was a little off on his atomic theory, but anyway . . .

MATT: Aquinas was real specific why he prefers Aristotle to Plato, and that was because Aristotle does not denigrate matter, whereas Plato puts matter down. And that is why he wrote over 10 commentaries on 10 of Aristotle's books and not a single one on Plato's books. So it's a huge shift for Christianity to move from Plato to Aristotle because it's about giving up the clash between spirit and matter.

TSOMO: Well, matter, motter, so there's the feminine.

MATT: That's right. If you look at it really strongly, Aquinas, with basic issues like that, is definitely in the feminist wing of things. And it's really what got him condemned three times before they canonized him. He insisted on the consubstantiality—that is, equality—of body and soul. And matter and spirit. And, as a dynamic play in everything—act and potency, too.

So there's a long history of this, and of course Nicholas of Cusa, in the fifteenth century, who knew Eckhart's work very well, and Cusa is just up the river, the Rhine River, from Bingen, where Hildegard hung out. He was a scientist of the first order and a mathematician of the very early Renaissance, late fifteenth century, and the modern physicist David Bohm says he owes more to Cusa than he does to Einstein. So Nicholas of Cusa gave him his whole idea of implicate and explicate order and all of that.

TSOMO: That's interesting, because Einstein himself, towards the end of his life, they asked him what he would do differently, scholastically, would there be anything, and he said, "Yes. I would have studied the mystics earlier."

MATT: Ooh, that's interesting. I didn't know that. I'm going to write that one down.

TSOMO: I know. I'm going to hunt down the quote and find out exactly where he said that.

MATT: Another thing he said was, "The older I get, the more precious solitude is to me." And that line comes to me every birthday at least.

Tsomo: Of course I feel the need to go into retreat for that reason. The word for "retreat" in Tibetan is actually the same word for "boundary." So in other words, you put yourself in the crucible, and put these elements of the practice together. And the body is seen as the place where this drama of enlightenment takes place.

Matt: The ground of it.

Tsomo: Yeah—there's this interaction between this mind and this body that's manifested in the energies that I was describing before.

Matt: So body is not a problem; it's a vessel.

Tsomo: It's a vessel. And of course there are imperfections in it, and we can work directly on that level as well as these other levels. One of the first things we study in the preliminary practices is this thought of the precious human birth. That this body is an excellent ship to enlightenment, a vehicle to enlightenment. So they actually just embrace the senses in the body and the material as a way to usher us to enlightenment. This is done with these skillful means that I was describing a bit of.

Matt: To go back to that idea, which is interesting, about the retreat as boundary. It's kind of like localizing it, because so much of our day is about interruptions, if you want to put it that way, phone, class, and issues and problems and bills and everything else, take us beyond our . . .

Tsomo: And yammering with other people . . .

Matt: Right, right— beyond really being centered. So I kind of like that.

Tsomo: When I spoke recently to my rabbi, who I keep hearkening back to—he's 93 and still alive—he said, "Isn't this meditation path awfully solipsistic?" So how would you reply to that?

Matt: Ha-ha, you're not going tell me how you answered him.

Tsomo: I have an answer . . .

Matt: First you want to hear me.

Tsomo: I already know what I'm going to say. I want to hear what you're going to say. [*Both laugh*]

MATT: A lot, I suppose, depends upon intention, but healthy meditation is the opposite of solipsistic; it takes you from, in Jung's language, from the self with the small *s* to the Self with the big *S*. So it takes you into the ocean of all beings. And is radically communitarian in that sense. But there's paradox.

TSOMO: Were you there when I answered him? [*Both laugh*]

MATT: No.

TSOMO: You could have been.

MATT: There's paradox. You have to bring solitude to healthy community. And to balance solitude, you have to bring healthy community to real solitude. It's a dance, it's a paradox, just like yin and yang and so many others. When you're dealing with spirituality, you're always dealing in paradox, I think.

TSOMO: Well, this is why there are three jewels . . .

MATT: So to an outsider this looks like solipsism.

CHAPTER 11

Communicating to the Collective

MATT: Otto Rank has a brilliant thesis about the artist, that the artist is often criticized because he or she has to go off alone and find their music or voice. And so the community, which is really made out of *artiste manqué*—failed artists or envious artists—says, "Oh, see, that guy doesn't like us. He hates us. He's not in community." But, no—you're going deeper, in fact, so you have a gift to bring to the community, something fresh.

TSOMO: Well, the art itself is communicating, the gems one received when plumbing those depths. And a good artist goes into the collective unconscious to bring something out which then they communicate to the collective. So there's this conversation.

MATT: Not only communicates but heals the collective.

TSOMO: Well, that's what it's for.

MATT: Real art is about healing. It's about celebrating what's really there. It's about compassion.

TSOMO: So that brings me to the three jewels.

MATT: Weren't you going to tell me, though, exactly what you said to your rabbi first?

TSOMO: Well, you did.

MATT: [*Laughs*]

TSOMO: I didn't have to say it.

MATT: Good Buddhist that I am, huh?

TSOMO: The three jewels are the Buddha, the *Dharma*, and the *Sangha*, so in doing the Dharma and communing with Buddha mind, that is one very important aspect of the path. But there's the Sangha, the community of people who are also on this path, so we're sort of traveling on it together. And that is one of the three jewels as well, because of course we're interacting with each other and infecting each other. Something that Jung talked about that most people don't, I don't hear them talking about, is centroversion. There's introversion, extroversion, and centroversion, and that has to do with being infected by the mind of the group. That sort of brings us to center, so you don't get off too far. We are infected by the thoughts and views of the people around us. So it's important for us to choose who we're with, and then the whole interaction that happens in between us keeps us honest—how much are we really realized here? There's a chance, here's a challenge, how can I work with that?

MATT: Criticism—positive criticism.

TSOMO: And there are practices to work with, not just compassion for our friends but to also bring our enemies in and sympathetic joy for our enemies. That's part of the practice as we expand that circle. And equanimity and so on of course. So this third jewel of the Sangha, then, speaks to just what you were talking about: First of all, going deeply within brings us to the all in everything. There's that, but then there's bringing it right to those at hand.

I was also thinking about what you were saying about the singers and the artists communicating to the collective, and thinking about William Irwin Thompson, a historian who studied the Renaissance—you were talking about the cusp of the Renaissance. It seemed to go through four basic societal groups. The first is the mystics, who are used to hanging out in what's not yet manifested, and what has no form yet. They can kind of be in those ethers, and that's where they hang out. So they act almost as transducers, energetically, to sort of infect the collective with what's still unseen, as far as everyone else is concerned.

Just like the shamans who were able to see the first ships that came to the New World. And nobody else could see them even though they were on the shore, and there were the ships. Their eyes physically were getting the imprint, but they couldn't cognize ships because they were so unfamiliar. But the shamans, who were mystics, could see first. So the people you're speaking of were the first ones to get the inklings of the new paradigm.

And then after that come the artists, because they can kind of hang out in that, too. But they can communicate it. So there were new art forms that came at that time. And now more in the collective begin to get infected by it. And so who then is most practical and not so imaginative but willing to apply what works are the merchants. They were the next ones. And the last ones, of course, were the political leaders.

MATT: Hmm, interesting.

TSOMO: Yeah. Once everyone's going that way, they run in front and say, "I'm leading." But they had a vested interest probably in the old way until the tide was already going this way, and then they run in front.

MATT: Hmm, that's interesting. It'd be interesting to compare that to what Otto Rank says when he says there are three levels of healing. One is one-on-one, which is what most therapists do. The other is the artist, who is healing pockets of a culture, groups. But the third is the prophet, who moves the whole civilization, moves the whole culture. And then it's interesting to ask, do we all carry this within ourselves?

TSOMO: "This" being?

MATT: These three elements. That we're one-on-one healing each other in homes and conversation and friendship and love.

And then in what way are we as artists kind of gathering with different Sanghas, different small communities?

In what way are we all called to be prophetic—to shift, especially at this time in history, when so much shift is obviously needed because everything's not working?

TSOMO: That's why the prophets have to speak. They have to sound the note because then it's much more likely that the prophet in all of us, the

Buddha nature in all of us, reverberates with that. When that note hits them, it's like, "Yes, that's true."

MATT: That's a very fresh way of putting it; I like that. The vibration of the note, it's almost musical, the tune it catches.

TSOMO: Well, that's my basis. I've played music since I was five, so it works for me.

MATT: Well, it's good you found a practice that is not hostile to . . .

TSOMO: . . . my musical background.

CHAPTER 12

Paradigms Shifting—
Embracing Pre-Modern Traditions

MATT: There are religious traditions that are iconoclastic and that are not friendly to art, certainly the whole Puritan movement and much of fundamentalism.

TSOMO: That's what I was saying about our picking these two traditions that are coming together. Because Catholicism is so rich with all of the senses involved and aesthetically beautiful and appealing, and that's also true of Tibetan Buddhism, and it's not true of other branches of our lineages.

MATT: Yeah, and I think the reason is that Catholicism is pre-modern, as is, obviously, Tibetan Buddhism; in other words, it's not based on textual books. The invention of the printing press in the fifteenth century, which launched the modern consciousness, obviously has a lot going for it. But we paid a tremendous price. And this post-modern generation, the young people, who are reading less—there's no question about it, they're reading less—nevertheless, they're picking up on more vibration. They're picking up on images more, and music. You go on a subway, and I mean everyone's got these earphones, and they're listening to music, and you watch their feet move and everything.

I'm not sure I'd want to listen to all the music they're listening to, but the point is they're moving beyond text and in that sense, they're much more vulnerable to pre-modern ritual and pre-modern spirituality, and this is one reason we have to get in touch. Whether you're doing it through the Buddhist path or I'm trying to do it through the Western path. We have to get in touch with these more ancient pre-textual ceremonies and practices.

Tsomo: We have to get past the left frontal lobe; there's more to us than that.

Matt: Yes, exactly.

Tsomo: This one neurosurgeon speaks on a scientific level, on a brain anatomy level, to exactly what you're saying. He believes that as soon as we had an alphabet that was not pictographs but a phonetic alphabet, that was when communication was restricted to the left frontal lobe. And that shifted us out of a balance of masculine and feminine.

Matt: Yes, are you talking about Leonard Shlain?

Tsomo: Yeah.

Matt: Yeah, he died recently, you know.

Tsomo: Did he? No, I didn't know that.

Matt: Yeah, yeah, he did.

Matt: Yes, I think it's a very important thesis, and he's not alone in it. Another thing is the traditions of alphabet are so new. Again, in China, the alphabet was pictorial, as it was of course in Egypt. But the alphabet became more and more abstract, in Latin and Greek, and then in English and German, these letters are abstractions. Whereas when you have pictures, it is a different use of the mind, literally; it's incorporating more of the right brain. So it develops a different kind of consciousness; it's more curved, more rounded, and less direct and left-brained.

Tsomo: And, yeah, just a small part of the brain. Much more of the brain and the body and the nervous system and so on are included with chanting and imagery, like you were mentioning earlier. And that completely just woos us, and, how can I say, inducts us into . . .

Matt: Seduces us.

Tsomo: Well, inducts us into states of consciousness.

Matt: Yes—well, sure.

TSOMO: I think.

MATT: Well, absolutely.

MATT: And the breath, you see, using the breath and calling on it and adapting it, being able to steer it.

TSOMO: The mind rides on the breath.

MATT: Well, there you have it. And the word *breath* is the identical word for "spirit," both in the biblical languages and in most languages around the world. The alliance between breath and spirit. And of course both are invisible, but they obviously both matter because without breath you're not going very far, for very long, right? [*Both laugh*] So, invisible things matter. No matter what Descartes says or modern science says as opposed to post-modern science, which is now acknowledging that not everything is quantifiable.

TSOMO: We don't have all of the equipment to perceive some of these things that we claim aren't there.

MATT: That's right, but we're developing them, as you know. At University of Wisconsin and some other places we're kind of creeping into this territory of being able to test how the brain waves are working and see. There's a lot more going on than anyone thought—well, than any scientist thought [*Both laugh*]—but that a lot of contemplative traditions have always known about.

TSOMO: In Buddhism, the way they worked with it was to use the mind as an instrument to study the mind, which is of course paradoxical, a little bit tricky. That's why we must train the mind in stability and kind of clean it up because otherwise it's not going to be a very fit instrument for the study. But when they did that, it was amazing the knowledge that they were able to gain.

MATT: That's one of the traditional arguments for the soul, that the human soul can reflect on itself. And this is very special, to be a mirror upon yourself. And it's interesting that your tradition has obviously developed so many sophisticated ways of exploring the mind, or the soul, in this case. And I think the West has really done more than it's aware of, including, of course, art and science itself. Science itself was also a way of examining our nature and even our inner nature if we start asking the right questions.

TSOMO: Yeah, well, in its plodding way it has come to . . .

MATT: In its plodding way, yes . . .

TSOMO: . . . to a meeting point.

MATT: Trial-and-error way, maybe, yes, that's right.

TSOMO: This is something to celebrate. This is why I'm so happy that scientists and the Dalai Lama are in such a lively conversation. And it's going into the laboratories. That laboratory you're speaking of, the people there are in constant communication with the Dalai Lama, and are getting a lot of the inspiration for their experiments.

MATT: They're hiring a lot of monks as guinea pigs, literally.

TSOMO: Yeah Richard Davidson is running that whole enclave there, and he's been working with His Holiness for 20 years or something.

MATT: Then you have people like Rupert Sheldrake in the West, and of course David Bloom and all, who are experts in exploring these areas of consciousness expansion, and what is consciousness, where is consciousness, and who is consciousness? [*Both laugh*]

One thinker I was reading the other day, I can't remember who it is, has this great line [paraphrasing], "God is consciousness; consciousness is God." I think it was Bede Griffiths, operating out of both a Benedictine and a Hindu tradition in India for 50 years, "God is consciousness." And of course Teilhard de Chardin in many ways incorporated that in his entire life work, as both a scientist and a mystic, and a poet and a Jesuit. He was forbidden to publish his books in his lifetime. But I think that he's being acknowledged 50, 60 years later as a real pioneer, who was right about a lot of things, in this regard.

TSOMO: There's that quote that Aaron loves to quote, by Milenko Matanovic, that in these times of paradigm shift, and I can only paraphrase this, that "what starts out as heresy, ends up as heritage." [*Matt laughs*] So that's just the evolution you're talking about, with Eckhart and Chardin and those people.

MATT: That's good, yeah. I like that.

Thomas Kuhn, in his work on paradigm shift, says [paraphrasing], "What happens in paradigm shifts is, what used to be considered peripheral, moves to center stage."

TSOMO: Exactly.

MATT: And that's wisdom as opposed to just knowledge. Wisdom has been banished in the Western consciousness for centuries, but now it's coming back. It's not only coming back; it has to move to center stage because knowledge alone is not going to save our species, obviously, or other species.

TSOMO: That's right: desperation we can actually rely on wisdom.

MATT: [*Laughs*] There you go.

TSOMO: When all else fails.

MATT: Well, so you have pursued wisdom vigorously. I think that is an amazing accomplishment in itself.

TSOMO: Well, you learned French enough to go to university, my gosh.

MATT: But French is a little easier than Tibetan.

TSOMO: Well, I didn't have to go to university.

CHAPTER 13

A Shared Mission in Wisdom Traditions

TSOMO: Since it was you that first proposed that we do this series, what was your mission statement, what was in your mind?

MATT: I think we're living at a time, obviously, where the human species needs all the wisdom it can get. On our path currently, we're unsustainable. Period. Any fool can figure that out. So what do we have to do? We have to call on whatever wisdom's available and bring it together. Not hold it in isolation. So I think that the goals I had, in terms of our dialogues, were to bring the wisdom of the East, the Buddhist, especially the Tibetan tradition, together with the wisdom of the West, Christianity, which is of course, in its depth, profoundly Jewish. Jesus was a Jew, which many Christians have forgotten over the centuries, conveniently so. To bring these together and see what third thing, really, we have to give birth to today, you might say. It's not just a matter of putting our cards on the table and dialoguing, but of, actually, within the context of the ecological crisis, and the context of economic breakdowns, and political upheavals, and religious fundamentalism, and all the contexts that we face today, what are some healthy ways to stay grounded and to find new directions? And I felt that these conversations can help us to do that.

TSOMO: So the reason I accepted this mission [*Laughs*] was first just to get the chance to dialogue with you. It was just too much fun not to do it.

MATT: Didn't want to pass it up.

Tsomo: Right. So I just have to confess that. But, hopefully, other people watching, seeing the joy of the interaction between these two human beings who are part of two lineages, feet strongly planted in each of those lineages, and appreciating the truth that's in the other tradition. I felt also that that's a good antidote for righteous wrath that seems to run rampant. I couldn't tell the difference between the righteous wrath of George Bush and the righteous wrath of Bin Laden. It seemed like they were actually saying the same thing. And maybe righteous wrath was the enemy. So this would be such an antidote to that.

And of course bringing forth wisdom traditions to people out there. I also found that whenever I mentioned this project to anybody, there's this immediate sort of transfixed look like, "Oh, I have to know about this." There's this hunger for meaning that I see out there that I'm responding to in my life, generally, as well as with this project. And a hunger that I saw in people's eyes when I would talk about this particular project because of the Christian tradition that they came out of perhaps. And their curiosity about meaning and about Buddhism. There was a general desire for something that's such a wholesome meal for them to be hungry for. So all of those reasons.

Matt: Maybe another word for "righteous wrath" is "reptilian brain." I think our species has been running on the reptilian brain for long enough.

Tsomo: Yeah. But we have the other lobes.

Matt: We want to include it, but it's got to be tempered with the mammal brain and the intellectual, really spiritual, brain. We're not running on all our cylinders.

Tsomo: But people who are running on righteous wrath are employing reasons for their righteous wrath, you know.

Matt: Oh, there's always a reason.

Tsomo: Which lizards don't bother doing. [*Matt laughs*] So that's how the humans do it.

Matt: And, of course, lizards have not invented nuclear weapons nor the devices to deliver them.

Tsomo: This is the wisdom without compassion. Yeah.

MATT: They aren't quite as dangerous as we are. Which is why they've been around millions of years longer than we have. And we're ready to end the Earth after about a hundred thousand.

TSOMO: Yeah. We're smart enough to destroy ourselves immediately.

MATT: Exactly. There's a renowned scientist, a Stanford biologist, who says we're the first species in four and a half billion years on the planet who can choose not to go extinct. So it's about choice and the choice to dialogue with different faith traditions, and to sort out what we have in common and what we can learn from each other—because we all have something to learn; no one tradition has all of the answers, or there would be heaven someplace on Earth—this is a choice, and I think that it's important that you and I are demonstrating, and witnessing to this, in front of an audience that, hopefully, will make its choices in favor of healthy dialogue.

I love what the Dalai Lama says, that the number one obstacle to inner faith is a bad relationship with your own faith tradition. As a Christian, I have to say most Christians have a bad relationship with their own faith tradition. And by that I mean they don't know their own mystical tradition. It's a scandal, and it's getting a lot of the world in trouble. So part of what we're trying to do, at least what I'm trying to do, is to kind of tell folks, "Hey, there's a Christian mystical tradition, too." And in many ways it kind of complements, matches, what's from the East. And in many ways we're saying very important similar things. And it's about waking up our compassionate and wisdom capacities.

TSOMO: And what I appreciate about the way we've conducted this dialogue is that it's not about throwing our religions in a pot and stirring it around and calling it New Age, and what we have is just mishmash, but rather mutual respect for each other's traditions. We're coming from long lineages that have distilled wisdom and skillful means to the point where now, today, we can compare notes, but standing on our own ground.

CHAPTER 14

Mystical Consciousness &
The Inner Experience

TSOMO: What struck me with Eckhart is, he was talking about the destination, these mystic experiences, and I wasn't getting so much of a sense of the path there, his methods or anything, but the destination was something I could really relate to, and that's really what he was speaking from. He was sort of reporting back from that place.

MATT: But there are passages, of course, where he is quite explicit about methodology. Where he talks about . . .

TSOMO: A little bit . . .

MATT: . . . letting go of all images and of all sound, and you know, being with nothingness, and being silent. I love that one phrase of his, "returning to your unborn self." Where you're perfectly free, free of knowledge, free of desire. But I always find that phrase very provocative, our "unborn self," and that we can get there. And I think the Buddhist tradition has . . .

TSOMO: They write of exactly that, the unborn self. Yeah, absolutely.

MATT: And you have methods for getting there.

TSOMO: Yep.

MATT: That are quite explicit.

TSOMO: They are—which helps me.

MATT: That's a good point. Some people appreciate the explicit more than others. But again Eckhart was part of this tradition, that I was, too, the

Dominicans, where there is a methodology to take you to these places, that's built into the training. But of course he was speaking for, preaching to, lay people, although he also taught young Dominicans. But the point is, he wasn't trying to make Dominicans of lay people or make monks of lay people, kind of like what the Dalai Lama's doing today in effect by leaving the monastery to instruct, so that we all have access to this, not just professional "pray-ers."

TSOMO: Professionals, right, exactly. But you're right, these were sermons that the book ended up looking at.

MATT: Yes, to the general public.

TSOMO: That's right. So of course he wouldn't be as detailed in any sort of map or the methods and exactly how to use them. Still, my sense just generally, in contrasting the two traditions, as we've investigated now for many hours together, is that there are many more, carefully laid out or laid out in great detail, methods that are sort of attempting to guide you from here to there.

MATT: Exactly. I so resent being called "New Age." I mean, is Thomas Aquinas new? He's 700 years old. Eckhart is 600 years. Hildegard is 800 years old. And Jesus's mysticism has been around at least 2,000 years, and the Jewish tradition far longer that that, and of course your tradition, 2,500. So, what makes this New Age?

TSOMO: Well, I'll tell you what does, is taking a smattering from all of that, and not really knowing any of them, mixing them together and having soup: New Age soup.

MATT: That's part of it. I think another thing is that journalists, and some academics, who have no clue about mysticism—even in themselves, where it has to begin—they want to belittle spirituality because they're so ignorant of it. They love to call it "New Age" and then laugh at it. The ignorance about mysticism is so profound in our culture. There's a mystical illiteracy, often in the name of religion or in the name of education. "Oh, I, I have my degree in journalism, so I know what's New Age and what isn't," or "I have my degree in philosophy or theology, and I'll label it what I want." So there is a belittling of mysticism still. And this is remnants, of course, of modern consciousness, which we can't afford to dally in any longer.

As a species we need all our capacities of working healthily to survive. And mystical consciousness is part.

Tsomo: We've spoken of a balance between the masculine and feminine. And I think another balance that you're now getting into is objective inquiry and subjective inquiry. Because the mystical experience, truly, is on a subjective level. And of course that's looked down on, in the Age of Enlightenment and modern times, and journalists like to think of themselves as only going the objective route. As a result, they're missing a whole lot. And they're not grounded at all in the other. They don't have their bearings in it.

What I loved about Jung is that he did both an objective and subjective inquiry. And this is what I think is needed in these times to have full knowledge. I just think you were pointing in that direction. I wanted to kind of bring that out.

Matt: I think I'd use the language "intersubjective" because "subjective" by itself almost feels solipsistic, whereas to me it's about the inner dimension of everything and everyone. In other words, my so-called subjective experience is not that different from your so-called subjective experience; there's an intersubjectivity. So there's common ground.

Tsomo: That would be a third one in a sense, where you'd begin to bring that in, is the way I would say it, because first we have to experience it within ourselves, and then we can apply it outward.

Matt: Uh huh. And that's what you mean by subjective. Inner experience. Taste.

Tsomo: Yeah, first having that inner experience.

Matt: By the way, I love that word *taste*; you know, it's the basis of the word for "wisdom."

Tsomo: Huh, really?

Matt: In both Hebrew and Latin, the word the word for "wisdom" comes from the word for "taste." And you have it in the Psalm: "taste and see that God is good." And I like *taste* because it's subjective, but it's not independently so. I mean, we can both agree on the wonderful taste of these oranges, so it's shared. It's something shared, eminently shareable.

TSOMO: That's part of the objective world out there.

MATT: That's right, the taste of life. Descartes was so intent on separating the subjective from the objective . . . see, I just don't want to yield ground on that. We now know, even scientists say, nothing's objective. The fact is, it depends on where you're standing—which part of the elephant you're touching when blindfolded.

So the whole objective quest is in some ways, I think, deconstructed, or demythologized, and that's why nothing is totally subjective either. If it affects you deeply enough, you're going to tell others and others, all, and then it becomes a community project. That's called art.

TSOMO: And when we land on the deeply collective unconscious experiences, everyone can relate to them; that's why great literature is immediately moving to everyone.

MATT: Exactly.

TSOMO: Because you come back to the whole if you go deeply enough into one, into yourself.

MATT: You go down the individual well, but you come to the common river of wisdom, of which there's only one to drink from.

TSOMO: Yeah. The aquifer.

MATT: The aquifer—there you go.

TSOMO: A new name for God.

MATT: Hah, there you go. Well, Eckhart had that. He said God is a great underground river, that no one could dam up and no one could stop.

CHAPTER 15

Synchronicity—The Lotus &
The Rose Project

TSOMO: So now we get to talk about how we met and how we decided to do this.

MATT: Oh, so give me your version.

TSOMO: Okay. My version was that I heard that somebody was going to the Bay Area, right about the same time I was, and they were going to get a chance to meet with Matthew Fox, and I was like, "Oh, I would love to do that." About 20, 30 years before that, I'd read your work and thought, "This is truth, this is making sense. Why haven't I seen this before?" It really spoke to me: the truth of it. And the brilliance of it as well. And so I was a fan, and I wasn't a Beatles fan, but, it's a strange thing, you know, what I'm a fan of. I'd always remembered you, and when I heard this person was meeting you, I was like, "I wish I were meeting Matthew Fox." So I mentioned that to David Korten, and he said, "Well, that can be arranged." "Really?" And he said, "Sure. I know him." "Okay, let's go for it." So he was the one who connected us.

I came to your office, I remember, and we were talking, and of course we fell into talking about our different traditions and what are some of the corollaries and this kind of thing, and it just got more and more interesting. You were looking for someone to bring in something about Buddhism into your program at the time. So you were thinking maybe I could teach something, and I thought that was very interesting, but I didn't have an actual PhD, which was necessary for the academic verification and that sort of thing—because being a lama doesn't quite translate. And we didn't think of that part, but as we talked more, they said, "Well, if she co-teaches with somebody with a PhD, then it would work." So then you gallantly said, "I'll teach with you." That was how we then taught that course. And during that course, you said, "Let's write a book together." You took the lead with this. I remember I said to you, "I think there are more qualified people who know more about Tibetan Buddhism than I do." But you said, "No—I want this to be the combination." And you can talk about your reasons for that. But anyway, so then we co-taught the course and you suggested the book, and soon thereafter you said, "What about a DVD series? Wouldn't that be more up-to-date and more of a full presentation ?" And I just kept saying, "Okay." And so here we are.

MATT: Well, I remember the course, and we did two texts; one was the Eckhart book, my book on Eckhart, and Rinpoche's book.

TSOMO: Trungpa Rinpoche.

MATT: Trungpa Rinpoche, yeah, *Spiritual Materialism*[29], those were our texts. And I remember I was impressed by what you got out of Eckhart, how kind of at home you were—even though you certainly don't come out of Christianity, and you barely come out of Judaism. [*Tsomo laughs*] But you and Eckhart were on the same page; you got genuinely excited in reading Eckhart and also in seeing these kinds of universal findings that Buddhism has come to, seeing them out of the Western tradition too.

TSOMO: So then what possessed you to ask me to, you know, write a book, which then ended up being a DVD series, and when I tried to back out why did you insist that it be me?

MATT: Your memory's better than mine.

TSOMO: Oh, I distinctly remember going, "I shouldn't be the one representing . . ."

MATT: Well, I thought you should because, for one thing, there aren't that many women lamas floating around who can speak good English and have their roots in Western culture. And having adopted as you have,

---

29. Chogyam Trungpa, *Cutting Through Spiritual Materialism* (Shambhala, revised ed. 2002)

by learning Tibetan and by learning those profound religious traditions, so we got along. And again I think it was your love of Eckhart. I've
already said, "Anyone who loves Eckhart is a friend of mine." [*Tsomo laughs*]
Because Eckhart takes you to depths of encounter, and anyone who
understands him is a friend of mine. *Les amis de Eckhart.* I think that was
kind of the test for me, if you will, if we could agree on this. And of course
we were dialoguing on Buddhism, too, and I was learning—I've always
liked learning. And I have things to learn from you, for sure. I knew it
wouldn't be boring, our, our conversations. [*Laughs*] I hate being bored.

TSOMO: Well, I don't think there's much danger of that whenever I'm in
the room with you.

MATT: And I did like the idea that, first of all, we're male and female,
and that you're from a Jewish tradition, too, so that you're kind of two for
one, you see, Buddhist and Jewish. [*Tsomo laughs*] And that we can talk the
same language. We can explore areas together, I think, of, of significance.
That kept me in the ball game. [*Laughs*] So that's kind of how all this has
come together. Your memory's very good, and I'm very grateful to David
Korten, whose most recent book I've been reading between sessions here.
I'm so taken with it. I think he's really talking about Wall Street the way
it has to be talked about.

TSOMO: Yes, and visionary in the economic sector. We need to envision
all the different facets of life in order to enter into the next paradigm

MATT: Exactly. He's doing such a great job with that and integrating both
history and ecology. He has a real consciousness of the plight of Mother
Earth today. And how all this is part of any sustainable economic vision.

TSOMO: So our first run-in was in Santa Fe. My friend Aaron Stern,
who is the founder for the Academy for the Love of Learning, heard
about our dialogue, and was intrigued by it and inspired by it, and
wanted to sponsor our first engagement. He knew Joan Halifax and
asked if we could do it at her center, which we did. It was a very small,
intimate gathering, and I really liked the feel of that. And it was a nice
introduction to us; that was the time when each of us really spoke about
our own spiritual journeys to arrive in the lineage we did, and how we
came to this moment.

It was also a good place for the experiential pieces because it was a small enough group we could really engage with them. So that was my recollection of Santa Fe. Do you remember anything else about it?

MATT: It's all blank. No, I think that explains the origins there, yes. And of course Santa Fe has such a wonderful history and such a powerful spiritual vibe about it, with the Native American tradition there and the Hispanic also, that I think it was a good place to begin.

Our second dialogue was held in Stanford University, Palo Alto, California. I was teaching there at the time, so we were able to get a weekend workshop place rather readily, and it was open to the public. The themes that we covered, you probably remember better than I, just because your memory's better than mine.

TSOMO: Actually, we covered a lot of different things. I think one theme that we ended up speaking quite a bit on was this question of methods, of the two different lineages. I seem to remember the audience being very interested in that.

MATT: Yeah, there was a lot of dialogue with the audience that weekend.

TSOMO: Mmm hmm. So it was nice to have a little bit more time in that installment to probe more of the depths of some of these, comparing and contrasting.

MATT: Right, and the audience was larger, and of course being on a university campus is a different flavor than being at that retreat center in Santa Fe. And it was a larger group of people that gathered.

TSOMO: Our third installment was in Houston, and we were invited to Houston just at the time you and I had talked about the fact that we were missing the archetypal piece; we wanted to do more of a comparing and contrasting of the archetypes of our two different traditions. And so in comes an invitation from the Jung Center in Houston, and they are actually the largest, most populous Jung Center in the country. It was to kick off their 50th anniversary year. We were invited to speak. So why say no?

MATT: It seemed perfect.

Tsomo: I know: It was synchronicity, which is a term invented by Jung.

[*Both laugh*]

Matt: And I think I was just finishing up my book on 10 archetypes to awaken the sacred masculine. We dealt with them and then the Green Tara, and the sacred feminine, so those topics were pretty strong that weekend.

Tsomo: Yeah, I took them through the Green Tara practice at breakneck speed, just to give kind of an overview of what it is. A person would have to really sink into it, and do it again and again, to fully experience it, but at least I was hoping to give people a taste of that. And Green Tara was hanging, the big *thangka* behind me. You brought the masculine, and there was a masculine figure on a thangka behind you. The room was packed to the point where people were actually out in the hallway. People were really wanting to know about the archetypes between these two traditions.

MATTHEW FOX

Author Interview

With Michael Frisbie and Katy-Robin Garton
August 28, 2017 • San Francisco, CA

MICHAEL: Since *The Lotus & The Rose* has become a multi-volume serial spread over several years, I'd be interested in any thoughts from your perspective on how this project came to be, how you feel about it, what you've learned from it over the process?

MATTHEW: [*Laughter*] You're testing my memory. Well, I remember our original dialogue in Santa Fe, in a home there, and there's been an evolution, I think, of our exchanges, of our getting to know each other, in our thought processes, in our deepening awareness of each other, and of the Buddhist tradition that Tsomo incarnates, and the Christian mystical tradition that I'm speaking to. I remember our original gathering at the home in Santa Fe, and then the Stanford weekend together, and the experience in Huston with the Jung Center, and then of course the experience in Tsomo's home. And hopefully there's been a growth along the way of our mutual awareness and exchange. I think it's assisted me to see the world through more Buddhist eyes. The last several books I've written I've certainly brought in the Buddhism in a big way. In my book on Meister Eckhart, for example, I have a chapter on Meister Eckhart and Thich Nhat Hanh—because Eckhart is so Buddhist in so many of his teachings. And then my most recent book is on Thomas Merton. And of course Thomas Merton was very important to the Dalai Lama. They met on Thomas Merton's last journey, his journey to the East. The Dalai Lama was 33 years old, and they fell in love with each other. They both canceled their next day's appointments to spend an extra day together. And the Dalai Lama actually was asked a year or two ago, he was asked by a journalist, "Do you believe in God?" And the Dalai Lama paused and said, "Well, yes, I do." And the journalist said, "Are you sure? A lot of Buddhists don't talk about God. So what kind of a God do you believe in?" And the Dalai Lama paused and he said, "I believe in the God of Thomas Merton," [*Laughter*] which is kind of fun. And Merton was important to my spiritual education because it was he who advised me to go to Paris to study. And that's where I met my mentor, Père Chenu, who named the creation spiritual tradition for me. So I owe Merton all the trouble that I've gotten in since I started out in consciously studying spirituality. So these stories, these synchronicities keep popping up. I keep running into all kinds of Buddhists, and I run into Buddhism in my own tradition. And of course Merton himself was very influenced by Buddhism his last ten years of his life, but he was even more profoundly influenced by Meister Eckhart. And it was a Buddhist, D. T. Suzuki, a Japanese Buddhist, who brought Zen to North America, who advised Merton to read Meister Eckhart in 1958. And Merton underwent this big conversion because of it. And Suzuki said to Merton, "Well, Eckhart is the one Zen thinker of the West. You've got to read him." And Merton wrote in his journal—his last journal—his Asian journal he wrote, "Eckhart is my lifeboat, Eckhart is my lifeboat." So the impact from the Buddhists on Merton, by way of Eckhart, was absolutely pivotal in Merton's awakening his last 10 years of his life. So all that, as I say, I'm constantly being alerted to the overlap between my Western tradition and Buddhism. One of the things so striking about Eckhart, he never read a Buddhist, he never met a Lama Tsomo or an ancestor of hers, and yet he talks in very Buddhist language a lot of the time. To me, this underscores the universal wisdom of the Buddhist tradition, that they've uncovered realities of the human psyche and of consciousness that are universal. Eckhart got there through his tradition, but they journeyed to the same place.

MICHAEL: Is there anything. any sort of deal-breaker, as much as you admire Buddhism—and as you said, as much as it's both interwoven into aspects of your tradition and your own personal growth—is there anything, though, about Buddhism that would make you go, "Yeah, I don't think I could really be a full-fledged Buddhist. I could be an ex officio member, but I don't know that I could ever fully embrace that tradition myself"?

MATTHEW: Well, even the Dalai Lama has said to Westerners, "Don't become Buddhist; [*Laughter*] become better Christians." So I'm at home with that advice. I do think that there are differences. I don't know if I've talked about this dream I had years ago. I was doing a workshop on a weekend in Malibu, California, and they put me up in a Buddhist home Friday night. And they said to me, "Now, some people may come early in the morning and chant." And there were a lot of Buddhist statues around; it was a very beautiful home. And sure enough, about 5 o'clock in the morning this group came in and started chanting in the living room. It was beautiful to wake up to these Buddhist chants. And when I went back to sleep I had this dream about Jesus and Buddha. And this is what

I learned, that Buddha lived to be about 84, and he saw all of life: he'd been a prince, and a husband, and a father, and a beggar, and a teacher, and a seeker, and all that, went through all of life, and died serenely. Jesus got himself killed at about the age of 30. There's a big difference there. So what I learned is to be human beings today, we need both the serenity and the patience of the Buddha, and we need the impatience and the prophetic outrage of the prophets like Jesus. So that's what I've learned. I don't think Buddhism has all the answers, and I don't think Christianity has all the answers. I think we have to forge, we have to create something today, including science, of course, which works. And time's running out on us obviously as a species. And we can't really afford the luxury of just staying in our little camps. I think we have to ask "What does the Buddha bring to Westerners? What does the Buddhist tradition bring, and what does the Western tradition bring to the East?" And then of course we don't want to leave out the indigenous wisdom either. Personally, I've been more affected during my own practice by Native American practice than by Buddhist practices. And I'm not real good at sitting for long hours. Now, I like walking and meditating, but I did that even before I met Thich Nhat Hanh. You know, the Dalai Lama gave a talk to his monks a couple years ago. He said, "We Buddhists are great at meditating on compassion and talking about compassion. We should imitate the Christians more in practicing compassion." Now, I don't know what Christians he's met, but I'm glad he's met a few that seem to be doing what Jesus talked about doing. So I think there is an emphasis on action in the West that is not always so prominent in the East. Because the Eastern notion of history is more cyclical, whereas the Jewish, the Biblical, notion of history is more linear, it's more about making some kind of improvements. And that's why Gandhi said, "I learned to say *no* from the West." So Gandhi learned his prophetic impatience from Jesus and from Tolstoy, who taught him Jesus, whereas the other Hindus in Gandhi's day were saying, "Don't worry about these untouchables. Next time around, if they're good this time around, they'll do better." And Gandhi's ire got heated up, and he said, "No, we want to do something about injustice this time around." So I think that the East has something to give the West, and the West has something to give the East.

MICHAEL: I'm thinking now partly of a comment that Pope Francis made clearly about President Trump, even though he never alluded to him specifically. He said basically if somebody acts like Trump does, he's not really a Christian. Is there anything for you that you would say is the core of what it means to be a Christian, that if somebody doesn't embrace a certain belief or set of values, or act in a certain way, they are not really a Christian, even though Christianity is obviously very embracing and involves a number of possibilities. But is there anything that would make you say, "You may call yourself that, but you're not if...?" Or the flip side of the question: "Is there any core element that you can say as long as you embrace and believe and follow this precept or these precepts, you can call yourself a Christian?"

MATTHEW: Well, first of all we have to make space when it comes to talking about who is an authentic Christian. We have to make space for for everyone's imperfection and failures and so forth. So no one's perfect. I like to point that out when I'm talking about hagiography and the saints, that they all have clay feet. And it's important to study the clay feet of saints; otherwise how would we ever identify with them or get up our courage and imagination like they had? So that's important. No one's perfect, and a quest for perfection, I think, is in itself a neurotic quest. We should learn to live with imperfection. Having said that, though, there are definitely some contours about authentic Christianity. For example, we're having this conversation the day after Hurricane Harvey hit Houston. And you have all over TV all these people on there. Now, first of all, the good news is people are being taken care of pretty well. So far there's been a very modest amount of fatalities, much wiser than the Katrina experience. And a lot of people come out in their boats, and everyone's calling for help, and all that is very inspiring. But what isn't inspiring is that the politicians of Texas—I'm talking about the governor who's on TV now telling us how awful it is, and the two senators of Texas, and all kinds of other politicians in Texas—are in complete denial about climate change. And the media is actually feeding that because I haven't seen any coverage yet about the cause of this greatest catastrophe ever. They say now that a lake the size of Lake Michigan—I know Lake Michigan; I'm from Wisconsin and Illinois—it's big. That's what's happening in Texas.

And yet all these loudmouth politicians are in complete denial—it's the know-nothing party of our time—about the cause. And talk to any scientist. I was with a group of 150 scientists this summer on an island off of New Hampshire for a week, and the theme was climate change. And they were all predicting this. They all said the wet areas are going to get wetter in the world, the dry areas are going to get dryer. And that's happening, and we have a president supported by his party who withdrew from the Paris climate change commitment and everything else saying, what, "Climate change is a hoax." I was in a conference a year and a half ago, it was January, in Florida, about seas rising, climate change and the seas rising. The conference began with a scientist who stood up, and he had slides of Florida today, Florida 10 years from now, chop, 20 years from now, chop chop, 30 years from now, chop chop chop. One thing I learned was, I wouldn't invest in real estate in Florida. Maybe rubber dinghies and rubber boots, but not real estate, and certainly swimming classes. But at that time there were two presidential candidates running for president—this is January 2016—both of them in denial about climate change. And the governor of the state was so much in denial about climate change that he put out a memo to all the government officials saying, "You cannot use the word 'climate change' in any email that you write on Florida stationery." At that time I visited South Miami, and there were six inches of water on the sidewalks. So this is pathological, the denial. It's a know-nothing party. Half of the political conversation in our country at this time is know-nothings, and I'm sick of it. And anyone who cares—don't tell me you love your children and you love your grandchildren; it's just nonsense if you don't care about the future of the climate, of the soil, of the waters, of the winds, of the animals that are disappearing at unprecedented, rapid state these days. It's just appalling. So I wrote a public letter to Speaker Paul Ryan a few months ago about this. I called it a "priestly letter" to Speaker Paul Ryan, who parades his Catholicism like all these politicians do, they're parading their Christianity. And I pointed out that the pope has written a wonderful encyclical on climate change and the environment, and you're a Catholic, why aren't you on board with the pope? He also writes about the relationship between climate change and the poor, how the poor will suffer the most and are suffering the most, and how Earth itself is now with the poor, because Earth is suffering just like the poor are suffering. And Ryan is chasing after the multibillionaires who are keeping him as a kept politician, and he's trying to get tax deductions for the billionaires instead of... And of course he's throwing millions of people off of insurance—poor people. How in heaven's name is this anything but pure hypocrisy? And Jesus spoke very strong language about hypocrites, and I quoted a few of those lines in my public letter. He's not written back yet, but a lot of other people have. We have to start doing just what you're talking about, call out crackpot Christianity and hypocritical Christianity, especially by public figures who want to parade their religion and get votes for parading it, wearing it like a coat. And that's all it is—it's 100 percent superficial. Their real gods, their real worship, is of Wall Street and of billionaires supporting them. It has nothing to do with justice, nothing to do with the people they claim to represent. So I get sick and tired seeing these Texan politicians on television telling us how full of woe they are that so much of their land is now underwater. Of course that's a woeful thing. But get smart and ask why. And this is going to repeat itself more and more and more in the near future. Ask any scientist. Of course if you belong to an ideology that's in complete denial, and won't even talk to scientists, well, then this is what you get. Amen.

MICHAEL: And as you say, it's ironic from sort of a hierarchical perspective and a philosophical perspective, that for these people who proclaim themselves as being such ardent Catholics or fundamentalist Christians, you would think one of the fundamental precepts of Christianity would be let's help each other. I don't think it gets any more fundamental than that. And then as you said, particularly in Ryan's case...

MATTHEW: ...as a Catholic who would I turn to for advice? Maybe the pope? I don't know. Just pulling a name out of a hat. But, yeah, it's more than ironic; I think it's bitterly ironic. And it's not just helping one another, but it's also in terms of religious philosophy and Christianity, it's about the sacredness of creation. Creation is sacred, if it's God-made and God-inspired, and divinity is present throughout creation—which is the teaching in all the world religions. The Buddha nature in Buddhism is paralleled with the Cosmic Christ teaching in Christianity, and with the image of God teaching in Judaism, and with teachings in Hinduism about Brahma being present in all creation. So if this is what religions are teaching us, then to ignore creation, to make our agendas just about Wall Street and just anthropocentric issues, this is in complete contradiction to what Jesus is about, what the Christ is about, what the Buddha is about, and so forth. And of course it is an act of hatred toward future generations, toward our children and great-grandchildren. And the media has of course played its role in contributing to this appalling denial. Like I say, the last 24 hours I've heard not a word on the media—now, I haven't been watching it all the time—but every time you listen to the radio or see something on TV, I've never heard anyone bring up the subject of cause of this catastrophe that they're all saying is the greatest catastrophe ever in the history of Texas. But let's look for causes. Isn't that what the intellectual mind is after? And scientists have told us the cause, and we're warned that: there are going to be a lot more events like this. Just as here in California we've just lived through seven years of drought. It's a big thing to live through seven years of drought. And it could come back anytime. So we can't take air for granted, we can't take water for granted, we can't take the soil for granted, we can't take other species, and animals, and birds, and fishes for granted. We can't take the oceans for granted. The acidic level of the oceans is rising at an alarming rate. And this could really be the death of the oceans, because it's the creatures at the lowest level of the totem pole, if you will, in the ocean who are being most affected by increase of acid. And that means the whole food chain is up for grabs. And no politicians are talking about this. And we have no leadership at all in terms of our elected officials, at least on the Republican side. So it's a scandal. It's a complete scandal, and it's an insult to anyone who believes that God cares about creation.

MICHAEL: I was talking with a fundamentalist Christian, and I said to him, "I think—leaving aside some of the other science/religion issues— it's disrespectful to not show some kind of passionate curiosity about this world" that he believes God has given us. It's a very intricate, complex, beautiful, subtle and nuanced, in some ways robust and some ways fragile world, and to deny science is really to deny or rebuff that gift, I think. Because science could tell us, "How does this work?" whether or not you believe it was divinely engineered. And to go, "Yeah, I don't care," is an insult. When somebody's made you a gift that profound, I think you'd better show some appreciative interest in it. And antiscience fundamentalists seem to have no interest, which I find distressing. You were talking a little bit earlier about the fact that no self-professed Christian is going to be perfect, so you have to take that off the table as a prerequisite. Are there ways in which you think you could be a better Christian?

MATTHEW: Well, sometimes I wish that I was more involved in a more intense experience of community. And in many ways that's behind the work I've been doing for twenty-some years now, and developing a cosmic mass to reinvent forms of worship that are more bodily, more inclusive, more delicious, and then incorporate the new postmodern art forms like DJ and VJ and dancing and rap and so forth. But it's such a struggle doing these rituals that there's not been the time for building the communities so much around them. So lately we've been doing them in many different cities, for example. And it's partly financial that we need support for that. But if I could, I would wish that I was deeper involved in a particular more intimate, community. But at the same time, things are changing so rapidly in our culture, especially as I notice through my work with young people in this, that there are new forms emerging. For example, I met a young physicist recently at a conference, and he's now starting a salon where we'll have regular gatherings in his home, maybe once a month, with scientists and some others to talk about...well, his favorite topic is synchronicity. But talk about spirituality and science. And I'm reading a book now on the spirituality in science, and of course my tradition as a Dominican goes back to Aquinas, who in the thirteenth century said, "A mistake about creation results in a mistake about God." So obviously those that explore creation, scientists, have a lot to teach us about God. Because, as Aquinas says, "Creation is the artwork. God is the artist of artists." So you learn about an artist often by examining their work. So why isn't that true of nature, too? And so we need to be working with scientists. And I've been doing a lot of that lately. And of course scientists come in a great variety of belief systems. It runs from atheism to scientific materialism on the one side, to all kinds of Buddhists, and Jews, and Christians, and other practices on the other side. I think it's real exciting to bring the two together. So my kind of hunger for more community is not a singular thing. I find a lot of people are not content with the communities that exist today. Going to church, for example, does not cut the mustard for a lot of people. On the other hand, being all by yourself, or just doing your thing, is isolating and is not necessarily building community either. So I think we're in one of those times between times when we have to kind of consciously give birth to new communities. And one thing I'm involved in today, we launched this in September, a book called the *Order of the Sacred Earth*[30]. I had a dream a couple years ago to start a new order. Not a religious order, but a spiritual order that's beholden to no particular religion. But it is about the sacredness of the Earth. So it's called the Order of the Sacred Earth. And everyone in it will take one vow: "I promise to be the best lover or defender of the Earth that I can be." That's the one vow that will unite us. And you can be atheist, or Christian, or Jewish, or Hindu, or Buddhist, or indigenous, or goddess, anything, if you want to focus on this one vow with the rest of us. So I have two young people—one's 33, one's 28, a man and a woman—who are kind of directing this, will be the leaders. I'll be an elder in the background. And we've done this book where each of us have written an essay and then we've invited about 20 other people to bring just two-page essays kind of in response to their take on the vision. David Korten has done the foreward for the book. And I'm excited about this because there's not time for a new religion or a new church and all that. We don't need new religions and new churches. But we do need communities, and we do need a focus. I know a 26-year-old young woman responded when I shared this idea. She said to me, "This is just what my generation needs. We're so dispersed because of social media. We need a focus. This would be a great focus," she said. "Count me in." I look at the history of, certainly, Western religion. And I notice, you know, religion often runs out of steam and goes down the wrong detour. But when it does, orders pop up. Like in the third century you had the desert fathers and the desert mothers, so these young men and women went out to the desert to get away from the empire and so forth, and distorted religion. In the sixth century, fifth century, you had Saint Benedict and his sister Saint Scholastica starting the Benedictine tradition, the monastic tradition, that

---

30. Matthew Fox, Skylar Wilson, and Jennifer Listug (authors), David Korten (Foreword), *Order of the Sacred Earth: An Intergenerational Vision of Love and Action* (Monkfish Book Publishing, 2018)

really did a lot of good work in the Dark Ages. But then it ran into maleficence. It got too aligned with the feudal system and privilege in the twelfth century. And then at the end of the twelfth century, the beginning of the thirteenth you had Saint Francis of Assisi and Saint Dominic starting a whole new version of a new order. And then the sixteenth century, you had the Protestant Reformation, which I interpret really as a series of lay orders. Each denomination has its own charism, its own ritual, its own theology. I interpret that historically as new orders with an emphasis on the lay people. And then, of course, also sixteenth century you had the Jesuits in the Catholic Church being born. But here in the twenty-first century nothing's happening. People are just leaving church. And so that's why I think this idea of an order makes a lot of sense. And of course you have orders in the East—Hindus and Buddhist orders and so forth. So it's not just a Western idea. But the thing about an order is, it travels much more quickly, and it's much more flexible and immediately responsive to the cultural zeitgeist than a "church" is or a "new religion" is. And we don't have time as a species. We're running out of time. So I think we need an order that's very portable and has only one vow and welcomes diversity of traditions, or no tradition, and diversity of lifestyles, like this Order of the Sacred Earth will do. I think maybe it may have something to contribute, and that's where I'm putting a lot of my energy these days.

MICHAEL: And as you said, a way of creating or catalyzing community is to develop that kind of order, a community that comes from a commonality whose origin isn't something that was narrow to begin with like a particular religion or a particular faith tradition, but something much broader and more inclusive. This just occurred to me, but do you think in any way it was a good thing or opened up opportunities that wouldn't have been opened up otherwise had you stayed in the Dominican order, had you not been encouraged to see other people? Do you think that being in that order and having that sense of community might've in any way constrained what you're doing now, would the community that you were already familiar with make you any less likely to have the vision that you have now? In other words, in a way, even though the intent was not to do you a favor, maybe were you being done a favor, looking back on it?

MATTHEW: Well, many people over the years have told me that I was blessed to be expelled from the Dominican order. It certainly gave me more freedom and wings to travel different paths. But even my interest in a new kind of order today is certainly partially related to the positive aspects of the Dominican order, of which I was a member for 34 years. And including the whole idea of "rite of passage." We need rites of passage today. Young people need rites of passage. And elders need rites of passage. And this was not talked about in that language in the Dominican order in my time, but it happened. You took serious vows as a young man or a young woman, if you were in the female wing of the order, and it did change your consciousness toward life. So the fact that I underwent that kind of commitment, but also that kind of acceptance into a larger community, certainly impacted on me, and was very positive. So in many ways you might say I'm translating my experience with the Dominicans into this new concept today. Well, I can look at the Franciscans, too. Saint Francis, you know, they took his order away from him, and then he died two years later, and I think he died of a broken heart. Because he didn't want his brothers to become priests. He didn't want them part of the hierarchy. And sure enough, they took it away, and then they made them part of the hierarchy, and within a generation after he died, Franciscans were running the Inquisition. And the same thing happened with the Dominicans. So there's a lesson there, a red flag, historically speaking, that there's a danger in a great vision being too closely allied with a religion institution. And so we can learn from the shadow experience of these orders, as well as from what's positive there. And that's I guess what I've been trying to do. So in my autobiography, you know, I— what should I say—I acknowledge with gratitude the many gifts that the Dominicans gave me. At the same time I refuse to back down at what my conscience was telling me, and I don't regret for a minute having left when I left. And I appreciate that the Episcopal Church offered me religious asylum when I needed it. And in a loose form within that tradition I've been able to do the cosmic mass and develop a tradition there where others are teaching, it, and learning it, and celebrating it. But also I've been able to do the rest of my work. So I am grateful in that regard.

MICHAEL: Do you consider yourself as an Episcopal priest, sort of an ex-Catholic, or are those not even meaningful distinctions under the broader umbrella of, say, Christianity or mystical Christianity?

MATTHEW: Well, having lived, what, fifty-five years or so as a Roman Catholic, and thirty-four years as a Dominican in that tradition, you don't throw that out. It makes an imprint on your soul, whether you like it or not. The same is true of Judaism. You can leave the Jewish structure, you can cease going to the synagogue, but you don't cease being a Jew. And Catholicism is like that. It makes a big imprint. I mean, Joe Campbell left the church when he was twelve or thirteen. He was a prodigy. [*Laughter*] But he also said many years later that he got his love of symbols and his love of metaphor from the Catholic Church. And I've never wanted to deny the gifts that Catholicism gave me, including the interest in the mystics. And as I say, I mean, look at my body of my work—a lot of my work has been exploring Thomas Aquinas. I've written three books on Meister Eckhart, three books on Hildegard of Bingen. These were all Catholic mystics and activists. And I carry them with me to this day. But the title of my auto-biography is *Confessions: the Making of a Post-Denominational Priest[31]*. I think we're living in a postdenominational time. That's part of what postmodernism is telling us. And so, yeah, I don't think anyone's stuck. I'm not stuck as an Episcopalian versus a Catholic. I'm not stuck in those two places either. And this is why I'm learning as much as I do from Lama Tsomo—I'm also part Buddhist. And I look for Buddhist presence in my Catholic and Christian forebears. Why not? So I don't think today the issue is what box are you in. That's Newtonian. That's modern. In this postmodern time, it's what's energizing you to give you the courage, number one, and the imagination, to assist the saving of our species and the planet, and the other species that we're here and responsible with. That to me is the issue. And it's like Jesus said, "By their fruits you'll know them." And I'm looking for the fruits of people's belief systems. And that's why I'm quite outraged when there's a Christianity wrapped in hypocrisy around the most important moral issues of our time, such as climate change.

MICHAEL: Thinking of you as a postdenominational, and also as a mystic, I want to talk a little bit about a couple of subsets of that. So when, for example, you pray, who are you praying to, or who are you communing with, and what is the nature and purpose of your prayers? And in that

---

31. Matthew Fox, *Confessions: The Making of a Post-Denominational Priest*
    (Harper San Francisco, 1997)

way is it any different from, for example, a more orthodox Catholic version of prayer?

MATTHEW: Well, my very first book was on prayer, what is prayer. I called it at the time *On Becoming a Musical Mystical Bear: Spirituality American Style*. Now the book has a new cover [*Laughter*] and a new title, a little less imaginative. But the title is *Prayer: a Radical Response to Life*[32]. That is the definition I came up for prayer with, about 40 years ago or so. And I still stand by it. I like it. Because for me prayer at its basis, it's not about talking—sometimes it's talking; it's also about silence, what we call meditation or contemplation. But it's deep. The key word is the word *radical* is the same word as *radix*, which means "root." So that's happening deep within our psyche, within our soul, within our consciousness, and some occasions at depth is joy, and awe, and wonder—it's what mystics call the via positiva. Sometimes that depth inside of us is a calling of silence and stillness. That's the via negativa; it's mindlessness. You cease entertaining images. You empty yourself of images. And of course suffering, too, is another form of the via negativa. And suffering of course, can be very, very deep. It's a radical response to life, how we respond to suffering. So addictions creep right into the via negativa to fill the void, whereas authentic meditative practices from the East or the West are about being with the emptiness, being in the silence, being with the void—what the mystics call the "dark night of the soul"—being with the suffering and the pain, letting it talk to us. Notice: let it talk to us. We have to shut up for it to talk to us. Like the Psalmist says, "Be still and learn that I am God." Then the third expression of prayer, I think is the via creativa, our creativity, when out of the emptiness comes something new. We give birth. And that may be to new political movements. It may be new social movements, economic movements, ways to do education, or ways to do worship and religion. But creativity is the work of spirit. Thomas Aquinas says that "The same spirit that hovered over the waters at the beginning of creation, hovers over the mind of the artist at work." I just love that passage because he's identifying , you know, that creation isn't something that was done 13.8 billion years ago; it's still going on with the same forces that brought the universe into existence. And we can tap into it. Our minds tap into

---

32. Matthew Fox, *Prayer: A Radical Response to Life* (Tarcher Perigee, 2001)

that, our minds and hearts. When he uses the word *mind* the medieval understanding of mind includes the heart and imagination. It's not a Descartes, a Cartesian notion of mind is just the head. But rationality, no, it includes intuition and creativity. And then the fourth path, the via transformativa is prayer, standing up to injustice, speaking out and acting out in a good sense. This, too, is prayer: taking a stand and doing something. It was exciting when I was at this conference this summer with scientists, to hear what some of them are doing. One of them, a young man—a young scientist, whose expertise is wind power he said we could be building floating islands 10 miles off the coast of the Atlantic Ocean, where it would be in nobody's backyard, no one would even see them, and these islands would be windmills, turbines, wind turbines. And we could provide all the electrical needs for North America. There'd be no coal, no gas, no oil needed from those turbines. And we could get started tomorrow. Well, that's the via transformativa. That's taking creativity into transformation. So think about that. As scientists and engineers and all human intelligence puts itself to the task at hand, all kinds of things are possible. That's prayer. People's work is prayer. The work of those scientists, that's prayer because it's deep. It comes from a radical response to life. From saying "no" to injustice, and to denial, and saying "yes" to the future of our species and the many other species. So that's how I see prayer. I don't see prayer as talking to God. You know, on occasion you might blurt something out. But, no, it's not talking—if it's anything, it's listening. But it's all those things. It's all those elements I think of what I call the "four paths of creation spirituality." So that's how I see prayer. And as a writer a lot of my work is the via creativa and via transformativa. I'm trying to give birth to ideas and language concepts that can affect a change in structures, in institutions, and forms. And that work is my prayer. I don't have to be talking to God to do that; I'm talking to people when I'm writing, or I hope I am. And that's my radical response to life. Hopefully I am working on behalf of life, on behalf of justice and compassion, love. And then that's prayer.

MICHAEL: Do you think that one fundamental difference is that most people seem to think of prayer as a form of asking for something, whether it's something concrete or something in them, and that your vision of it involves more connection and action, and less supplication and passivity?

MATTHEW: It's true that many people understand prayer as petition, asking for something. But, you know, that takes it back to Santa Claus. You know, that's such a childlike notion of prayer. You know, what did Paul say? "When I was a child I thought like a child. As an adult I think like an adult." Unfortunately many people who claim to be "religious" in America are still thinking like children. And I don't mean to insult children, but they are thinking of prayer as asking Daddy in the sky for something they don't have yet. And I think that's at the very bottom of the rung of what prayer means. The primary meaning of *prayer* is gratitude. Thomas Aquinas says, "The essence of religion is gratitude." And he puts religion as a virtue—that's how he sees it—in the larger virtue of thankfulness. And that's the via positiva then. And that's why the via positiva, the experience of awe and wonder and gratitude, is the kickoff for any prayer. And it all comes around to that again. And community worship is essentially about gratitude the word "Eucharist" that Christians apply to their worship, is a Greek word for "thank you." "*Eucharistein*" means "give thanks." And the sabbath experience of the Jewish people is about thanks, and to remember to give thanks. And I'm reading this book right now, I was reading it on the plane coming here, about air. There's a new book by scientists about air. And it really interested me because, you now, the word for "air" and "breath" and "spirit" are the same words, not only in the Bible, but in many languages around the world. So I say. "Oh boy, the more we can learn about air, the more we'll know about spirit." Well, the air, it turns out, is very, very complicated [*Laughter*]. There's all these chemicals in air. And it's really interesting how complicated air is. And yet we take our breath for granted, don't we? And so much of meditation, "East" and "West", is about meditating on your breath, you see? But the breath is a pretty amazing thing. It contains all these molecules. And the title of the book is called *Caesar's Last Breath*[33], because the author begins with Caesar's last breath, his being murdered in the senate in Rome, two thousand years ago, and how we are all breathing at least one molecule of Caesar's last breath [*Laughter*], whether you want it or not. So, you know, the utter interconnectivity

---

33. Sam Kean, *Caesar's Last Breath: Decoding the Secrets of the Air Around Us*
(Little, Brown and Company, 2017)

of breath, that we're all breathing one another's breath—and not just we who are, living, but our ancestors, too: we're breathing their breath. And not just human breath—we're breathing dinosaur breath, [*Laughter*] Sometimes it smells like that, you know, so you need some Listerine or something. But the point is that not to take for granted, I think, and therefore to be grateful is at the heart of the real meaning of religion, and the real meaning of prayer. To me, praise is the noise that joy makes. So praise is at the heart of healthy living and healthy prayer. It's about praise, which is another way I think of uttering thank you—thank you to be here. We're grateful to be here.

MICHAEL: Speaking of last breaths, you and I actually talked about this once, but I'd like to talk more about what do you think happens to us after we die?

MATTHEW: So what happens to us after death? Well, of course if I had a simple answer for that, I'd [*Laughter*] be a millionaire. No, I think that it's a mystery still. Whether you talk about reincarnation in the East, or resurrection in the West, or regeneration as the ancients talked about, I think that we do enter another world, and that that world is not divorced from this world. There are often many visitations from that world to this world. And our two-dimensional culture rarely celebrates that or instructs us about that. But I'll tell you a story. David Paladin was a Navajo painter who had a very difficult young manhood. He lied about his age, joined the army, and went to Europe, the Second World War times. When I say he lied about his age, he was underage. But he was captured almost immediately. Instead of putting him in a GI camp, the Nazis put him in a concentration camp where he languished for four years. And they tortured him. For example, one Christmas they nailed one foot to the floor and made him twirl for 24 hours. He was the only Native American in the concentration camp. When the Americans liberated the camp after four years they found his body at the bottom of a pile of dead bodies. He weighed 65 pounds, he was comatose, and paraplegic. They took him back to his reservation in Arizona, and he came out of his coma after two years. And his elders said to him, "You have a choice. You can go to a veteran's hospital where you'll be in a wheelchair the rest of your life, because you're paraplegic. Or we'll try to heal you in the ancient ways." He said, "Let's try the ancient ways." So they took him to an ice-cold river, this paraplegic, and threw him in over his head. He said when he hit the water he was more angry at his elders than he was at the Nazis who had done this to him. But it worked; he got his legs back. And he made several pilgrimages by foot to Mexico and back in his lifetime. Now, he was a painter—and fast-forward—he died, and his wife invited me to write some commentaries on his paintings, because she was doing an exhibit of his work. And he had known my work, especially my book, *Original Blessing*[34], and she said it was very important to him to combine his Native American spirituality with his Christian spirituality. So she invited me to her home where they had lived, and he had painted, and she said to me, "By the way," she said, "dead painters often came to my husband at night and dictated paintings." I said, "Really?" "Oh, yes," she said. And she disappeared, went into another room, and came back. And as soon as I saw the painting I said, "Well, that's Paul Klee." Sure enough it was signed "Paul Klee." She said, "I remember the night when Paul Klee visited my husband.

Now, this is a true story. I mean, it was true to her. I saw the painting. And what it tells me is that there are so many more dimensions to life than our culture whispers to us. Now, the elders told David Paladin the reason he suffered so much as a young man in the concentration camp was that he was being initiated as a shaman. And, you see, part of shamanism is that you live in two worlds at once. And this is why he was open and vulnerable to these visitations by the deceased artists. So to me that's just one example of, yeah, there's other things going on besides this world. Another example is that I've done some surveys lately. I have people shut their eyes—say I'm lecturing to a group—and I say, "Raise your hand if you have personally had experience of someone who died who you knew who died and appeared to you afterwards." And I remember the last time I did this. 75 percent, 80 percent of the people raised their hands. And then I often say, "Keep your eyes shut. How many of you know people you trust who have told you stories like that?" Another 75 percent of the people raise their hands. So all kinds of people having experiences of their loved ones coming back after they die. But we don't talk about these things. Our culture's

---

34. Matthew Fox, *Original Blessing: A Primer in Creation Spirituality* (Bear & Co. 1983)

so two-dimensional. And I have a good friend who's a blue-collar worker. He's not religious at all. He's not New Age at all. But three months after his mother died, she appeared to him at the end of his bed and they had a conversation. And every time he tells me this story, you know, his eyes tear up and so forth. It was just powerful, beautiful, and utterly real experience.

MICHAEL: I know a number of people who've had experiences like that. About four or five days after my wife's mother died, she appeared to her in a mirror. And my wife wasn't asleep and it wasn't some gauzy image. I mean, she was right there. And what she said to her was, "Be happy. Be kind. And do a little good in the world." And that's not the message necessarily you would've predicted from her. It's not something she'd ever said before. And in fact, I used that as the benediction at my wife's memorial service: "Be happy, be kind, and do a little good in the world."

MATTHEW: That's beautiful.

MICHAEL: You told me a story about—and I may be getting the details slightly wrong—about someone you knew who passed away and you went to his gravesite and talked to him. Could you tell that story if you recognize the story the way I'm angling it?

MATTHEW: No, I do. The last Sun dance I attended with Buck Ghosthorse and his community—he was a Lakota man who worked with me for years at Holy Names College, and then he went on to create his community. And then he died. And then I attended a Sun Dance a couple years after he had died, and it was run by his two sons, whom he left the responsibility to, and his wife. And there was a break during the Sun Dance in the evening, and I went to his grave. And I'd been at his funeral, where we had placed him in the ground, but now the grave had more stones on it and so forth. And I knelt on one knee, and I said, "Buck, you should really be proud of your sons and your wife for continuing to carry on this powerful and beautiful experience. And you really should thank them for it." Well, that was nighttime. The next morning, just before the Sundance began at dawn, his wife came up to me and said, [paraphrasing], "You know, something amazing happened last night. Buck came to me. And he thanked me. And he never thanks me." [*Laughter*] And she went on and on. It was just a very moving experience. And I'm glad Buck is still listening, and

I'm glad he's still acting. And I felt very good about it actually because I feel that his sons and his wife, you know, sacrifice, a lot to put on this elaborate ceremony, in addition to their dancing in it and fasting for days at a time, and doing the piercing and all the rest. But just to organize something like that is a huge undertaking. And they were doing a wonderful job. But to be reminded that our requests, people on the other side do not always fall on deaf ears is a good thing. And this, too, is ecumenical. Buck is Lakota in his spirituality, and I am Christian, and so forth. But obviously we're talking to each other. And another experience I've had since the last time we did these discussions, Lama Tsomo and me, is with Lorna Byrne. Lorna Byrne is a peasant Irishwoman who's been experiencing angels since she was two years old. And she's in her sixties now. They told her not to tell anyone until they told her she could. And it was only about, I don't know, seven years ago that they said, "Okay, you can tell people now." Her husband already died. And so she's dictated three best sellers since then about her angel experiences. And I say "dictated" because she's illiterate. She doesn't read or write. But she and I have had some wonderful encounters. I interviewed her at Grace Cathedral in San Francisco. Thirteen hundred people were there, because people have read her works. And she's so authentic. She's a very poor woman. She's been poor all her life, and simple, but she's had these experiences, still has them, with angels. And one of the things she said was this, when I interviewed her at San Francisco, [paraphrasing], she said, "There are many unemployed angels on the Earth today." I said, "Oh. I know lots of unemployed people." This was about three or four years ago during the recession. I said, "We have to be putting angels to work, too?" "Oh," she said, "this is the deal." She said, "God knows how much trouble humans are in today. So God is pouring angels on the Earth to help us, and no one's asking them for help." So there are a lot of unemployed angels wandering around. So I tell people, you know, when you go to bed at night, ask angels for help, and ask them to visit you. You don't have to be elaborate—angels are very smart and they're utterly intuitive, so they catch on real fast. But they want to be asked. They don't just want to show up and interfere with our lives. And of course Aquinas says angels reflect intuition. So as we develop our intuitions—which is what mysticism is, I think—angels will show up much more in our lives. You'll find angels hitchhiking on the highway of intuition. And so this is why a lot of artists and creative people encounter spirits all the time. We have a special word for this, a muse. A muse is an angel who shows up in our creative work. And so we're getting help from the spirit world. And we should be talking more about this. And so there are these dimensions of living that take us far beyond the television set if we open our hearts and minds to them.

MICHAEL: The focus of a lot of Christians in particular seems to be in some ways the persistence of the individual after death. And in some stripes, like in Mormonism, it's quite literally the same person in the same identity, in some cases it's a different form. But one of the things that struck me when we've spoken before is it isn't that you haven't thought about it or at some level don't care about it, but it certainly seems that your primary focus as a Christian person isn't, we've got to make it to the other side intact. It seems like something that interests you in a kind of incidental way compared to what other aspects of Christianity are more important. Does that seem like a fair assessment?

MATTHEW: Yes. Thomas Aquinas has this wonderful teaching. He says, "There are two resurrections. The first is waking up in this lifetime. And if you do that, you don't have to worry about the second." So I think that's very good teaching, and I think it comes very close to Buddhism, enlightenment, waking up. It continues after this lifetime. A phrase that is used in the Christian scriptures is *eternal life*. But eternal life is not something that comes after you die. It's something you taste in this lifetime. Again, it's about that radical response to life. It's a deepening awareness of the gratuity, the gift, the grace that life is, and the immense fullness of it, and the beauty of it. And beauty doesn't die; beauty lives on, and grace lives on. And, you know, one of the exciting discoveries a year ago by science is that our universe is not a couple hundred billion galaxies big; it's two trillion galaxies big. That is such astounding information—two trillion galaxies, each one with billions and hundreds of billions of stars. And if this doesn't kind of shock us... You know, Rabbi Heschel says, "The universe is not just here; it shocks us into amazement." Well, if we can't be shocked into amazement by facts like those, you know, and get over this ego concern about keeping your ego intact after you die, well, we've missed what life is about. So we have to become reincarnated again, I guess, start all over again. Or the Christian tradition doesn't talk that much about reincarnation; it talks about purgatory, which to me is a very parallel concept. If you don't love this time around, you can learn it someplace sometime around. So I think we're destined to have to repeat ourselves [*Laughter*] if we can't allow ourselves to be shocked into amazement and go with that. And what follows follows. But that's the first resurrection: waking up in this lifetime. And the rest will take care of itself.

MICHAEL: In much of your work, you're out there in the world communicating and doing various kinds of good—as JFK said, "Here on Earth God's work must truly be our own." And in order to get people to pay attention to you and what you're saying, you need to be as charismatic and emphatic as possible. How do you balance the value your spiritual tradition, or just you personally, place on humility and lack of egotism on the one hand, with *your* full attention-getting persona and presence as a public communicator?

MATTHEW: I'm not someone who denies ego. I think ego has a very important role to play in our lives. Ego is what we learn in a healthy adolescence—how you're separate from others, from your parent, how you're distinguished from others. So to me ego is a very important stage in life. And it's tragic when people are not able to develop their ego because they live under oppression or under such stress. But to be an adult is not to stop with a developed ego. It's to fold the ego in just as you fold the child into your whole self, into a living, breathing adult who is here to love and to serve as well as to be loved. So I eschew gurus who tell people they should kill their egos. I'm 100 percent against that. I think coming to a healthy ego is an achievement that's necessary for healthy living and healthy adulthood. The problem is stopping with the ego. That's the problem. And I think our culture is very ego-driven, and the majority of people end up stopping with the ego and just feeding that. And then they create a religion which is about saving that ego [*Laughter*], so the ego will live forever. And that's a pseudo-religion. It's false religion. It's certainly not what Christ taught. Jesus says, "You have to lose your life to save it." The seed has to die if a plant is to be born. So there is a dying that goes on. But it's not about murdering your ego; it's about recognizing the ego has this important place. The ego creates not only distinction but parameters, boundaries.

Boundaries are very important. And for the mystic, too. Yes, the mystic soars into boundlessness and beyond ego. But it also has to return to ego. You might say you're not in a mystical state 24 hours a day, 7 days a week. You've got to do the laundry. You've got to pay the bills and all the rest. So there's this dance that goes on between ego, and mystic, and adult, and all the rest. So, yeah, if you're teaching people, you've got to have boundaries. You know, there's already so much time in the class, for example, and there are books to read, and so forth. So it's both, and—there's a place for the rational, and the left-brain, and for ego; but there's also a place for intuition, for soaring, and going beyond the ego. And we all have to find that dance, that rhythm. And so we all have to because it's different in different people. We have different DNA and different personalities. In one family you can have personalities utterly different. So that's where diversity comes in and respecting diversity. But I don't think there's anything to be afraid of with the ego unless you've stopped your development with the ego. Then you're scary. You're stuck at about 17, 16 years of age, and that kind of adolescent excess is of course a very pitiful place to be stuck. And, now, I think men especially have a problem here, because more and more studies show that men do not develop our brains fully until about the age of 29 or 30, whereas women develop much faster. And certainly their social abilities develop much faster. And so men, I think, are more tempted to remain in an adolescent ego. And part of that ego is being afraid of responsibility. And so I think men have to be particularly aware of this. So I think it's very important, especially, that young men be involved in developing rituals today that give them an outlet for their energy, for their passions, for their dreams, for their anger, as well as for their joy. I think our culture is failing us dramatically in providing far too few rituals that are really effective, and that are more than just joining a team. That's useful. But there are many other ways we can be creating rituals today that could be effective too. You know this appeal with ISIS and all these radical groups, it's always to young men. And they join to join a group, and then they learn how to go around beheading people and so forth. I mean, it's strange, but I think it's related to the fact that we need a much healthier sense of the sacred masculine than our culture is giving us. And women need this as well as men, not only because they have men in their lives, but because the woman's soul is half-masculine, just like the male's soul is half-feminine. So women are walking around with toxic masculinity in them also, and so are men. So we have to shake the tree of masculinity up severely today and get back to something more real.

MICHAEL: If you were to go encourage someone to be more spiritual, for lack of a better word—although that word has almost become glibly meaningless, so I'm not sure it's a word that works anymore—and they were not already leaning in any particular direction, would you encourage them toward Christianity specifically? Or how would you guide somebody who maybe thinks, "I want to have some kind of spiritual or religious identity, but I really am not sure how to go about that, or even whether to go about that?"

MATTHEW: Well, I'm happy to report that a new school is opening in October called the Fox Institute for Creation Spirituality. It's grounded in Boulder, Colorado. Some former students of mine are birthing it. And I'll be teaching in it, but I'm not part of the administration as such. I've been there and done that—enough penance for my sins, as gross as they've been I'm sure. But I think we need centers like this where people can explore spirituality. I'm not at home with the word *Christianity* today. I think the word *Christianity* has been co-opted and highjacked by fascists, among others, and by hypocrites, among others, and by ignorant people, among others. You know, in the Middle Ages there was a parallel experience. The word *Christendom, Christianitas* in Latin, was used for centuries in the Dark Ages. But these radical groups, Saint Francis of Assisi and Dominic, were part of this movement that threw off the word *Christianitas.* They refused to use the word *Christendom* ever again. And they just moved on from there. Instead they talked about returning to the sources, and the poverty of Jesus, that Jesus was working with the poor. He was not part of this empire of Christendom. So I think today when you hear people like Jerry Falwell and others using the word *Christianity*, they're talking about the empire, today's empire, the American empire, and their version of a white Christian empire. And I want nothing to do with that. So I think it's a worthy debate to ask today whether we should even bother using the word *Christianity*. I don't use it. I use *Christ's path*, for example, or the *Christ way*. Of course I talk and write about the cosmic Christ. And I always point out how this is parallel to the Buddha nature idea. So I don't try to convert people to be a Christian. I speak to people about being their deepest, truest selves. I think that Jesus and his teachings—and many Christians through the centuries, the kind of people I've been exploring for years, such as Hildegard, and Aquinas, and Eckhart, and Mechtilde, and Julian of Norwich, and all these people, and now Thomas Merton and others, Pierre de Chardin, Pope Francis, Thomas Barry, Dorothy Day, there's so many people in history who I think have been modeling, or trying to live out in their time and place the teachings in the spirit of Jesus. And I'm proud to be part of that lineage. But the word *Christianity* is a little too big, and it's far too involved with imperialism for my tastes, and especially when it pops up on the American capitalist scene, and it really becomes gross. So I just think that, as we said earlier, that Jesus and the prophetic Jewish tradition from which he comes, and the wisdom tradition of his role from which he comes—which is nature-based mysticism, it's creation spirituality pure and simple—this has a lot to teach people today no matter where you come from. And I keep running into people, younger people, people in their thirties and twenties, all over the place who do not identify as "Christian," but they're very interested in Jesus. I have a friend who's Buddhist and he's in his thirties, teaches mathematics in high school, and he went and made the pilgrimage—Saint James Compostela pilgrimage, 480 kilometers—by foot several summers ago, and his feet bled halfway through so he had to quit. Went back home, taught for another year, flew back to finish it, which he did. And now he's talking about going back a third time and doing the whole thing over again. He's Buddhist. I find a lot of Asians are getting very interested in Jesus and what Jesus represented, just like a lot of Westerners are very interested in Buddhism. And I think that's a wonderful thing. We're human beings on one planet. We're one species. And why wouldn't we be borrowing from the wisdom of one another? So I'm not at home with the word *Christianity* anymore. I think it's been polluted beyond redemption probably. But we can come up with other phrases, like I say, *the way* and the "path." These were phrases that are found in the scriptures. This is the first generation talked about it that way. And notice that word, *the way, a way, or path*, it doesn't incorporate imperial ambitions or structures, not at all.

MICHAEL: As we've talked about before, one of the things I really admire about you is that you are such a 360 person, that you have what seems to me to be the full capacity for engaging the world emotionally, spiritually, personally, kinesthetically, and also analytically. You're a very sharp guy. So given all those various components, particularly your awareness of science and the scientific method, and verifying the truth of things as opposed to just the pleasantry of things, what do you think the role of faith is, or what does faith mean to you? How does it fit into these complexities and what do you have faith in?

MATTHEW: For me the primary meaning of *faith* is *trust*. And that's found in the gospels. The word for "faith" is is, *pistuein* in Greek, and it means to have trust. It doesn't mean to believe in a series of doctrines and dogmas. It's about trust. So when Jesus uses that phrase often, "Go your way; your trust has healed you," we've been translating it as "your faith", but it really means "trust." And Jesus himself is not out there offering up lists of believable dogmas. He was about healing people and getting people to heal themselves and one another. And to me that is the bottom-line meaning of *faith*, to "trust." To trust the universe. To trust your right to be here. To trust your own personhood, your uniqueness. I think everything changes when you can trust. Meister Eckhart says, "The main reason people don't create is that they lack trust." And of course good parenting will usually result in children growing up to trust their bodies, trust their minds, trust their intuition, trust their talents, trust their ability to learn and to know, and decisions they make, which is conscience—trust your conscience. But it seems to me a deformed culture does not want to teach us trust. I always say that original sin—which of course was Augustin's concept in the fourth century, which was a religious concept— has been taken over by consumer capitalism. In the secular world, capitalism begins with original sin. Capitalism is telling us, "You can't trust yourself. [*Laughter*] You've got to get salvation from the outside. You've got to go shopping. You've got to change your appearance. You've got to be like everyone else, or get the latest gadget, or the latest clothes, or whatever it is. But whatever it is, keep spending money." I really think there's not a deliberate, but a definitive parallel between original sin ideology and religion, and consumer capitalism that is in fact running our economic system. And neither of them is teaching trust. Both are an insult to the real meaning of *faith*. What they're teaching is a pseudo-faith, a faith in idols. And so I think there's grave danger there. I think that growing up means learning to trust.

MICHAEL: As you know, Buddhists have this concept of near enemies, something that seems to be the same thing but isn't really. And from what you're saying I think maybe that this culture does teach unthinking acceptance certainly of lots of things, but that's maybe the near enemy of faith. Faith is trust, this sort of informed, eyes-open trust, and just accepting something without thinking about it, which is what some people think of faith, might be the near enemy—it's the line in *Inherit the Wind* when the William Jennings Bryan character says, "I do not think about things that I do not think about."

KATY: I have a question. Especially in the culture of our time I've found that people really connect by hearing other people's personal stories. We crave that community, we crave that personal history. And so for me, of course, I'm sitting here listening, and I'm curious, what did it take for you to build that trust? Because faith—trust—goes from exploring, and looking in, and delving deeper. So can you share with us a little bit of how that trust was built for yourself?

MATTHEW: Well, I think I was blessed that my parents did not create dependence and codependence. My mother in particular was always eager to [*Laughter*] get us out of the house. And I think that even though she had seven children in 10 years, her goal in life wasn't to be a mom all her life; she wanted to get on with her life. She taught us to think for ourselves and to make decisions for ourselves. And she taught us to trust, therefore. And she trusted us implicitly. But above all she trusted herself. She followed her own intuition. For example, she would always take two hours off every afternoon for herself, no matter how many kids were running around in diapers, whether it was to read, or to join a sewing club, or go bicycling. She took care of herself. And she trusted us kids to take care of one another. And I think maybe risk comes in here, the willingness to risk, and the willingness to fail. And to me, the bottom line, can we trust the universe, you know? To me it's so important. There's been 13.8 billion years that brought us here, and that fine-tuned the air and everything else, and made this wonderful place for us. So that's why I think a lot of people recover their trust, even if they've been deeply wounded in childhood and so forth, in nature. Even though nature is wild, but you want wild. That's where beauty is to be found: in the wild. Nevertheless you can trust it. The sun will come up. And the rain will stop. And the soil will provide. And the animals will bless us, and so forth. And so to me all this is part of trust, it's part of living in the various worlds we live in, beginning with probably with our families, and then we grow our worlds. And so for me, like, even some prayer practice like sweat lodges, the very first time I was in a sweat lodge I was sure I was going to die there. The first 20 minutes I was looking for a fire escape. There was none. Then I was looking for a fire extinguisher. There was none. Then I said, "I'm going to die in here." And then I yielded to the experience. So in that I learned something about trust. And then you go into this altered state, and it was marvelous. And I came out feeling physically healed and wonderfully alive. So again, rituals, if they're done well, they can teach us trust. And we should be assisting others. Now, this new order that we're starting, what can I say? It's a big gamble. You know, it could just flop. Fine. I've already said I'd rather fail at something interesting than succeed at something pedestrian. So it takes trust to do this. And I'm trusting my dream, because it came to me in a dream to do this. And I'm trusting the young people I'm working with to launch this order. But we don't have any guarantee that it's going to work. Fine. We're going to give it a shot. You have to try something today, because obviously what we have isn't working. So you trust your intuition, you trust your dreams. I've trusted a lot of my dreams over the years and I've never regretted it. You know, there's something I'd like to bring up before we close. It's in my recent book on the cosmic Christ, *Stations of the Cosmic Christ*[35], which I did with Bishop Marc Andrus in San Francisco. And in there I quote this marvelous passage from Albert Einstein. He said that, "We're moving into the third era of religion. The third era of religion will be a cosmic religion," he says, "and it will have the capacity to create peace on the Earth, peace among all the religions, and beyond." But I just think this is a passage that few people have seen. And then when I shared it with these scientists this summer, 150 of them, they were blown away. They'd never seen this passage. And it has to do with the marrying of science and spirituality. In spirituality, we have this archetype of the cosmic Christ,

---

35. Marc Andrus and Matthew Fox, *Stations of the Cosmic Christ* (Kion Yamaguchi Press, edition, 2016)

the Buddha nature, the image of God, which is cosmic. But marrying that with the cosmos as we now know it, as this alive, birthing, fecund, generative organism that we call "the universe," it's really quite stunning. And I would hope that that's the future of Buddhism, and that's the future of Christian mysticism, along with the other traditions, that we move into this rediscovery of the sacredness of all creation, and that we learn to think cosmically, not just anthropocentrically, or what Pope Francis calls "narcissistically," which is how our species has been thinking during the modern era. For several hundred years we've been stuck on ourselves, and it's destructive. And we're killing the planet as we know it. So we've got to open up to this invitation from the cosmos. And as Rabbi Heschel says [paraphrasing], "It is an invitation that will shock us into amazement." And that's the beginning of mysticism in my opinion.

LAMA TSOMO

Author Interview

With Michael Frisbie and Katy-Robin Garton
August 28, 2017 • Montana

MICHAEL: We're going to start with the easy questions—it's like *Jeopardy!*: it'll get harder. So since this is kind of the 25th-anniversary tour for *The Lotus & The Rose*...

LAMA TSOMO: [*Laughter*] Just about.

MICHAEL: Just about. Looking back over the historical arc of this whole thing, can you talk a little bit about what drew you to this in the first place, what you've learned along the way?

LAMA TSOMO: What drew me to this dialogue in the first place was Matt Fox. I've been a fan for many decades, and I had the chance to meet him. We sat in his office and immediately we just fell into talking about our respective traditions and the fascinating corollaries. And I was trying to match this one thing, that didn't quite match, but then there were these other things that more closely aligned. And so those comparing and contrasting conversations....Anytime we got together we just fell into them immediately, and were both instantly engrossed.

MICHAEL: What had made you a fan of Matthew's from before you even met him?

LAMA TSOMO: When I read *Creation Spirituality*[36] I was struck by his combination of brilliant scholarship—piercing through the fluff to deep meaning—and, at the same time, levity. You know, he has a great sense of humor, and it was very alive. That combination is rare. So I was really struck by it and appreciated it. And what he had to say I felt was profound and true.

MICHAEL: Anything you learned about him spiritually or personally along the way of doing these dialogues that you hadn't run into in talking to him before?

LAMA TSOMO: As I've gotten to know Matt over the years I've discovered the breadth of his interests. And again, it seemed as though so many of our interests sparked each other. Just on the phone last night we were talking about yet another subject—nothing to do with these official *Lotus & The Rose* dialogues—and it happened again. And so almost anything we talk about,

---

36. Matthew Fox, *Creation Spirituality: Liberating Gifts for the Peoples of the Earth* (Harper 1, 1991)

whether it's politics of the day, or we were talking about nontraditional medicines from lineages other than either of ours, whatever it is, we would just go right to these profound levels, and there was so much consonance.

MICHAEL: Is there anything—and it's okay if the answer is no—is there any way in which you go, "I wish I were a little more like Matthew Fox in this particular way?"

LAMA TSOMO: Well, he is able to translate from, you know, Old German, and he literally brought some of these texts out of the basements of these monasteries, and brought them to us, our modern English-speaking audience, and illuminated them with his own commentary, and wove them into the concerns of our times. So I think that one thing that stands out is that, I mean, he also went to school in France, studying these very esoteric things in French…and then translating from the Old German. I'm just in awe of that, that he's able to do that.

MICHAEL: Sort of a flip-side question: I know you respect Matthew's intellect and his faith, but is there anything—and we've talked about this before—when you look at either his particular stripe of Christianity, or Christianity in general, you go, "Nah," you know, "that'd be a deal-breaker for me. I could never be fully committed to being a Christian myself, or Matthew's particular kind of Christian, because that's part of it that just wouldn't work for me?"

LAMA TSOMO: Yeah, there are a few things. So for me I'm finding that Tibetan Buddhist lineage and approach is so much of a great fit. Christianity less so, because I was really looking for, and still need, sort of a graduated path. You know, in math you have addition, then you learn subtraction, then multiplication, division, and so on. So needing to train my mind to be able to slowly but surely clear away more and more of my habitual way of seeing myself, my own mind, as well as reality out there, I needed to have a progression that I could follow. And as I got further and further in that progression, the practices were stronger, more direct, and more the channel changer, to get beneath the usual level of reality and configuration of the way we think it is, get much beneath that to how reality actually is, which used to only come for me just very occasionally in random epiphanies. But I wanted to be able to have the channel changer. And the methods in the practices in Tibetan Buddhism allow me to have those moments any time I sit down, and not just when I meditate, even faster than that. So over the years I've found them to be really effective in that way, and that's how they're intended. In most other religious traditions, spiritual traditions, you don't have that training, where you then have a way of having the channel changer in your hand, and you can actually switch to actually several channels.

MICHAEL: One of the things we've talked about before is that both what drew you to Tibetan Buddhism and a reservation you had about Christianity is what you're just talking about, which is Tibetan Buddhism is so much richer in practices—not just conceptually, but in application and practices—than other traditions, particularly Christianity. I hear that, and also the sense of progression, that there's sort of conceptual progression, which kind of leads me in a way to a couple of other differences. Depending on which stripe of Christianity you're looking at, there's a lot of focus on the redemption of and survival of the individual personality after death. Could you talk a little bit about what you think happens to us, as a Tibetan Buddhist, when we die?

LAMA TSOMO: Mmm hmm, mmm hmm. First I want to just backtrack and say that another feature of Tibetan Buddhist practice is that through the brilliant use of archetype I can tune into various aspects of myself, aspects of reality—I would say "principles" of reality, which can be useful on different occasions. And also if I feel like I'm kind of deficient in this or that one, there's a deity practice for that. A wonderful array of medicines I can take, depending on what I need. You can get too distracted by that whole array. But if you still focus on, look, I'm really trying to get to the end result, which is full awakening, still to have that array of practices, a full palette to use, that's wonderful. And it's not in Judaism, it's not in Christianity; it really is a full array in Tibetan Buddhist tradition.

So as far as what happens after life and the different traditions and the beliefs about that, to me it doesn't make sense if the soul does live, if there's some spark of awareness that lives beyond the physical body, then the idea that it would only incarnate in a physical body once doesn't make sense. So that's just a span of a very few short years, and then there's the rest of eternity. So how could it be that it's just once and then you go on somewhere else and you're there for the rest of eternity? That just doesn't make sense to me, so I wouldn't be able to sign up for a tradition that went like that.

MICHAEL: So when we die—not that either of us is planning on it...

LAMA TSOMO: I am.

MICHAEL: [*Laughter*] I know it's going to happen, I'm just not planning on it. I'm all penciled in for that day. In relation to what happens to us when we die, could you talk a bit about the practice that you've told me about—and I actually did with you at Spirit Rock—the sort of letting the parts of you that are your human identity evaporate, and what we lose of what we think of as ourselves when we die? Because I find that really interesting.

LAMA TSOMO: You want me to talk about that?

MICHAEL: Just, yeah, a little bit about it and what that involves, and why it takes that form and helps us from a Tibetan Buddhist perspective, see what does remain and what doesn't. Because in a funny, almost counterintuitive way, I actually find it consoling, even though I could see that some people would be freaked out by it. But actually I found it very useful and soothing for me.

LAMA TSOMO: When I practice Vipassana, a lot of times I do what I call the "what's left?" practice. And that is in a sense rehearsing my death. When we die, so much falls away. And so as those various layers of husks fall away, what's left, what's left, what's left? And...to go a little bit slowly through that, step by step, so that it feels real to me, then it allows me to get down to my true essence, and I'd like to know, who/what I really am. So as I begin I usually think in terms of, okay, now my ability to walk to the bathroom, gone. And, sort of like layers of the onion, my ability even to talk drops away. Then parts that I usually consider to be my identity drop away. So American drops away. I mean, as I leave this life that does drop away. English-speaker dropping away. And of course before that, you know, Tibetan-speaker dropped away. And so I move closer and closer in, and then even my name drops away. So what's left, what's left, what's left? What I come to is my awareness. And I used to stop there, but then I realized, "Wait, what's this 'my'?" That would mean that there's a boundary around awareness, but there's no boundary left. So as I leave my body, there's absolutely no container. So it's just awareness. And if there's no boundary to that awareness. then it's just part of the ambient awareness of the whole ocean. And so that wave went down, and now it's just ocean. And there is something comforting about that. We're all afraid of death. But when I rehearse it in that way I feel that coming home, and that ocean— feeling of joining with the ocean is—I mean, what's better than coming home? So it's bright, alive, strangely enough, and aware, and full of love, and deliciousness.

Michael: I remember the poem you wrote about your father's passing was really in many ways parallel to what you've said. He was losing various capacities: his wit, his intellect, his curiosity, his ability to walk. And I know part of the poem was about what he was losing, but the other part was encouraging him really to be willing to let go and move on. And I would imagine that was both personally and spiritually powerful for you in complicated ways.

Lama Tsomo: In that poem that's in *Why Is the Dalai Lama Always Smiling?*, I was writing about that through-the-eye-of-the-needle moment in the dying process that my dad was going through. So as the things are falling away—his capacity to be incredibly witty and knowledgeable and so on—and all these different capacities were falling away, he didn't know about this ocean piece, and didn't believe in it. And even for myself I have to say I'm still afraid I'll be afraid when I come to that eye-of-the-needle moment. And so as my capacities fall away, even though I've rehearsed it and I've sat in those places where I'm really just in the ocean, I wonder, you know, when I breathe out and I can't breathe in again, will I be in a place where I'm really ready and I just sort of dive into the ocean? That's certainly my hope.

Michael: One of the things that we've talked about before is how faith factors into Tibetan Buddhism. And I know it has a place in it, but we've talked before, and you've written before, about how blind faith is actually the worst kind of faith. So could you talk a little bit about that, how faith does factor in. And maybe more personally what's something either within the spiritual tradition or just more broadly that you have faith in?

Lama Tsomo: What I really have faith in is things I've experienced personally. And fortunately in Tibetan Buddhist understandings, that's the

one that's stable, that is worth something. At the beginning there's an aspirational faith, is how it's translated. So you hear about something and you
think, "Well, that makes sense and I'm really inspired by that. I want to
look into this more," and meanwhile, you know, I kind of have that as my
provisional faith. That would be, I think, how in Tibetan Buddhist studies
it would be held. My understanding of the way Westerners think of the
word *faith* is when you say "have faith," it's usually not telling you, "Oh,
well, you know this, so it's just the way it is." They mean you don't have
proof of it, you haven't experienced it yourself, so have faith, like, instead.
And that doesn't really work well for me; never did. So questioning, and
debate, and so on, are very much a part of Tibetan Buddhist tradition,
which I'm really comfortable with as a Jewish person because that was
the case when I was growing up. And, you know, good juicy questions the
rabbi delighted in, my dad used to delight in, and we needed to debate
points to get down to, well, what really makes sense here? If it doesn't
make sense then you don't just say, "Well, have faith anyway," in my book.
And so I was comfortable then with the Tibetan tradition, which was,
yeah, you need to see for yourself. So there are three aspects of teaching.
There's hearing, contemplating, putting into practice. First you hear, you
know, what is sort of the scaffolding of this understanding. And then the
lama starts to explain in examples and so forth. Then you go off and chew
on it. And that's what I really need to do. Does this really make sense to
me? And then I start thinking of examples to try it on for size. Well, does
it work here? Does it work there? How does this work? I come back and I
have asked Rinpoche a ton of questions, and he loves it. And then he and
his brother have invited me to do debate. And *invite* is the wrong word—it
was part of the curriculum—"Now we will debate." And I was, like, "Oh
goody. It's like my dinner table when I grew up." So then we hammer
these ideas against what each other is saying, and it helps me to hone
my understanding, "Oh, this is what they're talking about. Huh." Then I
chew on it some more. And then I take it into practice. And as I sit doing
practices that help my mind to sort of settle, and the waters to become
calm, and the silt to settle, and I can see to the bottom of the pond, if you
will, then I can see for myself. And that's quite different from any words.
But it's also then a very different "faith" that's actually knowing from your
own experience.

MICHAEL: So a couple of things occur to me. One is that Catholics have this idea of when something's inexplicable, that it's a "mystery of faith." And to me sometimes the deal is, yeah, it's a mystery why you'd have faith in that if there's no evidence for it. And I don't want to put those words in your mouth, but it's, like, it seems like kind of...

LAMA TSOMO: But they're so good.

MICHAEL: Feel free to use them; just don't drag me into this. So it sounds in a way as though what you have faith in is the process. In other words, that once you move from aspirational faith to something a little more active, that you have some faith that if you follow the process, not that you'll have to believe things that aren't proven out, but that it's worth following.

LAMA TSOMO: As sort of in an overarching way about the path?

MICHAEL: Yeah.

LAMA TSOMO: Yeah—yeah.

MICHAEL: But then at any given juncture you don't have to believe something if you go, "Wait a minute, this isn't ringing true, but it's a path worth following." If someone were considering starting on the path, if they were sort of at the pre-aspirational stage, and they're kind of on the fence, like, "I don't know where I'm going, I don't know if this is going to take me there," what would you tell them to encourage them to at least take a few steps on the path and see what's up, if they're either feeling faithless or contemplating various options, but have no idea where to turn?

LAMA TSOMO: Well, for me, I did need to sort of belly up to the spiritual smorgasbord, which America can provide in a huge array. And I felt that the way I was going to know whether a path was right for me was to go a few steps down it with somebody who knew what they were doing showing me about it, try it on for size. Because it can be intellectually appealing, but I need to know, does it actually work for me? So I need that faith-born of experience that in common parlance is called *knowing*. That's what we call that, when you've experienced something, this is actually how it is, you know it. One lama was in prison and the Chinese were trying to get him to change, to throw away Buddhism. But he had experienced things, and he knew them, and he couldn't un-know them. So he said finally, "You can make me say words—like 'this isn't true'—but that would be like saying my mother doesn't exist, when I know for sure from personal experience she exists." That did not endear him to the Chinese guards, but that's another story. But the point is, I think what you're talking about is trust. At a certain point if you've gone down a certain path... I think the word *faith* has so many connotations, I almost want to step around that a little bit and get to something we can all kind of understand on the same level. When I've gone a certain number of steps down a path and it's just feeling more and more right, and I'm learning more and more, "Yes, this is how it is," and I'm experiencing it, so then I know it, and it feels each of these steps is right to me, then I begin to trust. this path more and more. So that doesn't mean I'm still not going to need to evaluate, and ask a lot of questions. The process of hear, contemplate, and put into practice, those three aspects are still going to be needed at all levels. But I've been far enough down this path that I have a lot of trust that it's going to take me where I want to go. And I'm even more clear about where that is now that I've gotten further along. So, for me, more at the beginning, at a certain point I was trying different ones on for size, and what felt right to me. And I was kind of doing my own version of listening, chewing on it, and then trying the practices on for size, that I finally came down to, "Okay, this one feels right to me." And I wasn't making any commitments. I hadn't joined any clubs, or I didn't carry any cards. But I was, like, you know, "This feels right. I'm going to go a few more steps down." And so then I would go another few levels. That was incredible. And the further I went down the path, the stronger the medicines I was able to use, and the more benefit I was getting. I was starting to get feedback from other people around me— "Hey, you're doing better," you know? "Well, how bad was I before?" But anyway, I was happy the improvement was happening. So then I was upping and re-upping in increments to the point where finally I could say, "Yep, this is definitely the path for me."

MICHAEL: Would you say that some of that initial spark of trust came from your meeting with Rinpoche and feeling that you could both relate to him and trust him as somebody who was worth listening to, even before you heard that much about what he had to say or wherever he was going to guide you? Because obviously at this point he's guided your way along the path, but in those first steps was that meeting, your contact with him pivotal to this do you think, or...?

LAMA TSOMO: The very first meeting I had with Rinpoche I didn't know he was going to be my teacher. I was trying this path on for size. It seemed appealing, but I wasn't sure. I was just at the end of my first-ever retreat—again, trying it on for size. I had a meeting with him, and we debated about eating meat or not, and I learned a ton about it. I don't know that we ever fully came exactly to agreement, but very close. Fascinating debate. So I enjoyed it, I enjoyed him. The next time I met with him, he appeared on my doorstep to teach somebody else, and I got to sit in. It was then, in this concentrated and really rather advanced-level teaching, that I could really begin to experience how his mind is, and what he had to teach. And it was really jaw-dropping in its profundity. So that was when I felt, "Oh, this is my path. This is my teacher."

MICHAEL: What about his mind really appealed to you?

LAMA TSOMO: Well, there was the combination of his being very matter-of-fact, and he would just joke around and so on. And then when it was time to do an empowerment—which is like this transmission in which he's really a conduit of something much more vast from these principles of reality—I was able to experience directly quite a different presence that I didn't run into every day. It was quite powerful. Also, in his teachings he was quite precise and refined in what he was transmitting to me intellectually. So the combination of the vastness and power of his presence when he really took his seat, and his intellectual understandings and mastery, along with the fact that in between he could just goof off, joke around, we'd arm wrestle, whatever, so there was no show. You know, what you see is what you get. And what I got and what I saw was quite something. I felt this is the right lama for me. And as time went on and I got to know him better, and actually my mind was able to perceive more and sort of drop into more and more profound states with him, that's when I really began to see who and what he was. That was a process.

MICHAEL: As an official lama yourself, and also as a teacher and a writer across various media now, it's obviously important for people to feel that they're drawn to you, as well, especially if they're on the first step to the path, or to find you engaging, and trustworthy, and amusing and interesting. How do you balance that truth, which is very egocentric in a way, or ego-focused, with your tradition's emphasis toward humility as well as your personal inclination to avoid the spotlight. There seems to be an interesting tension between being a teacher and a galvanizing teacher, someone people are drawn to and will listen to on the one hand, and wanting to remain humble at the same time. How do you balance those two drives?

LAMA TSOMO: One wonderful thing about these practices is you learn a new habit for the relationship between small "s" self and large "S" Self, if you will—small "s" self being "ego," and large "S" self being like this vast ocean. So when I take the lama's seat I am being a conduit for something much more than my own personal small "s" self. Traditionally the Tibetan lama walks in to give the teachings, prostrates to the seat, then sits down in it, then prays to the lamas who have come before them, and also just the primordial Buddha to come through for the teachings. And so if ego is in right relationship with that, then ego has its own personality quirks, and, you know, can tell a joke, or speak English, or a bunch of other creative pieces that get added, so that the delivery is sort of this full range bridging from something that's beyond our normal perception to something that people I'm teaching will be able to grasp. And so it's kind of a delicious process really to open myself up to that. And I do pray before giving the teachings, and then find my own creative way of bringing the teachings to these people in this place at this moment.

MICHAEL: You just mentioned prayer. How do you pray in that case or other cases: who are you praying to and what are you praying for?

LAMA TSOMO: So we humans need to personify things. And as long as you know you're doing it, and you're using that as a bridge to the ineffable, that's fine. Whatever works. That's how I can use a channel changer, and tune into that ineffable awareness of the ocean. So I'm quite conscious of doing exactly that, and I do it every day in my practices, so I've had a lot of practice. So I tune into that, and I don't know if I'm answering your question exactly, but it's not that I'm imagining an actual person I'm praying to—even though I pray to the lama a lot, I'm praying to that essence of the lama that is no different from my essence or anybody else's, that is the ocean. We are all waves, therefore also all ocean. So it's really a bridge to tune into that.

MICHAEL: And do you pray for particular outcomes?

LAMA TSOMO: Well, I'm going to start by talking about one outcome that we think of with prayer, which is blessings. And that word for me was, like, "Huh? What do you exactly mean by 'blessings'"? And what I finally realized is that I want to be infected by that vast mind. So I'm praying for that when I'm praying for blessings. I'm praying to be infected by these masters who have come before my own master, who I still know, and who has that in evidence more than your average person, so that that helps me to tune in. And so then I can be infected by that mindset. So that's still about tuning in, the channel changer, that kind of thing. It's not as though it isn't always there. It's just that I am fixated on another channel and have to get some help tuning into that.

MICHAEL: I'm saying this from my semi-informed, ignorant perspective. Is Tonglen a form of prayer, would you say, or is it something else?

LAMA TSOMO: No, it's not a prayer; it's a practice that involves visualization. But you aren't uttering words for something.

MICHAEL: And the reason I ask is that, if I understand it right, Tonglen is somewhat outcome driven in that you are trying to get an outcome for the person, or the people, or the entities that are suffering in particular ways. Is it not a prayer because it doesn't require the visualization of an intermediary?

LAMA TSOMO: Well, there are no words. I think of prayers as having words. It's a compassion practice, so it does use visualization. But it's a practice.

MICHAEL: So prayer is word driven and other practices may be less so?

LAMA TSOMO: Yeah. I mean, you can have liturgy along with practices, but usually once you get to the point where you're really almost in this meditative practice kind of state, there can be visualization, there can even be mantra, but you're just repeating the mantra again and again, which is another avenue of tuning into the channel you're trying to tune into, a particular Chenrezi who's white and he's got four arms and he's holding this, that, and the other, and you're saying "Om mani pemey hung" because that's the archetypal sound that's associated with compassion. So you're kind of using all the avenues that we can tune into—which are things like images, and sounds, and so on—to tune into something that's really quite ineffable, the principle, the archetype of compassion.

MICHAEL: There has been some talk recently in public circles, from the Vatican for example, saying that Donald Trump isn't a Christian because he doesn't meet certain standards. Is there anything that you could say to someone, or have you ever run into situations in which someone proclaims themselves to be a Buddhist and you go, "I don't think so." Or is that really not the kind of judgment you would make about somebody who professes themselves to be a Buddhist?

LAMA TSOMO: I personally haven't run into somebody who's claimed, "I am a Buddhist," and I thought, "No, you're not." More the reverse is true, where people have said, "I'm not a Buddhist," and I'm, like, "Well, if it walks like a duck, talks like a duck, I don't know." The Dalai Lama, on his website, does speak of one group, of all the lineages out of Tibet there's only one that he's talked of as he didn't feel was Buddhist.

MICHAEL: If it walks like a duck, quacks like a duck, prostrates like a duck...

LAMA TSOMO: Yeah, there you go.

KATY: So when you've met those people, Lama Tsomo, who you've felt, "You sure act like a Buddhist," what are they acting like? Explain that to me. What do you see in a person you think, "They sure seem like a Buddhist," in how they live their life or how they practice?

LAMA TSOMO: So if—a person is working to become a better, happier person, a more compassionate person, and really putting it into practice whenever they can, and not afraid to see when they're off track and try to make that better, you know, that's one thing I would look for. Another is a view of reality that seems similar to me. For example, my rabbi, when I sat and talked for hours with him, I said, "Let's get rid of terminology and just say, 'If you were to describe the source of everything we see', how would you describe it?" And as he's sitting there talking, I'm thinking, "He's sounding like a lama." [*Laughter*] I mean, it was unbelievable. And then he asked me some very pointed questions, and I answered him from my training and my experience. And he just stopped and he's, like, kind of amazed. So I could see he was going through the same experience. So I don't believe everybody who doesn't think themselves a card-carrying Buddhist might not still be Buddhists at heart. Or then we don't even have to call it "Buddhist," but there's no difference.

MICHAEL: What's a way in which you think you could be an even better Buddhist? And it's okay to go, "No, I'm cool." But...

LAMA TSOMO: Oh, right. I'm perfect already. [*Pause*] Oh gosh. [*Laughter*] Let me count the ways. Well, I still have resistance to sitting down and practicing in the morning. So there's my little kid self who's, like, "Aw, do I have to? Let me just do this for— that for—oh, now there's no time." So there's that part of me. And then, you know, miraculously, I get myself to the cushion and I am able to practice. And not too far into it I realize "This is wonderful. What was the resistance? How come I don't know this is how I'm going to feel?" And then by the end of it it's just ... Even if somewhere in between something painful has bubbled up, something that I've kind of maybe been pushing into the background comes up into my consciousness, and, yeah, it's not comfortable. I've been trying to avoid it. But then I'm sitting there with these practices right at my fingertips, and almost without fail the practice I'm doing is the perfect medicine for what ails me. So, "Well, here we go," and I just plow that into the practice, and it can sometimes be really intense, especially if I'm feeling intense about this painful situation. And by the time I come through and out the other side, it isn't just like, "Oh, now I've found a great pleasant way to shove it under the rug." It's not like that at all. It's like I put it into the process and came to some realization. And by the time I'm on the other side of it, I'm really in a different position in relation to that painful thing. And if it's involving a person, which it quite often is—not 100 percent of the time; sometimes it's situational, but a lot of times it's with a person—I feel differently toward that person.

MICHAEL: Can you talk about any moments in your sort of non-practice, like, day-to-day life, when you think, "Eh, that wasn't very Buddhist of me the way I handled that"? I know the story, but maybe you could retell the anecdote about a friend of yours who was chided for not being Buddhist enough in a particular situation?

LAMA TSOMO: Well, I haven't ever told you the whole story around that, and it's not really important. It's just her response that's important.

MICHAEL: Well, just the elevator-speech version of it.

LAMA TSOMO: Yeah. So a mutual friend who was Buddhist was also friends with my dad. And my dad was sort of anti-religion and called himself an agnostic, but provisionally I would say he was an atheist. And so, you know, at one point the friend, was angry about something. And so then my dad said, "That's not very Buddhist." And she said, "Well, I'm a Buddhist, not a Buddha." So that would be my category. There are plenty of times when—actually pretty much all the time I'm not a Buddha, because there's no time that I am a Buddha. So I'm just somebody who is trying their best to move in that direction, meanwhile becoming a better, happier person along the way. And that much I've already seen. I hope that eventually I do become totally awake and totally enlightened. But meanwhile these methods are helping me to be better, happier today.

MICHAEL: In those kinds of moments do you find it harder to extend compassion towards yourself than you do to others? Or have you gotten to the point where you can be pretty much 360 compassionate to folks including yourself? Because I find that hard for myself.

LAMA TSOMO: Yes, well, I am a card-carrying Westerner. And we Westerners seem to be pretty terrible at compassion for ourselves or even liking ourselves. And I, too, find it challenging sometimes to give myself compassion. Luckily I have practices to help with that. And because of the visualization, and breath, and, the senses, and, sound, and all these different things we use, and the repetition creating a habit of mind and setting the pathways in, all of that has helped me so that I am definitely more compassionate with myself, more happy with myself, or content with myself, I think, is a better way to say it, and liking myself better.

MICHAEL: This is related to the book, which I want to talk about in a second, but how do you have to sort of align yourself differently when you're teaching Westerners, as you just brought up, than when, for example, you're teaching in Taiwan, where you've got a different audience?

LAMA TSOMO: One thing that's different for Westerners than, say, in Taiwan where I teach, is in Taiwan they've had Buddhism sort of the way fish are in water, they've been immersed in a society that has that as its underpinnings. It feels very different to me from a society where Christianity has been the underpinnings, and that's what's in the marrow of people's bones, that they're not even conscious of. Now, they're very modern in Taiwan and they like to know the reasons for this, that, and the other, as we do too here. But in Taiwan they very quickly fall into, "Oh, I see how that goes." A classic example is karma and reincarnation. They just kind of get it from having been raised with it. I have to back way up for Westerners, because we can't assume anything, and there's a lot of resistance, and I have to go very slowly and methodically and bring in science and so on. The other thing about Westerners is once we do have all the reasons, then we can really get on board, and it's a pretty clean understanding. I find with Taiwanese, sometimes they assume too much and they haven't really stopped and examined, "Well, how does this karma/reincarnation thing really work? Are you sure that's the way it is? Why do you have faith in the lama?" Because we don't want the blind faith. And so sometimes I'll challenge them with those kinds of questions. I don't have that trouble with Westerners. Then once we get to the point where people are accepting of the practices and they're really going to go for it, Westerners have a lot of trouble sticking with it, because what they've discovered in studies is you have to be in a context. Human beings are herd animals. So if there's at least a culture among a group of people who are sort of trying to go in the same direction, working on these practices together, they really go for it, and they support each other just by having a similar view and mindset and goal in mind. When Westerners don't have that, they stop practicing, just about guaranteed. In Taiwan they're more aware of the need for the group settings. You know, the three jewels of Buddhism are Buddha, Dharma, and Sangha. Sangha is the community. I think the Buddha was aware that we're herd animals, and baked that into his program. So there's a way that the culture there supports using a support of a group. And so they really take off with some of these longer practices and go ahead and learn them. Another thing is, Westerners have a lot of resistance to ritual, and I need to explain to them why the ritual, what that does for you. And then once they get, it they think, "Wow, this is great. This is very cool," and they really get into it. The Taiwanese can almost just go for it without any meaning. So then I want to back up and say, "Wait a second. Do you know why you're doing this? What does this do? Let me explain a little bit." And then they're, like, "Oh wow, that's cool. We had no idea. We were just banging the drum and doing the bells," [*Laughter*] just kind of having lots of fun, you know? And now they know more the reason and they love it.

MICHAEL: Which is why, as you said, the subtitle of the book *Why Is the Dalai Lama Always Smiling?* the subtitle is *A Westerner's Introduction and Guide to Tibetan Buddhist Practice* focuses on Westerners particularly as the audience.

LAMA TSOMO: Yes.

MICHAEL: Is there anything that you discovered about yourself or about your tradition in writing the book? And what are your thoughts on its reception since it's been published and how that fits in with your other teaching. Anything you've noticed about the reception that either surprised you, or pleased you, or ...?

LAMA TSOMO: Yeah. Well, my process in writing the book was that I thought I was going to do a little handbook, and now it's three large books. And I hope I can stick to three. [*Laughter*] Because I discovered that I had to keep backing up and explaining more, and bringing more in so that these basic practices that I wanted to cover, we would understand why to do them, and how to use them. Because these are highly sophisticated tools, and if you know how to use them, they're fantastic. And if you don't, you might lose the benefit and just kind of say, "Well, that didn't work." And that would be a terrible loss. So that's why the book kind of grew and grew. Then once the book was out there, the feedback I got was that some people still felt daunted, they scared themselves because, "Oh, it's about Buddhism and I don't know about Buddhism." But of course I was assuming no prior knowledge. So that was like my son who was bugging me to teach him piano before he went for his piano lesson, because he was afraid otherwise of showing up to the piano lesson without already knowing how to play piano, which was of course the plan. So I had planned that nobody know about Buddhism beforehand, but some people were unable to get past their own preconceptions. A lot of other people were surprised that it was actually accessible, and this was what was expressed to me. Some people could understand that I was really talking about Buddhist practice and giving you some context for that. And that's in the subtitle; this is a book giving you a couple of practices that you can road-test to see if this is for you. As I was recommending earlier, that's what I did. And that's what other people might want to do, and so this book is for them. Coming from a Christian society where there's sometimes a sort of missionary zeal and so on, wanting to save people from hell by making them sign up for your brand of religion, Westerners, I think, have a real knee-jerk reaction against that and almost against any religion. So then these practices that come from one of the world's religions get thrown out with the bathwater, if you will. And I've had students who are practicing Christians use these methods because these particular methods aren't in the set of tools in Christianity, so they can just take those and continue being Christians, but now they can also focus their minds better, they have a nice compassion practice, which works for a Christian. So there's been the gamut, in other words, of resistance for various reasons, and acceptance for various reasons.

MICHAEL: Do you approach your audiences any differently as an author than let's say you do as a teacher in person, or if you're doing something online like the e-course that you were working on earlier today? Is there anything different in your methods or your assumptions other than just the technicalities of the medium? Or is it pretty much the same voice and the same presentation, just in a different medium? So for example, in my own work sometimes I figure if I'm writing something, I can build into that the opportunity for people to pause and reflect. But if I'm teaching in person, I can't do that.

LAMA TSOMO: I can. I do.

MICHAEL: Yeah, good. So please, talk about that.

LAMA TSOMO: So my rhythm for teaching—and I do this in webinars as well as in person—is to give them an approach almost like hear, contemplate, meditate, a little practice. So a bit like that. I'll give them a bite-sized piece of something, input, to chew on. Then I have them just quietly try it. And then I have them turn to somebody nearby and kind of unpack that together. And then we unpack it together as a group, then I give the next input. So I kind of do a little bit of a circle like that quite often. We have built that into the e-course in a way because we have different media that we're weaving into each lesson.

KATY: You were talking about how you were balancing that humility versus sharing, right, and there's a sense of being a conduit for something that's bigger than yourself. And so in a sense I was hearing that it called to you to do that. Was there sort of a moment in time or an experience when it struck you that, "I need to be a conduit. I want to go that path?" Can you share that moment and kind of how that felt, and then when you were starting to do it how that felt, how you took on this other dimension of your being a Buddhist?

LAMA TSOMO: So I began to teach it way before I should have, in a way. I had moved here. Rinpoche hadn't yet moved here. He wanted me to sort of pave the way and get people prepared a bit. So he had me teaching the preliminary practices, the Ngöndro, before I'd even finished doing it myself. When I would sit down to teach a class, I would just go inside and do a simple prayer that calls Rinpoche and my teacher into me. And I was already doing the conduit thing, you know, that came quite naturally to me. I'd in my previous life been an acupressurist, and you're a conduit there, too. But there was another level to it then after I'd been ordained a lama. And I went to Hong Kong and gave teachings there. So everybody had been gathered in the room already, and then I was to walk in, make my entrance, which was already a little bit embarrassing for me. But I'm just about to walk in and I see that there is a throne, which is what Rinpoche usually sits on. But I said, "Well, who's sitting there?" And they're, like, "You are. We brought you here to give the teachings. Rinpoche's not here. This is you." And I was taken aback. And I said, "Well, I'm not used to sitting on a throne. Can you take that away?" And they said, "Well, no. Nobody's going to see you because we've got this all positioned, etc., etc. You just have to sit on that throne." So that actually was a way of dropping ego, and getting overly self-conscious and embarrassed can be a form of ego. So I had to drop even that, and just went in there, I prostrated first to the shrine, and those who have gone before me, and were actually fully realized, and then the Dharma in that seat is in a sense the conduit. And then I entered that conduit, sat down, and gave the teachings. And it was this wonderful combination of feeling the power and profundity of all that coming through while at the same time being able to play with exactly how to express it and so on in that moment. And so the personal and the far-beyond-personal got to come together to play. It was really a lovely experience. Continues to be.

MICHAEL: The last time I was here I mentioned that Grateful Dead guitarist Bob Weir was asked whether he had pride in his legacy. And he said that he distrusted pride. But he said that we can all be proud of the non-ego, collective "us." And it sounds like you've come to some of that yourself, that when you can make it about something more encompassing, that takes the focus off your own ego and it makes you less embarrassed, less worried about being egotistical, and more able to tap into not just the possibilities, but the beauty of what the ocean is as opposed to worrying about your own wave. If you could go back to , let's say, your 25 year-old self, and had only a couple of minutes, anything you'd want to give yourself a heads-up about that would have been helpful to you back then proceeding toward here?

LAMA TSOMO: The obvious one is find yourself a lama sooner and get started with practice. Because 25 is a wonderful age to begin using the practices to kind of let go of some of the pathways in your brain that are definitely not serving, and encouraging other pathways, the compassion ones and, things like that, and just being able to focus your mind and have it settle. I wish I had started all of that at that age. rather than what was close to twenty years later.

MICHAEL: Looking ahead on the path, is there something that you're particularly eager to master or learn about from where you are now? Or is it more just you want to get better at the what are already parts of your spiritual life and presence?

LAMA TSOMO: Well, I have recently started a new cycle of teachings that I am excited about, that I can't really talk about [Laughter] because that's how it works.

MICHAEL: Otherwise you'd have to reincarnate us?

LAMA TSOMO: [Laughter] I'd liberate you first. But it involves doing retreat in complete darkness, and it is a wonderful rehearsal for the bardo. And it's just a way to really turn up the Bunsen burner and accelerate. So again, stronger and stronger medicine. And also there are practices that I'm doing now that are really on the outer edge of my ability, and I'm still trying to push the envelope with those. And those are related to the ones I am continuing with.

KATY: I really like this question of what would you tell your younger self. But now as a teacher reaching out to all of these students, a lot of them who are younger, what do you see coming up as myths that people tell themselves about beginning on the path or starting meditation practice? Can you speak to that?

LAMA TSOMO: I think there are a lot of myths that people tell themselves as they're considering just daily meditation practice. And they may not even be considering following a whole spiritual path. At the beginning that's not really necessary. It's good to just sort of take it a step at a time. But I think people scare themselves with the idea even of spending a few minutes a day paying attention to their breathing. We're breathing all the time, so we've already got that down. We do a lot of sitting, so there you go. So it's just a question of paying attention to this breathing that's always happening. So I like to sneak up on people with it and just have them stop and pay attention to their breathing. And it's like, "See? No big deal." So that's a myth I really like to pop. [*Laughter*] And another myth I think is, "Well, if I do that then that means I have to become a card-carrying Buddhist." You know, "I can't just be a breather who pays attention to breathing from time to time." Another myth is, "I don't have the time to pay attention to my breathing for a few minutes a day." Then I just ask people, "So how much TV do you watch in a day? Could you spare a few minutes from that to watching this?" So there are a few myths that I like to sort of pop. Another one is, "I can't make my mind... my brain won't stop, so I'm a terrible meditator." So it's a little bit like my son with the piano lessons. He was a terrible piano player before he knew how. And he's a really good example because he's become a professional musician [*Laughter*]. So I just have to point out, you know, he started without knowing how to play the piano. And everybody who starts out meditating doesn't know how to meditate. So if you're starting out meditating and you don't know how to meditate, you're right where you should be.

KATY: That ties really nicely into that concept of, "I'm a Buddhist, not a Buddha." Guess what? Rinpoche talks about his mind wandering, too. We were speaking yesterday about how that gives you those moments throughout.

LAMA TSOMO: Those fresh moments.

KATY: Can you touch on that? Because I think it ties nicely into your idea of myths.

LAMA TSOMO: Yeah. So when I first started studying with Rinpoche he said, "Actually it's much better to have many short sessions within one sitting session, even if your sitting session is a few minutes." Because our brains will wander. The brain is a thinking machine; that's what it's designed for. And actually that's okay. The thoughts can come up and then go, and come up and go. But if we're following after and getting pulled off into some sort of whole story and movie or whatever, internal conversation, then we're not meditating anymore. So that session was over. So then we remember, "Oh yeah, I was meditating." Then we come back and there's this fresh moment of, "Ah." That's probably about the best moment in your meditation, so you want to have a lot of those. So instead of having a stagnant pond for many minutes, you can have water that bounces over mountain rocks. And I'd like to tell you that was my metaphor, but it was Rinpoche's. And I have a feeling he got it from somewhere. But, anyway, the water that bounces over the rocks is very fresh. So those many little sessions are actually good, and the more times you catch yourself following after thoughts when you're doing practice, the more that's practice for being mindful, aware, in your regular, off-the-cushion life.

About the Authors

LAMA TSOMO is an American lama, author, and co-founder of the Namchak Foundation and Namchak Retreat Ranch.

Born Linda Pritzker, Lama Tsomo followed a path of spiritual inquiry and study that ultimately led to her ordination as one of the few American lamas in Tibetan Buddhism.

Under the tutelage of Gochen Tulku Sangak[37] Rinpoche, international holder of the Namchak lineage, Lama Tsomo has done extensive spiritual retreat in the US and abroad and is fluent in Tibetan. Today, she is dedicated to sharing the teachings of the Namchak lineage with Western students, bringing greater happiness and meaning to life through meditation practice, community, and retreat. She is especially passionate about reaching young people and supporting those working for positive social change. Her teaching has inspired American and international students, who appreciate her informal, and often humorous, style.

Lama Tsomo holds an MA in Counseling Psychology with an emphasis in Jungian studies. She is the author of *Why Is the Dalai Lama Always Smiling? A Westerner's Introduction and Guide to Tibetan Buddhist Practice*, winner of a 2016 Independent Publisher award.

---

37. Sometimes spelled "Sang-Ngag"

MATTHEW FOX is an internationally acclaimed spiritual theologian, Episcopal priest, and activist who was a member of the Dominican Order for 34 years. He holds a doctorate, summa cum laude, in the History and Theology of Spirituality from the *Institut Catholique de Paris* and has devoted 45 years to developing and teaching the tradition of Creation Spirituality, which is rooted in ancient Judeo-Christian teaching, inclusive of today's science and world spiritual traditions; welcoming of the arts and artists; wisdom centered, prophetic, and committed to eco-justice, social justice, and gender justice.

Fox has reinvented forms of education and worship and awakened millions to the much-neglected Earth-based mystical tradition of the West, revivifying awareness of Hildegard of Bingen, Meister Eckhart, Thomas Aquinas, and Thomas Merton, among other premodern and postmodern spiritual pioneers. He has authored more than 35 books on spirituality and contemporary culture, among them: *Original Blessing, The Coming of the Cosmic Christ, The Reinvention of Work, A Spirituality Named Compassion,* and *Meister Eckhart: A Mystic-Warrior for Our Times.* His books, celebrated around the world, have been translated into 60 languages.

List of Matt Fox's books as of 2018

Original Blessing
The Coming of the Cosmic Christ
A Spirituality Named Compassion
Order of the Sacred Earth: An Intergenerational Vision of Love and Action
    (with Skylar Wilson and Jennifer Listug)
Prayer: A Radical Response to Life
Creation Spirituality: Liberating Gifts for the Peoples of the Earth
Whee! Weee, We Wee All the Way Home: A Guide to Sensual Prophetic Spirituality
Western Spirituality: Historical Roots, Ecumenical Routes (edited)
Natural Grace (with Rupert Sheldrake)
The Physics of Angels (with Rupert Sheldrake)
Christian Mystics: 365 Readings and Meditations
Passion for Creation: The Earth-Honoring Spirituality of Meister Eckhart
Meister Eckhart: A Mystic-Warrior for Our Times
Meditations with Meister Eckhart: A Centering Book
Illuminations of Hildegard of Bingen
Hildegard of Bingen, A Saint for Our Times: Unleashing Her Power in the 21st Century
Hildegard of Bingen's Book of Divine Works: With Letters & Songs
Sheer Joy: Conversations with Thomas Aquinas on Creation Spirituality
A Way to God: Thomas Merton's Creation Spirituality Journey
The Reinvention of Work: A New Vision of Livelihood For Our Times
Creativity: Where the Divine and the Human Meet
The Hidden Spirituality of Men: Ten Metaphors to Awaken the Sacred Masculine
The A.W.E Project: Reinventing Education, Reinventing the Human
Occupy Spirituality: A Radical Vision for a New Generation (with Adam Bucko)
Sins of the Spirit, Blessings of the Flesh: Transforming Evil in Soul and Society
Wrestling with the Prophets: Essays on Creations Spirituality and Everyday Life
The Pope's War: Why Ratzinger's Secret Crusade Has Imperiled the Church
    and How it Can Be Saved
Confessions: The Making of a Postdenominational Priest
One River, Many Wells: Wisdom Springing from Global Faiths
Religion USA: Culture and Religion by way of Time Magazine
A New Reformation
Letters to Pope Francis
Creation Spirituality: A New Story, a Deep Lineage
Naming the Unnameable: 89 Wonderful and Useful Names for God...
    Including the Unnameable God
Stations of the Cosmic Christ (with Bishop Marc Andrus)

Image Usage in L&R Video

1. **For the book cover from *Illuminations of Hildegard of Bingen*:**
   From the book *Illuminations of Hildegard of Bingen* Copyright © 2002 by Matthew Fox. Reprinted with permission of Inner Traditions, Bear & Company, Rochester VT. www.innertraditions.com

2. **For the book cover from *Meditations with Meister Eckhart,*** and certain quoted passages from *Meditations with Meister Eckhart*:
   From the book *Meditations with Meister Eckhart* Copyright © 1983 by Matthew Fox. Reprinted with permission of Inner Traditions, Bear & Company, Rochester VT. www.innertraditions.com.

3. For the images of **two paintings by Javier Garcia Lemus** ("Lemus") entitled *Green Man* and *Cosmic Black Madonna* (the "Artwork"): *Green Man* and *Cosmic Black Madonna* paintings courtesy of Javier Garcia Lemus.